"This is a riveting and all-engaging book. Not only does it provide context to yesterday's headlines, and perhaps tomorrow's, about the Iraq war and about our politics of personal destruction, but former Ambassador Joseph Wilson also tells captivating stories from his life as a foreign service officer with a long career fostering the development of African democracies, and gives us a behind-the-scenes blow-by-blow of the run-up to the 1991 Persian Gulf war. . . . Remarkably, Bush's White House continues to attack [Wilson]. . . . They should understand that they have picked a fight with the wrong fellow." —John W. Dean, *New York Times Book Review*

"Reads like the best spy fiction, but isn't fiction. What makes the facts even worse is knowing that the U.S. government would willingly expose the identity of Wilson's wife, an undercover CIA operative, for the sake of revenge. . . . A page-turner. . . . A fascinating read." —John W. Royal, *Houston Chronicle*

"Fascinating . . . Wilson's account of his service in Baghdad and of his fierce, face-to-face encounters with Saddam and his foreign minister, Tarik Aziz, are gripping. . . . This is dissent not from the radical fringe but from the heart of the establishment." —Tim Rutten, *Los Angeles Times*

"Full of suspense, betrayal and intrigue." —Ruben Navarrette, *Dallas Morning News*

"Wilson has written [a] book within the larger book, a non-sensationalistic, fascinating memoir of his unexpected decision to enter the U.S. foreign service. Wilson's account of his diplomatic tours in Niger, Togo, South Africa, Burundi, the Congo, Iraq, Gabon and Washington are superb, one of the most compelling and educational such accounts of dozens I have read. . . . Wilson's allegations carry the ring of truth. . . . No matter what a reader's views about the Iraq war, about Democrats vs. Republicans, Wilson's account of day-to-day life as a U.S. diplomat ought to educate and fascinate, an unusual combination in nonfiction about politics." —Steve Weinberg, *St. Louis Post-Dispatch*

"Wilson hits back hard with righteous anger against those who would jeopardize national security to score political points. . . . A vivid, engrossing account of a foreign service career that spans nearly three decades. Wilson is a lively storyteller with an eye for visual detail and brings a welcome insider's perspective on the political situations of the nations where he served." —*Publishers Weekly* (starred review)

The Politics of Truth

The Politics *of* Truth

Updated with a New Preface by the Author and an Investigative
Report on the Niger Documents Affair by Russ Hoyle

Inside the Lies that Put
the White House on Trial and
Betrayed My Wife's CIA Identity

Ambassador
Joseph Wilson

A Diplomat's Memoir

CARROLL & GRAF PUBLISHERS
NEW YORK

The publisher notes that the essay for the paperback edition of *The Politics of Truth*
by Russ Hoyle was reported independently and edited without the involvement of
Ambassador Joseph Wilson.

AVALON
publishing group incorporated

THE POLITICS OF TRUTH

Carroll & Graf Publishers
An Imprint of Avalon Publishing Group Inc.
245 West 17th Street
11th Floor
New York, NY 10011

First Carroll & Graf edition 2004
First Carroll & Graf trade paperback edition 2005

Library of Congress Cataloging-in-Publication Data is available.

ISBN: 0-7867-1551-0

9 8 7 6 5 4 3 2 1

Maps designed by Mike Morgenfeld and Suzanne Service
Interior design by Simon M. Sullivan
Printed in the United States of America
Distributed by Publishers Group West

To my wife Valerie, I cannot begin to tell you how sorry I am for what your government has done to you. If I could give you back your anonymity I would do so in a minute.

To Sabrina and Joe, who experienced so many of these adventures with me.

To Trevor and Samantha, in the hopes that by reading this you will gain some insight into events that took place before you could understand their significance.

To Dad and Mom, who will never read this but who, as Marines, did their best to teach me the meaning of duty to country.

*The hottest places in Hell are reserved for those who,
in times of great moral crisis, maintain their neutrality.*

—DANTE ALIGHIERI, *The Divine Comedy*

Contents

The Niger Affair: The Investigation That Won't Go Away

Russ Hoyle

T HE STORY OF THE NIGER–IRAQ URANIUM DEAL was a key prop in the Bush administration's case for war against Iraq—and the source of unexpected notoriety for former U.S. envoy to Africa Joseph Wilson. A year after the publication of Wilson's account of his clashes with the White House in *The Politics of Truth,* the Niger affair is not over. It has branched into three distinct and interconnected narratives with unforeseen consequences for the president, the U.S. intelligence community, and the American press.

1.

Most prominent in the headlines these days is the effort by federal prosecutors to intimidate two well-known national reporters with threats of jail for protecting their confidential sources. Special Counsel Patrick J. Fitzgerald, the U.S. Attorney for the Northern District of Illinois, has moved aggressively to compel Matthew Cooper of *Time* magazine and Judith Miller of the *New York Times* to name senior government officials who may have illegally leaked the identity of Wilson's wife, Valerie Plame, as a covert CIA agent. Fitzgerald, who has a reputation as a relentless prosecutor, was appointed special counsel by the Justice Department in December 2003 to investigate the Bush administration leaks. Wilson believes, reasonably, that the leaks were political retaliation for his role in opposing the shaky White House case that Iraq was seeking to buy uranium ore from Niger for its alleged nuclear-weapons program.

But Fitzgerald's attack on journalists' presumptive constitutional privilege is a sideshow next to the potential explosiveness of the criminal investigation now before a Washington, D.C., grand jury that is charged with finding out who leaked Plame's identity.

The grand jury probe has dragged on for more than a year now, but it is still directed at the heart of the Bush administration. The identification and indictment of high-level aides to the president, when and if it happens, would be the beginning of the end of a story that began on July 14, 2003, when *Washington Post* syndicated columnist Robert Novak wrote that "two senior administration officials" told him that Plame was an "undercover agent for the CIA." Confirmation that White House officials with top security clearances exposed a U.S. secret agent, a felony under the Intelligence Identities Protection Act of 1982, would likely result in a political firestorm, high-level firings, and a humiliating personal blow to President Bush.

But few in Washington see veteran Bush administration operatives standing by while Fitzgerald fingers culprits who may work just down the corridor from the president at the White House. The special counsel is, after all, a member in good standing of the Bush Justice Department and continues to hold down his high-profile Chicago job. Whether indictments are forthcoming or the case drags on because of appeals in the Cooper–Miller press case, possibly to the Supreme Court, the potential for political scandal only continues the longer the criminal probe remains unresolved.

The third and perhaps most important development in the Niger story since it flared up in mid-2003 has been the publication of the Senate Select Committee on Intelligence (SSCI) report and several related British intelligence reviews in the summer of 2004. The findings in the 511-page Senate document, drafted by the Republican-dominated committee, were limited to narrow judgments about key episodes in the Niger story that insiders believe were intended to divert attention from any White House role in shaping the intelligence. But the text itself was an indictment of the administration's meddling and the inadequate and contradictory evidence that supported U.S. intelligence assessments that Iraq had sought a deal with Niger for uranium—a conclusion Secretary of State Colin Powell arrived at independently when he refused to include the case in his February 5, 2003 speech to the UN Security Council.

The discredited Niger deal, along with the unraveling of more than two dozen other so-called statements of "fact and conclusion based on solid intelligence" by Powell, thoroughly undermined the Bush White House's legal case for war, but came too late to matter.

That did not dampen the ardor of the president's supporters, who cited the Senate report approvingly because it concluded that intelligence assessments about the Niger deal were reasonable "at the time" and it contained no finding that the administration knowingly tailored intelligence to suit its war aims, thus implicitly vindicating the White House in the intelligence fiasco. Indeed, it left that subject for a second report, which has not been completed as of this writing. While avoiding conclusions about who precisely was to blame for the failure, the committee strongly suggested that the blinkered Niger intelligence was due to CIA confusion, duplicity, and incompetence.

Wilson himself lambasted the Senate committee report shortly after it appeared for inaccuracies about his trip to Niger and the report's portrayal of him and his wife in a six-page letter to Senator Pat Roberts, the Republican chairman of the committee, and Democratic Senator John D. "Jay" Rockefeller, its vice chairman. The report was also widely criticized by Democrats as a narrow, technical account that blamed CIA bungling and let the Bush administration off the hook by soft-pedaling possible White House manipulation of pre-war intelligence.

Yet a careful reading of the Senate report, bringing to bear new details that have become public about the origins of the Niger story, provides the fullest account to date of a story that the Bush administration has so far effectively brushed aside. And that is how the White House prodded the CIA and other intelligence agencies to cobble together intelligence suggesting that Iraq had approached the government of Niger between 1999 and 2000 to purchase uranium oxide, or "yellowcake," for Baghdad's supposedly reconstituted nuclear-weapons program—which we now know did not exist. The administration declassified just enough of the Niger intelligence to help persuade the United States Congress and the American people to approve the president's "pre-emptive" war on Iraq.

Even so, the report is a virtual road map of White House involvement in the Niger affair and the sometimes reluctant complicity of then–Director of Central Intelligence George Tenet. It is this gathering version of the Niger story that deserves full-blown investigation by an independent prosecutor, and it is where an aggressive probe of the White House leaks would likely lead.

2.

The Senate committee's analysis of the Niger intelligence is important for several reasons. For a start, it focuses on a serious Bush administration mistake. White House officials conceded publicly that the famous sixteen words on the Niger deal in the president's 2003 State of the Union message never should have appeared in the speech. "The British government has learned that Saddam Hussein recently sought significant quantities of uranium from Africa," Bush declared on January 28. Stung by Joseph Wilson's *New York Times* Op-Ed piece six months later challenging the intelligence behind the statement, a "senior Bush administration official" admitted that "knowing what we know now, the reference to Iraq's attempt to acquire uranium from Africa should not have been included in the State of the Union speech."

Then–National Security Adviser Condoleezza Rice compounded the problem by first insisting that the sentence had been cleared by the CIA, only to later change her tune. "If the CIA, the Director of Central Intelligence, had said take this out of the speech, it would have been gone, without question," she declared. "We have a higher standard for what we put in presidential speeches."

That statement and others from Rice blaming the CIA were an outright admission on the eve of war that the intelligence on the Niger case was questionable. Although the White House apparently didn't know it, the CIA was then in possession of papers on the uranium deal—and had been for several months, without assessing their impact on existing intelligence—that were ultimately determined to be forgeries. That has left the Bush White House vulnerable to further questions about the credibility of the intelligence behind its case for war and about its truthfulness with the American public. The bully-boy tactics used against Wilson's wife have only added to the White House's self-inflicted injury and to an impression that administration and intelligence officials still have something to hide.

However misplaced, the administration's interest in the Niger deal was no accident. The story was deployed as critical evidence that Iraq had restarted its nuclear-weapons program, neatly complementing another key administration contention—that Iraq was purchasing special aluminum tubes to build gas centrifuges for making weapons-grade enriched uranium. It gave credence to White House warnings that nuclear weapons could end up in the hands of terrorists allegedly allied with Iraq. And it enabled the White House to use the aluminum tubes and the Niger uranium as rhetorical trip wires to spring the trap set for Iraq after the regime had submitted its 12,000-page accounting of its weapons programs in December, 2002.

It was also logical. Since the 1991 Gulf War, Iraq's indigenous sources of uranium oxide and its enrichment facilities had been destroyed by coalition forces. Both British and American intelligence assessments after the Gulf War noted that Iraq could speed up nuclear-weapons production by as much as two or three years by purchasing uranium ore, or yellowcake, on world markets. Iraq had bought uranium ore from Niger, Brazil, and elsewhere in the 1970s and 1980s. There was no reason it couldn't happen again if Baghdad and certain uranium-producing countries were willing to violate postwar sanctions.

The 2004 Intelligence Committee report established a number of facts about the White House's role in the intelligence-gathering process that, while not providing a comprehensive picture, raised serious questions about the timing of developments in the Niger affair and its shadowy origins. The committee reported that Vice President Cheney repeatedly pushed the Niger case forward—probably even setting in motion Wilson's briefing by the CIA at its Langley headquarters and his trip to Niger in late February 2002. The committee's reporting also casts doubt on White House claims that Cheney had not read the CIA report on Wilson's debriefing after his trip—thus suggesting that Cheney was unfamiliar with Wilson's conclusion that the Niger deal probably never took place.

The Senate committee's account of the flimsy and contradictory intelligence behind the October 2002 National Intelligence Estimate strongly suggested that the document was pre-cooked to White House order—and found that it was later used as the source of the controversial sixteen words in the 2003 State of the Union speech. The committee also documented a disturbing pattern of apparent CIA forgetfulness and self-contradiction about the mysterious suppression of the forged Niger documents once they were in the Agency's hands in the fall of 2002. And it presented contradictory impressions about whether CIA analysts and White House officials knew about the existence of the documents before they showed up in Rome and were forwarded on to Washington.

That the White House would take a strong hand in shaping intelligence is hardly shocking, but the truly historic dimensions of the intelligence failure that resulted are. Since the Civil War, American presidents have assumed greater powers in wartime, curbing civil liberties at home and asserting executive prerogatives in foreign affairs. Since the CIA was founded in 1947, the Director of Central Intelligence, or DCI, has served at the president's pleasure as his top intelligence adviser. Historically, when the best intelligence assessments of the DCI have failed to meet the political needs of the president, spy chiefs have learned to survive by accommodating the White House. The phenomenon, a source of classic passive–aggressive behavior on the part of the Agency, once led former Secretary of State Madeleine Albright to quip that the CIA "has battered child syndrome."

Such accommodation is also dangerous since it has often resulted in distorted and unreliable intelligence. Presidential control of the nation's intelligence apparatus, particularly when it has involved military operations or strategic planning—the Bay of Pigs invasion for John F. Kennedy, the public face of military success in Vietnam for Lyndon Johnson and Richard Nixon, the Team B assessment of Soviet military strength for Ronald Reagan—too often has meant spectacular failures of policy or costly political miscalculations. "No one can understand, much less predict, the behavior of the CIA who does not understand that the Agency works for the president," wrote Thomas Powers, the Pulitzer Prize–winning author and longtime expert on the U.S. intelligence community.

The commander-in-chief's surrogate this time around, as he was in many things during Bush's first term, was Vice President Cheney. Well before the terrorist attacks of September 11, 2001, President Bush asked the vice president, who had long experience in security matters, to oversee the intelligence community and assess U.S. vulnerability to terrorism.[1] In early February 2002, according to the Senate report, Cheney first directed his CIA briefer to find out more about sketchy reports of a "possible" African uranium deal. By then, the vice president was already familiar with intelligence "from a foreign government service" about an unconfirmed uranium deal with Iraq. And he wanted to know more about it.

The CIA had received its initial report about an alleged Niger deal in the weeks after 9/11. The name of the foreign government service is redacted in the Senate report, but columnist Josh Marshall of *The Hill*, a Capitol Hill newspaper, confirmed that the information originated with the Italian Intelligence and Military Security Service (SISMI).[2] The first Italian report reached the CIA on October 15, 2001, and a second and third came in February and March of 2002. The October report said that negotiations for a uranium purchase had been in the works since early 1999 and that an agreement was approved by the State Court of Niger in 2000. No mention was made of a paper trail or any evidence that uranium actually had been shipped. CIA analysts considered the report "very limited" and "lacking needed detail." State Department analysts at the Bureau of Intelligence and Research (INR) also considered the intelligence "highly suspect."

But the idea had been in the air for several years. A British report that surfaced in December 2000 was probably the earliest to suggest that "unconfirmed intelligence indicates Iraqi interest in acquiring uranium." Britain's Joint Intelligence Committee reported back then that Iraqi officials had visited several African countries, including Niger, in early 1999. Noting that Niger had sold Iraq uranium ore in the past, British analysts "judged that Iraqi purchase of uranium ore could have been the subject of discussions." On such gossamer threads of speculation regimes are toppled.

The CIA received a second wave of intelligence on the Niger deal on February 5, 2002. This, too, was from the same "foreign" service—that is the Italians. But there was more convincing detail this time, including what purported to be "verbatim text" of the actual agreement between Niger and Iraq. The report identified the Iraqi official who had traveled to Niger and elsewhere in Africa in February 1999 as Wissam al-Zahawi, Baghdad's ambassador to the Vatican in Rome. The information was also consistent with the 2000 British report. The Senate committee did not say whether actual documents accompanied the "verbatim text" of the uranium accord. But the second report clearly implied the existence of such documents, though no documents supporting the story would surface for another eight or nine months.

In early February, the Pentagon's Defense Intelligence Agency (DIA) wrote and distributed an "intelligence product" based on the new information about Niger's "agreement to sell 500 tons of uranium a year to Baghdad." That is a huge amount, enough to make fuel for fifty nuclear bombs, by a later CIA estimate, and lacked credibility to agency analysts. By all independent reports, Niger's two mines produced only three hundred tons in a good year. The vice president, the Senate committee reported, read the DIA report and asked the CIA for more information. In response, Tenet's newly established Center for Weapons Intelligence, Nonproliferation, and Arms Control (WINPAC), which coordinated overall intelligence on weapons of mass destruction for the DCI, issued an assessment saying that the "information on the alleged uranium contract . . . lacks crucial details" but that "we are working to clarify the information." WINPAC acknowledged that the intelligence was contradicted by reporting from the U.S. Embassy in Niamey. A separate version of the new CIA assessment was sent to Cheney.

Keeping the vice president in the loop was probably also on the mind of a State Department intelligence analyst who drafted a March 1 assessment that "a Niger uranium sale was unlikely." The analyst later told Senate committee staff that "the piece was in response to interest from the Vice President's office in the alleged Iraq–Niger uranium deal." The analyst's report was highly skeptical. As early as November 2001, the CIA had heard from the U.S. Embassy in Niamey that Niger's French-run uranium consortium claimed "there was no possibility" Niger had diverted any yellowcake to Iraq. In late February, U.S. Ambassador to Niger Barbro Owens-Kirkpatrick and U.S. Marine Gen. Carleton Fulford separately interviewed Nigerien officials about a possible deal and reached the same conclusion. The Senate report took care to note that the State Department analyst's assessment was not provided "directly to the Vice President in a special delivery" but delivered to the White House "through the routine distribution process."

The Senate committee's analysis of the March 8 CIA report on Wilson's trip to Niger in February did not identify the former ambassador by name and played down his detailed reasons why the Niger uranium sale could not have taken place. Instead it emphasized that intelligence analysts tended to dismiss Wilson's reporting as "nothing new." The CIA account, the committee reported, highlighted an offhand remark made by a Nigerien official to Wilson: that he had met with an Iraqi delegation at an Organization of African Nations conference in 1999. The official told Wilson it had occurred to him that the Iraqis may have been interested in purchasing uranium but that the subject had not been discussed in their meeting. That, explained the Senate report, "provided some confirmation" to the CIA of earlier reports by the unnamed "foreign government service" that Iraq was interested in purchasing uranium ore.

Early in March, Cheney asked his CIA morning briefer if there was any updated information on the uranium deal. Tenet's Center for Weapons Intelligence responded that the CIA would be "debriefing a source who may have information related to the alleged sale on March 5." That source was Wilson. The CIA report on Wilson's trip,

Agency analysts felt, did not add anything to "clarify the issue," so they did not "highlight the report for policymakers." Although the report was "widely distributed in routine channels," the Senate report explained that the "CIA's briefer did not brief the Vice President on the report, despite the Vice President's previous question about the issue." It had become clear that the CIA had chosen the wrong messenger with the wrong message.

The CIA's evolving angle of vision on the Niger affair could not have been clearer. The Senate report provided a snapshot of a skeptical and cautious Agency suddenly bent on dredging up dimly conceivable rumors, idle speculation, and outright gossip, ignoring contrary reporting from U.S. diplomats and intelligence analysts, and pushing forward selected "intelligence" that would build the case. In doing so, the committee also demonstrated that the vice president was the predicate and primary client for intelligence-gathering on the Niger sale. By detailing how the intelligence report on Wilson's trip may or may not have reached Cheney, the Senate committee may have even reflected an effort to head off possible political problems by providing answers to questions unasked in their report.

Was Niger intelligence tailored to the administration's policy needs and "stovepiped" to Cheney's office directly? Press reports to that effect had been circulating for at least a year. Had Cheney read the report? His office later denied it. By marginalizing Wilson's findings on the CIA-sponsored trip to Niger and broadcasting that the report was distributed through routine channels, Agency analysts handed Vice President Cheney that old executive-branch plum, plausible deniability. Yet the Senate committee also reported that the CIA report on Wilson was widely distributed, suggesting that the vice president could not possibly have missed it. No one would say it outright, but the CIA was feeling the heat from the White House and showing signs of a meltdown.

*   *   *

By late August 2002, some Democrats in Congress had grown uneasy with administration saber-rattling and increasingly skeptical about the administration's pumped-up rhetoric on Iraq's weapons programs. They wanted to see proof. Besides his frustration with criticism from the Hill and from former Republican officials like Brent Scowcroft and James Baker on the Op-Ed pages, Cheney was reportedly furious that the State Department had cut off funding to Ahmed Chalabi, an Iraqi dissident leader and U.S. intelligence asset whose defector sources had supplied abundant fresh intelligence on Saddam's resurgent weapons programs—all of which later proved wrong. The vice president, according to Bob Woodward's *Plan of Attack,* was ready to strike back.

On September 11, 2002, three days after Judith Miller published a spurious blockbuster on the front page of the *New York Times* reporting that Iraq had procured special aluminum tubes for its nuclear weapons program ("U.S. Says Hussein Intensified Quest for A-Bomb Parts"), National Security Council (NSC) staffers asked the CIA to clear language about the uranium deal for possible use by the president. The Senate report quoted the passage: "Iraq has made several attempts to buy high strength aluminum tubes used in centrifuges to enrich uranium for nuclear weapons. And we also know this: within the past few years, Iraq has resumed efforts to obtain large quantities of a type of uranium oxide known as yellowcake, which is an essential ingredient of the process."

The CIA okayed the NSC passage. Although it was never used by Bush, this was the first time the administration attempted to make its case that Iraq had reconstituted its nuclear-weapons program by linking Iraq's possession of aluminum tubes to the alleged attempt to buy African yellowcake. U.S. intelligence later determined that Saddam's nuclear program had been a shambles since the Gulf War, the aluminum tubes were actually intended for rocket parts, and no evidence ever emerged that a purchase of uranium ever took place or was even contemplated by the Iraqis. But at the time, no one, including the editors of the *New York Times* and the *Washington Post,* was the wiser.

Congressional grumbling in September led SSCI members to ask the CIA for a formal assessment of Iraq's weapons capabilities. The result, the 2002 National Intelligence Estimate (NIE) on "Iraq's Continuing Programs for Weapons of Mass Destruction," was more of the same.

Periodic national intelligence assessments are intended as authoritative statements of where the U.S. intelligence community stands on important issues of national security. The Senate committee's account of the rushed creation of the 2002 estimate by the CIA and the other government intelligence agencies was devastating. Key judgments in the document, provided to members of Congress only days before they voted to authorize the use of military force against Iraq, "were not substantiated by the underlying intelligence," according to comments appended to the 2004 Senate report by committee Vice Chairman Jay Rockefeller, Senator Carl Levin, and Senator Richard Durbin, Democrats from Michigan and Illinois, respectively. The Democratic senators called the 2002 NIE "a rushed and sloppy product" that "was hastily cobbled together using stale, fragmentary, and speculative intelligence reports and was replete with factual errors and unsupported judgments."

The NIE picked up phrasing from a September DIA report entitled "Iraq's Reemerging Nuclear Program" to describe the Niger sale: "Iraq also began vigorously trying to procure uranium ore and yellowcake; acquiring either would shorten the time Baghdad needs to produce nuclear weapons." As of early 2001, it added, "Niger planned to send several tons of 'pure uranium' (probably yellowcake) to Iraq," noting that "Niger and Iraq reportedly were still working out arrangements for this deal, which could be for up to 500 tons of yellowcake." The document concluded, "we do not know the status of this arrangement." The account of the Niger deal was a case study in what Rockefeller, Levin, and Durbin meant by "stale, fragmentary, speculative" and "unsupported" intelligence.

It got worse. When State Department intelligence analysts balked at the draft NIE, a statement was prepared for a text box indicating that "the claims of Iraqi pursuit of natural uranium in Africa are, in INR's assessment, highly dubious." The caveat, intended to show that the intelligence community did not unanimously support the Niger story, also undermined the administration position that Saddam had reconstituted his nuclear weapons program. Somehow, the Senate committee reported, the dissenting text box was "inadvertently" separated by "some 60 pages" from the section on the Iraqi nuclear program in the final version the CIA sent to Congress on October 1. No one could say how the text box had been misplaced.

Congress overwhelmingly gave President Bush the authority to use military force in Iraq. But the text box incident may have had the unanticipated effect of creating cold feet on the Niger case in some CIA quarters. A week later, a sentence about the African uranium deal included in a draft speech President Bush was to give in Cincinnati on October 7 went through several permutations before it was dropped altogether at the order of Deputy National Security Adviser Stephen Hadley.

On Oct. 6, the CIA faxed a memo to the White House to explain why it recommended deleting the sentence. The memo read:

> (1) The evidence is weak. One of the two mines cited by the source as the location of the uranium oxide is flooded. The other mine cited by the source is under the control of the French authorities. (2) The procurement is not particularly significant to Iraq's nuclear ambitions because the Iraqis already have a large stock of uranium oxide in their inventory. And (3) we have shared points one and two with Congress, telling them that the Africa story is overblown.

The Senate report does not identify who sent the explanatory message to the White House. But Hadley had received *his* orders to withdraw the sentence about Niger in the president's speech from DCI George Tenet. "The President should not be a fact witness on this," Tenet recalled telling Hadley in testimony before the Senate Intelligence Committee on July 16, 2003, nine months later. The "reporting was weak," said Tenet. Those remarks came ten days after Wilson's Op-Ed piece appeared, charging that the White House had "twisted" intelligence "to exaggerate the Iraqi threat"—and two days after Novak had outed Wilson's wife.

At about the time of the president's Cincinnati speech, the U.S. Embassy in Rome received photocopies of twenty-two pages allegedly documenting the Niger deal. The papers were made available to the embassy on October 9 for authentication by Italian journalist Elisabetta Burba, a reporter for the weekly *Panorama,* which is owned by Italian Prime Minister Silvio Berlusconi. Burba reportedly received the documents from an Italian businessman with financial and intelligence contacts whom she had dealt with before; he wanted $10,000 for them. The photocopies were sent to Washington in mid-October. At least one set went to the State Department INR group. Another eventually wound up at the CIA's Counterproliferation Division. Like Wilson, Burba traveled to Niger and decided that there wasn't anything to the story.

The reception the papers got at the CIA was muted, to say the least. Although the copies were widely distributed on October 16 to the various government intelligence agencies by the INR at a special meeting attended by least four CIA representatives, none of the four could remember getting a copy when questioned by Senate committee staff. At the CIA, the Niger papers mysteriously dropped from sight—for three months. After an investigation months later by the CIA's inspector general, one copy was found in a vault at the Counterproliferation

Division. The Center for Weapons Intelligence, Nonproliferation, and Arms Control (WINPAC), which reported directly to Tenet on key questions of concern to the larger intelligence community, did not receive a copy until January 16, 2003, when it had to ask the State Department for the documents.

As far as the CIA was concerned, the Niger documents seemed to be a nonissue. At the time, the Agency was preoccupied with the immediate problem of getting UN approval for U.S. military force if Washington could show that Baghdad was in breach of UN resolutions outlawing weapons of mass destruction. CIA analysts explained to the Senate committee that the "foreign government service" had already provided "verbatim text," therefore the documents wouldn't advance the case. Another said they were working on the reconstituted nuclear program, and the uranium reporting wasn't important. The lack of interest suggested that CIA analysts may have known about the existence of the actual documents that turned up in Italy—and not just the paraphrased or "verbatim" text of documents—long before the set of photocopies from Rome came over the transom in October. It also suggested that the CIA may have already believed they were bogus.

It didn't take long for analysts outside the CIA to sniff out problems with the documents. An INR analyst was skeptical and noted in an e-mail that one of the documents "bears a funky Emb of Niger stamp (to make it look official, I guess)." The suspicious INR analyst, the Senate report said, noticed that a separate document included in the photocopies mentioned a military campaign of Iran and Iraq against world powers being orchestrated by the Nigerien Embassy in Rome. "Completely implausible," he wrote.

After UN Resolution 1441 was negotiated by Colin Powell, the next hurdle was to develop a response to Iraq's 12,000-page disclosure, submitted on December 7, denying it had any WMD programs. On December 17, WINPAC produced an analysis of Baghdad's disclosure, pointing out that Iraq had breached its agreement by failing to explain its procurement of aluminum tubes to build centrifuges that could be used in a nuclear program. And Baghdad did "not acknowledge efforts to procure uranium from Niger, one of the points addressed in the U.K. dossier."

With this, the CIA had once more restored the Niger sale to respectability, even after Tenet himself had so carefully and thoroughly discredited it two months before by insisting on its deletion from the Cincinnati speech. On top of that, the CIA was attributing the intelligence to a classified British white paper that the CIA received in late September 2002 rather than to the original Italian reports. Once more the Agency was distancing itself from the Italian intelligence. Why was that?

The formulation by the Weapons Intelligence group also sprung the trap Cheney had set for the Iraqis. If the Iraqis admitted to having any unconventional weapons, they were in material breach of UN Resolution 687 of 1991, which banned them from building or possessing weapons of mass destruction. If Saddam tried to hide his weapons programs, well, he was also in violation. "That would be sufficient cause to say he's lied again, he's not come clean and you'd find material breach and away you'd go," said the vice president.[3] The White House declared Baghdad in material breach for attempting to conceal its "procurement" of aluminum tubes for enriching uranium fuel and for its "effort" to procure supplies of yellowcake uranium to feed the centrifuges.

The CIA had once more also failed to include mention of the State Department's well-known doubts about the actual use of the tubes and about the yellowcake deal in its report to the NSC. A December 23 exchange of e-mails, reported by Senate committee staff, between an analyst at the Department of Energy's (DOE) Intelligence section and a counterpart at INR made the obvious connection. "It is most disturbing that WINPAC is essentially directing foreign policy in this matter," wrote the DOE analyst. "There are some very strong points to be made about Iraq's non-compliance. However, when individuals attempt to convert those 'strong statements' into the 'knock out' punch, the Administration will ultimately look foolish—i.e., the tubes and Niger!"

On December 19, a State Department rebuttal to the Iraq disclosure mentioned Niger publicly for the first time, asking "Why is the Iraqi regime hiding their Niger procurement?" The U.S. response to Iraq's disclosure by then-UN Ambassador John Negroponte, who has recently been appointed to the newly created post of Director of National Intelligence by President Bush, elicited prompt denials from the Nigerien prime minister that Niger had sold uranium to Iraq or been approached to do since he took office in 2000.

By then, suspicions about the Niger documents from Rome were mounting. On January 13, the skeptical INR analyst spelled out in an e-mail to colleagues why he had concluded that "the uranium purchase agreement is probably a forgery." When an analyst at the CIA's Center for Weapons Intelligence, Nuclear Proliferation, and Arms Contro read it, he realized that the CIA did not have copies of the documents and requested them from the State Department. The CIA received the papers, said the Senate report, on January 16, 2003. Two CIA analysts studied the documents and later reported to Senate Intelligence Committee staff that "it was not jumping out at us that the documents were forgeries."

Jacques Baute, the director of the nuclear verification office for the International Atomic Energy Agency, asked the U.S. government for its evidence about the Niger uranium deal in January after Negroponte's speech, and was met with silence. His interest was piqued again when Colin Powell addressed the World Economic Forum in Switzerland on January 26, conflating the twin pillars of Iraq's allegedly reconstituted nuclear program. "Why is Iraq still trying to procure uranium and the special equipment to turn it into material for nuclear weapons?" Powell asked. On January 28, President Bush declared in the State of the Union address that Iraq "sought significant quantities of uranium from Africa," attributing the information to the British government. CIA Director Tenet testified that he never read the speech, but in the end took responsibility for the mention of the uranium deal, which had been borrowed by White House speechwriters from the problematic 2002 NIE and the September 2002 British white paper.

Baute was finally given copies of the Niger documents on February 4 after a flight from Vienna to New York. The next day, Colin Powell made his presentation to the UN Security Council stating the U.S. case for war. He did not mention the Niger uranium deal, an omission Baute noticed.

On February 3, the CIA had sent off a message that may explain why Powell dropped the reference to an Iraqi uranium deal—and perhaps even why the documents from Rome were turned over to Baute the very next day. The Senate committee reported in a heavily redacted passage on page 67 that the CIA sent a cable, apparently in response to Powell's tough vetting of the uranium deal, requesting "information from the foreign government service"—presumably Italian military intelligence—about an earlier report on the 1999 Iraq–Niger uranium deal. "The issue of Iraqi uranium procurement continues to resonate with senior policymakers," the CIA cable read, "and may be part of SecState's speech to the UN Security Council of 5 Feb 2003 if [a foreign government service] is able to provide a contract for the 1999 uranium deal, confirm that the information was not from another foreign government service. [Part of a lengthy redaction]."

"The same day," reported the Senate committee, "CIA [redacted] responded that the foreign government service does not have a copy of the contract, the information was of 'national origin.'"

Was CIA headquarters asking, say, the CIA station chief in Rome if Italian intelligence could provide a legitimate contract for the uranium deal? And could he assure Washington that the reporting on the 1999 deal did not originate with a third intelligence service, such as

Britain's MI6 or France's DGSE? Was the answer that Italian intelligence could not provide Secretary Powell with a legitimate contract? And that the documents on the 1999 uranium sale originated in Italy, with assistance from SISMI? Of course, this is only one possible interpretation of the redacted passage.

After Baute got the Niger papers in New York, he turned them over to IAEA investigators. A month later, on March 3, 2003, his office in Vienna informed the U.S. mission there that the documents were forgeries and, in the words of the Senate report, "did not substantiate any assessment that Iraq sought to buy uranium from Niger." Four days later, IAEA Director General Mohamed ElBaradei publicly declared that the documents were frauds.

Vice President Cheney responded on March 16 with an attack on ElBaradei. "I think Mr. ElBaradei frankly is wrong," he said. "And I think if you look at the track record of the International Atomic Energy Agency on this kind of issue, especially where Iraq's concerned, they have consistently underestimated or missed what it was Saddam Hussein was doing." Three days later, the U.S. "shock and awe" campaign against Iraq began. Two weeks later, the National Intelligence Council, the U.S. group responsible for national intelligence estimates, published a Sense of the Community Memorandum entitled "Niger: No Recent Uranium Sales to Iraq."

"We judge it highly unlikely that Niamey has sold uranium yellowcake to Baghdad in recent years," the memo read. "The Intelligence Community agrees with the IAEA assessment that key documents purportedly showing a recent Iraq–Niger sales accord are a fabrication. We judge that other reports from 2002—one alleging warehousing of yellowcake for shipment to Iraq, a second alleging a 1999 visit by an Iraqi delegation to Niamey—do not constitute evidence of a recent or impending sale." It did not say whether it still believed that Iraq had been "vigorously trying to procure uranium ore and yellowcake" from Niger.

The forged documents have raised suspicions that the entire Niger affair was a fiction cooked up by Western intelligence services. The IAEA pronouncement on the documents' lack of authenticity in early March, which may have been supported by the CIA cable traffic between Washington and Rome a month earlier, led Senate committee co-chairman Jay Rockefeller to request that the FBI investigate the origins of the forgeries. "There is a possibility," Rockefeller wrote to FBI Director Robert Mueller on March 14, "that the fabrication of these documents may be part of a larger deception campaign aimed at manipulating public opinion and foreign policy regarding Iraq."

The British were an early suspect. As Seymour Hersh noted as far back as the spring of 2003 in the *New Yorker,* both the British and the Americans used forged documents and disinformation in their dealings with Iraq, and Hersh reported that a sympathetic member of the UN weapons inspection team leaked unverifiable intelligence reports and tips to British MI6 agents who passed them along to London newspapers. He was also told by an Intelligence Committee staffer that "the Niger documents were initially circulated by the British." But British Intelligence's white paper about the 1999 Iraqi trip to Niger to buy yellowcake did not reach the CIA until September 2002, almost a year after the initial report. Hersh later reported that the documents may have been a setup arranged by disgruntled CIA employees eager to make the Bush administration appear foolish and credulous.

The French were also targeted by a British press report after French officials told the U.S. in November 2002 that France had also come by information on an Iraqi attempt to buy uranium from Niger. The following March, the United States learned that the French had based their assessment on the same documents the United States had turned over to the IAEA—a fine example of the Western intelligence echo chamber.

Recently, the Italian military intelligence service, SISMI, has come under closer scrutiny. Investigative reporters for a CBS *Sixty*

Minutes segment on the forged Niger documents identified an Italian businessman named Rocco Martino as a key player. Martino, who reportedly has connections to SISMI and other intelligence agencies, is believed to have been a conduit for the forgeries through an unknown source at the Nigerien Embassy in Rome, who apparently pilfered stationery for the operation. Martino offered to sell the phony documents to Elisabetta Burba for some $10,000. He is believed to have been working with another so-far-unnamed operative who apparently set up the deal and brought in Martino. Little more is known about the second man, who reportedly expected Martino to pass the Niger documents on to his foreign intelligence connections and who may have been a SISMI agent himself.

In the late summer of 2004, the CBS team brought Martino back to New York to film an interview, since law enforcement authorities in Italy reportedly had a warrant out on him. Fears that the FBI would pick up Martino in the United States to question him about the forgeries did not materialize, confirming the reporters' strong suspicions that the government wasn't pressing too hard to interview him. *Newsweek* reported that the FBI did want to speak to Martino but had "not yet received permission to do so from the Italian government."

That odd explanation fueled even more questions "about whether the right-wing government of Italian Prime Minister Silvio Berlusconi had helped manufacture evidence . . . to persuade Americans to support an invasion," according to the online magazine *Salon*. Martino, who has an arrest record and reputedly was once a SISMI agent himself, was questioned by Italian authorities in September 2004 about how the Niger documents came into his hands.[4]

The material on Martino was cut from CBS's final 30-minute version of the Niger report, which was scheduled to run before the 2004 elections. Copies of the segment were distributed to reviewers. Hours before the Niger story was to air, CBS shelved it and instead ran its now-infamous investigative fiasco about President Bush's National

Guard service, triggering an embarrassing internal CBS probe, multiple staff firings, and the retirement of news anchor Dan Rather. CBS News president Andrew Heyward later absurdly claimed that the Niger investigation was pulled because it was "inappropriate" during the presidential campaign.

3.

The reelection of George W. Bush in November 2004 put a damper on public interest in Special Counsel Patrick Fitzgerald's criminal probe into the White House leak, begun the previous January. At least half of the American electorate seemed willing to give this second-term wartime president a free pass, even if the truth about Iraq's WMDs was ignored and laws possibly broken in the rush to invade Iraq and protect the country from domestic terrorist attacks. Once it became clear that Iraq harbored no unconventional weapons or production facilities that posed a threat to the United States, the Bush administration quickly shifted its emphasis to making the Middle East safe for democracy. Iraq, it seems, had not been in serious breach of UN Resolution 687. The legal basis for the war had crumbled. Yet once Saddam was deposed and free elections were held in Iraq, even those many Americans who bitterly opposed Bush's reelection found it difficult not to hope that the administration's costly occupation of Iraq would be successful.

In this postelection atmosphere, Americans are hardly clamoring to learn who at the White House blew the cover of an obscure CIA operative. They forget that the president's own father called such a betrayal the act of "the most insidious of traitors." Yet, as historians such as Arthur Schlesinger, Jr. have written, Americans also have an instinct that is deeply protective of any president. They do not want to undercut the commander-in-chief's authority or credibility, especially in the face of threats abroad. Most are barely aware that this

White House is still the subject of a criminal investigation—and has been since before the election. Those with long memories point out that the public was not tuned in for some time to the early stages of the Watergate investigation or the Iran–Contra scandal either. Still, with public awareness at a low ebb, it is not surprising that even the staunchest anti-Bush Democratic leaders have shown little stomach for laying political siege to the Bush White House.

That could change, especially if the grand jury probe drags on inconclusively and the momentary elation at Iraqi elections gives way to clashes over forming a new government in Baghdad, further violence and bloodshed, or political unrest in the Middle East. As Schlesinger has pointed out, the expansion of presidential power during wartime and times of crisis is almost always counteracted by Congress and the American people cutting their leaders down to size when normalcy returns.[5] The domestic grace period for President Bush before the pendulum swings back may be even briefer, since the fight at hand with popular support is a war on terrorism to protect Americans from attack at home, not an internationalist impulse to export democracy to the Mideast.

It is difficult to decipher the current momentum of Fitzgerald's grand jury investigation. Many in the press believed the criminal probe was reaching a climax in June 2004 after Fitzgerald spent seventy minutes at the White House interviewing Bush and his lawyer, Jim Sharp. Some speculated that the leak must have come from a high-level official, if Fitzgerald's questioning led him to the Oval Office. But the grand jury has now been convened for fourteen months, and has been beset with problems from the start. Bush's newly minted second-term Attorney General Alberto Gonzales recused himself from the case in January 2005 as soon as he was confirmed by the Senate. The former attorney general, John Ashcroft, a close ally of the White House, had done the same in December 2003 after enduring growing pressure to appoint a special prosecutor.

Ashcroft's recusal came two months after he had appointed John Dion, a thirty-year veteran who headed the Justice Department's counterintelligence unit, to investigate the case. The attorney general finally stepped aside when the press reported that he was receiving regular FBI briefings on the progress of the case, including who testified, a clear conflict of interest.[6] Ashcroft turned the case over to his deputy, James Comey. Comey in turn appointed Fitzgerald, a former colleague and thirteen-year veteran of the U.S. Attorney's Office for the Eastern District of New York, as the new special counsel, a job that carried with it the power to subpoena witnesses. Fitzgerald had prosecuted the terror cell responsible for the 1993 World Trade Center bombing as well as other terrorist cases.

From the beginning, the investigation has been clouded with questions. Critics charged that the initial lag in getting the probe under way gave White House officials ample opportunity to destroy incriminating documents, e-mails, notes, phone records, diaries, and calendars that might have a bearing on the case. Such documents were also requested of Pentagon and State Department employees. Gonzalez held on to records submitted by White House employees for weeks before deciding which to send along to prosecutors. "I am very troubled by the fact that the White House counsel seems to be a gatekeeper," said Senator Charles Schumer of New York. "I want to know what precautions [the Justice Department] is taking to ensure that it gets all relevant information from the administration." Since the independent prosecutor legislation had expired, Schumer and other Democratic critics had little choice but to push for a government-appointed special counsel.

At the time, according to an ABC News/*Washington Post* poll, 70 percent of Americans wanted to see a special prosecutor assigned to get to the bottom of the leak. "This investigation is all blue smoke and mirrors," said Melanie Sloan, a former federal prosecutor and executive director of the Washington-based watchdog group Citizens for

Responsibility and Ethics. "It has the appearance of looking like an investigation without really doing enough to get to the bottom of this." White House officials still privately expected heads to roll. "Somebody will have to go before it's over," an administration official told the New York *Daily News*. "The only question is whether it's a low-level person following orders or somebody higher up."

Fitzgerald, who divides his time between his duties in Chicago and Washington's Judiciary Square, where the grand jury is convened, has come under heavy fire from liberals and conservatives alike. He is vilified by those on the left who believe he is conducting a witch-hunt against reporters and is in the pocket of the Bush administration for letting the grand jury probe drag on without indictments; his probe is under fire from the right for dragging out a criminal case against the White House that conservatives believe is without merit and for putting honorable journalistic traditions at risk.

In early 2005, the *Wall Street Journal* called on Fitzgerald to close down the grand jury investigation. Arguing that Wilson's "wife's role was bound to become public," the *Journal* editorial declared: "A wiser prosecutor than Mr. Fitzgerald might well have come to this same conclusion and shut down the probe. But like so many 'special' counsels who have only one case to prosecute, Mr. Fitzgerald seems to believe he'll be a failure if he doesn't charge someone with something. Thus his overzealous pursuit of reporters and their sources."

At issue was the *Journal*'s interpretation of the 1982 Intelligence Identities Protection Act, which makes it a felony to reveal the identity of an undercover CIA agent. The law was passed after rogue CIA agent Philip Agee identified CIA station chiefs in Beirut and Athens, both of whom were later murdered.

Victoria Toensing and Bruce Sanford, veterans of the Washington legal community who helped draft the law, wrote an Op-Ed piece for the *Washington Post* in January 2005 arguing that a high standard of evidence was built into the statute to avoid prosecuting people such as reporters or government employees who might unintentionally or carelessly identify covert agents. The agent's covert status must be classified, they wrote, and he or she must be either currently assigned to undercover assignments outside the country or have been assigned to such duty within the past five years. The disclosure must also be made intentionally with knowledge that the government has taken "affirmative measures to conceal [the agent's] relationship" to the United States.

In short, a guilty verdict under the 1982 law would have to show that the leaker either had security clearance and access to the agent's classified status or had inside knowledge from someone who did and intended to compromise the agent's covert identity. For conservatives, this narrow interpretation of the 1982 law raised the possibility that no crime had been committed. Why investigate the White House if there was no crime? Toensing and Sanford made no secret of their doubts that Plame's work with the CIA met the required legal standard. "It's time for a timeout on a misguided and mechanical investigation in which there is serious doubt that a crime was even committed."

Washington observers point out, however, that the CIA would not have referred a criminal case to the Justice Department unless it believed a law had been broken. And the Justice Department was under no obligation to take on a highly political Washington leak case, which is notoriously difficult to prosecute. In any case, the decision to gear up an FBI investigation and a grand jury proceeding connoted only that a crime *might* have been committed. It hardly guaranteed that anyone under investigation would be indicted or found guilty of a crime.

Plame's status as an undercover operative seems beyond question. Reporter Tim Phelps of *Newsday* confirmed her covert work with the CIA directly on the record. James Gordon Meek and Kenneth Bazinet of the New York *Daily News* quoted a former CIA counterterrorism official who told them that Plame "ran intelligence operations overseas" for the Agency's counterproliferation center, "recruiting agents, sending them to areas where they could access information about proliferation matters, weapons of mass destruction." Contrary to the Senate Intelligence Committee's reporting, former CIA official Vincent Cannistraro said that Plame worked undercover for the Center for Weapons Intelligence, Nonproliferation, and Arms Control, or WINPAC.

Without documentary evidence or witness testimony, however, problems might well arise in indicting lower-level administration aides without security clearance. They may have passed the word to reporters about Plame's CIA identity from their superiors but could credibly claim they had no knowledge of her status themselves. Applying a narrow legal definition, their cases might not meet the high evidentiary standards of the 1982 statute. Indeed, there is speculation in Washington that the White House legal strategy was organized around this reading of the law. Others believe the leakers could also be indicted under other laws involving the handling of classified material or on obstruction-of-justice charges.

Besides the president and vice president, Fitzgerald has reportedly met with two primary suspects in the Plame leak: Karl Rove, Bush's top political guru and deputy chief of staff, and I. Lawrence "Scooter" Libby, Vice President Cheney's chief of staff. Rove reportedly told MSNBC's Chris Matthews, the host of the political talk show *Hardball,* that the White House considered Wilson and his wife fair game for political payback. Libby was known as a no-holds-barred advocate of U.S. force in Iraq who played an active role as a spear-carrier between the CIA and the vice president's office on intelligence issues during the run-up to the war.

Other prominent Bush administration officials, including then–Secretary of State Colin Powell, former National Security Adviser Condoleezza Rice, NSC staffer and veteran GOP infighter Elliot Abrams, and former White House Counsel Gonzales, have testified before the grand jury or spoken with Fitzgerald. So far, however, no one has been officially identified by Fitzgerald's staff as a target of the investigation. That has led some to believe that he has been frustrated in identifying leakers he can indict under the Intelligence Identities Protection Act.

Others speculate that he may have identified lower-level administration officials who spoke to the press about Plame but is still gathering evidence on higher officials who might have given them orders. Some observers, noting the relentless and seemingly diversionary pressure Fitzgerald is putting on reporters Judith Miller and Matthew Cooper, believe that the special counsel is holding his cards close to his vest until all the witnesses under subpoena have testified.

4.

There is little question that the investigation of the White House leaks is now hostage to Fitzgerald's campaign to force Cooper and Miller to testify. On February 15, 2005, a three-judge panel of the U.S. Court of Appeals in Washington upheld the special counsel's right to do just that, sweeping aside the journalists' contention that they enjoy a privilege in this case under the First Amendment of the Constitution to protect the confidentiality of news sources and therefore should not have to testify. Cooper and Miller were initially found in contempt in October 2004 by U.S. District Court Judge Thomas Hogan and threatened with jail for as long as eighteen months if they did not tell the grand jury what they knew. Both have vowed to go to jail rather than expose their sources.

Although the circumstances differ that put Cooper and Miller at the mercy of Fitzgerald and the courts, both reporters and their news organizations have taken a strong stand that journalists are protected by the First Amendment against being compelled by the government to testify about their confidential sources. A journalist's privilege, in this view, is much like confidentiality privileges enjoyed by doctors and patients, lawyers and clients, or priests and confessors—a premise that has never sat well with jurists—or the public, for that matter.

Cooper, *Time*'s affable deputy Washington bureau chief, wrote an article for the magazine's Web site shortly after Novak's column appeared, questioning White House motivations in the leak. When he was first subpoenaed in mid-2004, Cooper testified for Fitzgerald, but only after Libby released him from his confidentiality agreement. When he was subpoenaed a second time and asked for evidence about other sources, Cooper drew the line. Miller, a onetime Pulitzer Prize–winning reporter who broke a half-dozen seriously flawed and misleading stories for the *Times* about Iraq's resurgent weapons programs before the war, had talked to administration officials about the Plame affair but had not written about it. She was subpoenaed by Fitzgerald anyway.

After the two were found in contempt by Judge Hogan, the *New York Times* and *Time* magazine combined forces and brought in Floyd Abrams, the nation's foremost litigator in First Amendment law, to defend them. Abrams knew that the 1972 Supreme Court decision, *Branzburg v. Hayes,* established that reporters who witnessed confidential sources in the commission of a crime could be compelled to reveal their identities if the public interest in justice outweighed the news that resulted. But ever since the ruling, reporters have enjoyed an informal agreement with government prosecutors, based on Justice Department guidelines, that has allowed them to protect their confidential sources in most circumstances.

Abrams saw an opening for what he hoped would be a better deal. Like other First Amendment lawyers, he argued that the late Justice Lewis Powell, in his concurrence to *Branzburg,* offered the promise that future legal developments might bring about a codification of the reporter's privilege in the law. For years after the decision, reporters were subpoenaed left and right. But the tacit agreement between reporters and the government held up. As Powell had predicted, thirty-one states now have shield laws on the books, and eighteen others have recognized some qualified reporter–source privilege. Abrams asked the appeals panel in December to recognize an unqualified confidentiality privilege for reporters.

The result was the unanimous decision in February against Cooper and Miller. Judge David B. Sentelle declared that the high court's "transparent and forceful" reasoning in *Branzburg,* a case in which *Louisville Courier Journal* reporter Paul Branzburg interviewed two Kentucky drug dealers about selling hashish in 1969, applied as well in the White House leak case. Sentelle wrote,

> In language as relevant to the alleged illegal disclosure
> of the identity of covert agents as it was to the alleged
> illegal processing of hashish, the Court stated it could
> not 'seriously entertain the notion that the First
> Amendment protects the newsman's agreement to
> conceal the criminal conduct of his source, or evidence
> thereof, on the theory that it is better to write about a
> crime than to do something about it.'

All three judges, including Judge David S. Tatel, a Clinton appointee, agreed that Fitzgerald had demonstrated that the grand jury's need for the reporters' testimony about the leaks overcame any protection due the reporters and their sources. Eight pages of the decision, presumably arguing the special counsel's case that information the reporters could provide was unavailable from other sources, were redacted from the court record to preserve secrecy in the grand jury proceedings. Tatel wrote that a common-law privilege based on qualified protections available in forty-nine states was an appropriate way for federal courts to balance the interests of the press and the grand jury. However, in this case, the judge said that protecting those who disclosed Plame's identity harmed national security while adding nothing of real news value, so that the reporters would have lost anyway.

Arthur Sulzberger, Jr., the publisher of the *Times,* said that if Miller went to jail, "it would create a dangerous precedent that would erode the freedom of the press," and promised that the newspaper would challenge the decision before the full Court of Appeals. "The protection of confidential sources was critically important to many groundbreaking stories, such as Watergate, the health-threatening practices of the tobacco industry and police corruption," said Sulzberger. He vowed to continue "to fight for the ability of journalists to provide the people of this nation with the essential information they need to evaluate issues affecting our country and the world."

Few journalists fault Cooper or Miller or their news organizations for the uncompromising stand they have taken. They know that Sulzberger is right about the critical importance of confidential sources in ferreting out government or corporate wrongdoing. But many wish Cooper and Miller had a stronger case to ride into this legal battle, and the journalistic community is split over the wisdom of staking such an important claim on the basis of a case in which reporters are protecting sources who were involved in a sleazy attempt to smear an outspoken opponent of the White House and who may have committed a crime in the process. The *Washington Post*'s Bob Woodward is also uneasy about the case. "This is not the Pentagon Papers," Woodward told the *Columbia Journalism Review* (CJR). "It's not the case I'd choose to make the law on."

At least five journalists have received subpoenas from Fitzgerald. Besides Cooper and Miller, Tim Russert of NBC's *Meet the Press,* veteran *Washington Post* investigative reporter Walter Pincus, and his *Post* colleague Glenn Kessler have all met with Fitzgerald and answered the prosecutor's questions—or negotiated what they would and would not discuss. The *CJR*'s Douglas McCollam reported that the *Washington Post* attempted to "defuse the impasse" with Fitzgerald with some success by demonstrating flexibility in responding to the subpoenas while drawing the line at testifying about confidential information. Pincus, for example, reportedly confirmed the time, date, and length of his conversation with a source other than Libby. The source had waived his right of confidentiality, but Pincus would not reveal his or her identity.

That lent credence to reports that Fitzgerald had subpoenaed records of every contact that White House personnel had had with reporters during the period in question and was engaged in a meticulous search to match such times and dates with records of meetings and telephone calls between reporters and Bush officials gleaned from calendars and telephone logs.

The sixth and most controversial journalist involved in the case is Robert Novak. Novak will not say whether he has been subpoenaed or if he has testified. Because he had contact with the officials who leaked Plame's identity, the presumption in Washington is that he was subpoenaed and has already talked. Lucy Dalglish, the director of the Reporter's Committee for Freedom of the Press, believes Novak may have cut a deal that enabled him to identify lower-ranking personnel involved who do not meet the stringent standards of the Identities Protection Act instead of the "senior administration officials" mentioned in his 2003 column.

Dalglish observes dryly that such a scenario would be consistent with increased pressure on reporters like Cooper and Miller, who have refused to cooperate with Fitzgerald. Is there any way out for the two? "The reporters will go to jail," Dalglish said.

The *New York Times* has declared it will seek a federal shield law for reporters to forestall this possibility. Two bills have been introduced in Congress, and although they have strong support in the journalistic community, many doubt that a Republican Congress will pass them any time soon. For his part, Abrams is currently seeking another appeal of the Cooper–Miller case before the full U.S. Court of Appeals, a process that could take months.

The final legal remedy is to petition the Supreme Court to put the case on its docket, which conceivably could push the resolution into 2006. However, the Supreme Court justices have been reluctant to take on First Amendment press cases in the past, preferring instead to leave such decisions to lower courts to decide on a case-by-case basis rather than establishing a hard-and-fast precedent. Fitzgerald is reportedly pushing Abrams to get the appeals moving. "We look forward to resuming our progress in this investigation and bringing it to a prompt conclusion," Fitzgerald said after the February ruling.

Michael Kinsley, the editor of the *Los Angeles Times* editorial page, made the obvious point in a column last October that "At least six prominent people know for sure who did the leaking." But Kinsley's sly reference to the six journalists in the know sharply underscored the difficulty of indicting government officials, who are protected against self-incrimination by the Fifth Amendment. Since Cooper and Miller are unlikely to testify, will Fitzgerald have to shut down the grand jury and declare that his multimillion-dollar investigation came up empty? Is some kind of negotiated, out-of-court settlement possible in which lower-level administration officials take the fall for the real culprits? Or will there be a whitewash along the lines of Lord Hutton's probe into the suicide of former British weapons inspector David Kelly, which exonerated government officials who may have "sexed up" pre-war intelligence supplied by Kelly about Iraq's weapons of mass destruction?

There are signs that that may be exactly what the Bush administration has in mind. In February 2004, the president created his own nine-member Commission on the Intelligence Capabilities of the United States Regarding Weapons of Mass Destruction to examine

U.S. intelligence agencies and assess their readiness to meet the challenges confronting American foreign policy. The report, which a commission spokesman said "will contribute to the understanding of what happened in Iraq," is due out in the spring of 2005. "It's for others to decide whether that's closure," he added. Vice President Dick Cheney has described the highly secretive work of the commission, which is led by retired federal judge Laurence Silberman and former Virginia governor and senator Charles S. Robb, as "one of the most important things that's going forward today."

Meantime, Senator Pat Roberts, the Republican chairman of the Senate Intelligence Committee, has declared that the second part of the committee's report on the White House role in the pre-war intelligence mess is on hold. "It's basically on the back burner," Roberts said in a March 2005 speech in Washington. "The bottom line is that [the administration] believed the intelligence, and the intelligence was wrong." Besides, said Roberts, the "WMD Commission in March will lay it all out." The Republican-dominated Senate committee has now turned its sights on the quality of U.S. intelligence on Iran's nuclear production network.

The jury is out on whether the news media and the American public will stand for a Lord Hutton–style cover-up on this side of the Atlantic. Could the benign post-election mood of the public shift, given the underlying polarization and uneasiness of the electorate on President Bush's handling of the war on Iraq? Any attempt to cover up possibly criminal behavior by senior White House officials, as alleged with such apparent precision by Novak, could backfire and set off obstruction-of-justice charges—with politically volatile consequences. Indictments could provoke the kind of public outcry that would force even the Republican-dominated Congress to call on the special counsel to widen his probe to include White House wrongdoing and Vice President Cheney's role in the pre-war WMD intelligence fiasco.

After all, if officials close to the president resorted to criminal tactics to undercut the credibility of potential opponents of Wilson's modest political stature, what might they have done to avert serious opposition to the invasion and occupation of Iraq? Four years after the Niger story first surfaced, many more questions have been raised than answered about the Bush administration's conduct of the Iraq war. Who was behind the forgery of the Niger documents? We have yet to see the results of the FBI investigation into their origins that was requested by Senate Intelligence Committee vice chairman Rockefeller two years ago. Will we ever?

Why did the CIA keep the forged documents under wraps for months before the war started? And who is responsible for the sixteen words on Iraq's pursuit of uranium that appeared in the president's State of the Union speech? We have yet to see the comprehensive probe into the effects White House political pressure had on the U.S. intelligence community that was promised by the Senate Intelligence Committee—and may never see it.

Who were the senior Bush officials who leaked Valerie Plame's identity? We don't know, despite a criminal investigation by a Washington grand jury that has been in progress for fourteen months now—and counting.

Russ Hoyle

New York City

March 14, 2005

[1] Bob Woodward, *Plan of Attack,* Simon & Schuster, New York, 2004, p. 29.

[2] See Josh Marshall, "There's More to Be Learned in the Niger Papers," July 15, 2004 and "Not Much on the Niger–Uranium Claims Has Changed," July 22, 2004, *The Hill,* Washington, D.C. Marshall independently confirmed through reliable sources that "the reports emanated from Italian intelligence." He also reported that a comparison of the subsequent U.S. and British intelligence reports, said to be summaries of documents on the uranium sale, and forged documents later provided to the U.S. indicates that the summaries included the same details as the forged documents. SISMI is the Italian

acronym for the Italy's military intelligence service, Servizio per le Informatzioni e la Sicurezza Militare.

3 Woodward, ibid; p. 222.

4 See Josh Marshall, Talking Points Memo, August 1, 2004; Michael Isikoff and Mark Hosenball, "The Story That Didn't Run," *Newsweek*, Sept. 22, 2004; and Mary Jacoby, "The Cowardly Network," Salon, Sept. 29, 2004, for discussion of the CBS investigation and the shelved *Sixty Minutes* Niger report.

5 Arthur M. Schlesinger, Jr., *War and the American Presidency*, W.W. Norton, New York, 2004.

6 See Murray Waas, "Ashcroft's Interest," *American Prospect*, July 8, 2004, for reporting on the former attorney general's conflicts of interest in the early stages of the Justice Department probe into the White House leaks that led to his recusal.

Anatomy of a Smear

I N THE MONTHS SINCE THE APRIL 30, 2004, publication of this book, I have traveled around the country and met literally thousands of Americans in bookstores, at universities, at local business forums, city clubs, and town hall meetings. Fellow citizens from all walks of life have reached out and expressed their anger and bewilderment at the vindictiveness of the Bush administration and what its allies have done to Valerie and me—from the compromise of her identity in the early days of this saga through the character assassination campaign waged against us in the summer of 2004.

Many of my colleagues in the Foreign Service have called to express their delight at the tale of a career in American diplomacy, pointing out similarities with their own careers. One friend, whose career was spent mostly in Bonn and Berlin, saw numerous parallels in our experiences. Other than the fact that I had also spent years in cities beginning with "B" (Bujumbura, Brazzaville, and Baghdad), I was hard-pressed to see the common threads until he pointed out that we had each been witness to tremendous change during our careers. His had been the end of the Cold War and the liberation of Eastern Europe from the vantage point of an office overlooking the Berlin Wall as it came down, while mine had been the first military action in the post–Cold War period, the deployment of 500,000 soldiers to the Persian Gulf, and the liberation of a small country invaded by a bellicose neighbor.

Many people who share my passion for Africa have responded appreciatively to the stories from that beleaguered and beautiful continent. Former president Bill Clinton took me aside at the Democratic convention in Boston to tell me that he had read the book and found the part about his trip to Africa to be a "perfect" rendition of that eleven-day odyssey.

These gratifying responses have, of course, not prevented Bush supporters from continuing—and indeed intensifying—the smear campaign against Valerie and myself. This is regrettable. And the lies and distortions have become magnified by the right-wing echo chamber that has unfortunately become so effective in our country, utilizing frequent repetition of the underlying falsehoods, and by a media that sees its role as giving equal space and time to lies as to the truth and then supposedly letting the news consumer decide. I wonder if some reporters and broadcasters are simply too beguiled by the administration's smoke and spin to look behind the veil for the truth. Indeed, as I wrote in Chapter Twenty-One of the book, we are in a media world that is a long, long way from the halcyon days of investigative journalism. Anne-Marie Cox, the irreverent "Wonkette" blogger, had it right when she argued at a conference broadcast on C-SPAN that politicians and political writers are all, in the end, part of one big company working for "the man." I somehow doubt that Bob Woodward, Carl Bernstein, and Ben Bradlee saw it that way when they were pursuing the truth behind the Nixon administration's cover-up of the Watergate scandal.

In July 2004, the Republican smear machine moved into high gear against Valerie and myself when the Senate Select Committee on Intelligence issued the first of what was supposed to be two reports on the prewar intelligence related to Iraq. (It is not clear whether the second report, on the political manipulation of intelligence, will ever be issued.) This first report was intended to "look behind the [Intelligence] Community's assessments to evaluate not only the quantity and quality of intelligence upon which it based its judgments but, also the reasonableness of the judgments themselves," as the preamble to the report reads.

Forty-one pages in the body of the report were devoted to the question of purported uranium sales from Niger to Iraq, my role in the investigation of the allegation, and whether or not Valerie had played a part in my being asked to travel to Niger. An additional three pages were devoted to the issue in the "Additional views of Chairman Pat Roberts, joined by Senator Christopher S. Bond and Senator Orrin G. Hatch." The report and the "additional views" of the three senators sparked a savage attack on Valerie's and my integrity. Driven by the Republican National Committee, the über-right-wing magazines such as the *Weekly Standard* and the *National Review,* the equally fanatical editorial board of the *Wall Street Journal,* and selected opinion writers, including William Safire, trained their poison pens on us. Even Bob Novak emerged from his self-imposed silence to take another whack at us.

The thrusts of the attacks were based on two tendentious conclusions in the senators' "additional views." These were: (1) "The plan to send the former ambassador to Niger was suggested by the former ambassador's wife, a CIA employee"; and (2) "Rather than speaking publicly about his actual experiences during his inquiry of the Niger issue, the former ambassador seems to have included information he learned from press accounts and from his beliefs about how the Intelligence Community would have or should have handled the information he provided." The senators' "additional views" also asserted that "during Mr. Wilson's media blitz, . . . [he] told anyone who would listen that the President had lied to the American people, that the Vice President had lied, and that he had 'debunked' the claim that Iraq was seeking uranium from Africa"; and that "The Committee found that, for most analysts, the former ambassador's report lent more credibility, not less, to the reported Niger–Iraq uranium deal."

Valerie and I were stunned and disheartened. She likened it to being hit full-force in the stomach—again. It took our breath away. Of course, since she was still employed by the CIA, she could not even defend herself. But it would not have mattered anyhow, since the Republican committee staff, with whom both Valerie and I had met and which was responsible for drafting the report and the "additional views" for the senators, had systematically misstated the facts and not even bothered to check with responsible officials at the Agency before coming to their conclusions.

They ignored, for example, a CIA statement issued to *Newsday* reporters Knut Royce and Tim Phelps barely a week after the Novak article had appeared in July 2003. The *Newsday* story read:

> A senior intelligence officer confirmed that Plame was a Directorate of Operations undercover officer who worked "alongside" the operations officers who asked her husband to travel to Niger. But he said she did not recommend her husband to undertake the Niger assignment. "They [the officers who did ask Wilson to check the uranium story] were aware of who she was married to, which is not surprising," he said. "There are people elsewhere in government who are trying to make her look like she was the one who was cooking this up, for some reason," he said. "I can't figure out what it could be.
>
> We paid his [Wilson's] air fare. But to go to Niger is not exactly a benefit. Most people you'd have to pay

big bucks to go there," the senior intelligence official
said." [Brackets in the original.]

This was not a difficult article to find, with the unnamed Agency official's quote featured in it. A simple Google search turned it up for me
in minutes, twenty months later. However, the committee staff apparently did not devote the effort to find it or else decided not to include
the official statement in their report. I called then–CIA spokesman Bill
Harlow, who confirmed to me that the formulation of "senior intelligence officer" was the CIA's way of conveying official information
without attribution. I asked him if the Senate staff had ever contacted
him to elicit the Agency's official position. He told me he had not
been contacted. Neither had Valerie's supervisor at the time of my trip
ever been contacted on this or on any other point by the Senate
Intelligence Committee. Had the Senate staff contacted Valerie's
supervisor, he would have been able to confirm that Valerie was not
responsible for the decision that led to my travel to Niger.

The Senate staff's case apparently rested on an anodyne comment in a paper that Valerie had drafted at the request of her supervisor in which she wrote that "my husband has good relations with
both the PM (prime minister) and the former Minister of Mines (not
to mention lots of French contacts), both of whom could possibly
shed light on this sort of activity." Nothing in that memo conveys anything more than a statement of my qualifications. The fact was that
she had not suggested me for the trip and had served only as a conduit when I was asked to come to the Agency to discuss the matter in
the first place. She had not been present at the meeting where I was
asked if I would go, so as to avoid even the appearance of conflict of
interest. Ironically, my bona fides for being asked to undertake the
mission were well established in the body of the Senate report: in
addition to my many years in Africa, including service as President
Clinton's senior director for African Affairs, I had undertaken a trip

to Niger in 1999 at the request of the CIA to look into other uranium-related matters. One reporter later said on a radio program that he had been told by the Agency that my name had been spewed out of a computer at the Agency when they had been looking for a candidate. After that, it would have been logical for Valerie's associates to ask her to write a sentence or two about me.

The "additional views" addendum to the Senate report also cites a CIA reports officer who stated that "the former ambassador's wife 'offered up his name.'" When that CIA officer read the quote in the report, he went to see Valerie to tell her that he had never said anything of the kind. He was so distraught that he offered to write a memo to clarify that it had been him, not Valerie, who had initially suggested that the CIA talk to me. Valerie made it clear to him that she could not advise him one way or another. Valerie told me he wrote such a memo and shared the contents with her, but that the supervisor would not allow him to send it to the committee.

Of course, even if Valerie had been responsible for the decision to send me, what difference would it have made? If the suggestion is that somehow nepotism was involved, what possible benefit accrued to either her or me from my pro bono time away from her and our two-year-old twins? More nefarious is the suggestion that perhaps this was a partisan political operation designed to embarrass the administration. That is the thrust of Novak's wondering in print why the administration would send a "former Clinton" appointee to make the trip, as if national security were partisan. Of course, my only presidential appointment requiring Senate confirmation had been by President George Herbert Walker Bush. My tenure at the National Security Council (NSC) had been a career detail from the State Department. My trip to Niger took place eight months before I ever wrote about my views on what our Iraq policy should be, and my first column was lauded by my erstwhile Republican colleagues from the first Gulf War, including former President Bush (who wrote "I agree with almost everything" in the column), and his National Security adviser, Brent Scowcroft. Again, a simple look at the calendar and the press would have shown that I did not become a critic of the war until many, many months after my trip. Even then, as my articles make clear, my criticism of the policy was not because I discounted the threat of weapons of mass destruction in the hands of Saddam but because I worried that the invade-conquer-occupy approach was not the best way to deal with the issue.

The second conclusion of the "additional views" charged me with having included information in my statements about which I had no personal knowledge. This charge was a reference to unidentified sources in articles in the *New York Times* and the *Washington Post* which said that the documents that had precipitated my trip to Niger were obvious forgeries and that the source of the documents had been the Italian intelligence service. In both cases, the information had been in the public sector for over three months before I had ever spoken on background to any journalist. In the case of one *Washington Post* article that cited the Italian origin of the documents, I had not been a source for any part of that article.

The *New York Times* article in question had been authored by columnist Nicholas Kristof and indeed had included, in addition to the story of my trip, a badly worded reference to the documents as forgeries, creating the possible impression that I had claimed to have seen them. Nothing could have been further from the truth, and I had called Kristof the day his article appeared to remind him that I had never seen the documents. When I wrote my own Op-Ed article for the *Times,* published on July 6, 2003, I made a point of stating that I had never seen the documents in question. But there was no reference in the "additional views" to my own statements. And nobody from the staff had bothered to ask Kristof about the article in question. I did, however.

As soon as I saw the report, I sent an e-mail note to Kristof asking if he remembered our conversation. His response was:

> Joe, thanks for that nice note. it finds me in salt lake city, where i'm driving through red states and talking to people about issues (here, they care about guns and abortion, but not about wsj attacks).
>
> don't worry. i remember you saying that you had not seen the documents. my recollection is that we had some information about the documents at that time—e.g. the names of people in them—but i do clearly remember you saying that you had not been shown them.

I said the same thing on page fourteen of this book. And the Senate staffers who interviewed me nearly a year after Kristof's article appeared made clear to me that they had read my book closely. So closely, in fact, that they took umbrage at a statement I made asserting that I knew that Cheney had been informed of the results of my trip. Was I a "witness of fact," I was asked. "No," I replied, but I did know how the government usually circulates information. Perhaps I should have used the word "assume" rather than "know" with respect to Cheney. Of course, the Senate report makes clear that the vice president was keenly interested in the Niger claim and had asked about it on several occasions. And the report points out that a report on my trip was circulated throughout the national security apparatus within days of my return. The vice president is, of course, part of that national security apparatus.

All of this was well documented in the report and in articles that had appeared in the press over the previous year, but none of that prevented the onslaught from the right.

*   *   *

The first article appeared in the *Washington Post* bylined Susan Schmidt, who in the 1990s had gained a reputation as a favored journalist of the Starr Whitewater investigation, often breaking stories with leaks from inside the Office of the Independent Counsel. Josh Marshall, the talented reporter and blogger at talkingpointsmemo.com, referred to her as the "Mikey" (of Life Cereal fame) for her willingness to consume Republican tales without critical reflection. Her article was replete with factual errors that could have been avoided had she bothered to read the text of the report or even done some basic research, such as looking up the CIA statement made the previous year in the *Newsday* article about Valerie's lack of involvement in the trip. But she did not. Indeed, her reporting was so sloppy that from the lead sentence she conflated what the three Republican senators—and not even a majority of their own party's representation on the committee— asserted with what the actual report concluded. She even confused Iraq with Iran, a significant error of fact. She also quoted a phrase from this book that Valerie "had nothing to do with the matter" without the qualifying phrase in the beginning of the sentence: "Other than serve as a conduit." Schmidt asserted that my report, rather than debunking intelligence about purported uranium sales to Iraq, had bolstered the case for most intelligence analysts. She went further, noting that "contrary to Wilson's assertions and even the government's previous statements, the CIA did not tell the White House it had qualms about the reliability of the Africa intelligence that made its way into 16 fateful words in President Bush's January 2003 State of the Union address."

Both these assertions were patently false, and even a cursory reading of the body of the report dedicated to the Niger case would have borne that out. The corporate view of the American intelligence community was communicated to the Senate Select Committee on Intelligence on October 2, 2002, almost four months before the State of the Union address, by the deputy director of Central Intelligence. In response to a question from Arizona senator Jon Kyl, the deputy responded: "The one thing where I think they [the British] stretched a little bit beyond where we would stretch is on the points about where Iraq was seeking uranium from various African locations."

Four days later, again nearly four months before the State of the Union, the director of Central Intelligence called the deputy National Security adviser and, as he later testified, told him, "the president should not be a witness of fact on this issue" because "the reporting was weak." A subsequent fax to the National Security adviser's office a day or so later explained further why the CIA recommended that the White House not use the assertion in presidential statements: "(1) The evidence is weak. One of the two mines cited by the source as the location of the uranium oxide is flooded. The other mine cited by the source is under the control of the French authorities. (2) The procurement is not particularly significant to Iraq's nuclear ambitions because the Iraqis already have a large stock of uranium oxide (yellowcake) in their inventory, and (3) We have shared points one and two with Congress, telling them this is one of the two issues where we differed with the British."

It could not have been any clearer. The American intelligence community did not believe the British claim and told both the White House and the Senate that it did not—months before the president uttered his infamous sixteen words. As fundamentally flawed as Schmidt's article was, it became the primary source for the spate of opinion pieces that soon appeared in many right-wing editorial pages. None of these pundits apparently took the time to read the report, for the simple reason that the Schmidt article gave them cover for the vitriol they would soon spew. And vitriol was the reason for these articles; truth was something to be consciously ignored. The goal was character assassination, not investigative journalism or critical analysis.

Key to generating momentum was the Republican National Committee, sending blast e-mails and blast faxes on a daily basis to its coterie of propagandists. Jim Moore, the author of *Bush's Brain*, a book about the president's senior political adviser, Karl Rove, wrote to me that that it had all the hallmarks of a Rove campaign. A Republican, disenchanted with his own party, told me that it was done to "take you out of the national debate because you have been effective."

The *Wall Street Journal* made clear in an editorial the objective of its attacks on Valerie and me: to get the special counsel looking into a possible crime—cited as treason by the first President Bush—to "fold up his tent."

Valerie had been devastated by the continuing attacks, now directed not just at me but at her too. But she could only sit by in silence. As an employee of the CIA, she could have no contact with the press without prior approval, and the CIA was unwilling to allow her to speak out. She finally drafted an Op-Ed in December and submitted it to the CIA prior to sending it to a newspaper, only to be denied the right to publish it because "the publication of your article has the potential to affect your ability to perform your official duties and the Agency's ability to perform its mission." In an oral comment to our attorney, Agency officials were blunter, saying they did not want to do anything that might undermine their relationship with the Senate Select Committee on Intelligence by perhaps giving the appearance of taking sides. I was not surprised. After all, the recently installed director of Central Intelligence, former Congressman Porter Goss, had made it clear in comments made nearly a year earlier that he would not pursue Congressional hearings in the leak case unless somebody produced "a blue-stained dress." With that attitude from the top, how could an employee expect support from management? While I would love to be able to share Valerie's article with readers, so long as her Agency refuses to allow her to defend herself, there is nothing she or I can do.

Despite my admonitions that she not read the articles I've been referring to, she could not help herself. When the *Wall Street*

Journal's editorial board weighed in, however, she was comforted by her recognition of the goal of the hate campaign: to derail a criminal investigation.

In mid-July, I appeared on PBS's *NewsHour with Jim Lehrer* with Senator Christopher Bond to discuss the Senate Report and the additional views. The senator was adamant and hostile even in the face of my explanations, at one point noting that the White House had sent the uranium claim to the CIA nine times for clearance and that it had been cleared for use in the State of the Union. In so stating, he confirmed one of my most controversial charges: the intelligence had been manipulated for political purposes. The White House and the NSC are not intelligence-collection or -analysis agencies. When the director of Intelligence had told the White House that the "President should not be a witness of fact" in the matter, efforts to obtain CIA clearances should have immediately ceased. That the White House had continued to press the case was clear evidence that the charge was important—not for its intelligence value but to support political decisions that had already been made. One key quote from the Senate report said it all. A CIA analyst cited an NSC staffer as saying that we had to use the British allegation because we did not want to leave the Brits "flapping in the wind." If that is not the manipulation of intelligence for political purposes, I don't know what is. The NSC staffer in question conveniently did not remember saying that but also did not deny it.

During the Democratic Convention in Boston, the Republicans stayed on the attack. According to a journalist, they opened every one of their morning press briefings by trying to discredit me further—by simply asserting that I had been discredited.

I addressed the charges at a gathering in New York in late August during the Republican Convention, later carried on C-SPAN. I pointed out that there were two reasons to be concerned by the attacks. First, as the *Wall Street Journal* had acknowledged, the goal was to derail the special counsel's investigation. The head of the Republican Party is the president of the United States. Key Republican leaders include Vice President Cheney and Karl Rove. All three had hired lawyers and had been questioned by the special counsel. The fact that the organization they led was attacking me certainly gave the impression of tampering with that ongoing criminal investigation.

More seriously, what the Republicans and their flacks were doing was a clear signal to all Americans that they were determined to destroy those who would dare to criticize them—and their families. Be afraid, be very afraid, was my warning; I said that it was un-American and undemocratic and must be confronted.

What I faced in the days and weeks before the convention was but a prelude to the beating John Kerry took when the so-called Swift Boat Veterans for Truth launched their campaign of lies. I have often wondered if the attacks on Valerie and me were a test run for the latter campaign, designed to see how far they could go with an often craven and uncritical press corps. In both cases it turned out be very far indeed.

The scurrilous lies overwhelmed the substance as the press raced to keep up with the eye-catching, *National Enquirer*-style headlines promulgated by such yellow journalism sources as *Fox News*. The shameless attacks were consistent with the well-known legal strategy of diverting attention from the facts by impugning the integrity of the accuser. In Kerry's case, the challenge to his heroism called into question the very system by which we as a nation honor the service of those who put their lives on the line for their country. All holders of silver or bronze stars or purple hearts had to wonder if their own meritorious service had been called into question by the Republican campaign. It was outrageous, all the more so since it was apparently so successful in blemishing Kerry's reputation and service.

For well over three decades, I had looked upon American presidential elections as a celebration of our democracy, of the vitality of a system of government that promoted liberty, strove to protect minority views, and celebrated the rights of the individual. The election of 2004, however, was a referendum on us as a society. The election of George W. Bush in 2000 could have been interpreted as the result of Clinton fatigue or a natural turn away from eight years of one party holding the presidency. However, Bush's reelection in 2004—after the debacle of Iraq, the failed promise of compassionate conservatism, and the shameless pandering to the most venal and least tolerant elements of our society—could only be interpreted as a national espousal of the radical turn taken by the incumbent administration. For foreigners, many of whom had seen imperial armies march across their lands in their histories, this had to be a chilling moment—the endorsement of American imperialism through the aggressive use of force.

Bush's administration was not a conservative one. It had not exercised fiscal discipline; rather, it had added over a trillion dollars to the national debt. It had not limited the growth of the federal government; this was the largest government since the first Bush administration. It had not gotten government out of Americans' lives; between the Patriot Act and the crude campaign against gay Americans, there was no limit to how much time or political capital the federal government was prepared to spend peeking in the windows of its citizens.

Indeed, the Bush administration had taken American governance into uncharted and undesirable waters; and everywhere I traveled around the country during the campaign, people were worried, even Republicans. I met very few people who had voted for Al Gore or Ralph Nader in 2000 who were going to vote for Bush in 2004. By contrast, at every stop, from Seattle to Cleveland to Trenton, New Jersey, people would tell me that they were switching their vote from Bush to Kerry, even if they remained Republican in their political views. John Eisenhower, the son of the president and a general and ambassador in his own right, wrote that his father would not recognize today's

Republican Party. A member of the Taft family told me the same thing in Cleveland.

The Republican victory in the 2004 election was a testament to their campaign of fear, lies, and character assassination and to their determination to stay in power whatever the cost to the country. And it has come with a cost. The message to the rest of the world is clearly that we are out of control; that we as a society not only failed to rein in our radicals but reconfirmed them in power. The views of the neo-conservatives that our national security is enhanced through aggressive use of military force will be further entrenched and difficult to root out. The prevailing view that religion (their fundamentalist brand of it) not only has its place in the public square—but should also be taxpayer-supported—is also on the ascendancy. When evangelicals say, as they often do, that "truth is absolute, it is not democratic," we need to worry about intolerance in our diverse and heterogeneous society.

And now the rest of the world will either have to accommodate us or attempt to constrain us. Many of them have ingrained in their national memories the plundering of their countries at some point by marauding imperial troops. That is what they see the United States doing today, with its unbridled military power. Their response will not be to confront us directly militarily but to do so through a combination of economic, cultural, and other flanking actions. Both Saudi Arabia and Iran are already forging deeper ties with China. One of the ironies of this second Gulf War might well be that we drive moderate powers into alliances to be better able to defend themselves against us. With China holding an increasing share of our national debt and with the euro now a legitimate competitor reserve currency, will we continue to be that "indispensable power"? Not for long, if fear of American intentions drives other nations into each other's arms.

These are increasingly perilous times for our democracy, which is threatened not only from international terrorism but from the affront to our democracy by those who value their own power above our two-hundred-year constitutional history. Karl Rove, the architect of George Bush's ascendancy and often called the meanest man in American politics, said it best at the opening of the Clinton Library in November 2004. According to Sidney Blumenthal, writing in the *Guardian*, Rove, shortly after being told that he didn't seem to be so dangerous, was heard saying to himself as he walked away "Yes, I am. I change constitutions. I put church into schools." However powerful Rove might be, he is not an elected representative of the people of this country, and his comments are profoundly antithetical to the very nature of our great nation.

Benjamin Franklin is reported to have said at the conclusion of the Constitutional Convention that a republic had been created "if you can keep it." And if we want to keep "it," we must be better stewards of our democracy. It is necessary but not sufficient that we vote in record numbers; we must also have a clearer understanding of the underlying issues on which we are voting. And our political leaders must be held to some standards of integrity and truthfulness.

Thirty years ago, the American people, our representatives in Congress, and the press rose up to throw out an administration engaged in dirty tricks that in today's political environment pass as business as usual. Whatever differences our parties might have philosophically—and I for one don't believe that either party has a monopoly on wisdom in public policy-making—there should be no more room in our politics for the dirty tricksters today than there was then. We owe ourselves and our great country more vigilance in the public square. We will not achieve that until the charlatans are exposed for what they are and our press coverage is less dependent on the ratings war that favors rants over thoughtful debate and sensationalism over serious discussion of issues.

Valerie and I never aspired to more than good citizenship and public service. Indeed, the greater part of this book is a recitation of one citizen's service to country. The attacks of the past several months have left us dumbfounded. At the conclusion of one interview, Wolf Blitzer commented to me that "it is just politics." But it has *not* been "just politics"; it has been a concerted effort to destroy our reputations, just as they tried to destroy John McCain in the 2000 primary campaign and John Kerry in 2004. The facts have remained the same: the sixteen words in the State of the Union should never have been there, and the White House and the Senate knew it several months before the speech. While everybody knows Valerie's name and mine, nobody knows the name of the person who inserted the lie into the president's speech nor who revealed Valerie's identity to Robert Novak and other journalists.

The president could get to the bottom of this if he truly wanted to. After all, he gave the order in October 2003 that all members of his administration should cooperate fully with the Justice Department investigation. According to reporting, some of his staff refused to sign Justice-requested waivers of confidentiality with journalists on self-incrimination grounds. While they are certainly entitled to do so in our legal system, should they continue to enjoy presidential patronage after violating his direct order? Instead, the administration continues to stonewall, while the press becomes understandably exercised over the possibility that a couple of journalists might have to go to jail for refusing to disclose their sources. Matt Cooper of *Time* magazine and Judith Miller of the *New York Times* have been held in contempt of court for refusing to divulge the names of those who apparently shared with them some aspects of the leak, perhaps including Valerie's name and employment. They are arguing that the First Amendment guarantee of freedom of the press permits them to protect their sources. The case is before the courts as this is being written, but most observers with whom I have spoken believe their case is very weak. As one former Justice Department official said, "they are not relieved of their responsibilities as citizens to report crimes and to cooperate in the investigation of criminal activities." He added that the government has a long-established need to collect intelligence and hence a right to protect those officers who are collecting it, and that that right overrides the press's right to protect sources.

Valerie and I are clearly not part of this debate, even as our names are invoked. It is between the government and the press. As a citizen, I regret any circumscribing of the press's ability to do its job. But in this case, it is not as though the press is protecting a whistle-blower against an all-powerful government; it is, rather, a case where a vindictive government has used the press in order to try to destroy an opponent.

In our democracy, the press and individual citizens have a duty to hold our government to account for what that government has said and done in the name of the people. We do that every day as citizens, at city council meetings, in our statehouses and in our Congress. Ask any mayor or congressman. I intervened in an area where I had some relevant information. Nothing more, nothing less. It was no more an act of courage than it was treachery: it was civic responsibility.

And for that, Valerie and I have been subjected to a heinous hate campaign, abetted not just by right-wing extremists and their allies on the editorial board of the *Wall Street Journal* but also by the unfortunate descent into shoddy journalism by the *Washington Post,* a paper that prides itself on being a national paper of record. But I would do it again in a minute, because I am an American. The most solemn decision a government ever has to make is the one to send its citizens to kill and to die in the name of its people. We have a right to insist that the debate leading up to that decision be based on facts, not on information that simply supports the administration's view irrespective of its veracity. Exposing government lies is what our system was set up to encourage.

Of course, debates on going to war should also take place before, not after, more than 1500 Americans have been killed, $150 billion spent, our international standing reduced to tatters, and countless thousands of Iraqis killed, injured, and their property destroyed. We best support our troops by not sending them to war unless and until we are certain there is no other way to defend our national security or to attain our objectives. What Valerie and I have endured in this right-wing paroxysm of hate is nothing compared to what the administration has inflicted on tens of thousands of American troops and their families in this monumental breach of faith with the armed forces. My only regret is that we as a nation were not able to prevent this ill-advised war before so many of our fellow citizens were put in harm's way.

Washington, D.C.
March 14, 2005

NB: I would like to refer inquiring readers to two pieces of important documentation.

The first is my letter to the chairman and vice chairman of Senate Select Committee on Intelligence, responding to their committee's July 2004 report on intelligence before the invasion of Iraq: http://archive.salon.com/opinion/feature/2004/07/16/ wilson_letter/print.html

The second is to David Corn's October 20, 2004, article in the *Nation* magazine, responding to the demands of some Republican House members that the Nation Institute and the Fertel Foundation rescind the Ron Ridenhour Truth-Teller Award I was given in 2003: http:// www.thenation.com/capitalgames/index.mhtml?bid=3 &pid=1922

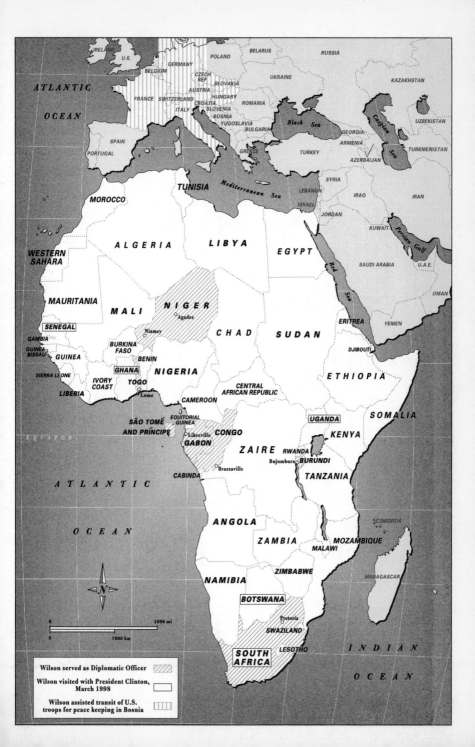

Wilson served as Diplomatic Officer

Wilson visited with President Clinton, March 1998

Wilson assisted transit of U.S. troops for peace keeping in Bosnia

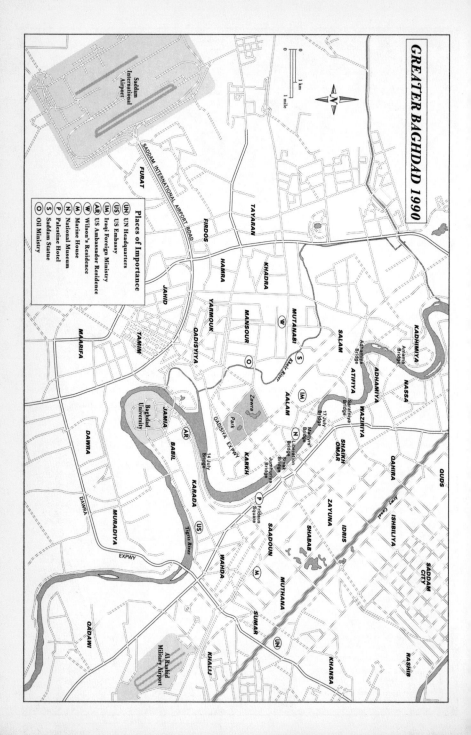

GREATER BAGHDAD 1990

Places of Importance

- **UN** UN Headquarters
- **US** US Embassy
- **IM** Iraqi Foreign Ministry
- **AR** US Ambassador Residence
- **W** Wilson's Residence
- **M** Marine House
- **N** National Museum
- **P** Palestine Hotel
- **S** Saddam Statue
- **O** Oil Ministry

Saddam International Airport

SADDAM INTERNATIONAL AIRPORT ROAD

FURAT

FIRDOS

JAHID

TAMIM

MAARIFA

DAWRA

MURADIYA

QADAWI

KHALIJ

KHANSA

SUMAR

WAHIDA

KARADA

BABIL

JAMIA

Baghdad University

QADISIYA EXPWY

14 July Bridge

Zawra Park

KARKH

AALAM

SALAM

MANSOUR

QADISIYA

YARMOUK

HAMRA

KHADRA

TAYARAN

MUTANABI

Khar River

ATIFIYA

ADHAMIYA

WAZIRIYA

SHAIKH OMAR

Adhamiya Bridge

Sarafiya Bridge

17 July Bridge

Maytora Bridge

Liberation Bridge

Sinak Bridge

Jumhuriya Bridge

Ahrrar Bridge

Aimma Bridge

KADHIMIYA

NASSA

QAHIRA

ISHBILIYA

QUDS

SADDAM CITY

ZAYUNA

IDRIS

SHABAB

SAADOUN

MUTHANA

Firdaus Square

RASHID

Al Rashid Military Airport

Tigris River

EXPWY

DAWRA

Al Karkh River

0 1 km
0 1 mile

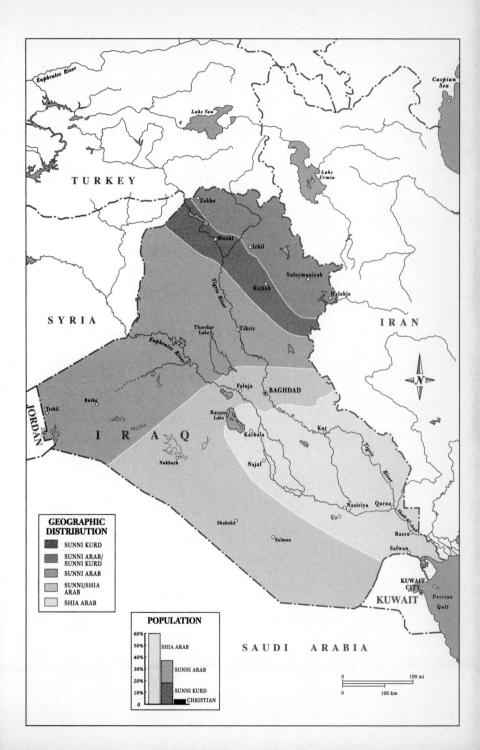

Chapter One
The Sixteen Words

"'Wilson's wife is fair game.'" Those are fighting words for any man, and I'd just had them quoted to me by MSNBC's Chris Matthews. It was July 21, 2003, barely a week since a column by Robert Novak in the *Washington Post* had named my wife, Valerie, as a CIA officer, and now the host of *Hardball* was calling to tell me that as far as the White House was concerned, they had declared open season on my family.

In his signature staccato, Matthews was blunt: "I just got off the phone with Karl Rove. He says, and I quote, 'Wilson's wife is fair game.'" Before abruptly hanging up, Matthews added: "I will confirm that if asked." As head of the White House political office and one of President George W. Bush's closest advisers, Rove was legendary for his right-wing zeal and take-no-prisoners operating style. But what he was doing now was tantamount to declaring war on two U.S. citizens, both of them with years of government service.

Together, my wife and I had been on the media equivalent of Mr. Toad's Wild Ride since the appearance of a piece I had written for the *New York Times* op-ed page on July 6. In it, I stated that the Bush administration had been informed a year and a half earlier that their claims of Iraqi attempts to purchase uranium from Niger were false. I knew what information the administration had about Niger because in early March

2002 I had briefed the CIA on the results of a trip I had made for them to that African country. As a former diplomat with years of experience in Africa, I had been asked by the Agency to go to Niger to investigate whether reports of a uranium deal that may have been made with Iraq were credible. I had found nothing to substantiate the rumors. But my report—and two others from American officials—had apparently been disregarded, while an unsubstantiated report that first appeared in a British white paper in September 2002 had somehow found its way into the president's State of the Union address delivered on January 28, 2003. Speaking before Congress, the nation, and the world, President Bush had confidently declared: "The British government has learned that Saddam Hussein recently sought significant quantities of uranium from Africa."

But his confidence was misplaced. The documents that formed the basis for that flat assertion were not submitted by the State Department to the International Atomic Energy Agency (IAEA) until early February 2003, after the president's speech. On March 7, the IAEA went on the record with the verdict that the documents were "not authentic." The next day, the State Department claimed that it had been taken in by the forgeries.

However, while the administration was admitting that the reference in the State of the Union address had been based on now-discredited sources that claimed there had been a Niger–Iraq deal, White House officials also continued to dissemble what they had actually known at the time of the president's speech. In fact, they had chosen to ignore three reports that had been in their files for nearly a year: mine as well as two others—one submitted by the American ambassador to Niger, Barbro Owens-Kirkpatrick, and the other by four-star Marine Corps General Carleton Fulford, who had also traveled there. Instead, the administration chose to give credence to forgeries so crude that even *Panorama,* the Italian weekly magazine that first received them, had declined to publish. The administration had ample evidence that there was nothing to the uranium charge but went ahead and placed the inflammatory claim in the State of the Union address anyway.

For four months, from March to July, I did what I could to encourage the White House to come clean on what it knew, including speaking to people close to the administration, senior officials at the State Department, and to the staffs of the House and Senate Intelligence Committees. One senior official told me frankly that I probably would have to write the story myself. I also spoke on background to reporters and voiced openly to Democrats and Republicans alike my dismay at the continued administration stonewalling in the face of reasonable queries from the press.

In late June, the story began to spin out of control as journalists started to report speculation as fact. At this point I was warned by a reporter that I was about to be named in an article as the U.S. official in question. Learning this, I concluded that the time had come to speak out in my own name in order to set the record straight. Over the article I wrote for the *New York Times* op-ed page ran the words "What I Didn't Find in Africa." Instantly, the media spotlight found me, and the subsequent uproar included not-unexpected attacks on my credibility and my motives. I was accused of being a partisan Democrat who had long been against invading Iraq, and characterized as someone who had no particular qualifications to undertake such a mission. However, none of this criticism was credible, given my background and the positions I had taken with regard to Iraq and the possibility of war.

The problem for the White House was that despite their orchestrated efforts to focus attention on me as the subject of the controversy, there was still its own admission, made the day after the publication of my article, that the Africa uranium claim "does not rise to the level that we would put in a presidential speech."

I spoke to a number of people from both parties in the days

immediately following my *Times* appearance. Sandy Berger, President Clinton's national security adviser, was as cogent as he was concise. Since the Bush people never backed down, he pointed out, the fact that they had been so quick to admit their error this time meant that they must have something more important to protect. A Republican from the first Bush administration offered a different take, noting with delight that now "real" Republicans finally had the ammunition they needed to confront the neoconservatives whose influence permeated this administration. My favorite reaction came from John Prendergast, who worked with me at the National Security Council from 1997 to 1998. No doubt alluding to my many years in Africa, he had this to say: "Congratulations, you're like the baboon who's thrown the turd that finally hit the target and stuck."

Clearly, a consensus was emerging that the credibility of the president had taken a hit.

Eight days after my article appeared, on July 14, the focus of attack abruptly shifted when conservative pundit Robert Novak, writing about me in his syndicated column in the *Washington Post,* asserted that "his wife, Valerie Plame, is an Agency operative on weapons of mass destruction. Two senior administration officials told me Wilson's wife suggested sending him to Niger to investigate the Italian report." No administration official came forth to acknowledge being the source of this leak—which was definitely a breach of national security and, quite possibly, a violation of federal law. David Corn, from *The Nation* magazine, had alerted me and later written the first article pointing out that the disclosure by way of the Novak article might have violated the 1982 Intelligence Identities Protection Act. But, whether illegal or not, it was still an unwelcome intrusion into my wife's private life.

Then came the call from Chris Matthews. *Now I have a name,* I thought. The political director of the White House, Karl Rove, condoned the attack on Valerie and was retailing it to reporters, whether or not he had actually been the source behind it. For a president who had promised to restore dignity and honor to the White House, this behavior from a trusted adviser was neither dignified nor honorable. In fact, it was downright dirty and highly unethical even in a town where the politics of personal destruction are the local pastime.

After Matthews's call, I started cursing a blue streak, for he hadn't been the first to tell me that the White House was actively promoting the leak of my wife's name and employment. The night before, on July 20, NBC's Andrea Mitchell had phoned to say that "senior White House sources" had stressed to her that "the real story here is not the sixteen words in the State of the Union but Wilson and his wife." But, unlike Matthews, Mitchell had stopped short of naming her sources to me.

After a deep breath and a pensive moment staring out my office window down onto Pennsylvania Avenue barely a block from the White House, I tried to figure out why the administration would take this tack. What were they trying to suggest to the press? Were they suggesting that my wife had somehow influenced a decision to send me to the middle of the Sahara Desert? Were they implying that this had been nepotism, or some kind of a junket? At the time of my Niger trip, Valerie and I had had two-year old twins at home, a full-time job for both of us. My trip had cost the government nothing except travel and expenses, as I had given my time pro bono. Niamey was not Nassau in the Bahamas, but rather the capital of one of the poorest countries in the world.

Apart from being the conduit of a message from a colleague in her office asking if I would be willing to have a conversation about Niger's uranium industry, Valerie had had nothing to do with the matter. Though she worked on weapons of mass destruction issues, she was not at the meeting I attended where the subject of Niger's uranium was discussed, when the possibility of my actually traveling to the country was broached. She definitely had not proposed that I make the trip.

Then it struck me that the attack by Rove and the administration on my wife had little to do with her but a lot to do with others who might also be tempted to speak out. There had been a number of anonymous leaks to reporters from the intelligence community during the late spring and early summer of 2003, claiming that Vice President Cheney, his chief of staff, Lewis "Scooter" Libby, and even former Speaker of the House of Representatives Newt Gingrich had pressured analysts to skew intelligence analyses to back up the administration's preconceived political intentions.

On June 12, Walter Pincus filed this report in the *Washington Post*: "a senior CIA analyst said the case 'is indicative of larger problems' involving the handling of intelligence about Iraq's alleged chemical, biological and nuclear weapons programs and its links to al Qaeda, which the administration cited as justification for war. 'Information not consistent with the administration agenda was discarded and information that was [consistent] was not seriously scrutinized,' the analyst said.

"As the controversy over Iraq intelligence has expanded with the failure so far of U.S. teams in Iraq to uncover proscribed weapons, intelligence officials have accused senior administration policymakers of pressuring the CIA or exaggerating intelligence information to make the case for war."

Congressional leaders had expressed a desire to hear from these analysts, and had spoken out to reassure them that there would be no negative consequences for coming forward.

This attack on Valerie may have been the White House's way of saying that yes, indeed, there would be consequences if anybody else dared to speak out publicly. The message to mid-career intelligence officers was clear: Should you decide to speak, we will come after you and your family. Anyone not accustomed to the rough-and-tumble of Washington politics would naturally wonder if the game was worth the candle.

But how stupid, I thought. The suggestion that Valerie might have improperly influenced the decision to send me to Niger was easy to disprove. The White House had already acknowledged that the Niger uranium link was unsubstantiated. Yes, I had been among those who early on reported this but at the moment, it should have been the administration's priority to find out who had betrayed the president by putting lies in his mouth, rather than to attack someone who had brought the truth to him.

The White House gained nothing by publicizing Valerie's name, and actually stood to lose a lot. It marked a terrible breach of faith between the clandestine service of the CIA and the government it served, and it made my wife a victim. What the White House seemed not to understand, however, was that this attempt to divert the media's attention from the lie in the State of the Union address was only going to complicate matters for them. In addition to the question of who was responsible for putting the offending sixteen words into the president's speech, the press now had a possible violation of law to pursue, not to mention an ugly violation of the code of cowboy chivalry promoted by this administration as the warmer, fuzzier side of its image.

Whoever had okayed dragging my wife into my disagreement with the administration wanted to punish me for bringing to light a lie—a lie that, when exposed, undermined the administration's public rationale for invading Iraq. This was the situation as I understood it, and no part of it was acceptable to me. I was committed to the truth, and it was clear that that meant not just speaking out about it, but also pursuing any untruths to their source, no matter how highly placed.

Seventeen months earlier, on a cold, clear morning in early February 2002, I had driven across the Potomac River ten minutes from my Washington, D.C., home to CIA headquarters in Langley, Virginia, to discuss the Niger uranium industry. This meeting was not unusual for me. During my twenty-three-year career as a diplomat, I had often met with members of the intelligence community to share my knowledge of the countries I worked in. It is the job of the CIA's deputy directorate for intelligence (DDI) to analyze the millions of bits of data the U.S. government receives daily. Like researchers everywhere, the analysts are a close-knit group of experts in a cloistered world of paper and computers, working side by side in windowless cubicles. Their exposure to real life, as it goes on every day out in the field, is limited. They don't often come into contact with the subjects of their study or have the chance to walk the ground, smell the smells, and immerse themselves in the habits and mores of the cultures from which this information is steadily being gleaned.

And while we policy types rely on the analysts to provide necessary underpinning for decisions the U.S. government makes, so too do the analysts want to hear what we have to say. It gives them a chance to test their working hypotheses and also to get closer to the nitty-gritty. It is not unlike the sports bettor, whose chances for a winning wager are enhanced if he has access to insider information on the health and fitness of the players in the contest.

On that cold day in Langley, I was the insider increasing their store of information, supplying that perspective missing from their raw data. I had served as a junior diplomatic officer in Niger in the mid-1970s, a period that happened to coincide with the growth in the uranium business there. We had followed this issue closely from the American Embassy in Niamey, Niger's capital, just as my staff and I had when I was ambassador to Gabon, another uranium-producing country, from 1992 to 1995. When I worked on the National Security Council in the Clinton administration two years later, among my areas of responsibility was the African uranium industry. Rarely did conversations with Africans from uranium-producing countries fail to touch on the subject. Niger, where I had traveled frequently over the years, was always of particular interest.

The 1990s were an era of serious political upheaval in Niger. A military coup had toppled the elected government in 1996 and brought General Ibrahim Bare Mainassara to power. As a consequence, the United States was obliged by law to suspend all development assistance. A Francophone country, Niger, since achieving its independence from France in 1960, had depended on foreign assistance in order to survive. With a population estimated at eleven million living on land that is arable only when there are abundant summer rains, it had suffered two debilitating multiyear droughts in the previous twenty years, and these had led to widespread hunger and famine. Since it shared borders with the more aggressive nations of Libya, Algeria, and Nigeria, Niger was often preyed upon by its larger and wealthier neighbors.

Prior to the 1996 coup, U.S. relations with Niger had been excellent. We had provided food shipments during the droughts, and we had helped them defend themselves against Libyan aggression. Niger had even sent soldiers to fight alongside our troops during the first Gulf War. Thus, this suspension of normal relations and assistance was difficult for both sides. But nothing was going to change for the better until the ruling military junta left office and a representative civilian government was restored. When I was senior director for African Affairs at the National Security Council from 1997 to 1998, I met frequently with Niger's prime minister, Ibrahim Mayaki, and other senior officials. I had known some of these men for twenty-five years, and our long experience with one another helped them to understand my perspective when I pressed them to work toward the reinstatement of a civilian leadership government so we could ease the restrictions on assistance.

After I retired from the U.S. government in 1998, I traveled to Niamey at the personal invitation of then-President Mainassara to participate in a cultural festival in the Sahara Desert outside the northern Nigerien town of Agadez. But there were other reasons than just the festival for my trip. I went prepared to engage with

Mainassara in unofficial discussions on how to cede power, also at his request. Mainassara was not inherently a bad man, just badly out of his depth. Of modest stature, he was reserved and thoughtful, but he had allowed himself the delusion of believing he was his country's savior. When he had staged his coup in 1996, the political class had been embroiled in never-ending squabbles that paralyzed the country. Niger's precarious economy could ill afford the luxuries of endless debate.

Mainassara, a paratrooper widely regarded as his country's most respected soldier, sought to re-create himself in the image of the country's first military dictator, Seyni Kountche. Kountche had been revered in Niger for his tremendous discipline and national commitment during the droughts that ravaged the country in the 1970s and 1980s. He was a man of ascetic tastes, and no hint of scandal or personal corruption had tainted his twelve-year rule. After his death from illness in 1987, the country had floundered from one poor president to another.

As much as he tried to project himself as the new Kountche, however, Mainassara's failures were evident to all. He careened from one political disaster to another, including rigging elections to hold on to power. With such deficiencies of character and vision, Mainassara was incapable of taking the actions required if his country was ever to regain the much-needed support of the U.S. and European countries.

It was only a matter of time before the ills of the country manifested themselves in a new political crisis. Coups in African nations occur with depressing regularity, and Niger was no exception. The coups that had brought both Kountche and Mainassara to power had been largely bloodless, with the deposed presidents arrested and jailed, but not killed. It came as a shock, therefore, when in April of the year following our meeting, while walking to his airplane to travel to an international meeting, Mainassara was mowed down in a hailstorm of machine-gun fire from his own security detail. His violent death left everyone in Niger and abroad fearful for the country's political future.

I returned to Niamey in 1999 not long after Mainassara's assassination and met with his successor as president, Major Daouda Malam Wanké, at the request of the same civilian prime minister, Ibrahim Mayaki, with whom I had worked so closely during my time at the National Security Council. Mayaki, a political activist and scion of one of Niger's leading families, had played a bad hand as well as anybody could have during the period, managing the government bureaucracy and services and seeking international economic support while trying to persuade the military junta to return to their barracks. He became a good friend in the course of my efforts to help him move the soldiers out of the presidential palace and out of politics.

At Mayaki's urging, I gave Wanké a crash course in what he would need to know if he was going to succeed as chief of state. There was no question, I told him, that so long as he held the office of president, he would be treated as a pariah by the West, as well as by many of his fellow African leaders. Military coups were unacceptable to Niger's development partners, and his African counterparts would recoil from dealing with the man who had been personally responsible, in his capacity as head of the Presidential Guard, for the death of his predecessor. The only way he could ever hope to gain even a measure of international respect would be to restore civilian rule to the nation as soon as possible, and such a plan would, of course, require that he step down as president.

I was frank: "Whoever is elected as your successor will be very nervous with you in the background, fearing that you will do to him what you did to Mainassara if he does not meet your expectations. You should plan to retire from the army and leave the country for a decent interval to give him time to solidify his power and rule."

A year later I met Wanké again, at the airport in Niamey, just after the presidential election that seemed to promise the return of civilian politicians to power. He was on his way to neighboring Nigeria to meet with that country's leaders to thank them for their assistance and support during the transition. He had heard that I was in town and had expressly asked that I come to meet with him at the airport.

There, mingling with the diplomatic corps summoned to bid farewell to the president every time he left the country and welcome him every time he returned, I was culled from the herd of ambassadors and ministers by one of Wanké's aides. Under the harsh stare of Hussein al Kuma, the Libyan ambassador, a man who had been in Niamey for fifteen years, and who was widely suspected of everything from financing rebellions in the north of the country to trying to rig the recent presidential election, I was escorted to the president's private salon. The president greeted me warmly. After a ceremonial glass of tea, he recalled our previous meeting in his military compound and said: "You see by the elections that I have done everything you said needed to be done."

I agreed that he had led a remarkable political transition.

"I am now off to Nigeria on a state visit to celebrate this success," he continued. "But I am also going to inspect and take possession of the keys of my new house there. I will be spending most of my time in Nigeria in private business. As you suggested, I am leaving Niger so that my successor does not have to worry about me. Nobody else knows." He broke into a huge smile at the idea of sharing the secret with the one person who had dared to confront him soon after his arrival in power, and to press on him a scenario for leaving power. We embraced, and I left, winking at the wondering Libyan as I passed.

In short, I knew the country—its uranium industry and its leadership—intimately.

Therefore, it was not surprising that the CIA thought my observations and opinions on Niger worth soliciting. It was my first time inside the

Agency in several years. The CIA campus covers several acres nestled in a wooded glen, isolated from the hustle and bustle of the neighboring suburbs. Beyond the forbidding security gate guarding the entrance, a tree-lined lane meanders to the visitor's parking lot next to the Agency's original building. The front entrance is made of highly polished marble and glass, and one proceeds through it toward the inner courtyard, where a statue commemorates the codebreakers who achieved such momentous success in World War II. There is also a memorial to fallen intelligence operatives, recognized not by name but by stars on the wall, their anonymity preserved even in death.

It is a poignant reminder that security precautions do not end even with death. Protection of the identity of CIA officers is a sacred responsibility. Compromising the officer means compromising a career, a network, and every person with whom the officer might have ever worked. Slips of the tongue cost people their lives.

I was escorted to a meeting room in the basement, down a long nondescript corridor devoid of decoration, past a series of cubicles with shoulder-high dividers occupied by people busy at their computers, the hum of the air circulation system audible above the quiet.

Inside the conference room, there was one change since my last visit: gone was the battleship gray of chairs and tables past. The furniture now was in lighter pastel colors, the idea obviously to create a more cheerful ambiance. It was still drab.

The participants in the meeting were drawn from the intelligence community's experts on Africa and uranium, and included staff from both the CIA and the State Department. As I shook hands with a group of mostly young men and women, a couple of them mentioned that they had met me at previous briefings over the years. I did not know any of them personally nor did I recognize anyone by name or by sight. They were interested and interesting professionals but as anonymous as you would expect in a bureaucracy that places a premium on secrecy and discretion. That said, they were a knowledgeable and dedicated fraternity of public servants, and I was struck by their commitment and their professionalism, toiling in obscurity so that the rest of us can be safe.

My hosts opened the meeting with a brief explanation of why I had been invited to meet with them. A report purporting to be a memorandum of sale of uranium from Niger to Iraq had aroused the interest of Vice President Dick Cheney. His office, I was told, had tasked the CIA to determine if there was any truth to the report. I was being asked now to share with the analysts my knowledge of the uranium business and of the Nigerien personalities in power at the time the alleged contract had been executed, supposedly in 1999 or early 2000. The Nigeriens were the same people I had dealt with during and after my time at the National Security Council, people I knew well.

The report, as it was described to me, was not very detailed. For example, it was not clear whether the reporting officer—not present for this meeting—had actually laid eyes on the document or was simply relaying information provided by a third party. The amount of the uranium product—a lightly processed form of uranium ore called yellowcake—involved was estimated to have been up to five hundred tons but could also have been fifty, suggesting that the account had been written from memory (and an imperfect one at that) rather than with the document at hand. It would have been of keen interest to me to know who might have signed the contract on behalf of the Niger government, but no information was provided on this either.

I was skeptical, as prudent consumers of intelligence always are about raw information. Thousands of pieces of data come over the government's transom on any given day, but a lot belongs to the category of "rumint," rumors passing as fact, no more reliable than Bigfoot sightings. Rumint is a necessary if unfortunate reality in a world where many people will sell you what they think you want to hear, as opposed to simple facts.

The American intelligence business makes use of many different sources and methods in order to arrive at a reasonable picture of the truth in a given situation. No one source provides all the answers, but taken together they contribute to a clearer picture of what is going on. To help decision makers figure out what is wheat and what is chaff, a phalanx of analysts sift through all the bits of information, weighing each one against what else is known, forming hypotheses against which to test it, inviting people like me to share their experience.

The CIA is devoted to this task, but there are also organizations within the State and Defense Departments that provide additional expertise and deliberate redundancy. The goal is to give decision makers the best possible background for formulating policy. The welfare of the nation depends on it.

Since my most recent visit to Niger had been two years earlier, the background I could supply was not about the current situation. However, the former Nigerien minister of mines, the man overseeing the industry at the time of the alleged sale, was a friend of mine. When I had seen him on my last trip, we had discussed the uranium mining sector of the national economy, but we had not talked specifically about any sales to countries outside the consortium of companies from four nations—France, Germany, Spain, and Japan—that, with Niger, own the concession. The organization and ownership of the Nigerien mines had not changed over the quarter-century they had been operating. Niger had not actually sold uranium on its own since the collapse of the uranium market in the mid-1980s, when a major Canadian mine began producing uranium at a far lower cost. Niger's mines were located in the middle of the Sahara Desert, far from ports and even farther from customers.

At the end of the briefing—after I'd answered questions on topics ranging from security arrangements to transportation routes for the yellowcake—I was asked if I would be willing to travel to Niger to check out the report in question, which, if credible, would be very troubling. As the last American diplomat to meet with Saddam Hussein before his army was driven from Kuwait, I knew it was critical to maintain the containment that the U.S., with the U.N.'s help, had thrown over his military ambitions since the end of Desert Storm in 1991. If he was breaking out of his box, it was a very serious matter indeed.

I wanted to help my government learn about it, but before answering their question, I had to point out the obvious: "I am not a spy; I did diplomacy, not clandestine, in my career." I wanted them to understand that I didn't know the tradecraft of spying and had never in my life carried a suitcase full of cash to pay for information. Moreover, I could hardly be described as having a low profile in Africa. During my stint at the National Security Council, I had been one of the principal architects of President Clinton's historic trip to that continent in 1998, and as one of the few senior American officials to speak fluent French, I had often been interviewed for Francophone African newspapers and magazines. Niger was one of those countries where I was well known.

The fact was, though, I did know the officials who would have made the decisions and signed the documents, if the sale had really taken place. Ambassador Owens-Kirkpatrick had arrived just as the new elected government was taking power. Her current contacts were undoubtedly excellent, but since most of the officials of the former military regime had by now melted back into private life, she could not know those potentially useful figures as well as I did.

We discussed whom I might see and what questions I would pose were I to undertake the mission. We plotted it out, as if we were moving pieces on a game board, with a number of possible outcomes, trying to determine whether there was any value in such a trip. I did not know at the time that other American officials were also looking into the matter. For my part, I made it clear that I would require the approval of both the Department of State and the ambassador before traveling. I also stipulated that I would have to be open with my contacts, not concealing the fact that I was traveling on behalf of the U.S. government. I would accept reimbursement from the CIA for my expenses, but I expected no wages for my time. At the conclusion of my trip, the Agency would receive my oral report. As the two-hour meeting ended, my hosts said they would make a decision and get back to me soon, and I told them I would need adequate advance notice to clear my calendar and make the necessary arrangements.

A few days later, I was asked to go to Niamey. Within hours, I went over to the State Department to see the assistant secretary of state for African Affairs, Walter Kansteiner, and his principal deputy. I had known Walter since I'd served on the National Security Council and had admired his leadership of the Bureau of African Affairs in the State Department. Under Walter, morale in his bureau was high, and progress had been made in resolving conflicts from Sierra Leone in the west to Sudan in the east. This was impressive, since resources for Africa were always scarce and the Bureau was chronically underfunded and undermanned. Embassy staff had been reduced and intelligence assets had been largely withdrawn from Africa after the end of the Cold War, as the CIA focused on other targets; this had left our embassies without an essential capability. To fill the gap, different approaches had been tried, including the mounting of temporary intelligence "platforms" whenever crises emerged. But considerable time is required to develop good intelligence, with the obligatory cultivation of contacts, relationships, and networks, all being parts of the equation. Quick fixes rarely work, as they depend on untested sources and offer only a partial picture of any given situation. Despite the inherent difficulties, Walter was managing his portfolio with purpose and aplomb. He agreed to my trip and contacted Ambassador Owens-Kirkpatrick, who also agreed to it.

A visa was easy to obtain, as I had been friends with Niger's envoy to America, Joseph Diatta, and his family since my time in Niamey in the mid-1970s, and worked closely with him when I was in government. Now there remained only the travel arrangements.

There were only two flights a week to Niamey from Europe, and they arrived within eight hours of each other. The flight I took arrived in the evening, the other got in the following morning. Both planes would depart later the same day, which would have left me in Niamey for only twelve hours. If I waited for the next week's flights, I'd be in town for eight days—far longer than necessary for the task, but realistically my only option.

The plane settled into a long slow turn, easing first west toward the sun setting over the scruffy Sahelian buttes and mesas bordering the Niger River, then dipping back to the east. The brown river meandered through the city and under the John F. Kennedy Bridge, the only crossing point for the capital's 750,000 inhabitants and the lifeline for food and supplies arriving from the Atlantic Coast via Ouagadougou, Burkina Faso. The banks of the river with their truck gardens stood in bright green contrast to the muddy water. One last turn, and we were on final approach.

As I looked down at Niamey, I could see the camel caravans crossing the bridge. They arrived every morning laden with firewood, the principal cooking fuel, gathered through the destruction of the few remaining stands of trees and bushes in the country. Deforestation had been one of the most serious development problems we had identified when American aid was first brought to Niger thirty years earlier. Peering through the smoke-charged haze at the camels, I couldn't help but think that we still had not helped them solve the problem.

The city had not changed much over time. There were a few new buildings, and the south side of the river had grown considerably; but, mostly, it remained a sleepy town of low-slung earthen dwellings, dirt alleys, and open sewers. I could see the cooking fires in the court-yards where the foufou stews of millet, okra, and bits of goat meat were being prepared for the evening meal.

We set down on the airport tarmac on the edge of town, and I noticed the remnants of a DC-8 cargo jet that had crashed, killing two of its four crewmen, when I had been posted there. The jet had landed a half mile short of the runway and erupted in a fireball as it skidded down the tarmac. It had been carrying a cargo of cigarettes and record albums that were strewn for miles across the hardscrabble landscape. Hundreds of French expatriates and Nigeriens had witnessed the horror from the airport observation deck while waiting for a passenger plane from Abidjan carrying friends and relatives scheduled to arrive at about the same time. For several minutes after the crash, they had feared they had just watched that plane and the deaths of its two hundred-plus passengers. The two crewmen actually killed in the crash were Americans, and those of us working at the embassy immediately became responsible for the repatriation of their remains to the U.S. The DC-8 had never been removed, and it served as a kind of rusted memorial to the crewmen that now reminded me of my earlier years in the city.

After deplaning, I made my way through immigration, controlled in Niger by the military. Here young officers, chosen primarily because they were among the literate minority in the country, staffed the checkpoints and were trained to be suspicious of any foreigner entering the country. I wondered why it was that bureaucratic functionaries so often seemed to have been born with chips on their shoulders. I decided to trot out my few words of Hausa, the local language, and succeeded in breaking through to the friendly, humorous, and welcoming African lurking just beneath my interrogator's stern veneer. I mentioned that I had lived in Niger probably before he had been born and, suddenly, we had established a friendly rapport. After he amiably told me about an American Peace Corps volunteer he had known a decade earlier, he left the counter, commandeered a baggage handler, and with a flourish packed me into a dilapidated and filthy Renault taxicab. Soon I was rattling down the highway toward the city less than five miles away.

I checked in at the Gaweye, a modern hotel in downtown Niamey, and took a room with a view of the river. The site of the hotel, right next to the bridge and across from the National Museum, had been a refugee camp when I lived in the city. Filling it had been Tuaregs, desert nomads, driven to the capital by the devastating droughts of the 1970s that had decimated their cattle herds. But now in its place was a gleaming concrete-and-glass seven-story L-shaped structure, and the Tuaregs were back in the desert, returned to their pastoral wanderings.

Communications in West Africa are always problematic. Antiquated telephone systems, not modernized since the end of the French colonial period in 1960, are frequently out of order. But cities like Niamey are small enough that everybody knows everybody else, and word of mouth is often the best way to make contact. I managed a couple of phone calls, hired a cab driver to deliver a message, and settled in for the night, knowing that within a day friends, contacts, and people who simply wanted to meet me would start dropping by. Appointments were not easy to schedule, but that didn't matter. The first day would be slow, but then the pace would pick up as it became known around town that I was there for a visit.

My first formal stop was to meet with Ambassador Owens-Kirkpatrick. She was a career foreign service officer who had been in Niger for two years. Though this was her first post in Africa, my impression was that she had penetrated the local culture and society and enjoyed a position of trust and confidence. She understood both the needs of Niger and the limitations of Washington's willingness and ability to help, managing to satisfy the most urgent priorities of the one without alienating the other with unrealistic demands. I liked her.

Her briefing was crisp. She gave me an update on the progress the government had made since the last time we had met, on my visit two years earlier. President Tandja and Prime Minister Hama had managed to consolidate their authority and keep the military in the barracks. Last year's rains had been good, so the harvest was satisfactory and the population content. The political parties were still traumatized from the period of military rule and were on their best behavior. Debates no longer degenerated into the impasses that had long paralyzed Nigerien governance and opened the way to the military interventions.

In return, I explained what I hoped to achieve from my mission. At this point, she told me that she had already discussed the allegation with President Tandja and said she was satisfied with his denial and his explanation of why such a uranium deal could not possibly have taken place. She had also, she said, accompanied Marine General Carleton Fulford—the deputy commander in chief of U.S. armed forces in Europe, and the officer in charge of our military relations with the armed forces of African nations—to meetings with President Tandja and members of his government. General Fulford, she told me, was equally persuaded that the story of Niger uranium sales to Iraq could not be true. Their reports to the State and Defense Departments, respectively, had been widely circulated in the American intelligence community. It was a surprise to her when she learned of my mission because she had believed she and General Fulford had already definitively discredited the yellowcake rumor.

While this was the first I had heard that the allegations I was here to investigate had already been looked into, she and I agreed that the contribution I could make would be to establish contact with officials from the former government. While they were still invited to embassy functions, they were no longer among her principal contacts. By contrast, I had spent many hours with them over the years, working on the most sensitive issues they had faced as they tried to maneuver the military junta out of office, and I had no doubt that I might still learn much from them.

Over the next several days, I renewed my relationships with these former government ministers and bureaucurats. We spoke of many things, uranium among them. The pace of business in Niger—as it is around the world in places where time isn't measured in fifteen-minute segments—is unpredictable, to put it politely. Meetings may not occur at the time agreed upon, or may not happen at all. Patience is crucial.

When meetings do finally take place, business is often the last thing to be discussed. Even in relationships that are already well established, the rituals are to be observed. In the local Hausa and Djerma languages, rituals are enshrined in the greetings, which often last several minutes. "Hello, how are you?" is only the beginning. Each question is answered "Thanks be to Allah," even if one is not Muslim. Only after both parties are satisfied that everything is well, and that God is indeed all-merciful, is the guest invited to sit and offered a drink, which cannot be refused without giving offense. The choices range from traditional sweet tea or instant coffee to Johnny Walker Black Label scotch. Despite being Muslim, many Nigeriens drink or do not object to others drinking. The local beer, Campari and soda, and Johnny Walker are the favorites. Another popular drink, and my personal favorite, is a shredded ginger juice, sweet and tangy, poured over a full glass of ice. With the drinks are served locally produced peanuts, or, on special occasions, cashews imported from neighboring Benin. They are not packaged in hermetically sealed tins, like we buy, but in old liquor bottles, retrieved from the trash, cleaned (more or less), filled with the nuts, capped, and sold on street corners. You ask yourself how many dirty hands have handled the bottles and the contents, and wonder if the frequent bellyaches that residents of Niamey suffer might just be on account of the lack of simple sanitation. But soon the tasty nuts become too tempting to resist.

Then and only then does conversation begin, a conversation that moves at its own pace, meandering like the Niger River itself, from topic to topic.

Nigeriens are naturally reserved and wary. Unlike the tribes along the coast of West Africa, they remained isolated from European contact far longer and resisted colonization more vigorously. Even after the French triumphed as the colonial power there, Niger was always considered an exotic outpost of little commercial value to its foreign masters. While trade flourished and French communities prospered in other West African countries, Niger remained a backwater, its people regarded even by neighboring Africans as quaint and simple "country folk."

I was soon having a steady series of appointments with former officials, European expatriates, Nigerien businessmen, and international aid workers. Not all of the conversations focused on the uranium industry; some of my callers were interested in discussing the local business climate, while others wanted to talk about America and Americans.

From these conversations, three pertinent areas of discussion emerged: the business of uranium mining; the bureaucracy that would have governed any decision to sell yellowcake; and the general atmosphere in the country at the time of the alleged sale.

Niger's uranium is extracted from two mines, both located in the center of the country in the Sahara Desert, a day and a half's drive from the capital along the road to Algeria. The mines are owned by a consortium, comprising foreign companies, along with the Niger government through a state-owned corporation. The day-to-day management of the mines is in the hands of a French mining company, COGEMA. German, Spanish, and Japanese companies are partners, but only COGEMA has actual possession of the ore from the time it is in the ground until it arrives at its destination.

In the 1980s, when large Canadian deposits of uranium began to be exploited at a much lower cost than the mineral could be mined for in Niger, it coincided with the general decline of the worldwide nuclear power industry. This meant that Niger's two mines were soon producing yellowcake at a loss. The mines are kept open in order to ensure a dedicated supply of product for the nuclear power industries in the consortium countries. No market for Niger's uranium exists, however, beyond these countries. In fact, the Nigerien government has sold no uranium outside the consortium for two decades.

Uranium production schedules are established annually at a meeting of the consortium partners and are set to meet their current needs. They are reviewed every couple of months to take into account possible changes within those narrow parameters. In order to accommodate some hypothetical extraordinary demand by the Nigerien government for an extra supply of the product, the partners would have had to meet to adjust everything from the volume of production to the size of the workforce, as well as ramping up transportation and security. The volume of the alleged sale—five hundred tons—would have represented close to a 40 percent production increase. There is no doubt that such a significant shift from historic production schedules would have been absolutely impossible to hide from the other partners, and most certainly from the managing partner, COGEMA. Everyone involved would have known about it.

A government decision authorizing the sale of five hundred tons of uranium to Iraq would have required several decisions, each of which would have been fully documented. Because the conduit for Niger's participation in the uranium consortium was via a state-owned corporation, the government ministry in charge of the corporation, the ministry of mines, would have had to be informed and to concur in the decision to make the sale. The alleged transaction was between two sovereign countries, so the foreign ministry would also have had to agree to the sale, taking into consideration such niceties as international law, at a time when Iraq was subject to international sanctions. The sale would also have been subject to a Council of Ministers decision representing the interests of the government as a whole. In short, any documentation covering the sale would have to carry the signatures, at a minimum, of the prime minister, the foreign minister, and the minister of mines. If any documents did not contain the valid signatures of those officials, then they could not be authentic.

Furthermore, a government decision authorizing such a sale would have automatically been published in the Nigerien equivalent of the Federal Register, and it would have had tax and revenue implications that would quickly have become known to the bureaucracy, which would be salivating at the prospect of such a windfall. In a country chronically short of cash, an unexpected infusion of money would have been eagerly anticipated and much talked about. A five-hundred-ton sale would have had to be negotiated at a premium of above-market prices, both to cover the costs of production and to ensure a reasonable profit. Even with uranium prices down 80 percent from their mid-1970s peak of over fifty dollars a pound, the premium on five hundred tons might still have yielded up to tens of millions of dollars, quite a sum to sweep under the rug in a poor country.

But what about an off-the-books transaction? Theoretically, this was a possibility, given that a military junta had been in power at the time of the alleged sale. Neither the Mainassara regime, nor the short-lived Wanké regime, had been responsible to any other authority in the land. But the transfer of five hundred tons of uranium yellowcake would have been impossible to conceal. Even an illegitimate transaction would have led to the acquisition of thousands of barrels, adjustment of shipping schedules with bills of lading and other documentation to cover the lightly refined ore's movement out of the country. There would have been records somewhere reflecting this significant increase in production. It simply could not have happened without a great many people knowing about it, and secrets widely known do not remain hidden for long. And again, COGEMA, as the managing partner, would have had to know and be complicit.

Finally, the American response to the droughts of the 1970s and 1980s had prevented mass starvation in the country. Mainassara and Wanké, who were in power respectively in 1999–2000 at the time of the alleged sale, were career officers of an age to recall the American response to the country's humanitarian crises. Though unschooled in many areas of leadership, Mainassara nonetheless was acutely aware of his dependence on the West, and the U.S. in particular. I had personally observed this on many occasions, such as the time we flew to Agadez, in 1998. On that trip Mainassara had asked me to sit with him in his small forward cabin.

Shortly after I'd taken my seat, al Kuma, the ubiquitous Libyan envoy had muscled his way into the same cabin, asserting what he believed was his right as the dean of the diplomatic corps, and sat down across the aisle from us. Al Kuma had served in Niger for well over a decade by that time, and was suspected of having coordinated rebellions by northern nomadic Tuareg tribes that convulsed Niger for several years. While he strained to eavesdrop on our conversation, President Mainassara whispered in my ear about his continuing concerns over Libyan efforts to undermine the country's security. He clearly understood where the threats to Niger came from—Libya— and where he would have to turn for help: The United States of America. And getting involved in a secret transaction with Iraq was certainly not going to help him win America's favor.

During the eight days of my fact-finding visit, not all of my time was spent in formal meetings. After many years of friendship with local residents, I was invited to dinners at private homes. There I was introduced to family and friends as the American who had finally persuaded the military to return to their barracks, and stay there, after the nightmare era of military coups and assassinations. Goat *mechouis,* a special delicacy, were prepared in my honor. (To make a *mechouis,* a whole goat is stuffed with couscous and roasted on a spit for several hours. The meat is served to the women on plates, but the men, typically, stand around and pull the meat directly from the carcass. Experience counts in goat grabs. Not all meat is the same. Some is tender and some is sinewy. I always found the meat along the backbone of the goat to be the tastiest, so I pulled mine from there.)

As is common in Muslim practice, only the right hand is used for eating, with a bucket full of water on the side to rinse after the meal. Utensils are rarely in evidence, and the men never touch them, at least not at informal gatherings. *Mechouis* are social events where the male guests remain standing around the goat until the last morsel has been stripped from the carcass. Many subjects are touched upon, and the fact that a foreigner is present never inhibits the flow. If he has been included in such a private gathering, then he is, by virtue of the invitation, already accepted into the inner circle. Local politics always dominate the conversation, and gossip is as animated as at any Georgetown dinner party. After a couple of these occasions, as well as dinners with Americans and other expatriates living in Niamey, it was clear to me that there had been no underlying change in Nigerien attitudes toward Americans, despite the cutbacks in U.S. assistance that followed the military coups.

Before dawn one morning, I slipped out of the hotel to indulge one of the pleasures I had always relished during my many postings in Africa: observing indigenous wildlife up close. Niger had long been home to Africa's most northern and western herd of giraffes, though it was thought that they had died off during the droughts of the recent decades. Now I had learned that a herd had survived the privations, so I hired a guide and we drove sixty miles east of town to a rudimentary reserve. Amid the small landholdings of the local population and the millet fields were majestic giraffe families elegantly strolling among the scrub trees, oblivious to the comings and goings of the local population; these wild animals were wholly integrated into their world. My guide pointed out a family with twin foals. The gangly kids were unsteady but rambunctious, not unlike my own two-year-old twins back home with Valerie.

Before I left Niger, I provided a member of the American Embassy staff with an extensive briefing. In it, I outlined all that I had learned about the uranium operations. Additionally, I described a conversation with one of my sources. He had mentioned to me that on the margins of a ministerial meeting of the Organization of African Unity (OAU) in 1999, a Nigerien businessman had asked him to meet with an Iraqi official to discuss trade. My contact said that alarm bells had immediately gone off in his mind. Well aware of United Nations sanctions on Iraq, he met with the Iraqi only briefly and avoided any substantive issues. As he told me this, he hesitated and looked up to the sky as if plumbing the depths of his memory, then offered that perhaps the Iraqi *might* have wanted to talk about uranium. But since there had been no discussion of uranium—my contact was idly speculating when he mentioned it—there was no story. I spoke with this Nigerien friend again in January 2004, and he recollected our conversation in 2002. He told me that while he was watching coverage of press conferences in Baghdad prior to the second Gulf War, he recognized the Iraqi information minister, Mohammed Saeed al-Sahaf, known to Americans as "Baghdad Bob," as the person whom he had met in Algiers. He had not known the name of the Iraqi at the time he told me about the conversation in 2002, and so this had not been included in my report.

I also mentioned in my briefing that, while I was satisfied personally that there was nothing to support allegations either that Iraq had tried to obtain or had succeeded in purchasing uranium from Niger, if there was interest in investigating the matter further, my suggestion was simple: approach the French uranium company, COGEMA, that had direct responsibility for the mining operation, since it would have had to have been party to any irregular increase in production, or to a transaction with a customer outside the consortium.

I met with Ambassador Owens-Kirkpatrick before leaving the country and shared with her what I had learned. She offered again that my conclusions mirrored hers, as well as those of General Fulford.

Within an hour of my return to Washington in early March 2002, a CIA reports officer, at my request, arrived at my home. Over Chinese takeout, I gave him the same details of my trip and conclusions that I had provided to Owens-Kirkpatrick in Niamey before my departure. These included the account of the meeting between my Nigerien contact and the Iraqi official on the margins of the OAU meeting, as well as my observations about where our government might inquire further if it was not persuaded by my report or those of the ambassador and the general whose inquiries had preceded mine. He left, and I went back to my life as a business consultant, with no further official contact with the CIA for the next year and a half.

Chapter Two
Getting Started in a Diplomatic Career

IN MY FAMILY, THERE IS A LONG TRADITION of politics and service to country. The history of San Francisco—its drydocks and shipbuilding industry, its banking sector, its politics, as well as its social life, including the Bohemian Club and the San Francisco Yacht Club—is replete with the names Rolph, Moore, and Finnell: relatives all, and not a Democrat among them.

My mother's uncle, James ("Sunny Jim") Rolph, served as mayor of San Francisco from 1912 to 1931, the city's longest-serving mayor, and subsequently as governor of California until his death in office in 1934. He was also a delegate to the Republican National Conventions in 1920 and 1932. His brother Thomas was a member of the U.S. House of Representatives from California's 4th congressional district during World War II. Politics was a staple around the table of our proud Republican family. We still talk about the time a couple of uncles, brothers of Sunny Jim, motored down to Phoenix, Arizona, in the early fifties to pay a call on my mother's sister and her new husband. At one point during their stay, the uncles took their new brother-in-law aside and confided that they rather liked that new, young congressman, Barry Goldwater, "but isn't he a bit liberal?"

Both of my grandfathers had fought in World War I and served again in World War II, and, until his death, we called my father's father "Colonel." Not Granddad or Poppy, but Colonel. My brother and I still refer to him that way fifty years after his death. He was a recipient of the British Flying Cross and the French Croix de Guerre for his exploits in World War I. My father was a Marine pilot in World War II and was among the last pilots to take off from the deck of the aircraft carrier *Franklin* just before it was hit by two bombs dropped from a Japanese dive-bomber, one of which exploded amid planes waiting to take off. The resulting damage included the deaths of more than seven hundred American servicemen. Had a plane in the slot to take off not stalled and been pushed to the side, my dad would have still been on the carrier when it was hit. He did not talk much about the war, but he never forgot how lucky he was to have survived—not to mention that my younger brother and I would never have been born.

But the Vietnam War was different, or so it seemed to many of us who came of age in the late 1960s. My college years were tumultuous. Antiwar demonstrations at the University of California at Santa Barbara, from which I would be graduated in 1971, convulsed the campus for several years, and included the burning of the Bank of America building, the death of a student, and several periods of dusk-to-dawn curfews. When in 1967 Muhammad Ali declared that he had nothing against the Vietcong, it made sense to me and my friends even as it sent chills down the spines of our parents. We did not trust the government to tell us the truth, and the credibility gap, epitomizing the gulf between official pronouncements versus truth on the ground in Vietnam, pitted parents against kids in my family just as it did in many other households around the country.

I was born in 1949 and found myself with a low number after the draft lottery began in 1969. With my family background, military service, even war itself, was not something I shied away from. But the fact that I had a student deferment from the draft that would last only until graduation, and was staring Vietnam in the face, was sobering.

A couple of friends and I celebrated our bad luck the day after the lottery draw by planning a hike up one of Santa Barbara's creeks into the coastal mountain range that formed the backdrop to the town, with majestic views of the Pacific Ocean and the Channel Islands some twenty miles offshore. Since we had heard that when we got to "Nam" we would only be able to get beer in cans, we bought a case of bottled beer to haul up with us. Arriving at the trailhead, we pulled the case out of the back of the car to load into our backpacks. The cardboard bottom fell out of the case and the beer bottles shattered, leaving us staring down at a foamy mess. We were certain it was an ominous sign foretelling our future career as GIs in the jungles of Southeast Asia.

Unexpectedly, the Nixon administration decided that it did not want our class in the military after all and suspended the draft in June 1971. The suspension lasted through March 1972, the period that covered our period of eligibility, so on April 1, 1972, I was no longer subject to the draft.

I had gotten lucky, yet I still hadn't, at that point, a clue about what I wanted to do with my life. Many of my peers were increasingly disillusioned with the "establishment" and had begun embarking on "counter-culture" adventures. My own was to learn the trade of carpentry. After joining the local Brotherhood of Carpenters and Joiners, an AFL/CIO union, I learned to build houses and condominiums in Santa Barbara, and later at Lake Tahoe. This left me enough time to surf and ski, until in 1973 I broke a leg skiing and was sidelined. Being in a cast and on crutches, however, didn't prevent me from falling in love with a young woman I had known in college and had always had my eye on, albeit from afar. Susan Otchis was an effervescent blonde from the San Fernando Valley, just north of Los Angeles. The following year, we married in a ceremony that brought together my Episcopalian family and her Jewish family to dance the hora after we'd said our vows before a Lutheran minister. It was a decidedly nondenominational affair. We started our new life together by moving out of California to experience the great Northwest. We left Santa Barbara with the intention of driving north until we came upon a town that struck our fancy.

Sequim, Washington, then a community of fewer than three thousand people, was where we landed, about an hour and a half northwest of Seattle, on the Straits of Juan de Fuca that separate Washington from British Columbia on the Olympic peninsula. It is in what is called the banana belt because, in comparison to the rest of the area, it is dry, averaging only seventeen inches of rain a year. The massive storms that hit the Pacific Northwest from the Aleutians every winter, dropping twelve feet of rain along the West Coast forests, are blocked by the nearby Olympic Mountains, leaving Sequim—pronounced "Squim"—in the rain shadow, relatively dry. But for a restless young man from Santa Barbara, even this made for far too wet and cold a season for driving nails to be much fun. After a long winter, it was time to look for something else to do.

I had spent my high school years in Europe following my parents in their quixotic quest to be expatriate journalists and authors. We had first traveled to Europe in 1959, driving around in an old Citroën taxi that was low-slung like the gangster cars in old movies. My parents had fallen in love with the Hemingway lifestyle, including the corridas and toreadors of Spain. We had spent the spring when I was nine following the bullfights from village to village.

In 1963, the family returned to live in Europe. My father had a couple of jobs bringing American products to European customers, but the enterprises didn't work out, so my parents turned to writing. They wrote principally about cultural activities they believed would be of interest to North American readers at a time before mass travel to Europe, and sold their stories to the *San Francisco Chronicle,* King Features syndicate, and the *International Herald Tribune.* We lived in Nice, Mallorca, and Montreux, and spent all four summers of our European sojourn in Biarritz, France, where my brother and I surfed along the Atlantic beaches.

(The first Americans to surf in France were author Peter Viertel and his wife, actress Deborah Kerr, who once loaned me a safety pin to keep my bathing trunks up after the button had come off, a kindness to an embarrassed teenager that I never forgot.)

Given my experiences living abroad, and an interest I had developed in foreign cultures, it was natural to think about international affairs as a new career choice, even if there was no international policy being made anywhere near Sequim. From this unlikely springboard, I looked into the School of Public Affairs at the University of Washington in Seattle and met a couple of times with the dean, Brewster Denny. It was a good program, but in order to gain admission, an applicant had to demonstrate a commitment to public service. Understandably, those who were already pursuing a career in the public sector stood the best chance of admission.

My only experience with the public sector up to that point had been collecting unemployment insurance during the winters at Lake Tahoe, and these trips to the unemployment office had been just about my only contact with public servants. That did not strike me, nor do I suspect Dean Denny, as evidence of a strong commitment to a career in public service; so, in order to bolster my application, I decided to take the Foreign Service examination. Back then, the test was offered every December and typically attracted more than 20,000 applicants for fewer than 150 jobs. I had no expectation of passing but hoped merely to do well enough to convince Dean Denny of my potential. To my surprise, I squeaked by and was invited to the next stage, the oral examination.

On a beautiful spring day in 1975, I made my way from Sequim across the Hood Canal on the Pontoon Bridge, and the Puget Sound via ferry, to downtown Seattle. The Kingdome was in the final stages of construction and competed with the Space Needle for the attention of gawkers on the ferry. I ambled nervously through the Pike Place Market in my suit and tie, feeling completely out of place. The day before, my hair had fallen well below my collar and I had been sporting a wispy but earnest attempt at a beard. I had not worn a tie in at least four years, and my suit dated back to before I had left home for college. But all that had changed in a few short hours. Gone were the long locks and the beard. Off came the Pendleton shirt, replaced by a starched white shirt, my dad's hand-me-down blue and gold school tie (University of California colors), and a suit that was a bit tight in the shoulders and short at the cuffs. Freshly shined loafers replaced hiking boots, and, for all the world, I looked like an aspiring young executive, or just maybe a diplomat-in-waiting.

The oral examination turned out to be a nightmare in every way. First of all, I had never been inside a federal building before and was completely out of my element. The head examiner was a lady named Sarah Nathness, and when she greeted me, she thrust out her hand in a way that caught me completely off guard. The world of carpentry and contracting at that time was pretty much a male preserve, and I had never encountered a female executive. Even the courtesy of handshaking was unfamiliar to me, strange as that may seem. You just don't get much practice at it when you're wielding a hammer all day. She introduced herself, and I responded by mispronouncing her name—three times: "How do you do, Miss Nessnath . . . Miss Nassneth . . . Miss Nethnass," until finally stammering it out correctly.

After that, it only got worse. The opening question was about what books I might suggest to a foreigner planning a visit to the United States. This was not long after Alistair Cooke had published *America,* his 1975 best-selling tribute to the finest our country has to offer, which probably would've been an ideal answer, but that was not the book that came to mind. Instead, I volunteered titles from sociology courses I had taken several years previously: *Tally's Corner,* a book on the plight of the urban black in the ghetto; *Delano,* a book about the migrant farm workers of California; and one of the satires

on the midwestern American character by Kurt Vonnegut thrown in
for good measure. After an hour of questions that just got more and
more difficult, I was banished to the outer office to await the decision
of the three examiners. I was not optimistic as I sat there with the
temp secretary the examiners had hired for their brief stay in Seattle.
Several minutes later, Miss Nathness came out and told me I had
passed. The secretary about fell off her chair. In the two weeks she
had been there, she told me, she had seen only a few applicants pass,
out of the dozens who had appointments.

A security investigation, which came next, included the random
questioning of friends and neighbors. One of my former room-
mates—he's now a well-respected cardiologist—was enjoying a Saturday morning joint with his girlfriend when his doorbell rang.
Assuming it was a buddy, and always willing to share a toke, he
opened the door, only to find a man in a suit flashing a badge. Ever
alert and polite, he excused himself, half-closed the door, swallowed
the remainder of the joint, and then invited the security officer in to
discuss his good friend, the candidate for the Foreign Service.

As I waited to hear from the State Department, I pursued my
graduate degree, moving to Cheney, Washington, on the other side
of the state near Spokane. I had recently accepted a fellowship
from the economics department of Eastern Washington State College, which was running a joint public affairs program with the
University of Washington in Seattle. I had also opened a basement
remodeling business and was settling into the graduate student life,
when one day the phone rang. It was the State Department offering
me a job. I had taken the Foreign Service test to get into graduate
school so that I might be better qualified to join the Foreign Service, and now here they were offering me a job! I proposed post-
poning my entry into the service, suggesting that surely a master's
degree would only make me more valuable to my future employer.
Unfortunately, the mechanism for such a postponement did not

exist. If I did not accept, my name would go to the bottom of the list and there was no guarantee that they would ever make another offer. It was hard to imagine that I would ever be able to pass the written and oral exams again, so I bailed out of school and prepared to move to Washington, D.C., a city I'd been to only once, when I was nine years old.

Several weeks later, the sale of my Chevy pickup truck and the purchase of a pinstripe suit behind me, Susan and I arrived in the nation's capital in the midst of a snowstorm and deep freeze, conditions pretty unwelcoming to California natives.

The matching up of employees to job openings at the State Department is always a delicate minuet, even for the new recruits. Everybody wants to go to Paris, and nobody volunteers for Niamey. Everyone wants to be the aide-de-camp to the American ambassador to France; no one wants to be the general services officer, responsible for the motor pool and plumbing problems in Niger. In the early years of a Foreign Service career, officers are generally interchangeable parts, serving in the junior consular or administrative positions where energy and stamina are at least as important as expertise. It is often trial by fire, as anybody who has served on the visa line in Manila can testify.

My case was no different. I had no particular talent that would qualify me for a specific opening. I was not an expert in a part of the world where there was a shortage of experts, nor was I an attorney or a scientist. I was just an ex-carpenter, in the mix with all the other candidates. My only potentially distinctive value lay in my knowledge of French, which I could speak fluently as a result of my time in French schools during my family's expatriate years.

About halfway through my third week in Washington, D.C., the personnel office began to interview new officers. For many of the openings, especially the junior-level jobs, it is a matter of filling vacancies with warm bodies. I was summoned to meet with my "career development officer." Mr. Jesse Clear turned out to look a little different from the other diplomats striding the halls of the State Department, and this seemed to me a good thing. He had a sharply cut beard and worked on America's relations with organized labor in foreign countries. I immediately felt some affinity with him, since I had recently been in the ranks of organized labor, had not long ago sported a beard, and, moreover, liked to think I was not cut from the same cloth as the others in my training class. Most of them had come from academia or buttoned-down junior management positions, not from the world of surfing, skiing, and building houses. At a time when I was feeling more than a bit lost, here was a fellow who seemed to have come from a similar background, and who looked like I had before I cleaned up for my new career.

Jesse asked me where I wanted to be posted. I gazed out the window, and so, looking at the bustle of people moving through the cold February afternoon, I shared with him my dreams and aspirations.

"I have lived in France and French-speaking Switzerland. I speak French almost as well as English. I studied French history and French literature in college. It seems to me that it would be in our nation's interest to send me to Paris, Bordeaux, Nice, or Marseille, where I could put this experience to immediate use." I left out our consulates in Lyon and Strasbourg, France, because I knew the winters in both places were cold and wet. My interest in France did not extend to "cold and wet" except for Paris.

My new friend Jesse, the man with whom I had felt such an immediate affinity, and who now held my future in his hands, replied: "Well, son, I think we have just the place for you. It is a little to the south of France, but they speak French there. And you will be able to use your carpentry skills. We have an opening for a general services officer in Niamey, Niger, and I think you would be the perfect candidate for the job."

When Jesse called me "son," I knew I was in trouble. General services officer where? I did not have a clue about what he was offering. It had never really dawned on me that I would go anywhere but Europe. Maybe France would not be the first tour for my wife and me, I remember thinking as I had gone into the meeting, but I would settle for Spain or even Italy.

I politely thanked him for the offer but made no commitments, saying I wanted to discuss it with Susan—a holding action to collect my thoughts, and since I really didn't know what she would think. Leaving his office, I walked around the corner to the third-floor State Department library and searched for an atlas to find out where in the hell this Niamey place was. I finally located it in the middle of the Sahara Desert, in West Africa. To the south of Paris, indeed. I checked out a copy of a State Department post report on Niger to take home to Susan. It contained pictures of adobe-style dwellings, camel caravans, and sand. Sand everywhere: sand floors in homes, sand streets, sand in the eyes of the natives, and, of course, sand dunes. Sand, sand, sand.

I realized then the first truth about the personnel process at the State Department: "career development officer" is really a euphemism for the guy who drives the square pegs into the round holes that are the jobs. The needs of the service are what must be met. And among the most difficult jobs to fill are the administrative ones in Africa. Nobody wanted them, and many candidates refused to take them.

Susan and I looked at the post report closely. Our first reaction was that people assigned there obviously had managed to survive the experience. Our embassy had been there since Niger's independence in 1961. But our second response was more personal. Though I'd been dreaming of a diplomatic career in European capitals, Susan reminded me that when we'd first started discussing living in foreign lands, we had looked into the Peace Corps because the idea of a foreign adventure appealed to us. Niamey sure ranked as an exotic destination. We were young, without children, and open to challenges in faraway places, so we decided to view this as our "National Geographic" experience and signed up. We did not negotiate, we did not hold out for a better job, we did not angle for something else. We signed up—and we never regretted it.

I came to be eternally grateful to Jesse Clear for having so expanded my horizons—for launching me on what became a lifelong love affair with a continent, its peoples, and their cultures. The only thing I've ever found to reproach him for is his comment that I'd be able to use my carpentry skills in Niamey. Niamey is on the edge of the Sahara Desert. Apart from the occasional oasis, there are no trees in the Sahara Desert. Without trees, there is little lumber. Without lumber, people build shelters using other materials. In short, there were few things, interior walls included, that one could drive a nail into. But I forgave Jesse on this score, since I soon discovered that my other handyman skills would be useful in Niger.

We left for Niamey in May 1976, having received our Foreign Service class award for "most exotic" posting. Typically this honor goes to the junior officer sent to Ouagadougou, the capital of neighboring Burkina Faso (then called Upper Volta), but there were no postings there from my class. The award was a pith helmet, fitting for a safari to the heart of Africa.

With more than a bit of trepidation, Susan and I clambered aboard an old Pan Am 707 for the red-eye flight to Dakar, Senegal. This was one of two weekly flights that flew direct to Africa from New York at that time. These flights were typically full of returning Africans—Senegalese, Ghanaians, Nigerians, Kenyans, and South Africans—waiting to be disgorged in their homelands. The cabin was a loud and rowdy place, reflecting the excitement of travelers going home. There was little opportunity to sleep on the long journey across the Atlantic Ocean.

We landed at the Dakar airport shortly before sunrise. Back then, Dakar's terminal was a colonial-era building designed for fewer travelers than were using it in the mid-1970s. Arrivals strained the immigration and customs capacities. But since Senegal was a former French colony, there was no queuing up. That most quaint of English habits—orderly lines and everybody waiting his or her turn—had not made it across the channel, or to the faraway lands colonized by the French. Pushing, shoving, and squeezing to the front of the line was a common practice. It was only after much commotion that we made our way out and found the embassy car to take us to our hotel in downtown Dakar.

As we drove into the city, the sun rose over a flat barren landscape, revealing scruffy bushes among the rocky outcrops and the majestic Atlantic Ocean crashing onto the beaches below. People were already making their way into town, striding ramrod-straight in their flowing robes (called grand boubous). They were tall, slim, and ebony-colored, and they carried themselves with great presence. An indelible memory is the visible dignity of these proud people.

Several days later, after a stop in Abidjan, Ivory Coast, we arrived at our destination: Niamey. Stepping out of the airplane was like walking into a hot oven. It was so hot and dry that we found it hard to breathe. The afternoon sun beat down relentlessly on the parched, baked clay earth. Hearty shrubs sprung from the hardpan, only to be munched by herds of goats grazing wherever they spied something to eat. The airport balcony, extending the length of the building, was full of Nigeriens and Europeans awaiting the arrival of loved ones. I later learned that airplane arrivals were one of the few "modern" distractions in the capital. Television had not yet come to the country, and there was only one cinema in town—and it operated outdoors.

We were pleased to see that our new home had cement, not sand, floors, as we had half expected from the post report. There was one air conditioner in the living room, ceiling fans to move the hot air around, and a contraption called a "desert cooler" attached to the back of the house. A fan blew air into the house through a moist membrane on the cooler, taking the edge off the stifling heat and providing some humidity in the otherwise extremely arid climate.

The property was located on the other side of town from the European quarter, next to the American Club with its swimming pool, tennis court, and snack bar. It had a large yard, was ringed in flamboyant trees—no candidates for lumber, these—and bougainvillea hedges that were always in bloom, giving our yard the feel of an oasis amid the dust. Across the street were the poorer neighborhoods of Niamey, with their open sewers, dirt alleys, and the adobe-style houses we had seen in pictures.

The two years we spent in Niger were marked by a tremendous American effort to help this impoverished people cope with the ravages of drought. The American presence doubled each year, as we were inundated with assistance workers from the U.S. Agency for International Development (AID). AID projects ranged from improving the seed stock of millet and sorghum in an effort to replicate India's "Green Revolution" of the 1960s, to inoculating the cattle and goat herds against disease. Our growth was such that by the end of the second year, there were often traffic jams in the capital involving only Chevrolet Suburbans, the big vehicle favored by American project workers.

I handled logistical support for the growing mission. This involved everything from importing the supplies used by the embassy to leasing houses for our personnel from local property owners, plus providing all the services that Americans are accustomed to, even in one of the most underdeveloped countries on earth.

At embassy receptions, where local politics and the efforts of the Soviets and the Libyans to subvert the delicate political calm were common topics, I was approached with questions about plumbing and requests for new curtains.

Among the logistical duties for which I soon found myself responsible was repatriating to the U.S. the bodies of the two DC-8 crewmen who had died when their plane, later a rusted memorial on the tarmac, crashed at Niamey's airport in 1977. The corpses were stored at the only morgue in the city, while a team of American forensic surgeons was dispatched from the National Transportation Safety Board to perform autopsies on them. It is the practice in Niger, as elsewhere in the Muslim world—as it is in other religions, including the Jewish faith—to bury the dead within a day of death, so a large morgue was not necessary. In fact, the local facility had room for only six bodies, while serving a city of over 350,000 souls at that time. I had to commandeer two of the facility's six refrigerator units for ten days. I visited the bodies daily, and once the American surgeons arrived, I found myself assisting in the autopsy, since the morgue staff considered the idea of cutting into the bodies sacrilegious and would have nothing to do with it.

When it came time to ship the bodies home, I wrapped them in formaldehyde-soaked shrouds to preserve them—I hoped—in lieu of embalming, which was not practiced in Niger, and then planned to put them into custom-made coffins. I learned that shipment of unembalmed remains from Africa was often a problem. The coffin, in addition to being lead-lined and copper-sealed, had to have an air-escape valve to allow for the decomposition of the body and to vent the build-up of gases. A coffin from neighboring Chad had exploded a few years previously in the 120-degree heat in an airplane's cargo hold, spewing body parts across passengers' luggage. It couldn't have been a pretty sight.

The one coffin maker in the city was straight out of central casting. He was Belgian, short, stout, with a foul-smelling unfiltered cigarette perpetually glued to his lower lip. He had no more than half a dozen strands of hair left on his head, and he tried to make the most of them. They wrapped around his skull in an elaborate comb-over. But, should a puff of wind come along, what was on top became a long, stringy tail that hung down to his shoulders. Most of the time, he kept his head covered with a soiled black beret. Under my breath, I called him Igor, as he reminded me of Dr. Franken-stein's laboratory assistant.

While I struggled with the bodies and the shrouds, Igor welded and hammered together the coffins in the 100-degree heat of the after-noon, near the dusty entrance to the morgue. I vainly tried to wrap the shrouds mummy-style around each of the bodies as they reposed on narrow gurneys. The Nigerien who was supposed to help me was driven away by the overwhelming odor—a combination of decom-posing flesh and chemical vapors—coupled with what was to him the unnatural act of wrapping the bodies, only loosely stitched back together after the autopsies. It was all too much for him to bear. Left alone, I had great difficulty maneuvering the muslin shrouds over and under the dead weight of the corpses. I finally gave up and settled for rolling each body onto a length of the shroud, making sure it was cov-ered from head to toe, and tying the bundle together. I then manhan-dled the rigor mortis–stiffened bodies onto wheelchairs and rolled them out into the bright sun of the desert afternoon toward Igor and the coffins he had constructed. He helped me with the bodies, which were finally placed into the containers and flown back to the grieving families who waited to bury them back home.

Though it was hardly funny at the time, I chuckle ruefully now, thinking of the stereotypical pinstriped ambassador, white wine and canapé in hand, waxing eloquent amid the glitterati of an exotic for-eign capital. It is in distinct contrast to the morbid scene that still lodges in my memory: the stench of death mingling with formalde-hyde, two stiff specters, each in its wheelchair, and the coffin maker in his ash-and-dandruff-speckled blue worsted sweater. The heady romance of a diplomatic career just cannot be overstated.

The job itself brought me into close contact with the upper strata of Niger society. Since only about 10 percent of the country was in the monetized economy, with the remainder surviving as subsistence farmers or nomadic shepherds, there were a limited number of vendors of essential supplies and of landlords for our burgeoning population of American AID workers. I got to know all the vendors, while also supervising a workforce numbering several hundred, from stock clerks to mechanics to security guards. That made me the face of one of the largest employers in the country, and every local businessman and bureaucrat saw our operation as a cash cow. Despite the embassy's exemption from local taxes, nearly every hour brought a creative new attempt to extract fees from us. Each day was a negotiation. Leases, tax exonerations, maintenance contracts, importation of goods through customs, and airport fees for our monthly supply flights—these were just some of the daily challenges I learned to meet, speaking French, in a country far from home, with a people for whom our dollars meant their salvation.

Niger is a landlocked country, with only laterite roads linking it to the coast. Laterite is an iron ore–based road treatment that, while not asphalt, at least provides minimal erosion protection. Such roads remain passable during the rainy season as the water drains off, leaving little ridges spaced a few inches apart. However, the washboard effect created by the drainage patterns makes them very uncomfortable to ride on. To survive the unceasing pounding, four-wheel-drive vehicles with stiff suspension are required, and cars must travel at relatively high speeds to "float" over the ridges. Anything less than about forty miles per hour relegates the passengers to a very bumpy ride. For goods coming into the country, the breakage rate was extremely high. I remember seeing entire pallets of toilet bowls reduced to shards from the incessant bouncing over eight hundred miles of washboard roads.

Our solution was to charter a monthly flight from Lagos, Nigeria, where the U.S. government had established a supply depot. We had a contract with a small American company that would fly a DC-6 full of goods to Niamey every month. We negotiated an arrangement with the Nigerien customs authorities to permit us to take delivery directly from the aircraft and submit the paperwork later. We had to do it this way because we never had the exact inventory for what we were going to receive until the plane actually landed. I worked with the head of customs to overcome his bureaucratic inclination to impound all of our goods and supplies until the paperwork had the appropriate stamps from the foreign and finance ministries, a process that would have held up delivery by several weeks at least. He and his staff were invited to check the inventory against the goods delivered as they were coming off the aircraft, just as I did, and to look into every box that was delivered.

The first time we ran the operation this way, it took almost a day to complete the offloading of the aircraft while the local minor bureaucrats asserted their power. They had a tendency to be officious. In the face of this, we cheerfully complied and aggressively opened every box, insisting that they take a look before we loaded the goods into one of the twenty trucks we'd rented for the day. After a few months of this, our cooperation with the authorities had completely disarmed them and we wound up enjoying free run of the airport. The customs officials became our friends and allies, helping to expedite rather than slow the turnaround of the flights, to the point where we were able to take delivery and put the DC-6 back in the air within two hours. It was a great lesson in how to work around the heavy bureaucracy in third-world countries to get things accomplished reasonably efficiently, all without violating the integrity of their procedures.

Susan and I took advantage of our time in Niger to travel throughout the country. In the south, along the border with Benin and Upper Volta, we visited a game park called "W," after the bends in the river. It was home to many species of antelope, lion, elephant, and hippopotamus in the river and streams. We drove across the John F. Kennedy Bridge in Niamey, along the washboard roads, and finally met the river again at the park entrance. For three days we wandered through the park, searching for game and camping along the stream. At night we heard the lions in the distance, and around our campsite a family of baboons gathered, hoping for some handouts. In the morning when we washed at the stream, we saw the footprints of hippos that had emerged from a pond upstream to forage in the grasses bordering the water. One morning we came upon a troop of elephants and found ourselves caught between a mother and her young. Preparing to charge us, she trumpeted loudly and flapped her ears. I panicked; I could not get our Toyota Land Cruiser into reverse. Finally, as she was bearing down on us, the car slipped into gear and we raced backwards away from the stampeding mother.

One time I accompanied our ambassador, Charles James, to Bilma, an oasis settlement surrounded by sand dunes. Bilma's location, in the northeastern part of the country in the Sahara Desert, made it Niger's first line of defense against Libyan aggression. The Nigeriens liked to say that when Muhammar Qhadafi looked at a map on the wall, he saw that Niger was below Libya. He knew that water flowed downhill and assumed the same for oil. He worried that all of his oil was going to run down into Niger and therefore was prepared to take Nigerien territory to keep control of his oil. Bilma, and the airfield of Derkou, some forty-five minutes away, was the first outpost of settled population east of Agadez, the regional capital, south of some recently opened uranium mines, along the road to Algeria. To get there involved a trek of several days in four-wheel-drive caravans across some of the harshest land imaginable.

I got a taste of desert travel after arriving by plane at the Derkou airfield. A delegation of Nigeriens, including the senior government authority, met us at the airport and loaded us into the ubiquitous

Land Rovers. Off we set across the sand, no roads in evidence. The Land Rovers fanned out, and the only rule of the road was that no vehicle could move ahead of the government official's car in which Ambassador James was riding. Several times we edged up to the lead car, only to have our driver back off. Driving flat-out, we topped sand dunes at full speed and slid down the other side until we finally entered a date palm–filled village, in the middle of which was a fresh-water spring feeding small truck gardens and providing the water supply of Bilma.

Susan and I also enjoyed canoeing on the Niger River, putting in about twenty miles north of the capital and taking the whole day to float downstream, while birdwatching in one of the best birding areas in West Africa and coming upon villages along the river that had vir-tually no contact with the outside world, far away from roads and out-side influences. For these villagers, the river was almost the only source of life and sustenance. Our passage would bring the whole vil-lage to the banks to watch the white strangers paddle by, a sight they rarely experienced.

Two years later, our tour was up and Susan and I returned home for vacation. From Niger, we wanted to continue our 'round the world odyssey, and so I bid on several openings in India, another devel-oping nation, but one with a much different culture and society. Madras, Bombay, Delhi, and Calcutta were on our list, but almost as soon as I sent it off to Washington I was contacted by an ever-helpful career development officer—not my buddy Jesse Clear this time, but someone I had never met. He offered me a position in Lome, Togo, as administrative officer. His note to me said: "This is a challenging position that will be career enhancing and professionally rewarding." It was only later that I learned this was code for "We can't find anyone else to take the job."

Lome is about eight hundred miles south of Niamey along the Atlantic coast. While it would take a very long time to see the whole world if I was going to move only eight hundred miles every two years, I jumped at the offer. The Togolese are a gregarious and hard working people, as Susan and I had discovered in a brief trip there the previous spring. Lome, with its palm trees and ocean views, was completely unlike Niger, and the house to which we would be assigned was one block from the beach. The position was a promotion and signaled my arrival as a manager in the Bureau of African Affairs.

Considerably smaller than Niger, Togo is bordered by Ghana and Benin. There were plenty of excursions to make, and every morning I went body-surfing in the Atlantic Ocean. We also bought a small sailboat that we kept at the lake outside town for weekend jaunts. Susan worked as a teacher in the local American school, and I served as a member of its school board. I was, in my official post, responsible for the administration of an American community that comprised more than a hundred Peace Corps volunteers and a large USAID population, in addition to our small diplomatic contingent. As the second posting in my diplomatic career, I really enjoyed our pleasant routine that included trips to the interior and the neighboring countries, along with an active social life. I even bought a surfboard to sample the waves in nearby Benin.

Chapter Three
Back to Africa with Twins

NOW THAT WE SEEMED TO BE LAUNCHED ON OUR NEW LIFE and career, Susan and I took the next step and decided to start a family. Within just a few months of our arrival in Togo, Susan became pregnant. She grew, and grew, and grew over the next several months. Each time she visited the overworked German doctor at the local hospital—the only medical service available—he seemed not to recognize her, and though this was a distinct possibility given his heavy workload, she was certainly one of the few European-looking blondes in this African setting. He would give her a cursory examination, pronounce her healthy, and inevitably ask her if she was three months more pregnant than she was, because she was so large in the belly. We took that as a sign that the baby was going to be a big one. At seven months, she returned to her parents' house in Tarzana, California, to wait for the baby to arrive. Although she had grown so big, the pregnancy had otherwise been uneventful.

My first surprise came when she telephoned and, through a typically bad connection, yelled that we were having twins. She had been to the doctor we'd lined up in California, and in the course of his routine examination he had announced that he felt two heads. She called to urge me to return home sooner than planned because twins typically come early.

I flew to Paris on an overnight flight and then on to Los Angeles, arriving about twenty hours later. I hadn't slept at all on the plane, but when I got to my in-laws' there was no time for a nap, as the family had planned a dinner out and a Woody Allen movie. About halfway through the movie, Susan turned to me and announced, "My water has broken." She was about to go into labor. From the theater we drove straight to the hospital in Van Nuys, where, after twelve hours of Lamaze breathing with a sleep-deprived and utterly untrained husband, she gave up on the idea of a natural childbirth and had an epidural. Unfortunately, the drug went up her spine instead of down, so she still felt the pain but was unable to push from the diaphragm down. The delivering doctor finally used some forceps and pulled the first baby out. When he turned her around I was face to face with the most beautiful thing I had ever seen, my daughter, Sabrina. Five minutes later, my son, Joe, appeared, butt-first in all his glory, crying lustily to announce his arrival. Both kids were in perfect condition, and all of us were ready for some sound sleep.

Our second surprise came when Susan just didn't recuperate after her difficult labor. Each day, the obstetrician would come by, give her a cursory examination, and leave. But she had fevers and was retaining water, so much so that she had regained most of her pregnancy weight in the week she remained in the hospital. After three days, we began to worry; after five, we were truly alarmed and couldn't understand why she was not recovering. Finally, when a week had gone by, the doctor who had delivered the babies threw up his hands, said he had no idea what was wrong, and had her taken by ambulance to the UCLA Medical Center. I followed in my car about forty-five minutes later, after dropping Joe and Sabrina off with their grandparents.

When I got to UCLA I met Dr. Amy Rosenman, who told me that my wife was suffering from clostridia and had only about a one-in-twenty chance of survival. Clostridia is gas gangrene. It is not an exotic disease. In Susan's case, it had begun during the birth of the twins. It is caused by infection of a cut and was among the most common causes of death during the Civil War. Doctors have known about it for well over a century. Dr. Rosenman diagnosed it in ten minutes, while the physicians attending Susan for a week at the other hospital had completely missed the signs, despite the fact that the person suffering with it gives off an unmistakable odor. Their failure to diagnose and treat her correctly was absolutely incredible and unconscionable.

Shortly after I arrived, Susan was taken in to surgery. According to Dr. Rosenman, her only chance for survival lay in their ability to cut out the infection, which by this time was spreading. I remembered a Peace Corps volunteer in Togo who had contracted gas gangrene after a traffic accident. Over several days, multiple amputations up her leg were performed, trying to keep the clostridia from spreading, but it was too late, and she had died a horribly painful death.

I called my old college roommate and one of my dearest friends, Bob Moore, an attorney in Beverly Hills. He came immediately, and we sat together in an empty room waiting for news. John Wayne was in the same section of the hospital, dying of cancer just a few doors down. He heard about what we were going through and had the nurse bring us a bottle of wine with his best wishes. We sipped and waited for almost four hours. Finally a nurse came in and told us that Susan had survived the surgery and that they were going to send her to the hospital in Long Beach, some thirty miles south, by helicopter. The hospital there had the only hyperbaric chamber in the area, and she would be administered several sessions a day in a super-oxygenated environment to keep the gas gangrene, which thrives in low-oxygen environments, from growing.

But what she also said was that Susan had only a 10 percent chance of survival. At that news, Bob became faint and lay down on a bed nearby. I told the nurse, "Those odds are twice as good as what I heard just a few hours ago." The nurse looked puzzled, so I added that the last person to talk to me before the surgery had offered that she had a one-in-twenty chance of survival: 5 percent.

The nurse took me by the arm and said, gently, "Five percent or ten percent, you need to understand that it is highly unlikely that your wife is going to survive. In fact, she will probably not live through the transfer to Long Beach. We are doing our best, but she is dying. The gas gangrene spread so far into her tissue, and we had to cut so much out, that it would be a miracle for her to survive. And if on the off-chance she does live, she will probably never walk again."

Bob and I watched from the parking lot as the helicopter lifted off from the roof of the hospital, lights flashing in the dark night, a sky full of stars as a backdrop. It swooped south, and we followed in Bob's car, not knowing if Susan would be alive or dead by the time we arrived at the next hospital.

Long Beach is about a half hour south of West Los Angeles, where UCLA is located. The freeways were not congested, and we made good time as the helicopter disappeared in the distance. There was not much to say, and we sat silently with our thoughts. I prayed for Susan, for her survival and for her recovery.

By the time we got to the correct wing of the hospital, she was on the gurney ready to enter the hyperbaric chamber for her first session. She was ghostly pale, and all the water weight of the previous week had drained off in the surgery, leaving her now looking skeletal. She was awake and in obvious pain. She could barely talk, but all she wanted to know was how the kids were doing and when she could see them. I promised they would come soon, and then she was wheeled into the cylinder.

Over the next several days, Susan had several more surgeries as the vestiges of the gas gangrene were cleaned out of her tissue and excessive bleeding was staunched. At one point, when I learned that she was going to be operated on for the fourth or fifth time, I went to the chapel and prayed that she not be allowed to suffer any more.

The memories of the Peace Corps volunteer and her multiple amputations haunted me. How many times does one have to be carved into before enough is enough?

Susan's parents took wonderful care of Joe and Sabrina and brought them to the hospital every day to see their mom. They were as strong and supportive as any two people could possibly be, and an inspiration, even as they feared they might lose their daughter. Weak though she was, Susan cherished every second with her beautiful, healthy babies. Her determination to live, her courage in the face of such long odds, came from her maternal love for her new children. She simply was not going to leave them.

After five days of treatments in the hyperbaric chamber, she seemed to stabilize and turn the corner. She was going to live. Amy Rosenman and her timely intervention had saved her. As incompetent as the doctors were who failed to see the most obvious signs of infection, Amy's quick thinking and swift action kept Susan from dying. Moreover, deft cutting with the scalpel had spared the nerves in her leg so she did not become paralyzed and would walk again. In fact, she would do better than just walk, taking up tennis and hiking as she resumed a normal life.

Susan remained in the hospital for over a month, and then in convalescence for several more. It was not until December, seven months after the birth of our twins, that she had her final major surgery. By then we had moved back to Washington, D.C., and were trying to cope with all the issues that a young couple with two small children has to deal with. I was going to work by bus and Metro at 6:30 every morning and returning no earlier than 7:30 every night. We had no extra money, so Susan had no help with the kids. It was a very difficult time for her.

A year later, at the end of 1980, I was asked to move to the American Embassy in South Africa to take over the general services operation after a major scandal involving my predecessor had been uncovered. He had been discovered stealing property on a massive scale, buying a farm and then leasing it back to the embassy, effectively having the U.S. government buy it for him. His corruption had been widespread, and he had engaged in a number of other fraudulent activities. Where there was a dollar to be skimmed from the operation, this guy had found a way to do it.

We jumped at the chance to move. It would put us in a position where Susan could have help with the kids and where we might be able to save some money—an impossibility in Washington—and, for me, the job promised to be very interesting. South Africa was still in the clutches of apartheid, the odious system that institutionalized racism against the black majority and was maintained by a minority numbering less than 25 percent of the population.

Susan was now well enough to travel and no longer needed medical attention. The operations were behind her, and she was as fully recovered as she would ever be. We arrived in Pretoria in January 1981, only days before the inauguration of Ronald Reagan. In an interview before the ceremony, President-Elect Reagan had been asked about America's relations with South Africa's white government. He responded that South Africa had been allied with the United States in all the wars we had fought in the twentieth century and that its repository of mineral stocks was important to the U.S. Not surprisingly, the South African government took his answer to mean that there would now be less pressure on them to change their system under the new American administration.

In June 1981, when a senior American delegation visited the region, led by William Clark, a California associate of Reagan's and newly confirmed as deputy secretary of state, the South Africans tried to press their luck and secure an official shift in American policy. The regime's aggressive approach was exposed the first evening at dinner in Cape Town. Roelof (Pik) Botha, the foreign minister, and Magnus

Malan, the defense minister, managed to cull Clark from his herd of advisers, ostensibly to give him a tour of the historic "Castle" where we were gathered. After several minutes, the embassy's political counselor, Dennis Keogh, and I set out to find the missing trio.

(Dennis was one of my first mentors and one of the finest Foreign Service officers of his generation. His career was cut short when he was killed three years later in a terrorist attack in Namibia. He taught me the value of proactive diplomacy and steady commitment to goals. He was also the father of twins, and with his wife, Sue, provided us with much needed support and advice.)

We stumbled upon Clark in one of the antechambers, backed into a corner with Botha and Malan verbally pummeling him from both sides. The oral mugging was designed to take advantage of Clark's inexperience and lock the U.S. into the pro–South African policy they had inferred from Reagan's interview. However, they badly overplayed their hand with the genial Clark, who was deeply offended by the actions of his hosts. Once extricated from their clutches, he retreated to the company of his delegation, which included Chester Crocker, the very capable assistant secretary of state for Africa and architect of the policy approach that came to be known as "constructive engagement."

Incredibly, the following day the South Africans renewed their efforts. They commandeered Clark's motorcade and whisked him out to the military airport to take him up to a South African military base in Namibia. If they succeeded, the impression left in Africa would be that the U.S. supported the South African government in the region's wars, and Crocker's policy would be stillborn. Dennis and I raced to the airport, panicked that Clark might have succumbed to the South Africans' entreaties. We found him resolutely refusing to make the trip, even after he was told that all the arrangements had been put in place, including a military band to receive him. "But the band is already up there in place," Botha said lamely.

Our next year in South Africa—1981—afforded us the opportunity to travel extensively, from the Cape to the northern scrub veldt prairies, from the jagged Drakensburg Mountains to the southern beaches on the Indian Ocean. South African society was just beginning to come to grips with the profound issues of racist governance and to accept the fact that change was coming. Crocker's constructive engagement, while derided in many liberal circles for being too modest in its approach, was predicated on the principle that evolutionary political change could yield a better outcome than revolution, with all the violence and upheaval it would entail. In order to successfully influence constructive change, Crocker preached how crucial it was that diplomatic contact be maintained and mediation efforts be kept robust.

In my next two postings, I would have to defend the policy of constructive engagement in two of the African nations most vehemently opposed to the South African apartheid regime—Burundi and Congo—not easy when it was routinely mischaracterized as a compact with the hated racist Boers. The policy was ultimately successful, particularly after it was supplemented by economic sanctions passed by a Democratically controlled Congress over a presidential veto in 1985. The lesson was that, often, diplomacy is the art of occupying space and time while the facts on the ground evolve in a direction that will permit antagonists to find the necessary compromises without resorting to violence. In South Africa, the emergence of new leadership, as F. W. De Klerk took over as prime minister and, most importantly, Nelson Mandela's enlightened leadership after his release from his Robben Island jail cell, provided the keys to unlock the process. Patience and a willingness to use all of the tools we had available—from diplomatic pressure to economic sanctions—yielded peaceful transitions in both South Africa and Namibia.

Early in 1982, the American ambassador to Burundi, Frances Cook, was evacuated to South Africa for her own safety after a report had reached the American government that a "female ambassador" was the target of a Libyan assassination plot. Frances, an imposing and high-profile personality, was the only diplomat fitting that description in the region at the time.

Muhammar Qhadafi had already demonstrated an interest in broadening his influence in the region, and Libyan troops had recently been deployed to Uganda to prop up Idi Amin's regime. There they were soundly defeated by Tanzanian forces, but, hardly stopping to lick his wounds, Qhadafi had been lavishing money and Islamic libraries on the impoverished countries of the region. Burundi had been vulnerable and largely isolated since the time of a genocide perpetrated by the minority Tutsi government in 1972. Though the president of Burundi had since been deposed, the successor government was still overwhelmingly Tutsi. Frances had been active in promoting democratization and respect for human rights in the regime and had, by dint of her forceful personality, established a number of positive programs designed to move the Burundi government in the right direction. Since Qhadafi was actively engaged in undermining such efforts, an assassination plot against her was not at all out of the question.

Frances and I went to lunch together one day while she was cooling her heels in Pretoria. It was then that she offered, as she put it, to elevate me from the motor pool to the front office. Would I like to come to Bujumbura, she asked, to serve as her deputy? I was too junior in grade for the job, with less than six years' experience, but she understood that many of the problems an ambassador faces in managing an embassy in Africa are administrative in nature, and she wanted someone with such a background to complement her own political strengths. My administrative and management skills had been tested in three African countries, my knowledge and understanding of African issues were solid, and I spoke the official language of Burundi—French.

The job of deputy chief of mission (DCM) is a key position in an embassy, with responsibility for the operation's day-to-day management as well as the coordination of the various U.S. government agencies and programs operating in the country under the supervision of the ambassador. When the ambassador is out of the country, generally for at least a month each year, the deputy is in charge of the operation. The biggest attraction for me was that my own personal goals had changed with the arrival of my twins: a desire to see the world had given way to the business of having a career, and the pinnacle of a career in the State Department is service as an ambassador. I knew that the road to an ambassadorship generally includes at least one stint as DCM.

The choice of a deputy was at that time the absolute prerogative of the ambassador. The problem was that because I was so young, thirty-two at the time, and relatively inexperienced, there was considerable resistance in the personnel system to my getting the assignment. Even though it was common knowledge that a DCM assignment was a big step up the career ladder, I actually received a letter from my ever-vigilant personnel officer (again, one I did not know), discouraging me from accepting the offer. Far from agreeing that the assignment would be career-enhancing, as well as personally rewarding, she actually suggested that it might not be good for my career.

That letter quickly found its way to my circular file. I accepted the assignment and prepared to move my family several thousand miles north, from cosmopolitan Pretoria to an isolated city in the heart of Central Africa.

When we arrived in Burundi in July 1982, the capital, Bujumbura, was a sleepy backwater nestled in the foothills arising from the Ruzizi plain along the banks of Lake Tanganyika, not far from the spot where Henry Morton Stanley greeted a fellow Englishman with the enduring question, "Dr. Livingstone, I presume?" There was only one stoplight in the town, and it rarely worked. The Burundians were reserved and formal toward outsiders and also very wary, no doubt a consequence of the periodic bloodlettings that plagued the society.

Unlike the peoples of most other African countries, the two major ethnic groups of Burundi, the Hutu (85% of the population) and the Tutsis (14%), lived mingled together in the hills of this Central African nation. There were no tribal zones. In the period before colonization, the country had been ruled by a royal group called the Ganwa through a chief known as the Mwami. In pre-colonial Burundi society, cattle, and the milk they produced, were signs of status and wealth. The Tutsi clan that came to dominate the government after independence had once been of such low caste that their members were not permitted even to milk the Mwami's cows, a tangible measure of how discriminated against they had been.

After colonization by the king of Belgium (the Belgian colonies were property of the king, not of the country), the traditional royal system of governance in Burundi gave way to the authority of poorly trained and uneducated administrators drawn largely from the Tutsi tribe. At the time of independence in 1962, there was only one Burundi national who had even attained a university education. The Belgians had also conscripted an army made up mostly of low-caste Tutsi. Unable to touch the Mwami's milk cows, they were nonetheless trained to wield modern weaponry. It was only a matter of time, once independence had been achieved, before the army emerged as the best-trained—and the only armed—organization in the country. The takeover it staged was brutal; in the intervening years, there had been paroxysms of violence so horrific that "genocide" is the only word to describe them. During the intensely violent era of the early 1970s, several hundred thousand Hutu were hacked to death by machete, or lined up in the national football stadium and massacred by the army. In interludes between the fits of killing, there were Tutsi governments that tried to ensure their own survival through less violent means. My stay there coincided with one of those interludes.

My embassy colleagues and I stayed busy for the next three years with activities ranging from the financing of health clinics in the interior to coordinating and overseeing the Peace Corps and USAID, and working with the Burundi government as it tried to write a constitution and empower a National Assembly. In the end, the government, still overwhelmingly made up of the minority Tutsi, could not shake off its paranoia and the conviction that the majority Hutu were bent on overthrowing them. They reverted to authoritarian rule and cracked down on the civil rights and liberties we and other Western governments had been encouraging them to install and respect. There was no understanding of concepts that we take for granted, including the linkage between majority rule and minority rights, or even the rule of law. The mistrust among the parties would not allow them to take the plunge and forge new political or legal arrangements.

Despite the country's troubles, life outside of work could be very pleasant. The embassy had a boat on Lake Tanganyika that Susan and I took out frequently, looking for hippos and crocodiles. Our house was on a hill overlooking the town, the river, and the Ruzizi plain, and across to the mountains of eastern Zaire. We learned to play golf there, and our kids thrived, enjoying the warm weather and the French schooling. Susan went to work for the Cultural Center in Bujumbura, but after two years, life in Africa had lost its appeal for her. Instead of adventure, she saw Bujumbura as another outpost a long way from home. She spent increasingly long periods at home in California, where she could be closer to her parents and family. I began unreasonably to resent the times apart and, frankly, did not handle the problems in our marriage very well. There was no marital counseling available in Bujumbura, and even if there had been, I doubt I would have been a very good candidate for it. My work and outside activities began to crowd my family life, something I have regretted ever since.

Susan and I grew distant, and she returned to the States with the kids. Although our split was more or less amicable, it was definitive.

I left several months later, in the summer of 1985, after three years in Burundi, for a sabbatical in Washington, D.C., as a Congressional Fellow under the auspices of the American Political Science Association.

Twice in a normal career, a Foreign Service officer can take a year-long training assignment, once in mid-career and again for senior training. Mid-career training could be at a university for an advanced degree or else at one of our military war colleges, or could involve practical training in business or government. I applied for the Congressional Fellowship because it offered academic training at the Johns Hopkins University in Washington on how the congressional process worked, as well as hands-on experience in the offices of senators and representatives.

Ideally, a Fellow serves in both chambers of Congress and for members from both parties, but it often happens that the entire fellowship is in one house or with one party. I interviewed with several Republicans, including the offices of Pete Wilson from my home state of California, and Frank Murkowski of Alaska, before being offered a post in the office of the junior senator from Tennessee, Al Gore. It was not a partisan decision, although my personal views on domestic issues such as abortion and gun control were definitely better represented by the Democrats than by the Republicans. I saw myself, then as now, as center–left in my outlook on social issues and as a realist in foreign policy. I was by no means either extreme left or extreme right, then or now.

In Gore's office, I handled issues related to domestic agriculture and the passage of the 1985 Farm Bill. I also had the chance to travel to Tennessee with the senator and to accompany him to a series of town meetings, driving across the state from Memphis to Nashville one crisp autumn Saturday.

The night we arrived from Washington, D.C., we stayed with Al's uncle in Jackson, about forty-five minutes from Memphis. The next morning, I dressed in my finest double-breasted suit with a nicely pressed shirt I had carefully packed and a fancy tie. My shoes were polished to a high shine. I was not going to let the senator down by looking anything less than my best. Unexpectedly for me, he came to the breakfast table in a shopworn blue suit, a slightly frayed pale blue shirt, a nondescript tie, and shoes that looked like they had not seen polish in months. When we arrived at the first town meeting, I suddenly understood. The senator's constituents were regular folk, dressed for Saturday activities in their coveralls, jeans, and ball caps. They were there to have their issues addressed by "Al," their man in Washington, not to be overawed by some city slicker out to impress them with his wardrobe. I discreetly made my way back to the senator's car, removed my coat, loosened my tie, and rubbed some dirt on my shoes to try to blend in a little better. What could be worse that an overdressed senator but an overdressed senator's aide?

I learned a lot from that trip about American voters and their interests and concerns. And I watched as the senator treated his constituents with interest, compassion, and real friendship. He seemed to know the name of everyone he saw, and asked about family members by name as well. His very real comfort in front of audiences contrasted starkly with the unease he projected then and later in front of a television camera. He was approachable (I knew him even then as Al) and very funny. And he loved to be out there. He drew energy from his audiences, listening carefully and answering every question with passion and enthusiasm. He was with his people, and however mundane their concerns, they became his concerns.

Al was also dedicated to the issues, some of which—his support for the information technology revolution, for example—were far ahead of their time, generating no public interest then, and offering no political return. But he kept plugging away at them until they saw the light of day. In his senate offices we already had a rudimentary intra-office E-mail system that permitted us to communicate directly with the senator and office colleagues. We were on the cutting edge. Even Newt Gingrich later acknowledged, in a panel discussion, that Al Gore's efforts had been instrumental in creating the regulatory framework that led to the rapid expansion of the technology we know today as the Internet.

In the spring of 1986, I moved to the House side, into the suite of offices in the capitol rotunda occupied by the majority whip, Tom Foley. The House was a completely different experience. I served as the congressman's staff assistant on subjects that he dealt with in his capacity as whip. He was frequently asked to speak at events having little to do with his legislative agenda: the North American Association of Pakistani Physicians was one such event, the meeting in Washington of the American Association of Nuclear Power Plant Managers another. I would draft his talking points and try to figure out what questions might come from his audience. He took me to all the speeches he delivered and showed delight in introducing me to audiences as his "State Department aide."

Foley was from Spokane, Washington, a conservative district on the eastern side of the state, and had been in the House since 1964. He and his wife, Heather, are two of the most thoughtful and friendly down-to-earth people I know. Heather served as the unpaid administrative assistant in the whip's office, managing the schedule and the staff, and keeping Tom moving in the right direction. She would bicycle in to work from their apartment across town in the Kalorama neighborhood with her dog, who was a fixture in the office. Gently, but resolutely, she would bring order to the chaos that reigned as a result of the pace of work in the chamber. There are 435 members of the House, all with needs and demands that eventually find their way to the whip's doorstep. Though most members are fine, affable public servants, they did not get to hold elective office by being wallflowers.

Assertiveness is a trait of all politicians. The whip's office was the arbiter of who got what; and since the whip was elected by his fellow representatives, care of the constituents was an essential part of the job description. Heather was acutely sensitive to the delicate balance between catering to the members and keeping them in line.

Tom's office did not have a desk, but was outfitted to look like an English club drawing room, with deep cordovan leather couches and chairs and an elaborate stereo system that played opera with a fidelity worthy of the great opera houses of Europe.

He allowed me to sit in on every meeting that my workload permitted. In fact, I could perch in his office or follow him around when not doing my research in my own office upstairs, just behind the visitors' gallery off the floor of the House. His knowledge of the history of the House was profound, and he could quote at will pithy aphorisms from earlier times. Tom was, and still is, one of Washington's most eminent raconteurs.

There were regular Tuesday meetings with all the assistant whips, chaired by Speaker Tip O'Neill, to set weekly agendas and discuss strategies. These were free-flowing occasions, with the unruly House members passionate and loudly sharing their ideas. Finally Tom would gently sum up the debate and he, Majority Leader Jim Wright, and the Speaker would rein in the herd and dole out assignments.

We would also often be with Speaker O'Neill when he carried out his ceremonial duties. On one occasion, he received the newly arrived Soviet Ambassador Yuri Dubinin, who had replaced the long-serving Anatoly Dobrynin, a fixture on the Washington diplomatic circuit since 1962. Ambassador Dubinin sported a silver-colored Elvis-style pompadour that caught Tip's attention. He could not get over it, and spent the first several minutes commenting to the ambassador on his haircut. The ambassador, new to Washington and wanting to make a good first impression, was obviously uncomfortable. He had doubtless assumed that in meeting the man third in line to be president of the United States, he would be treated to a learned discourse on American foreign policy as viewed by our elected representatives. Instead, all he got was a discussion of his high hair.

Just before I departed Washington at the end of the fellowship, Tom and Heather invited my twins and me to watch the Fourth of July fireworks of 1986 with them from the balcony of the Capitol building. We spent a wonderful evening celebrating the national holiday from the vantage point of one of our most illustrious institutions. After the fireworks were over, Tom opened the floor of the House Chamber and gave my seven-year-olds a guided tour. They sat in the Speaker's chair and listened as he explained the importance of the mace as the symbol of the House in session—without the mace in place, no work could transpire on the floor. If the mace were withdrawn, work ceased. He showed them how new voting cards worked, permitting representatives to place votes from their desks on the floor. I treasure a picture in my office of Joe and Sabrina, wearing Statue of Liberty crowns on their heads, sitting at desks on the House floor next to Tom Foley, who would soon become Speaker of the House.

I left Washington not long after this, in July 1986, for my next assignment, deputy chief of mission in the Republic of the Congo. Congo's capital is Brazzaville, located on the northern bank of the Congo River, across from Kinshasa, capital of Zaire, the former Belgian Congo. I had first been to Brazzaville in December 1978 to help reopen our embassy that had been closed after the 1967 Arab–Israeli war. Congo had been convulsed by politics since its independence from France in 1960, and had been ruled by military dictators who found friends in the Soviet Union and among its allies. The government's rhetoric was rabidly socialist, and they even displayed a hammer and sickle on their flag, which did not prevent the leadership from enriching itself at the expense of the population. The bureaucracy there was woefully slow, inept, and corrupt.

By contrast, most of the Congolese people were animated and vibrant, politically, culturally, and socially. The art school in the Poto Poto neighborhood was renowned for its creativity, and was home to many of the continent's most distinguished and imaginative artists of the seventies and eighties. Political discourse, while heavy on socialist and anti-colonial rhetoric, peppered all walks of life. One of Africa's most famous singers, Zao, made his name singing about African veterans of the French military ("Ancien Combatant"), a satirical song about those who fought for the colonial masters in Europe's wars. Yet for all their egalitarian zeal, they loved their dark Pierre Cardin suits, their Mercedes, and their regular trips to Paris. Education in Moscow at the Patrice Lumumba University, perhaps, but vacations in France. Or as one Congolese official put it to me, "Just because we are socialist does not mean we have to be poor."

The Congolese economy was fueled by oil. Huge reserves had been discovered off the coast of the southern city Point-Noire (Black Point), and the horizon was dotted with derricks of flaming natural gas. The oil business was controlled by the French state-owned Elf Aquitaine. Elf was a force unto itself. At times, it was even difficult to differentiate between the company and the French state, and indeed, as we later learned, a number of clandestine state activities were run through the company. More sinister, Elf also served to advance political parties' interests, both in France and in Africa. A French journalist once told me that a good way to gauge when elections were going to be called either in France, or in an African nation with an Elf presence, was to watch the suitcases coming in and out of the Elf headquarters. If they were heavy coming in, it signaled that money was arriving to finance the election of the Elf favorite in the country. If they were heavy leaving, money was being repatriated to finance French elections.

Congo proved to be far more interesting than I had expected. I had recently remarried—my new wife was a Frenchwoman who had been raised in Africa and had returned there to work with the French Ministry of Cooperation, the equivalent of our USAID. We would spend weekends playing golf at the regional headquarters of the World Health Organization, where she worked. Afterward, sipping drinks at a riverside bar called les Rapides, right on the Congo River rapids just below the capital, we would watch an impromptu fashion show of young Congolese men and women sporting garb only they could wear. They called themselves Sapeurs, which stands for *Societe des ambianceurs et personnes elegantes* (the Society of Trendsetters and Elegant People). It was a movement that had sprung up in Kinshasa across the river, spearheaded by Congolese singer Papa Wemba. Picture men in zoot suits, fedoras, and spats, and women in boas and spike heels, parading back and forth on the banks of the Congo River and turning it into a fashion catwalk. That was the "la Sape" fashion movement.

Professionally, Brazzaville was very satisfying, though I got off to a rocky start there. Shortly after my arrival, on the eve of a visit to Washington by President Denis Sassou Nguesso, his foreign minister equated Zionism to Nazism in a speech at the United Nations. It was a more virulent formulation of the historic African comparison of Zionism to racism; there were few more offensive statements that he could have made. The uproar that ensued in Washington was bipartisan, full-throated, and fully justified. Already there had been little enthusiasm for a meeting in the Reagan administration between President Reagan and Sassou Nguesso. After all, in the halls of the State Department, Nguesso was referred to as the "Marxist–Leninist devotee of *Afrique-Asie*" (a left-leaning French-language magazine on Africa). The only reason a meeting with Reagan was even entertained was because Sassou Nguesso had recently been elected head of the Organization of African Unity (OAU), and it was protocol for the president to receive the heads of the regional organizations.

After the debacle at the United Nations, at the embassy we were told by a deputy assistant secretary for Africa that a significant gesture was required to put the visit back on track, and it would have to be something like the firing of the foreign minister, who just happened to be the president's uncle. Nothing short of that would ensure that Reagan would see Sassou Nguesso.

I was dispatched by our ambassador to convey the bad news to the Congolese president's chief of staff. In the car en route, I thought about how I was going to phrase it. I came up with a formulation along the lines of "Far be it from me to tell you how to handle the internal affairs of your country, but I will say that my government would not be displeased if you removed your foreign minister from his position." Predictably, as I learned later, the chief of staff reported to the president, and later to a cabinet meeting, that I had insisted they fire the foreign minister. The discussion then turned to declaring me persona non grata—diplo-speak for kicking me out of the country. But Sassou Nguesso correctly understood that such an action would only make his problems with us worse and that I was too small a fry to waste the gesture on. Several months later, when our relations had improved, I asked that he read the memorandum of my conversation with his chief of staff. It had been prepared by a staff member of his who'd been at the meeting. Nguesso did read the document, and word was sent back to me that it confirmed my version of events. We have remained friendly ever since.

Nguesso's trip to Washington was anticlimactic. He was not received by the president, who instead made a phone call to him in his room at the Willard Hotel, a block away from the White House. The Congolese president commented wryly about the exchange to intimates: "It would have taken no longer for us to have gone across the street to meet him than it took to talk on the phone." It was unprecedented for the American president not to receive the OAU chairman, but Sassou Nguesso was undaunted and had a montage of doctored photos featuring him with President Reagan published on the front page of the government newspaper in Brazzaville, literally papering over the contretemps for his own people.

Sassou Nguesso knew that Congo's relations with the United States would continue to be characterized by American apathy, at best. The Soviets were too involved in the politics of the country and supplied much of the military assistance, while the French managed the economic relationship and greased the palms of those who counted. Both were suspicious of us.

The Congolese president needed, however, to mark his time as head of the OAU with some visible success, and that played into our own policy goals. For all the pressing issues facing Africa at that time—everything from the debt shadowing the continent to Namibian independence—there was one that the Congolese might be able to help us with. That was the Angolan war.

For a dozen years, Cuban troops had passed through the Point-Noire port on the Congolese coast on their way to fight on the side of the MPLA† government against the insurgency of Jonas Savimbi and his South African and U.S.-supported UNITA movement. Many of the MPLA's senior people had been in exile in Brazzaville during the last days of Portuguese rule in the mid-1970s, and relations between Sassou Nguesso's political party and the MPLA were very close.

Soon after he returned from his disappointing trip to Washington, Sassou Nguesso sent his adviser, Dr. Seydou Badian, to meet with the ambassador and me to discuss how we might restart the moribund negotiations with Angola. Badian, a Malian national, had been a minister in the first post-independence government of Mali in the 1960s. He was a highly respected author, as well as a politician who in his youth had been an avowed Maoist. As minister, he had been

---

† *Movimento Popular de Libertação de Angola,* Angolan political party founded in 1956.

Mali's point man on Communist China. He had also spent several years in a notorious prison in the Sahara Desert after a military coup when he had been on the losing side. This incarceration had left him no less passionate about the future of his continent, albeit less enamored of the Chinese model of governance. Although he was still a socialist, the years in jail had cured him of his passion for revolutionary regimes. He was in semi-exile in Brazzaville with his adopted daughter, helping Sassou Nguesso manage the OAU portfolio. Though he was an unlikely interlocutor for the U.S. government, his acumen and wisdom outweighed his communist background for me, and, eventually, for Chester Crocker and his team as well.

By this time, close to fifteen months had passed since the last time we had spoken to the Angolans. Positions had hardened and hostilities had increased, and the flood of troops from Cuba and South Africa had given the war a nasty international flavor. South African troops and American military assistance supported the rebel army of Jonas Savimbi, while Soviet arms and Cuban troops came to the aid of the government. It was a hot war during the waning days of the Cold War, with proxies doing the fighting and killing and dying. Battles over control of our Angola policy were paralyzing Chester Crocker and the Africa Bureau at the State Department. The South African government, American lobbyists, and conservatives in both the administration and in Congress were effectively undermining any initiative that was not directly related to unabashed support for Savimbi. The newest darling of the American right, and a bad actor, Savimbi had a terrible record of human rights violations, and, having received his guerrilla training in China, he could hardly be called a democrat.

From my perspective in Brazzaville, it was simply not acceptable for us to be doing nothing in the face of the worsening situation in Angola. Continuing the war would only serve to leave all sides embittered, and while the Angolan government was admittedly not pro-American, neither was it the rigidly Communist regime that the American right wing liked to set up as a bogeyman. While lobbying for a renewed effort on the part of my government, I knew that in most diplomatic careers, hewing to the administration line is what's expected of a diplomat. And yet, I also knew that Foreign Service officers in my position often endeavor to influence the future direction of that line. Diplomats must sometimes act like lawyers, frequently defending positions they may not believe in. The similarity doesn't go far, though, because in diplomacy, you have the opportunity to offer constructive alternatives. In the event the differences with your government are too great, you may resign. But when one shares strategic goals, the fact of tactical differences in approach is not a reason to resign. As it was, I shared a key part of Chet Crocker's vision for the continent: evolutionary change in southern Africa. Even where I might have differed with the tactics, I saw his approach vindicated years later in the independence of Namibia and the peaceful transition to black rule in South Africa.

But Crocker did not have a particularly high opinion of Sassou Nguesso at that time, given Sassou's relationship with the Soviets, his socialist bent, and Crocker's sense that Sassou was not serious about brokering a peace and probably could not produce one even if he tried. So, when those of us at the embassy in Brazzaville were told that Sassou Nguesso wanted to use his good offices and his position as OAU chairman to help bring the Angolan war to an end, and duly informed Washington of these facts, we were met with a steely silence. In the ensuing months, the embassy kept pushing the State Department to give the Sassou Nguesso gambit a chance. We even sent Badian to Washington to meet with Crocker and make the Congolese case directly.

Finally, in April 1987, Crocker and a delegation arrived in Brazzaville to test the waters. Sassou Nguesso had promised that a senior Angolan official, Manuel Alexandre "Kito" Rodrigues, then the minister of interior and number two in the government, would be the Angolan representative. This had been the hook to persuade Crocker to come.

Crocker and his delegation arrived for the meetings only to find the Angolan delegation headed by Vice Foreign Minister Venancio de Moura, a hard-working bureaucrat but no political powerhouse. Kito was still in Luanda because his president, Jose Eduardo Dos Santos, had traveled to India, and according to Angolan protocol, he and Kito could not both be out of the country at the same time. Thus, the meetings were threatened before they even started. Sassou Nguesso pulled every string he could and, by sending his plane down to Luanda, managed to produce Kito the next day. The meeting itself lacked substance, but it marked a turning point in the negotiations. It was the first time Crocker had directly engaged the Angolans since January 1986, and the eventual result was an agreement, signed in December 1988, to withdraw both Cuban and South African troops from Angolan territory. The Angolan civil war wasn't over, but at least the proxy armies were going home.

It had been a slow but patient negotiation, and it validated the underlying principle of constructive engagement: that the process has to be constant and paced to minimize the negative impact that change always brings. It involved several trips to Brazzaville of Cuban and South African delegations, as well as Americans and Angolans, and bilateral discussions elsewhere. The tangible benefits included the withdrawal of international forces from Angola, and the first de-escalation of one of the proxy wars we were involved in against the Soviets around the world.

I never thought that I would see South Africans like Magnus Malan and Pik Botha set foot in rabidly socialist Congo. But the photo of the delegations to the Angolan talks, which included both Cubans and South Africans, on the front page of the Congolese newspaper said it all. As Crocker himself noted, South African Foreign Minister Botha was caught looking at the others in the photo as if "they were cockroaches walking across his dinner plate." The feeling was mutual, but necessity made them all bedfellows.

In late 1987, one of Crocker's chief assistants, Robert Cabelly, traveled to Brazzaville. I had known Robert for several years and liked him very much. He is one of the smartest Africa hands I know, discreet and very effective. We went to lunch, and over coffee in a Brazzaville cafe, he said that Crocker had been impressed with what I had accomplished there and wanted to reward me with "whatever job you want that he controls." I jumped at the chance to have the position I had always lusted after—the Africa/Middle East–watcher slot at the American Embassy in Paris. The person in this job followed what the French were doing from the Arabian desert to the South African Cape. I had always harbored a not-so-secret desire to live in Paris, and this was the one time I thought I might be able, finally, to land an assignment there. Robert told me that the job was mine and that he would fix it with Crocker when he got back to Washington. Jaunty in the belief that next autumn would find me in the sidewalk cafes of the Champs-Élysées, I saw him off at the airport.

Unfortunately, while he was on his flight home, another good friend of mine who was serving at our mission at the United Nations, Reed Fendrick, learned that his wife, who had worked for me in South Africa, had just taken a job of her own in Paris. Reed got on the phone to Crocker, who, not knowing of my interest, agreed that he could have the job I thought I had just been promised. By the time Cabelly was back in Washington and broached the subject with Crocker, the job was gone.

I was keenly disappointed. As I adjusted to the news that I wouldn't be going to Paris, it became all the clearer to me that I had arrived at a point in my career when it simply was time to get out of Africa. I'd been on the continent or working on African Affairs for over a decade, with little respite. It was time to do something else, put my foot in some other geographic region. I bid on DCM positions in Algiers, Kathmandu, and in about a half dozen other capitals. I had served five years as deputy at our embassies in two difficult countries and was a known and experienced quantity. I was not interested in returning to Washington at this point, so another deputy position was a natural move.

As I was making my way through the assignments process, I received a cable from yet another career development officer, advising me that "You are in the running for a number of DCM jobs, but nothing is certain at this stage. The Kathmandu DCM position has 142 applicants for example. In Algiers our Ambassador has not yet been named, so there will be no decision on his Deputy for several months at least."

Because DCM jobs are the key ticket to be punched en route to an ambassadorship, the competition is always fierce, and it is not enough just to have prior experience in the position. Geographical experience and time in Washington in the relevant bureau also factor in. Most importantly, as I have said, it was still, at this time, the one job that an ambassador personally controlled, an appointment not subject to the rules of the personnel assignment system.

My personnel officer also asked: "Would you be interested in going to Baghdad, Iraq?" Apparently, nobody was bidding on Baghdad. It was, after all, on the front lines of an extended and bloody war with Iran, which had been going on now for more than seven years and was still raging without an end in sight. I thought about it for a while and decided what the hell, why not? I knew hardship posts and had lived in places most people would consider dangerous, but I had never been in a real war zone. I thought it might be very exciting, and I knew that the Middle East was a key region to work in. I put my name forward and began waiting impatiently for a response.

Chapter Four
Coming to Baghdad

APRIL GLASPIE, THE NEWLY APPOINTED AMBASSADOR to Iraq, found that her requirements for a deputy and my resume matched up neatly. She wanted someone with management skills, an experienced person who would help her rebuild the embassy—at that time still suffering from the results of the break in diplomatic relations between the United States and Iraq dating back to the 1967 Arab–Israeli war. In 1984, agreement had been reached between the two countries to reestablish a diplomatic presence in Baghdad, only to have any steps in that direction halted during the Iran–Iraq war. Glaspie, a career officer, was only the second American ambassador to be named to Iraq since the shuttering of the embassy in 1967. With the decade-long Iran–Iraq war finally winding down, she clearly grasped that the United States would soon be moving to reestablish a presence in Baghdad, with a range of American interests to be pursued in this key Middle Eastern country.

The idea was that I would help her oversee the growth of the embassy, and, in exchange, she would give me an on-the-spot education in Middle Eastern diplomacy. It was a part of the world in which I had no experience, while she, by contrast, was one of our most experienced and knowledgeable Arabists. She had served in most of the Arab capitals and in key jobs at the State Department. Widely acclaimed as one of the best of her generation, April Glaspie understood all the issues and knew all the players very, very well.

It was a great opportunity, and I jumped at it. The Middle East Bureau was always seen in the State Department as an entity unto itself, insular and very difficult to break into, especially at senior levels if you hadn't come up through the ranks within the Bureau. I didn't know who else might've bid on the DCM job in Baghdad, but there was grumbling in the Bureau that an outsider like me got it. I was not a career Arabist, and I would have to work to overcome my outsider status.

In a coincidence that produced uneasy laughs and some anxiety, the day I received official word that I was being assigned to Baghdad, bold headlines in the *International Herald Tribune* announced that the missile war had suddenly resumed between Tehran and Baghdad. With scud missiles being lobbed back and forth between the two cities, I couldn't help but read the letter assigning me to Baghdad with mixed feelings. On the one hand, it was an opportunity to be involved in diplomacy of great strategic importance; it also offered a logical progression from the work I'd done on the Angolan peace process. Nothing could be more satisfying than being part of a team that helps to end wars.

There was no doubt that real danger was involved. However, my wife and I didn't hesitate to accept the assignment, figuring that newspapers always inflated the risk in any situation. We thought that if the people of Baghdad could adjust to the dangers and go about their business, as long as our embassy was still open, even if there *were* occasional missiles exploding in Baghdad neighborhoods, we could manage too.

We arrived in Iraq on Labor Day, 1988. Iran and Iraq had agreed to a truce under the auspices of United Nations Security Council Resolution 598 on August 20, bringing active hostilities, including the missile war, to an end. Despite this fact, one's peace of mind was hardly assured; when I landed in Baghdad, Iraq had just used chemical weapons against its Kurdish population in Halabja, a village in the eastern part of the country. The photos of thousands of dead women and children, killed indiscriminately in a most vile fashion—including the use of chemical weapons dropped in bombs and launched in artillery shelling of the villages—were just beginning to be circulated by the international media.

The resultant international outrage against the actions of Saddam Hussein and his murderous regime was swift and merited. By 1988, he had been in power for a decade and had been a Baath Party thug ever since his attempt to assassinate Iraqi Prime Minister Abdel-Karim Kassim in 1958. His rule had become a veritable case study in torture, murder, and intimidation, and, beginning in 1979, also came to be characterized by disastrous wars with its neighbors and, ultimately, with the United States. But though the Reagan administration was vocal in its diplomatic condemnation, neither our efforts nor the broader international condemnation included penalties. There was no cost to Saddam Hussein for his actions.

Some of the harshest criticism came from the American Congress. Claiborne Pell, the Democratic senator from Rhode Island, was chairman of the Senate Foreign Relations Committee at the time. One of his staff members, Peter Galbraith, advocated vigilant monitoring of Saddam's brutality and human rights violations. Peter's concerns reflected Senator Pell's own conscience-driven policy agenda. He traveled frequently to Iraq and to Iraqi Kurdistan, often accompanied by one of our embassy officers, to catalog the human rights abuses of the Saddam regime. Peter was a steadfast proponent of a harder line toward Iraq and a fearless critic of the sitting Republican administration.

From our vantage point at the embassy, we shared the Foreign Relations Committee's concerns, harboring no illusions that we were dealing with anything other than a shockingly brutal regime. The human rights reports we sent to the U.S. Congress over the three years I was in Baghdad pulled no punches, as we cited example after example of Saddam's willful excesses and his penchant for making opponents vanish or for summarily executing them.

In pursuing the bilateral relationship, the administration was always faced with the question of how to calibrate our approach. We recognized that Saddam was a sociopath and that his regime was an ugly totalitarian dictatorship, and we wanted to encourage better behavior. Could that best be achieved by isolating Saddam's regime, as the United States had done with Fidel Castro's Cuba and Muhammar Qhadafi's Libya? Or did a better approach mean cultivating relations in the hopes that contacts and incentives might eventually yield more moderate behavior by the Iraqi regime?

There are always limits to diplomatic influence, all the more so when there are few common interests at stake. Governments, not surprisingly, put their own agendas first and typically resist foreign intrusions into their internal affairs. Isolating a regime often results in our simply isolating *ourselves,* and we then lose any leverage we might have to influence outcomes. On the other hand, when dictators are treated like any other leaders, it's often interpreted by them as a free pass to continue in their autocratic ways, while critics label it as appeasement. "Soft on thugs" is an accusation democratic leaders try to avoid. The merits of ideologically driven diplomacy versus a more pragmatic approach have been a recurring theme of foreign policy debates throughout the history both of international relations and America's own domestic politics.

Iraq's Arab neighbors unanimously urged us to tread lightly. They argued that after almost a decade of a grinding war with Iran, Saddam had learned his lesson and that his natural radicalism would now be tempered by the harsh experience. He might still be unpredictable, so the logic of his neighbors went, but it was better to tie him to relationships that would be hard for him to jettison than to leave him free to make trouble with no encumbrances. Engaging with him at least kept him in our sights.

Virtually everything Iraq had done during the war and against its own citizens was an affront to our own value system. At the same time, Iraq had emerged from its conflict with Iran as an important player in Gulf and Arab politics, albeit one deeply indebted to its neighbors, with enormous wealth and military power that would make it a formidable force with which to reckon in the future. In the first months of 1989, the incoming Bush administration joined the debate pitting those who thought we could moderate Saddam's behavior through incentives against those who believed the regime was incorrigible and irredeemable. The problem with the latter position was that acting upon it would leave us with virtually no tools at our disposal to isolate or contain Iraq. Meanwhile, our relations with Iran were still colored by the virulently anti-American sentiment there, as well as by the equally strong anti-Iranian views that Washington policymakers held after the humiliating takeover of our embassy in 1979 and the holding of over a hundred American government officials hostage.

As far as the rest of the Gulf went, there was no interest there, and especially not in Saudi Arabia, in a presence of American military forces on Arabian soil to discourage adventurism by Saddam. All of Iraq's neighbors continued to argue for a softer approach; and since they clearly had at least as much at stake as we did, the Bush administration was willing to follow their lead.

Even as the embassy produced human rights reports, which were accurate in their depiction of Iraq as a totalitarian regime, the Bush administration adopted a policy enshrined in National Security Decision 26, formally promulgated in October 1989 but in effect, practically, from the middle of that year. It laid out our goals and objectives, proclaiming that "Access to Persian Gulf oil and the security of key friendly states in the area are vital to U.S. national security." The order specifically directed federal agencies to seek economic and political incentives for Iraq to moderate its behavior and to increase American influence.

Armed with this policy statement, we sought to implement it. One of the tools in our diplomatic kit at the time was the Department of Agriculture's Commodity Credit Program that had been put in place during the Iran–Iraq war. At the height of this program, the United States had about a billion dollars of commodity credits extended to Iraq—second only to Mexico in the program worldwide. Yet it had become subject to considerable—legitimate—criticism from Congress, even as the American government and American farmers were profiting on the investment every year. One view was that this program, which facilitated American agricultural exports, was in fact an unjustified reward to Iraq. There were also concerns that Iraq was overextended and might default, and that it might even be diverting funds into arms programs. With these thoughts in mind, we began downsizing the program and limiting our exposure, even as Iraq's demand for American farm products was increasing.

We continued to actively support other U.S. business efforts to expand commercial relations with Iraq and to bid on major Iraqi infrastructure projects. For their part, the Iraqis made very clear their preference for American products. The most visible example of this during the more than two years I worked in Baghdad was the transition of the Iraqi automobile fleet from Volkswagen to Chevrolet as the national automobile of choice. The Chevrolets sold in Iraq were seen as a symbol of the United States (though shipped from a General Motors plant in Canada), representing our improving relations with Iraq. Our products were welcomed, just as Americans were. Nearly all Iraqis were eager for peace, yearned for a reduction in domestic oppression, and wanted improved relations with the United States.

Unfortunately, even with the increase in goodwill between our two countries, America's relationship with Iraq remained very difficult, owing to Saddam's leadership style and the resulting paranoia that pervaded the country. Travel by a foreigner required advance permission, which took three weeks to obtain from authorities, and most trips more than twenty-five miles outside Baghdad included some sort of active surveillance—either a tail or intensive scrutiny at government checkpoints around the country.

Baghdad was a bustling city in 1988, with about four million inhabitants stretching along both sides of the Tigris River. Date palm trees lined the streets of the affluent neighborhoods, and much of the city had been rebuilt from the days when Agatha Christie made her home there in the 1930s. Few parts of town still had the old-style structures, built up topsy-turvy, with floors stacked above another in precarious fashion, casting their shadows over narrow alleys. One such neighborhood bordered the river directly across from the city's *souk*, or market, where rugs, clothes, copper pots and decorations, and many other goods were sold. It was also one of the few places in the river where boats were allowed to cross. My wife and I used to explore this quarter frequently on Saturdays, taking a flat-bottomed canoe across the river, eating dates and almonds sold from pushcarts, and shopping for Kurdish prayer kilims, the lightweight tapestry-style floor coverings that were traditionally carried by Muslim travelers stopping to pray on their journeys. Crossing the river and looking back at the old neighborhood, I couldn't help thinking back to the history of the caliphate that had dominated Baghdad for so many centuries.

Even before my arrival in Baghdad, the Iraqi government had embarked on an aggressive campaign to convince the United Nations of the validity of its positions on issues related to the cease-fire and peace negotiations with Iran. During the early months of my tour, we were regularly invited to meetings that amounted, essentially, to seminars on the hegemonic ambitions of Persia, Iran's precursor empire, and its designs on Iraqi territory over the previous 150 years. Senior Iraqis from Tariq Aziz, the foreign minister, on down, would take out their maps to show us how the Iranians had been encroaching on the Shatt al Arab, the river that merged the Tigris and the Euphrates, and which had served as the historic border between the two countries since the middle of the nineteenth century. The Iraqis claimed that with every successive crisis or war between the two countries, the Iranians were attempting to move the border farther west, from the high-water mark to the center of the river. And, inevitably, the Iraqis feared their enemy would keep moving it until they reached the Iraqi side. In a region where water and water rights are precious, a border like this one had resource implications as well as significance as a demarcation. Tariq Aziz would often say, "We defended the Arab nation against the Persian onslaught with the blood of our sons."

Aziz was an interesting and complicated character, very bright and very articulate. I used to say that although he learned his English at school in Iraq, he could express himself far better than I could in my native tongue. He was a committed Baathist, but as a Christian he had no tribal or clan political base independent of the party. All his power and authority was derivative, based on his relationship with Saddam. With great bravado, he projected the public face of the Iraqi government and Saddam. But the continual question for me about Tariq was always: could I trust him? I found over time that I could not.

The relationship between Iran and Iraq often played out through the Kurds, who served as surrogates or proxies in the ongoing struggles between the two countries. Iranian Kurdish dissident groups operated in Iraq, and Iraqi Kurdish dissident groups were based in Iranian territory, each being tolerated by the host country for the mischief they could make against the other. They engaged in low-intensity operations against the central government's troops and outposts in the traditional Kurdish area, and then would slip back across the border to safety.

The Iranian Kurdish Democratic Party (IKDP) leader, Dr. Abdul

Rahman Ghassemlou, became a close friend of mine. His headquarters were in the hills outside Sulaymaniyah, in the northeastern corner of Iraq. He would often visit me at my home in Baghdad, bringing burlap sacks full of pistachios and tins of Iranian beluga caviar to share. Ghassemlou was a highly educated man, having attended schools in Paris and Prague, where he had received his doctorate, and where he had also taught over the years. Because of the travel restrictions, I was never able to visit him in his headquarters near Sulaymaniyah, even though he would often joke that if I wanted, he'd arrange to have me kidnapped and thus out from under Iraqi surveillance long enough to spend a couple of days in his camps. As an Iranian Kurd, he was freer to pay visits to foreigners than other Iraqis, and as an ally of Saddam in the fight against Iran, he might well have been reporting our conversations to the government. It did not matter to me, since I assumed that everything we said was heard and recorded by the intrusive Iraqi intelligence services.

We did meet one time in Paris for dinner at the Brasserie Lipp, a well-known restaurant on Boulevard St. Germain on the Left Bank. I was there on vacation in early July 1989, and Ghassemlou was passing through on his way to Vienna. When we met, he was accompanied by his European representative, who was carrying a heavy bag that made a resounding thunk when he set it down. I could only guess that it contained weapons, as protection against ambush on the streets of Paris. Ghassemlou held me spellbound for hours with tales of Kurdish fights for autonomy and democracy against the former Shah of Iran and, after that, against the theocracy of Ayatollah Khomeini. Though he was then in his late fifties, he had the twinkle in his eye and the bounce in his step of a much younger man. He was an enchanting individual and a true leader.

Four days after that dinner, I opened the *International Herald Tribune* to see that he and his colleague had been assassinated in Vienna, shot several times at point-blank range while attending what he thought was a negotiating session with the Iranian authorities. Politics in the region were never simple, and always dangerous.

At the end of the Iran–Iraq war, the Iraqis had brought back to Baghdad immense quantities of war booty captured on the front. In a new neighborhood on the outskirts of Baghdad, they eventually displayed the treasure, inviting all to come and see. Laid out in neat arrangements were helmets—many with bullet holes in them—armaments ranging from rifles to artillery, and heavy equipment, such as tanks, armored personnel carriers, trucks, and bulldozers. Citizens by the thousands would come out to stroll for miles up and down past rows of equipment. I found it dramatic testimony to the enormity of the war's toll—watching pensive Iraqis examine the detritus of the conflict, seeing firsthand these not-quite mementoes of friends and relatives lost in battle. Over the decade of the war, the world became inured to the death and destruction caused by it, but living there, it was impossible not to feel the lingering pain deeply. Prior to the war, Iraq had had a population of 17,000,000, of whom roughly 1,000,000 had not come back from the front. Virtually every Iraqi family was in mourning.

It was also a war that, by necessity, went unquestioned by the population, simply because no one dared challenge the wisdom of the regime. Saddam, after all, had come to the presidency in full control of the Iraqi security forces. By the time of the war, there were, under his devious management, as many as seven concentric and overlapping circles of Iraqi intelligence services, some of which existed just to spy on the others and all of which spied on the population at large. We used to say that if you wanted to do your Iraqi friends a favor, never be seen with them. Very senior Iraqi officials would routinely report on social conversations with other senior Iraqis. Open, candid dialogue about the war or about any aspect of Iraqi politics did not exist. The war was simply what the official government line said it was: Iraq defending the Arab nation, in the broadest sense of that term, against Persian encroachment.

For all of the oppression, the heavy hand of totalitarianism, and the daily stresses of living in such an environment, if you had only one time to work as a diplomat in the Middle East and one country in which to serve, this was the time and Iraq was the place. Working there as the deputy chief of mission involved me in just about every issue in the entire region. Now that the Iran–Iraq war was ended, the Iraqis were increasingly asserting themselves as a Middle East power. Saddam was sending signals on the Arab–Israeli peace process that encouraged some U.S. senators to think that post-war Iraq might moderate its hard-line position on the Palestinian question. Republican senators Arlen Specter from Pennsylvania and Larry Pressler from South Dakota, and Democrats Wyche Fowler from Georgia, and Richard Shelby from Alabama (who later switched parties), came and looked closely at all aspects of the relationship with Iraq. Senator Specter was sincerely interested in, and very knowledgeable about, the Middle East peace process, to the extent that he visited twice to try to ascertain whether there was a positive role that Saddam might play in moving the process forward. It was not an unreasonable hope, given Saddam's influence on Yasser Arafat, a frequent visitor to Baghdad and a recipient of considerable financial and political support from Iraq.

It was only in the context of these meetings between the visiting American senators and Saddam that Ambassador Glaspie and I had the opportunity to meet him. Saddam did not as a matter of practice meet with resident ambassadors. In fact, even the presentation of credentials—that protocol-laden initial encounter between a newly arrived ambassador and a country's chief of state—was delegated by Saddam to his deputy, Izzat Ibrahim. This was highly unusual, since ambassadors are traditionally the personal envoys of one chief of state to another.

Though the bulk of embassy work is government-to-government, the personal nature of the ambassadorial assignment is still respected in ceremony, if not in fact. Even in Washington, where the president's time is his most precious commodity, he still receives new ambassadors in staged ceremonial welcomes. But the only two times we saw Saddam for substantive meetings were when April Glaspie met with him on July 25, 1990 and with me, less than two weeks later, on August 6. Both meetings concerned the tension with Kuwait and, in the case of my meeting, the Iraqi invasion of that country four days earlier.

One of the most controversial issues that we grappled with during my tenure concerned Lebanon. The Iraqis saw Beirut and the ongoing Lebanese civil war as a way to avenge what they considered the Syrian betrayal of Iraq and the Arab cause when Syria refused to support Iraq in the war with Iran. The Syrians were in the process of seizing control of Lebanon and imposing military force on the feuding Lebanese factions that had been at each other's throats more or less since the mid-1970s. Getting back at Syria through the medium of Lebanon offered the Iraqis a way to avenge this insult.

Iraq quite openly tried to ship surface-to-surface missiles from Baghdad to Beirut through the Jordanian port of Aqabah in the spring of 1989. The U.S. reacted aggressively to this transaction, committed to dissuading the Iraqis from adding yet more fuel to the fire in Beirut. Surface-to-surface missiles in an urban environment would mean a major escalation of the violence. April Glaspie met with senior Iraqi officials daily as we applied diplomatic pressure to thwart their efforts to arm the Lebanese Maronite Christian prime minister, General Michel Aoun, in his losing struggle against Syria. The U.S. even mobilized a ship to patrol the Mediterranean, to intercept and turn back any missile shipments before they arrived at Lebanese ports. One of the ironies of Iraq's position, as April frequently pointed out to Tariq Aziz, was that General Aoun was a friend of Israel. Thus, the Iraqi support for him put them in tacit alliance with

Israel, still their sworn enemy. For the Iraqis, of course, it had nothing to do with Israel, or Aoun's position in Lebanon; it had everything to do with giving Syrian President Hafez al-Assad a bloody nose and using Beirut as the cudgel with which to bash him. For the Iraqis, the road from Baghdad to Damascus went through Beirut.

Saddam's weapons programs kept a permanent hold on our attention in the embassy as we aggressively strove to learn everything we could about his attempts to procure weapons of mass destruction. We also closely followed his research and development of missile technology and other exotic weaponry. One such exotic weapon program was the so-called long gun, an artillery piece developed by a shady Canadian engineer named Gerard Bull, who was later assassinated in Brussels. The cannon was supposed to be able to project shells much farther than conventional artillery pieces, possibly reaching as far as Israel. At the embassy we worried that if Bull's long-range weapon were ever to really work, it would put Israel under threat of chemical attack, since we knew that Iraq had earlier been able to put chemical weapons into artillery shells. It was never clear whether the concept was even viable, and the cannon itself was so unwieldy that it could easily have been destroyed by an air attack. Bull's death brought development of the program to a halt. We suspected that Israeli intelligence had been responsible for the assassination, not because of his work on the artillery piece but for other activities involving Iraq's ballistic missile program.

While we tried, with our limited diplomatic and intelligence assets, we were hard pressed to keep close tabs on such developments in unconventional armaments. Our actual diplomatic contacts with Iraqis were very formal and highly restricted. There were established channels and procedures, all of which involved going through the foreign ministry with little opportunity for any deviation. Virtually all of our contacts with the Iraqi government passed through the undersecretary at the ministry in charge of relations with the

U.S., Ambassador Nizar Hamdun. After first ascertaining the nature of our business, Hamdum would then play the role of traffic cop, directing us to the appropriate office within the foreign ministry or setting up meetings at another ministry. Substantive discussions outside this tightly controlled access were rare. Occasionally we might have formal meetings with ministers such as Saddam's son-in-law, the infamous Hussein Kamel, Minister of Industry and Military Industrialization, who seven years later would defect to Jordan and tell U.N. officials about the Iraqi nuclear program. (Kamel subsequently returned to Iraq, only to be killed a day later, allegedly by Saddam's son Uday in a shootout.) These meetings were perfunctory and never offered anything in the way of detailed substance. We met more regularly with the minister of commerce or minister of agriculture, usually in connection with some specific program we were working on. For example, there were American companies whose bids we were supporting, or there might be issues relating to the Commodity Credit program—but even these encounters were infrequent.

Social contacts with Iraqis were also very limited. Rarely were they permitted to visit us in our houses. A very few—only six—whom we referred to as the "tame Iraqis," freely circulated in the broader international community. But it was difficult, if not virtually impossible, to discuss issues with them and to hear something other than the government-approved line.

Because contact with Iraqis, official and otherwise, was so restricted, about the only way to learn what was going on in Iraqi government circles was to be active on the diplomatic cocktail party circuit and attend the various embassy celebrations. There were close to a hundred embassies in Baghdad, so there were almost a hundred different Independence Days celebrated, just as we would invite the diplomatic corps to celebrate the Fourth of July with us. Most of these embassies also had military attachés in the country, as Iraq had just fought a major war deploying significant military power, much of which had been purchased from these same foreign countries. That meant at least another hundred military celebrations similar to our own Veterans Day observances.

On about two hundred days of the year, then, a foreign diplomat could expect to be invited out to some pomp and circumstance commemorations of a nation's hard-won freedom or to honor its exalted—and often all-powerful—military. Circulating among the diplomatic corps, our own embassy officers made it their business to chat up their counterparts and try to learn which ones were speaking with the Iraqis and about what subjects. Gossip was the stock in trade, and it was a commodity freely traded at these functions.

The Soviets had a close relationship with the Iraqis, built on their role as principal arms supplier of the Iraqi armed forces, and thus enjoyed more frequent contact with the Iraqi government than any other delegation. Their deputy chief of mission, my counterpart, was Alexander "Sasha" Kalugin, the son of the renowned KGB officer and later Soviet critic Oleg Kalugin. The Egyptian Embassy, too, had frequent dealings with the government, and with 4,000,000 Egyptians living in Iraq, they could not help but have a finger on the pulse of Iraqi life, given the myriad needs and complaints of their expatriate community.

But the best source of information and analysis, across the range of issues, was undoubtedly the Turkish Embassy. Several hundred years of Ottoman domination had created deep historical and trade ties between the two countries. The Turkish Embassy had some of the best and most effective diplomats I had ever met anywhere. Their ambassador, Sonmez Cocsal, would later go on to serve as chief of the Turkish Intelligence Service and as ambassador to France. He was a meticulous man who took copious notes on every meeting, every exchange, and every observation. When we would sit down and discuss a subject, he would inevitably bring out his little bound notepad, both to consult as he was sharing his information and jot down what we were telling him. I believe that when he writes his diplomatic memoirs, they will be the definitive history of the period leading up to the first Gulf War.

His deputy, Ahmed Okcun, was equally capable, if a much different personality. In contrast to his discreet superior, Ahmed, who had already served in Baghdad for several years, was a flamboyant playboy, given to hosting elaborate theme parties and conducting trysts with some of the most desirable women in town. He was, nonetheless, one of the most astute analysts of Iraq and its politics. Ahmad's store of useful information was supplemented by his many contacts among Turkish traders who moved back and forth between the two countries, and with the Turkmen population in northern Iraq that was in continual conflict with Saddam's regime, and often with the Kurds who shared the same region.

We also had a number of reliable contacts among the Kurds. One of our key employees at the embassy was a Kurd, and although his clan had long ago been co-opted by the regime, he kept us apprised of the despicable acts that Saddam was committing against the Kurdish population. This included the forced removal of Kurds from traditional villages into settlements in new government housing projects, where they could be more easily controlled. This man was also an active trader in his spare time and kept our embassy staff supplied with a steady supply of Kurdish rugs and kilims. We could not travel to Kurdish territory as easily or as frequently as we would have liked because of government-imposed travel restrictions. Still, in my second year in Iraq I was able to go as far north and east as the Iranian border—to Rania, Rowanduz, and Dahuk, returning through Irbil, all Kurdish towns. Despite the regime's heavy-handed oppression, life in these towns was busy, the markets full of goods, and the streets bustling with activity.

Also of interest to the U.S. Embassy were the relations among the great Kurdish clans. Kurdish alliances were famously short-lived. On any given day, one Kurdish group might be in cahoots with the Iranians and on another tied to Saddam. But that could easily change, and frequently did as fortunes waxed and waned. The overriding loyalty of any Kurd was to his clan's survival. For so many centuries a persecuted minority surrounded by enemies—the Turks to the north, the Arabs to the south and west, and the Persians in the east—they had learned how to maneuver to make the best of whatever situation they found themselves in. And when they were not fighting their external enemies, the inevitable clan rivalries meant that they were called upon to fight one another.

Despite all of America's efforts, and those of our Arab allies, to wrap a commercial trade and investment cocoon around Saddam that would moderate his behavior, we did not succeed. As early as April 1990, less than two years after the end of the conflict with Iran, Saddam was preparing to go to war again.

At the end of the Iran–Iraq war, Saddam had not demobilized. Instead, he had maintained his huge military machine. Nearly 20 percent of the population either was still bearing arms, or had died or been injured fighting the Iranians. All of this was at enormous cost to the Iraqi economy, already laboring under the burden of close to $70 billion in external debt, plus whatever the government owed to domestic suppliers. At the same time, Saddam was bent on convincing his citizens that the Iran–Iraq war had been a victory; a massive importation of consumer goods masqueraded as a war dividend. It was a classic guns-and-butter budget. But having already mortgaged his country's future waging the Iran–Iraq war, Saddam needed debt relief from his neighbors in order to be able to afford both his large standing army and the ambitious domestic expenditures he was undertaking. In short, he was desperate for a source of revenue, and Kuwait—small, rich, and despised—lay there on his southern border, ripe for the taking.

Kuwait had financed much of Saddam's war effort with substantial loans in the late 1980s. But it had balked at converting the loans to grants and was unwilling to extend more credit to Iraq. Kuwait was also suspected by Saddam of regularly exceeding its OPEC oil quota, thereby driving oil prices down and preventing Iraq from maximizing income on its own oil exports. Iraq also accused Kuwait of stealing Iraqi oil, by using sophisticated slant-drilling techniques to tap into an Iraqi oil field, Rumaillah, just north of the border between the two countries.

Iraq had issues of strategic concern with Kuwait as well. The government wanted to execute a land swap with Kuwait in order to better defend its one remaining port city with access to the Persian Gulf. The historic port of Basra, legendary home of Sinbad the Sailor, is located in the delta where the Shatt al Arab River flows into the Persian Gulf. However, in order to function in the modern world of deep-draft ships, constant dredging operations were required to keep the passage open. During the Iran–Iraq war, when the same waterway was also a matter of contention, the channel had become hopelessly mired in silt. Moreover, unexploded artillery shells, many chemical-laden, were sitting on the bottom of the river, adding considerable risk to any dredging project.

Iraq's solution had been to build a new port farther west, at Um Qasr, along the narrow part of the Iraqi territory that actually bordered the Gulf. Across a narrow strait from the port were two islands, Bubiyan and Warbah, which belonged to Kuwait. These were largely uninhabited, save for an Iraqi garrison established with Kuwaiti permission to provide security for the port access. Iraq wanted to make the arrangement permanent and had offered some territory along its land border with Kuwait as compensation, but the Kuwaitis had balked at the deal.

On April 2, 1990, in an extremely inflammatory speech, Saddam suddenly announced that Iraq possessed weapons of mass destruction and threatened to "set fire to half of Israel." At the same time, he had put troops on spring maneuvers down in the south of the country, and the word coming back to us was that his soldiers had been told that Israel was the enemy they were training against. We were alarmed by Saddam's rhetoric and determined to calm the situation before it escalated out of control. While we were concerned about the tensions in Iraq's relations with Kuwait, we did not suspect that the southern military exercises were, in fact, a first signal of Iraq's intention to invade *that* country. We were more worried that Saddam's hard line toward Israel would further inflame Arab passions and contribute to making any lasting settlement between Israel and the Palestinians that much more difficult to achieve.

At the urging of the embassy, President Bush requested that a delegation of American senators, already in Egypt, detour to Baghdad to deliver a message to Saddam. The delegation was headed by Republican Bob Dole of Kansas and included other Republicans: Frank Murkowski of Alaska, Jim McClure of Idaho, and Alan Simpson of Wyoming, as well as Democratic Senator Howard Metzenbaum of Ohio.

The senators arrived in Baghdad on April 12 and were whisked immediately by air to the northern city of Mosul, along with Ambassador Glaspie, myself, and a number of senior mission employees. We met Saddam, not at his palace but at the one luxury hotel in Mosul, recently opened for the few tourists who actually braved the oppressive political climate to visit Iraq. Mosul is the closest city to the ancient towns of Nineveh and Nimrud, dating back to the thirteenth century B.C. Archeological excavations there had, just the year before, yielded one of the greatest finds of gold jewelry ever, which had gone on display in the Baghdad Museum of National Antiquities.

Senator Dole delivered the presidential message—which we had drafted at the embassy—conveying faithfully the tone that we wanted to strike with Saddam. Dole urged Saddam to eschew chemical and nuclear weapons programs, at the same time reassuring him that the United States remained dedicated to improving relations between our two countries.

After Dole had spoken his piece, Saddam replied in a long-winded statement. "I didn't really say I was going to set fire to half of Israel," he protested. "What I said was that if Israel attacks me, *then* I will set fire to half of Israel." The difference, he went to painstakingly great lengths to emphasize, was that he would take action only in response to Israeli aggression. However, if he were obliged to react, that response would come in the form of a devastating counterattack showcasing his new weaponry. Saddam also made clear his irritation at what he thought was an orchestrated American–British effort to undermine him by scaling back economic and commercial programs, and by engaging in a smear campaign against him. His complaints were a reaction to American and British criticism of his execution of an Iranian-born British journalist for espionage, a recent Voice of America editorial attacking him, and the fallout from an international banking scandal involving kickbacks and misuse of funds associated with the Agricultural Commodity Credit program.

When Saddam had finished his remarks, he invited the other senators to comment. After Senators Murkowski and McClure had spoken, Senator Metzenbaum, an outspoken supporter of Israel, made the most incongruous statement to Saddam: "Mr. President, I can tell you are an honorable man." I was the note taker at this meeting, and as he spoke, I remember thinking to myself that whatever beneficial impact the president's message and Dole's statement may have had on Saddam, it had all just been negated by this obsequious boot-licking. To make matters worse, Alan Simpson, who is about six foot seven inches tall, leaned way far forward in a chair so low that he looked like he was on bended knee before this potentate, and averred: "Mr. President, I can see that what you have here isn't really a policy problem; what you have is a public relations problem. You've got a problem with the haughty and pampered press. I know all about that, because I've got problems with the press back home. What you need is you need a good public relations person."

Saddam no doubt took away from the meeting not the admonition to stop developing weapons of mass destruction and threatening his neighbors, but rather support for his own misguided belief that he was an honorable man who didn't really have policy problems at all, just clumsy press relations. After all, one of Israel's champions had told him so, and another American leader had knelt before him to reassure him that he had no problems with the American government.

I know now that Saddam's rhetoric against Israel was largely camouflage for his real intentions. Under the cover of this rhetoric, he hoped to increase pressure on neighboring Arab nations to forgive his debt and cough up even more money for Iraq's reconstruction effort. In an earlier meeting of the Arab Cooperation Council, in February 1990, Saddam had already warned the Gulf countries: "Let the Gulf regimes know that if they do not give this money to me, I will know how to get it." If nations outside the region bought his line of bluster and saw Iraq as a looming military menace to Israel, Saddam might be able to wrest economic concessions from them as well, in order to ease the threat.

By July, it was clear that the Iraqis and Kuwaitis were on a collision course, though the Kuwaitis feigned blissful calm. On July 17, 1990, in an address commemorating the anniversary of the Baath Party takeover in Iraq, Saddam excoriated those Arabs who he believed had conspired with the Americans and Israelis to sabotage Arab development. His attack was highly personal, as he accused leaders in the region of being bought off with gleaming villas and Mercedes-Benz luxury cars and failing to stand up to Western efforts to thwart Arab ambitions. By this time, it should be noted, Iraqi debt amounted to about $80 billion, or 150 percent of its GDP—much of it in short-term notes owed to Japan, the United States, and European countries. Saddam also claimed that low oil prices, the result of overproduction by a couple of countries, namely Kuwait and the United Arab Emirates, were a "poisoned dagger" in Iraq's back. The message to the region was clear: pay me off or else. When three days later, on July 20, the British military attaché shared with the embassy evidence of a large movement of Iraqi troops into the south again, it underscored the idea that Saddam meant business.

With an OPEC pricing meeting scheduled for July 26 in Vienna, the Kuwaitis finally awakened to Saddam's intention to drive the price of petroleum from $14 a barrel to $25 and to do it immediately, risking international economic turmoil because he needed to raise cash to meet his obligations. If Kuwaiti overproduction didn't stop, he clearly was willing to threaten military action to stop it.

On July 25, April Glaspie went to the Iraqi foreign ministry to deliver to Tariq Aziz a copy of a statement made earlier in the week by the State Department spokesperson, Margaret Tutwiler. The statement had noted that although the United States did not have a mutual defense pact with Kuwait, "Iraq and others know that there is no place for coercion and intimidation in the civilized world." April went alone, which was not unusual for these meetings. As an embassy, we were understaffed and overworked, and a routine meeting did not require a second person just to take notes. Ambassador Glaspie was blessed with a keen mind and a profound understanding of the issues, and was also an inveterate note taker. Shortly after she returned from the meeting with Aziz—during which she emphasized her desire that the information she was sharing be transmitted to Saddam—she was summoned back to the foreign ministry, put into an Iraqi government car, and driven to meet Saddam himself. This was unprecedented. During the two years she had been ambassador, Saddam had never held a private meeting with her, delegating all contact to Aziz or other underlings. It was only when she had escorted visitors from Washington that she had been part of meetings with Saddam, and then as a bystander, not as a principal.

The one-on-one meeting with Saddam was fateful for Ambassador Glaspie. Out of it emerged the charge that she had not been tough enough with him and had somehow given him a green light to invade Kuwait. Nothing could be further from the truth; Glaspie has been made a convenient scapegoat for a more complicated and complex failure of foreign policy. I was with her immediately after the meeting and had several discussions in the few days between the meeting and her departure from the country on a long-planned leave. Her explanation of American policy toward Arab disputes did not waver from our standing instructions. The United States did not take positions on the merits of such quarrels between Arab nations, although the policy was to, in the strongest terms, urge that the parties to a dispute resolve it diplomatically or through international mediation, and not via military threats or action.

During the meeting, Saddam made clear to Ambassador Glaspie that Iraq had no intention of taking any military action against Kuwait, so long as there was an ongoing negotiation process. The meeting was interrupted when Saddam took a call from Egyptian President Hosni Mubarak. Mubarak had been very active in mediating the dispute between Iraq and Kuwait, even engaging in some secret shuttle diplomacy, traveling from capital to capital in the region in quest of a peaceful solution. At the conclusion of the call from Mubarak, Saddam returned to Glaspie and informed her that he had just told the Egyptian president the same thing—that he would not invade Kuwait so long as there was a negotiation process. (It was later reported that Saddam had asked Mubarak not to share with the Kuwaitis what he had told him, in order to keep his bluff alive.) The Egyptian president must have honored Saddam's request, for the attack was a complete surprise to the Kuwaitis, with the royal family barely fleeing with their lives. The double-cross may also explain Mubarak's anger at Saddam in the aftermath of the invasion.

Though Ambassador Glaspie was frequently criticized after the invasion of Kuwait and after the release of the Iraqi transcript of the meeting for not having been tougher on Saddam—for supposedly failing to give him a red light—the Iraqis themselves have, in fact, stated that they understood perfectly what she had said in defining American policy. Even Tariq Aziz has publicly acknowledged this to be true.

Much more recently, on April 2, 2003, I met for lunch with Nizar Hamdun, the former foreign ministry undersecretary, once Tariq Aziz's right-hand man and present at the meeting between Glaspie and Saddam. I had not seen or spoken to Nizar since January 11, 1991, the eve of my departure from Baghdad before Desert Storm began. We had occasionally exchanged personal messages through third parties, and I often received a Christmas card from my Muslim friend. But direct personal contact had been out of the question while I was still a government official. Despite the intervening years with little direct contact, we met as old friends, once having shared the profound responsibility of trying to avert war. In fact, Trudy Rubin, a columnist for the *Philadelphia Inquirer,* had written in early 1991 about our relationship, saying that if war should be avoided, credit would have to go to the two of us for our efforts to find a diplomatic solution to the crisis.

When Nizar arrived at the midtown New York City restaurant a few minutes after I sat down, I was dismayed by his appearance. He was clearly dying; for the third time in twenty years, he had been obliged to submit to chemotherapy for lymphoma. He was under no illusions about his chances of survival, and when I asked him point-blank if he was going to make it, he flatly acknowledged that he did not think so. He was most worried, however, about his wife and daughters, who were still in Baghdad, where the second Gulf War had begun two weeks earlier. He had recently had only intermittent contact with them, on the occasions when sympathetic journalists would arrange a call on a satellite phone. Nizar had made a lot of friends in his life, and they were always happy to accommodate him in his personal needs.

He died on July 4, 2003, knowing that his family had survived the "shock and awe" bombing campaign but still worried about their safety in post-Saddam Iraq. He had left an extensive set of personal notes with a friend and instructions not to share them with anyone until it was certain that his widow and daughters were out of harm's way. To my knowledge, as of this writing, his family is still in Iraq.

Nizar and I compared notes on our experiences in Baghdad before the first Gulf War. I even suggested that we consider writing a book together, examining those issues we had once confronted from our separate points of view. For health reasons, he demurred, and because of the danger to which he feared it could expose his family. He also declined an invitation to sit for an interview with the History Channel. (I was then appearing weekly as a commentator on the 2003 war.) Looking back at the events of 1990, I brought up the Saddam–Glaspie meeting and shared with him my recollections that the position she had put forward to Saddam had been consistent with U.S. policy and was in no way tacit permission for Iraqi action. Nizar was emphatic: April's comments had not deviated from what was known U.S. policy, and she had not encouraged Saddam to invade Kuwait. The Iraqi leadership had not come away thinking she had tacitly indicated that the United States condoned the use of force. On the contrary, he knew exactly what the American position was— opposition to Iraqi military action, under any and all circumstances.

Therefore, Nizar continued, the Iraqis had been startled by the positive tone of a letter from President Bush, delivered a couple of days later by Glaspie, just before she left the country. That letter was far too conciliatory, Nizar had felt at the time, and left the impression that the American desire for good relations with Iraq might override its concerns about Iraqi aggression. He thought that the president's note had sent the wrong signal to Saddam by not explicitly warning him against taking any military action, and not threatening harsh retaliation if he did. He intimated that Saddam had concluded from the positive tone of the letter that the U.S. would not react militarily and that he could survive the political criticism resulting from the aggressive action he was considering toward Kuwait. This letter, much more than any other United States statement, appears to have influenced Saddam's thinking. Nizar's memory in this regard was vivid and unflinchingly critical of the letter.

President Bush's letter to Saddam, in fact, followed the same approach that we had been using for some time, to try to extract good behavior with as many carrots as sticks, particularly in our highest-level exchanges. The letter itself contained language that was conciliatory, but it also reconfirmed our interest in a peaceful resolution of the Iraq–Kuwait dispute. However, it did not, nor did Glaspie's oral presentation, nor did even my own remarks to Saddam four days after the invasion, contain threats of U.S. military action should he fail to heed our entreaties not to invade Kuwait.

The operative passage in the president's letter went as follows:

> I was pleased to learn of the agreement between Iraq and Kuwait to begin negotiations in Jeddah to find a peaceful solution to the current tensions between you. The United States and Iraq both have a strong interest in preserving the peace and stability of the Middle East. For this reason, we believe that differences are best resolved by peaceful means and not by threats involving military force or conflict. I also welcome your statement that Iraq desires friendship rather than confrontation with the United States. Let me reassure you, as my ambassador, Senator Dole and others have done, that my administration continues to desire better relations with Iraq. We will also continue

to support our friends in the region with whom we have had long-standing ties. We see no necessary inconsistency between these two objectives. As you know, we still have certain fundamental concerns about certain Iraqi policies and activities, and we will continue to raise these concerns with you, in a spirit of friendship and candor. . . . Both our governments must maintain open channels of communication to avoid misunderstandings and in order to build a more durable foundation for improving our relations.

When all is said and done, American influence with Saddam was limited. To him, U.S. government actions in investigating and ultimately suspending the one economic program we had with Iraq—the Agriculture Commodity Credit program—along with hostile Voice of America editorials, and congressional efforts to toughen the policy, all contradicted any professions of friendship. Saddam's view of the world was limited and heavily influenced by his relations with his neighbors and his ambitions to be the regional power. Long infatuated by the idea of dominating the Arab world, his emergence from the Iran–Iraq war with a large battle-tested military machine gave him the means to flex his muscles. His dire economic straits and the continuing reluctance on the part of his neighbors to submit to his strong-arm tactics provided him the rationale for doing so.

Kuwait was not a country popular among many Arabs, who saw it as an artificial creation of British colonial officials doodling on a map over a glass of port one afternoon in 1922. Iraq was a leading proponent of this position, long claiming Kuwait as a province cleaved off by the British to weaken Iraq by denying it significant access to the Persian Gulf. Saddam reasoned that if Israel could get away with repeated invasions and occupation of Palestinian territories in flagrant disregard of U.N. Security Council resolutions, why could not Iraq restore Kuwait to its "historic status" as a province of Iraq? Such an outcome would alleviate Iraq's debt problem, provide it greater access to the Gulf, and punish the sclerotic royal family in Kuwait for its bad behavior toward Iraq.

On July 31, State Department Assistant Secretary of State John Kelly appeared before an open session of the House International Relations Committee, chaired by Congressman Lee Hamilton, an expert on Middle East affairs. Hamilton asked Kelly a question point-blank to which he must already have known the answer: did the United States have a mutual defense pact with Kuwait that would necessitate an automatic American response should Iraq invade? The State Department spokesman had already addressed the question several weeks previously, but Hamilton asked it anyway. John Kelly gave the correct answer, the only answer that he could give: "We don't have any defense treaty with the Gulf States. That's clear. We support the independence and security of all friendly states in the region. Since the Truman administration, we've maintained naval forces in the area because its stability is in our interest. We call for a peaceful solution to all disputes, and we think that the sovereignty of every state in the Gulf must be respected."

For me, sweating it out in Iraq, that was a defining moment. A senior administration official had testified in open session to our Congress that we did not have a defense pact that would lead us to come to the defense of Kuwait. Within minutes, Kelly's testimony was transmitted to Iraq. Despite the qualifiers that Kelly put into place about America's preference for peaceful solutions to disputes, the only thing the Iraqi regime heard was that we had no legal obligation or even any mechanism to react to an invasion. That had far more effect than anything that April Glaspie may or may not have said in her meeting with Saddam Hussein. It substantiated that she was in no position to threaten Saddam, nor that if Kuwait was invaded would we bring the B52s over and bomb Iraq back into the Stone Age. There was no legal or political basis before the invasion to make that threat, and Glaspie was never going to so grossly exceed her instructions. She could not in fact have gone any further in her response to Saddam than she had actually gone.

In the region, Saddam agreed to a negotiating session with Kuwait brokered by Mubarak's intense efforts, set for August 1 in Jeddah, Saudi Arabia.

The members of the Iraqi delegation were formidable thugs with nary a diplomatically inclined bone in their collective bodies. They were enforcers, pure and simple, and the Kuwaitis clearly had miscalculated when they assumed a negotiated settlement could be achieved. Izzat Ibrahim al-Douri, the nominal number two in the Iraqi regime, headed up their contingent, with Taha Yassin Ramadan, another hard case given to wearing pearl-handled pistols backwards in twin holsters in order to effect the cross-handed draw of an Old West gunslinger in the event of a shootout. They were accompanied by Ali Hassan al-Majid, the infamous "Chemical Ali," who had earned his nickname as the Butcher of Kurdistan during the gassing of the Kurds in the north of Iraq; he would later reign as the temporary governor of post-invasion Kuwait, where he pursued his murderous ways and became known as the Butcher of Kuwait. There were no Americans, or any other third party, at the negotiations, and the Kuwaitis should have understood that the Iraqis were there only to deliver an ultimatum.

During this period, most of the leaders in the region continued to urge us to do nothing, simply because they feared that anything we might do would provoke Saddam into the very actions we wished to avoid. They claimed he was bluffing and that they would solve the problem with Arab-led diplomacy. Even the United Arab Emirates, who had asked us to undertake a quick military exercise with them, criticized us for making the joint exercise public, concerned that it might bring a negative Iraqi reaction.

On July 31, Ambassador Glaspie left Iraq for her long-planned home leave and to participate in consultations in Washington. Most of the other ambassadors assigned to Baghdad now also made their way out of the city during the infernally hot months of July and August, as was customary. At the time of the invasion of Kuwait, almost all were out of town, having left their embassies in the hands of their deputies, my direct counterparts. This left me the most senior official at the American Embassy in Baghdad.

Chapter Five
How to Shake Hands with a Dictator

IN THE DAYS BEFORE THE INVASION of Kuwait, our embassy military attaché reported regularly on the massing of Iraqi troops in the south, the logistical support that was moving forward, and the establishment of supply lines. But to most of the analysts in Washington, indicators from the field did not lead to definitive proof of an impending invasion. By the time it was completely plain what was in the offing, it was too late to do anything to forestall it.

On the evening of August 1, about six hours before the invasion was launched, I was the dinner guest of an Iraqi national whose principal residence was Paris, where he served as Iraq's arms procurement liaison officer. He was quite likely the one responsible for the purchase by Iraq of the French-made Exocet missiles that Iraq had used to strike the USS *Stark* in a 1987 incident in the Persian Gulf that resulted in the deaths of thirty-seven American sailors. It was one of the hottest days of the summer, probably close to 120 degrees outside. Pulling up to his opulent home on the banks of the Tigris River, I could see the air shimmering just beyond my windshield. The front door opened, and I was ushered in to a living room that by contrast seemed to be chilled to sweater temperatures. It felt to me, just coming in from the heat of the day, like 45 or 50 degrees, but it was probably 65 or 70. There was a fire roaring in the fireplace, while just beyond were floor-to-ceiling windows opening to a backyard on the river. It made for quite a surreal scene. Adding to the ambiance, in one corner of the living room a mustachioed gentleman, looking more like a gangster than a concert pianist, was playing a sonata on a white baby grand piano.

I was the only guest and sat down to an intimate meal with my host, his two sons, and four bodyguards, whom I guess were there to ensure that I would not attack their boss and also to report back to Iraqi intelligence on the evening's conversation. The dinner itself was a classic Arab meal that went on, course after course, for several hours. In the Arab world, social intercourse takes place prior to and during the meal. Guests generally leave right after rising from the table, so dinners tend to involve a lot of time in the dining room itself.

We stood up from the table shortly after eleven, and I left soon thereafter. We had talked about a wide range of international and domestic issues, including alliances in the Arab world, Arab relations with the West, and Arab–Israeli affairs. But we did not broach the subject of Kuwait, even though the August 1 meeting between the Kuwaiti and Iraqi delegations had ended in disarray in Jeddah and Saddam's team had returned to Iraq. The subject was just too sensitive.

I finally got to bed that night about 12:30, pleased to have had an interesting evening with an Iraqi, however weird the scene had been. It had been only the second time I had been invited into an Iraqi home in the two years I had been in the country.

At about 2:30 in the morning, the telephone rang. Naked in the sweltering night and sound asleep until an instant before, I jumped out of bed to answer the shrill ring on the other side of the room. On the way, I tripped over our wire-haired fox terrier sleeping at the foot of the bed, whose yelps added to the sudden clamor in the room. I picked up the phone and heard the voice of one of the embassy's Marine security guards: "Sir, I have the White House on the line," he said. My head cleared as I thought, *"My God, the president of the United States is calling."*

I snapped to attention as I suppose any patriotic American would do with his president on the line and saluted, stark naked, while the dog was still barking behind me. Then the line went dead. Once I had gathered my wits about me, I realized, of course, that it probably hadn't been the president himself calling me, so I phoned back to the National Security Council and spoke with Sandy Charles, the deputy responsible for Iraq and the Gulf. My decision to not call the president back directly was well founded. The caller had in fact been Sandy, trying to get through from Washington, D.C., to alert me that Iraqi troops were moving into Kuwait, and that our ambassador in Kuwait City, Nathaniel Howell, had reported gunfire outside his embassy compound. The embassy had been surrounded by Iraqi troops, and Iraqi tanks and infantry were quickly overrunning the light Kuwaiti defense forces.

I got off the phone with Sandy and called Nat Howell directly down in Kuwait. He had just begun to brief me on the situation there when the line went dead again. Despite several efforts to reestablish contact with Nat, I could not get another international line, leading me to conclude that the Iraqis had cut direct international service. They had done the same thing throughout the Iran–Iraq war, forcing international calls through their operators to ensure maximum surveillance. Stories abounded of Iraqi intelligence officials breaking in to telephone conversations to exhort the participants to speak more slowly, or in the case of a Japanese diplomat to speak a language that those who were listening could understand.

Now thoroughly awake, I took a shower, dressed, and drove to the office about twenty minutes away. My house was located across the river from the embassy, and the drive, as the sky was just beginning to lighten, took me down one of Baghdad's main boulevards, past a large park and parade ground with the two huge crossed swords in hands that local legend suggested were molded from Saddam's own. I crossed the river at the July 14 Bridge. To the right was the street leading to Ambassador Glaspie's house and to the home of my host from the previous evening. I turned left and drove through the residential area leading to the embassy, a block from the Tigris River. As I walked into the reception area, the Marine standing guard gave me the customary salute reserved for the head of the embassy, and let me in. Little did I know at the time that I was about to embark on the most intense period of my life, marked by twenty-hour days, seven-day work weeks, and sleep limited to short, fitful naps during the few hours when both Iraq and Washington were asleep. Desert Shield had now kicked off, and I was in for the ride of my life.

I had not yet received any instructions from Washington, but I knew that I wanted to take some initiative and confront the Iraqis on the invasion. I immediately paid a call on Tariq Aziz, the foreign minister, meeting him about 8:30 in the morning. I was careful to use language in keeping with what the U.S. government had been saying for several weeks. "What you have done is inconsistent with commitments that President Saddam made to Ambassador Glaspie," I said. "Inconsistent with the Charter of the United Nations, inconsistent with the Arab League Charter, and inconsistent with the draft Iraqi Constitution, all of which outlaw invasions of neighboring countries to resolve border disputes," I continued. For perhaps the only time since I had known him, Aziz was flustered and seemed confused, as if he was improvising.

In his reply, he lamely argued that Saddam had promised only that Iraq would not take military action so long as there was a negotiating process ongoing, and that since the negotiations in Jeddah had failed, Iraq was within its rights to exercise its military option. I angrily responded to Tariq that he knew better than me, from the many failed negotiating sessions with Iran over the past two years, that a single failed negotiating session did not add up to a failed process.

After several diplomatic thrusts and parries, it was clear that I wasn't going to succeed in securing an immediate Iraqi withdrawal from Kuwait. So I turned to the issue of communications with Washington, and with Kuwait, pointing out to Aziz that with Iraqi troops surrounding our embassy in Kuwait City, and with the U.S. Navy patrolling the Persian Gulf, it behooved us both to ensure that we had done everything in our power to minimize the potential for an accidental confrontation between our forces. One of the obvious ways to do that, I argued, was to enable our respective embassies, and our respective capitals, to have direct contact.

I asked Aziz to restore the direct-line communications capability from the embassy, though I had little expectation that he would accede to my demand. After all, the embassy had been forced to forgo direct communications throughout the Iran–Iraq war, and there seemed little chance that the Iraqis would now respond favorably to this demand. Much to my surprise, however, within about three hours I was able to pick up my telephone and call anybody in the world without going through Iraqi operators. The entire embassy compound was hooked up, including the Cultural Center, which was across the blocked-off street, outside the embassy walls. Later in the crisis, we converted the Cultural Center to a press filing office, enabling the American press covering the story to file their stories electronically rather than having to dictate them across insecure lines.

One appreciates the minor victories when one achieves them, and this success did give me some satisfaction. We immediately established an open line to the operations center at the State Department, manned at our end by embassy officers twenty-four hours a day. It became our primary means of communication with Washington.

Within hours after the invasion, President Bush issued an executive order that stopped all commercial trade with Iraq and imposed sanctions on essentially all transactions between Iraq and the United States. Ironically, this included telecommunications, so that despite our having been reconnected by the Iraqis, our own telephone service providers would disconnect us about every eight hours. I imagined that with every shift change at the telephone company, a new foreman would realize that there was an active link to Iraq and, having been briefed on the executive order, would cut us off.

We assumed that as the U.S. government we were automatically exempt from the order, but nonetheless, like clockwork our line would go down every eight hours. It was nerve-racking, to say the least, as we were organizing evacuations of families out of Iraq, which required much rapid coordination. We would have to send a flurry of cables to Washington from our communications center, alerting them to the problem, and after a couple of hours, the line would be reestablished. This continued for several days until the appropriate paperwork by the Treasury Department was generated to grant us a waiver from the executive order, permitting us to keep the line open without interruptions.

It struck me during those first days—as serious issues occupying myself and my colleagues began to mount, with the number and frequency of telephone calls to and from Washington also increasing—that to control the management of our part of the crisis, we were going to have to be aggressive in our approach. It would be better to risk doing something wrong than to hold back and do nothing. There is always a tendency in these situations for Washington, with its massive bureaucracy, to think that it knows best and to try to micromanage from afar. This approach inevitably results in every conceivably concerned government office demanding that the embassy respond to its set of requirements. It is typical behavior of managers to want to cover their bureaucratic behinds and avoid the criticism that they failed to do enough. But it's also the tendency of strong-willed people—and the senior ranks of government are full of these types—to assume that they have a monopoly on wisdom and to try to impose that wisdom, in the form of tasks, on an embassy.

We correctly identified security as our highest priority in those first few days. After all, we reasoned, there would be a real threat to Americans in Iraq if the United States reacted vigorously to the invasion.

Accordingly, I ordered an extensive review by embassy employees of all our routines and practices, and then took action on their recommendations, reporting to Washington what we had done. In that way, we were able to make it clear that we were not waiting around for instructions but were taking necessary action promptly.

We painted the windows of the embassy white to make it more difficult for potential snipers to see us. We burned almost all of our classified files within the first few days. We moved people from their homes to locations closer to the embassy compound in order to be better prepared in the event we had to evacuate quickly. We drew up extensive evacuation plans, including automobile assignments, and designated embassy officials we deemed nonessential to our operations in this crisis situation. I knew that as we went forward the numbers of our staff would need to be reduced, and I wanted to know who was really necessary, and who we could manage without.

On the diplomatic front, I learned that a number of Americans had been caught up in the invasion and were detained by Iraqi forces. One of them was a twelve-year-old California girl who had been flying from San Francisco to spend the month of August with one of her parents in India. She was traveling alone, and her plane, unfortunately, had landed at the Kuwait City airport just as Iraqi troops had taken control of it. Like the other passengers, she had been taken into custody. She was the only child, and we were very worried about what might become of her in the hands of the Iraqi army.

I made several passionate demands to Nizar Hamdun that she be released to our custody, stressing that she was just a child and would not have the coping skills of an adult. I added that the Iraqis would not want the added burden of her security and therefore should turn her over to the embassy. Nizar agreed, and within a short period of time she was in our hands, our first liberated hostage. We kept her busy with the Marines, shredding documents in the morning and swimming at the Marine House in the afternoon. She turned out to be very self-confident and assertive and appeared to be having the time of her life. To her, it was a great big adventure. While she was not shy about making her needs known, she was a real trouper and pitched in wherever she could.

We documented everything we did from day one in comprehensive reports sent to Washington. The tone we consciously tried to strike was one of efficiency and confidence. We understood that if we didn't control the action in Baghdad, it would be controlled for us from Washington.

Apparently we were successful. According to John Kelly, one of the first National Security Council (NSC) meetings after the invasion of Kuwait was chaired by President Bush. The president was brainstorming with his cabinet-level national security team, and suggestions were being thrown about, when Kelly leaned forward to the president and said, "Mr. President, you will see from the executive summary here, a number of things being suggested, Joe Wilson has already done." According to Kelly, the fact that we had already acted in ways consistent with the collective thinking at the highest levels of our government gave the embassy great credibility in Washington.

I was later told by David Welch, then on staff at the NSC, that in subsequent meetings of the president and his "War Cabinet," when people came up with ideas, President Bush would frequently ask "What does Joe Wilson think?" Of course, such presidential confidence can be a two-edged sword in Washington. In a town where reputations are made on the ownership of ideas and policies, people rarely care about what those in the field think. For someone sitting in meetings with the president to be reminded that ideas were best run by Joe Wilson first had to be somewhat galling. These folks, who were the power players in Washington, weren't used to coming second.

The day of the invasion, August 2, the Iraqis closed their borders and prohibited travel outside the country, both for their own citizens and for foreigners in Iraq and Kuwait. All flights in and out of the country were likewise cancelled, a situation that would persist after the imposition of United Nations sanctions on Iraq. Our efforts to organize an evacuation east across the desert to Jordan or up north through Turkey were delayed by the border closures and by the long-standing requirement that we provide three weeks' advance notice of any travel beyond twenty-five miles from Baghdad.

Additionally, in the midst of all the activity, with everybody's emotions raw, one of our most popular employees died of a brain hemorrhage. He was a communications officer, responsible for transmitting and receiving classified cable traffic. A relatively young man, in his early forties, he was single and very active within our community. It was a real shock to our embassy family. Even in the best of times, the unexpected death of a friend and colleague is traumatizing. In our small community far away from home, people became very dependent upon one another. We worked together, worshiped together, and played together. Relationships were important, as the support system was so people-intensive; to lose not just a coworker but a friend reverberated through us all.

In a time of such controlled chaos and high stress as we were living through in those first days after the invasion, his death could have really been seriously debilitating for our community. But we took comfort from one another, and everyone held together. In the midst of everything else we were working on, I contacted the lay reader of the local Church of England, the only English service in Baghdad, and asked him to celebrate a memorial service in our embassy courtyard. The vicar was on leave, and the reader was conducting services in his absence. Americans and Iraqi staff alike, we took an hour to pray, to cry, and to reminisce about our fallen friend. And then it was back to work, without the luxury of extended mourning.

This colleague was one of only two Americans to die in Iraq during the entire period of Desert Shield. The other was a businessman who succumbed to a heart attack later in September while in Iraqi custody. As for the rest of the Americans—those who were in hiding in Kuwait, those who were taken hostage by Saddam, and those whom we housed in embassy homes to keep them out of Saddam's clutches—all survived and returned home after several months of intensive effort on the part of the embassy.

In the first two weeks of the crisis, I worked literally twenty to twenty-two hours a day. My wife had left in the first evacuation convoy soon after the crisis began, and for a few hours a day, I would try to get home to be alone, relax, eat, and sleep. My house was in Mansour, one of the tonier, more recently developed neighborhoods of Baghdad. It was a two-story modern plaster-and-glass building with a small swimming pool along the side of the house. The dining room could seat ten, while the living room was large and circular with floor-to-ceiling windows opening onto a large lawn in front. My bedroom was above the dining room, down a long hall that would later serve as my pacing track as I tried to think through ways to resolve issues with the Iraqis. Even during the few hours I was away from the embassy, I would receive calls from Washington. Several times they told me that Nat Howell had just reported the massing of Iraqi troops around the American embassy compound in Kuwait City—with their formation suggesting that they were about to scale the walls and overrun the embassy. American flag flying proudly above the right front wheel of my car, I would make my way over to the foreign ministry, enter by the back door, and meet with Nizar Hamdun, tell him of Nat's concerns, and urge him to call off the troops and to stop threatening Americans in Kuwait City.

He would offer only to "pass my demand to higher authority"— the latter a euphemism for Saddam himself. I would return home only to be awakened a couple of hours later by Nizar, who would inform me that the "higher authority" had said not to worry, they were not going to overrun the embassy. I would relay that message back to

Washington and, in another hour or so, would be awakened again with news from Washington that the Iraqi troops had backed off from the embassy compound. The same scenario played out almost nightly for several days, ensuring that neither our colleagues in Kuwait City nor those of us in Baghdad were able to enjoy even a few hours of uninterrupted sleep. I often wondered if harassment was the objective of the nightly Iraqi troop movements. I doubted that it was just routine.

In addition to more than a hundred Americans behind the walls of our embassy compound in Kuwait, there were a couple of thousand Americans in hiding throughout Kuwait City and several hundred more who had been rounded up by the Iraqis during the invasion and taken hostage. On August 4, the Iraqis transported a number of them, mostly oilfield workers, up to Baghdad and lodged them at one of the local hotels. My consular officer and I went over to the hotel intending to meet with them, but the Iraqis refused to allow this, ostensibly because they feared that the workers, who had last been in Kuwait, might have some militarily sensitive information they could share with us. The Iraqis were calling all foreigners in their custody "guests," even though the guests were not permitted to move around or even to meet with their embassy officials.

No, they sure seemed like hostages to me, and I urged the administration to let us confront the Iraq government on this issue. I called Washington and spoke with Bob Kimmit, the undersecretary for Political Affairs. Bob was reluctant to call them hostages until their situation had been more fully clarified, and I learned that this was the administration's position too. Their reasoning was that if we started referring to them as hostages, we might give Saddam the idea that holding on to them as hostages would be a good idea. The situation at that point was so fluid, said Kimmit, that we should wait to cross this rhetorical divide. It was possible that Saddam was holding them only until the conquest of Kuwait was fully achieved, after which he would release them. In those first days, though, the Iraqis released only the twelve-year-old girl to our custody, and no one else.

By August 5, with the international phone service at the embassy back up, American television reporters and anchors began to arrive. Forrest Sawyer, then with CBS, was the first of the big-name newscasters, followed shortly by ABC's *Nightline* host, Ted Koppel. Dan Rather, the CBS *Evening News* anchor, was not far behind. Unaccustomed to hosting news professionals, we permitted the first wave to sit in our executive offices and work around us. It soon became clear, however, that we needed to be able work away from the inquiring gaze of the press, and retain our privacy. So we quickly converted the United States Information Service (USIS) Cultural Center across the street into a filing center for both the American and the international press, thereby getting them out of our hair and still giving them the advantage of being able to file without impediments using our direct connections.

It was a mutually beneficial relationship since, from the beginning, we thought it important that the story be covered as fully and as openly as possible from Iraq. For the same reason, I made myself available to the press almost every morning for a background briefing to discuss the issues we were concerned about and to try to answer questions.

On August 6, when I arrived at the office, I was told that I was expected at the foreign ministry at 10:30, ostensibly to meet with Foreign Minister Aziz. I took the embassy political officer, Nancy Johnson, with me to serve as note taker. By this time, I had gone four days straight with virtually no sleep. My mood was a bit surly, and I was ready to unload on Tariq. When we got to his office, however, we discovered, to our great surprise, Saddam himself, decked out in his Baath Party uniform complete with the characteristic pistol on his hip. Less than two weeks after his unusual meeting with April Glaspie, Saddam was again sitting down with an officer of the U.S. government for a substantive meeting.

With cameras whirring to record the handshake and the introductions, we were ushered into Tariq's outer office, where Saddam
was standing in front of heavy drawn curtains and an Iraqi flag. Along
the wall to his left were several senior officials from the foreign ministry, including, in addition to Tariq Aziz, Nizar Hamdun; Wissam al-
Zahawi, the other undersecretary at the foreign ministry; and Riyad
al-Qaysy, the foreign ministry's chief lawyer and formerly ambassador
to the U.N. They were motionless, at attention.

Over the two years I had been in Baghdad, I had had many
opportunities to observe and participate in these greeting ceremonies, and I had always noticed that Saddam did everything he
possibly could to intimidate his guests and create a pose in which
his guest would be photographed bowing to him. Typically, he
approached his guest and stopped closer than normal, breaking the
social space and automatically putting his guest on edge. The handshake would not take place until after preliminary courtesies were
exchanged through the simultaneous translator, while Saddam fixed
the visitor with an unblinking stare. Some have described it as a
snake hypnotizing his prey. I was actually reminded of the many
games of "Who is going to blink first" that I used to play with my
twins. There may have been many things I could not do, but one
thing I *could* do is go for minutes without blinking. I thought: *"If
Saddam thinks he's going to outstare me, he is sadly mistaken."*
Finally, when the time came for the handshake, I knew that
Saddam's practice was to hold his hand low, forcing his guest to
look down to take it, lest his visitor grab some other, less socially
appropriate part of Saddam's anatomy. When my moment came to
take Saddam's hand, I continued to stare directly into his eyes, kept
my back ramrod-straight, and groped blindly for his hand, which,
thankfully, I found. No cameras were going to catch me "bowing"
to the dictator.

Months later, back in Washington, seated in the office of Tom

Foley, the Speaker of the House of Representatives, in the rotunda, I recounted the story of the handshake. After I explained about groping for Saddam's hand, Tom leaned forward in his cordovan leather wingback chair and said: "You mean to tell me that you were this close to having Saddam Hussein by the short hairs and you didn't go for it? Instead, we had to send Norm Schwarzkopf and five hundred thousand of America's finest soldiers to finish the job?"

The cameras were still going when Saddam and I sat down, with him adjusting the gun, still on his hip. "Well, what's the news?" he began. I was angry. We were four days into the crisis, during which I had hardly slept; there were the remains of a deceased colleague to ship home; there was an ambassador in Kuwait worrying every night about possible Iraqi attacks on the embassy there; there were American citizens being held hostage in Kuwait and in Iraq. I could well have shown how I really felt, but I chose, instead, to make a little joke.

I said, "Look, if you want to know what's new, you really ought to address that question to your foreign minister and not me, because your foreign minister has a satellite dish that allows him to get American news stations such as CNN. I've been fighting with him for two years now to try and get a satellite dish for our embassy, with no success. So if you want to know what's new, ask him, not me." Saddam laughed heartily. He no doubt knew of our failed efforts to import satellite dishes for the embassy. Given to appreciating my own jokes, I almost joined Saddam in his laughter. I started to lean back and smile when I remembered that the cameras were still there. I caught myself and straightened up, trying to look as stern as possible.

My meeting with Saddam ran well over an hour. During much of the time Saddam attempted to justify the invasion in historical terms and also ranted against the Kuwaiti royal family for its callous disregard of Iraq's needs. While he did not reveal what he intended to do with Kuwait, Saddam at one point made a comment that his interpreter had trouble translating. Tariq Aziz interrupted from his seat against the wall, saying, "The al-Sabah family is history." It was the only time that any other Iraqi spoke. Whatever Saddam had in mind for the future of his neighbor, apparently it did not include the return of that particular royal family.

It soon became clear that the purpose of the meeting was to allow Saddam to outline the deal he wanted to make with the United States. If the United States were to refrain from interfering with whatever Iraq was going to do with Kuwait, Saddam would guarantee uninterrupted supplies of oil for a reasonable price, and as the dominant power in the Gulf, Iraq would assume responsibility for policing it. He also promised that he would take no action against Saudi Arabia—a country with which Iraq had a mutual defense pact—unless the Saudi rulers allowed their country to be used as a platform to launch efforts to destabilize the Iraqi regime. If, on the other hand, the United States reacted militarily to the Iraqi invasion, Saddam scoffed that we had neither the tenacity to remain engaged as long as it would take to drive Iraq from Kuwait, nor the political will to sustain the "spilling of the blood of ten thousand soldiers in the Arabian desert." There it was then, the carrot of cheap oil coupled with the stick of dead American soldiers.

When it was my turn to speak, I began by commenting on the roiling of international oil markets occasioned by the invasion. This prompted a spirited interruption by Saddam condemning the Kuwaitis for their refusal to accommodate reasonable Iraqi demands, while they also undermined international petroleum prices by their overproduction. Saddam was clearly agitated, claiming now that the Kuwaitis were to blame for everything.

I returned to what I thought I might achieve in the meeting, arguing that the invasion of Kuwait was a violation of Iraq's international obligations. I also expressed our concerns about Iraqi troops looting American diplomatic properties in Kuwait, as well as threatening our personnel at the embassy there. There was also the closing of Iraq's international borders, which, contrary to the Geneva and Vienna Conventions, prevented Americans and other foreigners from leaving Iraq.

"Are you talking about just Americans?" Saddam now asked, and I responded, "Well, I'm only empowered to speak on behalf of Americans, but I would think that, more broadly, you ought to open your border so that all foreigners can leave." He then asked me, "Why? Do you know something that I don't know about a potential American response?" I replied, "Well, Mr. President, I can assure you that if I knew something about American intentions, I would not share it with you, but what I will tell you is that I intend to be here so long as there is a role for diplomats to play in resolving this situation peacefully." Saddam's question made it clear that he was fishing for clues as to whether the United States might intend a unilateral military response to his actions.

It was a tough meeting. Shortly after I began to speak, Saddam reached down for his gun. I could not help but wonder if I had said something to provoke him, as I watched in slow motion while he moved toward the weapon. He must have noticed my consternation, for now, as he removed the gun belt and holster from around his waist and placed them on the table next to him, he commented on how uncomfortable it was to sit while wearing it. The cameramen had by now left and the weapon was evidently no longer necessary as a prop. It offered me quite a telling window into Saddam's pretensions and his choice of symbols for projecting power and manhood.

After the meeting was over and we were walking out together, Saddam relaxed noticeably, put his hand on my shoulder, and said, with a smile, "That was a good meeting." I was still preoccupied with the plight of Americans in Kuwait and Iraq and in no mood to humor the dictator or help him feel good about our exchange. On reflection, the notion that Saddam needed me to reassure him about our conversation is bizarre.

In the years since those meetings—first with Ambassador Glaspie, and then with me—I have come to the conclusion that Saddam was worried about the possible American response to his actions and may have concluded that the confusing statements coming from different parts of the U.S. government meant there would be no consensus to respond militarily to his invasion of Kuwait. I believe that he met with Glaspie for the express purpose of deceiving us about his intentions, as he did with Egypt's President Mubarak at the same time. In this way he maintained the element of surprise. His meeting with me, then, was to try to insure there would be no military response by the U.S.

I have also often thought that whatever one concludes about Saddam's sanity—and he was clearly a sociopath—the invasion of Kuwait, given the circumstances, was a rational, if high-risk, act. After all, a successful invasion of Kuwait, leading to its annexation, would have eliminated many of his strategic and financial problems. And if he were able to avoid a military counterattack, he could engage in endless international negotiations while he flooded Kuwait with Iraqis to change the demographics and ensure himself a favorable outcome in a future ballot of some kind. His own experience with international organizations had shown him that he stood to win in a prolonged showdown: the two U.N. resolutions dealing with Iraq's use of chemical weapons had been toothless, and even the resolutions concerning Israeli occupation of Palestinian territory had not resulted in Israeli withdrawal for the previous twenty years. Absent an American military response, Saddam might well have concluded that a lengthy occupation of Kuwait, followed by a rigged referendum, would succeed. That is why when dealing with such a determined leader, diplomacy be backed by both sustained international will and the credible threat of force when necessary.

Whatever Saddam's thinking, he was clearly going to attain his financial and strategic objectives at Kuwait's expense one way or another, either by threat or military action. The timing of the decision to invade Kuwait, however, may well have been an emotional response to the tone of the failed negotiations in Jeddah. Patrick Theros, our deputy chief of mission in Jordan, was called to King Hussein's palace the night before the invasion, because the king had just gotten off the phone with Saddam, whom he described as furious with the Kuwaitis. He told Theros that he had no idea what Saddam might do but that his anger had made the Iraqi dictator irrational. Nizar Hamdun later told a close friend of mine that when the Iraqis were pressing for financial relief, the Kuwaitis responded that if Iraq needed money, it should do what it had always done—"put its women on the streets," an unspeakable insult to the proud Iraqis.

Back at the office after the meeting, Nancy Johnson and I wrote three cables for Washington. She took responsibility for writing the formal memorandum of the conversation between Saddam and myself, while I composed a short message outlining the main points of the meeting and then a slightly longer memo that included my analysis and commentary. Washington was anxious to have these cables as soon as possible and kept interrupting our drafting of them to ask when they were going to be transmitted. It turned out that at the same time we were drafting the cables—early in the afternoon, Baghdad time—the National Security Council, with President Bush as chair, was ready to convene an early morning meeting. But they were waiting until our cables arrived. We rushed what we had onto the wires, hastily written and only lightly edited, so the NSC meeting could begin. They were highly classified, sent "Secret NODIS Babylon." NODIS is the acronym that means no distribution beyond those officials within our government directly involved in managing the issue. Babylon was the code word used to identify the Gulf crisis, or Desert Shield.

Notwithstanding our best efforts to protect the security of our communications, within two days of my meeting with Saddam, the text of Nancy's long memorandum was reproduced in the *New York*

Times, including many of the editorial errors that we had overlooked in our haste to get the information to Washington. It had no doubt been leaked by a senior official in our government. At the same time, one reporter asked President Bush if he had received the message from Saddam, to which the President replied "no."

The Iraqis were furious—and not about the editorial oversights. Nizar Hamdun called me in to complain, vociferously, "You put a confidential message from my president to yours on the front page of the *New York Times,* but you don't bother to give it to the president himself." After he had let off steam, Nizar reminded me that the Iraqis were still waiting for President Bush's reply.

Licking my wounds and very unhappy with Washington, I called John Kelly's deputy, Edward "Skip" Gnehm, to complain that I had been undermined by the leak and to urge a prompt reply from the White House. Skip glossed over my irritation, telling me, quite appropriately, to suck it up, and instructed me to go back to Nizar with the message that the president had indeed seen Saddam's message and that if the Iraqis wanted to know his response, they needed only to turn on CNN.

I went over to the foreign ministry and was ushered into Nizar's office, where I delivered Washington's message. When I finished, we both turned our eyes to the television monitor in the corner of Nizar's office. On the screen was CNN televising U.S. Air Force transport planes taking off from bases all around the country. Every few seconds, another of the huge C5s took to the air filled with military equipment destined for Saudi Arabia. The American deployment had begun.

Now Saddam had his answer, and it was not lost on Nizar. Although I met with him several times a week from then until my departure on January 12, 1991, the only other time I was invited into his private office with the television was the day I delivered the diplomatic note announcing that the United States was suspending diplomatic relations with Iraq, the day before I left the country.

Between those two occasions, my access to news on television was limited to the daily Iraqi English language propaganda broadcast every evening at eight o'clock. Without satellite dishes my colleagues and I had no means of receiving the blow-by-blow coverage. Of course, we were living it instead.

While I was meeting with Saddam, Secretary of Defense Richard Cheney was in Saudi Arabia showing the rulers of the kingdom satellite photos of the Iraqi troop deployment throughout Kuwait, close to its southern border with Saudi Arabia and not far from the fabulously lucrative eastern Saudi oil fields.

President Bush had drawn his "line in the sand," the line being between Kuwait and Saudi Arabia, and he had declared that Iraq's invasion of Kuwait "would not stand." Our immediate objective, however, remained the protection of Saudi Arabia. When King Fahd, the Saudi monarch, invited us to deploy our troops in the kingdom after Cheney's presentation, the armada was launched.

On August 8, Saddam announced that Iraq had annexed Kuwait, making it Iraq's nineteenth province.

Our primary concern at the embassy continued to be the welfare and whereabouts of our citizens, as well as their safe evacuation from the region. We had succeeded in rounding up close to a hundred Americans in Baghdad and offering them refuge in embassy quarters. Most of them were employees of the American firm Bechtel, in Iraq to work on major construction projects. We were in a grim race against the Iraqis, who now had taken about 115 Americans hostage and were putting them in what they considered "strategic sites" that American forces might bomb in the first hours of a military conflict. In Kuwait, where the Iraqi army was terrorizing the population, about 2,000 Americans were still in hiding or behind the walls of our embassy there. The situation was grim.

On the night of August 8, I met in my office with the embassy's defense attaché, two of our political officers, and the consul. For five hours, from ten until three o'clock the next morning, we drew upon our collective knowledge of Iraqi history since the revolution in 1958—when several American citizens had been dragged from their hotel rooms and killed in an orgy of bloodletting—and tried to "game out" all the possible scenarios the next few weeks might hold in store. Iraqi response to high-stress situations such as this one had consistently involved lashing out at whomever they considered to be the offending parties. In addition to the Americans killed in previous uprisings, for example, an entire Iranian delegation in Baghdad at the outbreak of the Iran–Iraq war in 1980 had simply disappeared, never to be heard from again. Thus, the chances were very good, we concluded, that some of us, or perhaps all five of us in that meeting, might not survive.

With that sobering thought in our minds, we turned to how we thought we should comport ourselves. If, in all likelihood, we were going to die anyway, did we want to go meekly to our deaths delivering useless diplomatic notes to a brutal regime, or did we want to be defiant, treating the Iraqi actions as the outrages they were? We opted for the latter code of conduct.

That decision—to stand up and confront Saddam at every opportunity—set the tone at the embassy from that moment on. (Months later, after I'd left Baghdad, a psychologist at the CIA told me that the only way to deal with a personality like Saddam's is to stand up to him: to be defiant, antagonistic, and intimidating. We had not had the benefit of such CIA wisdom back in August, but our instincts were still on the mark.)

In September, several weeks after that long late meeting in my office, the Iraqis expelled four American Embassy employees. I drove these colleagues to the airport and walked them to the gate, where they would board a charter flight out of the country. As they proceeded through customs, I realized that I was saying good-bye to the other participants from the meeting where we had each recognized we might not make it out of this crisis alive. They were leaving, I was staying. I thought to myself, *boy, you really did draw the short straw this time.*

Chapter Six
Of Hostages and Convoys

B Y THE MIDDLE OF AUGUST, we had made the embassy as secure as we could under the circumstances. Our executive suite had been transformed into a war room, complete with clipboards on the wall containing all of the cable traffic of the past forty-eight hours, which was as long as we kept anything on file. We had shredded and burned many documents and were at a point where we could destroy all remaining classified information within five minutes. We had evacuated all of our family members and most of our staff, and were running two twelve-hour shifts daily with the remaining nine employees to maintain constant contact with Washington on our hot line.

The debate over who should stay and who should go had been a very difficult one among us. Almost every employee at the embassy wanted to stay. Each felt an obligation to do his duty, and no one wanted to be considered nonessential. Washington, on the other hand, wanted as many people as possible to leave, fearing for the safety of anybody left in Baghdad. Both positions were legitimate, but this was one time when Washington was going to prevail. The fear of exposing more than the absolute minimum of Americans to danger trumped our need to ideally staff an embassy in crisis mode. We were simply going to have to do more with a lot less.

Among those deemed nonessential were our Marine security guards. We had a detachment of seven Marines assigned to the embassy to provide twenty-four-hour-a-day security coverage of the premises. Their role was to protect classified material from falling into the hands of potential intruders and did not normally extend to protecting embassy personnel, except as directed by the chief of mission in the event of a riot or attack. I had already issued orders to the Marines that they were not to use their weapons to resist unless they felt their lives were threatened. I would have forbidden use of weapons even then, but the Marine Corps standard operating procedure was that they must always have the option to use their weapons in self-defense. My rationale was that if a breach of embassy security were to take place as a result of an extremely determined demonstration, the use of force by the one Marine normally on duty would be of limited effectiveness and would only further enrage the survivors of any armed confrontation. Our chances of survival would be better if we were taken hostage than if an enraged crowd fought to avenge fallen comrades.

Confident that we could quickly dispose of the little classified material that hadn't already been destroyed, there was no longer any reason for the Marines to remain. However, it was all but impossible to convince these young patriots, whose loyalty to the mission was paramount, that their services were no longer required and they could leave. So long as any American official was in Baghdad, they wanted to stay to defend him. I finally persuaded the gunnery sergeant in charge of the detachment that we needed his Marines in the first evacuation caravan to ensure that the convoy managed the desert crossing with a minimum of problems. Given a fresh task, the Marines rose to the new challenge.

Iraqi permission for that evacuation of our diplomatic personnel and their dependents finally came through, almost two weeks after the invasion of Kuwait. By then, we had organized the details of the convoy, including the vehicles to be used and assignments of people to those vehicles. Personal goods had been limited to a couple of suitcases per person, but that maximum was soon exceeded as every available space in the cars was crammed with items.

Although the Iraqi government had authorized the departure of Americans holding diplomatic passports and their family members, we were nonetheless very concerned about a potential double-cross. We worried that our families might be attacked or otherwise harassed en route to Jordan and were determined to do everything we could to make it difficult for the Iraqis to do so. All the evacuees, close to a hundred people, gathered at the ambassador's residence, some three miles along the river from the embassy compound, the night before their scheduled departure so that the convoy could leave promptly in the morning and not have to wait for stragglers. We moved the departure time up several hours so that our people would be on the road well before sunrise. We wanted them to do as much driving as possible in the cool of the early morning before the desert became unbearably hot, and like the ancient Israelites' exodus from the recalcitrant pharaoh who wouldn't let them go, we hoped to get our convoy well outside of Baghdad before the Iraqis realized they were gone and caused some trouble.

Managing land evacuations was one of the most nail-biting activities I had to undertake. As a rule of thumb, each car added to a convoy added at least ten minutes to the time it took to arrive at the destination. The convoy, close to forty cars, could travel no faster than its slowest driver, and pit stops were inevitably time-consuming as each individual had personal needs to satisfy. We did not realize all of this at the time of that first evacuation, and so were anxious about the fate of our friends and loved ones from about eleven in the morning, six hours after their departure from Baghdad, when we thought they might arrive at the Jordanian border after their 350-mile trip across the desert.

It was not until late in the evening that we finally heard that the convoy had been stopped at the border and could not cross. Apparently, the Iraqi permission for their departure had not been transmitted to the border crossing. Telephone contact was close to impossible, since it was dependent on willing Iraqi bureaucrats, of whom there were few. I instructed the convoy to remain at the border while I raced to the foreign ministry to upbraid Nizar Hamdun. Two hours later, the appropriate approvals were transmitted, but by then it was too late; the convoy had turned around and was heading back to Baghdad. Despite our best efforts to have them stopped and turned around at one of the intermediate Iraqi checkpoints, our people arrived back at the ambassador's residence shortly after midnight, bedraggled and angry, but still unbowed by the ordeal.

We put them to bed for four hours and sent them on their way again early the next morning, this time confident that the approvals were in place to permit their departure from the country. Late that afternoon, we received word from our embassy in Amman, Jordan, that they had arrived safely. With a heavy sigh of relief, we were able to resume our other responsibilities with our new lean staff of nine Americans, including me. I called us the expendables.

CBS news anchor Dan Rather arrived in Baghdad on the evening of August 14, accompanied by his longtime producer and friend Tom Bettag. They had been traveling in the region since early August and had finally been able to secure their visas, arriving just after the departure of Ted Koppel. Dan was intent on interviewing Saddam, as were all the journalistic heavyweights. They swept into the embassy and took over the office recently vacated by Koppel, where Rather found a piece of paper purporting to note the time of a Koppel appointment with Saddam. It had been left as a joke. I did not get to see whether Rather was amused or disconcerted by the prospect that his competitor had landed the big interview before he could.

With the departure of our families, we were able to move other Americans to whom we had offered safe haven into the ambassador's residence, where our diplomatic rights and privileges afforded us some protection against Iraqi intrusions. So long as our citizens were on the embassy property, they could not be taken hostage. It was tough for them in the ensuing months, and some opted to take their chances in the streets of Baghdad rather than remain cooped up at the residence, which, while on a site covering at least two acres with a swimming pool, was nonetheless confining. Behind its high walls there were few diversions for the thirty-plus Americans residing on top of each other in the half-dozen bedrooms.

I invited a representative of the group to attend our daily staff meetings so they would remain abreast of what we were doing. We also held frequent meetings to address more general concerns. The daily management of their needs was delegated to other key officers in the embassy, who worked tirelessly to make their lives comfortable. Meanwhile, I was trying to get them out of Iraq as quickly as I could. We all made an effort to socialize with them as much as possible, given the other demands on our time, but I went out of my way *not* to learn their names, since, as I told them, I refused to concede the possibility that they were going to be with us long enough for us to get to know each other.

Above all, we tried to instill in the new arrivals the same "in your face" attitude that we ourselves had adopted toward the Iraqis. We were determined not to let the Iraqis think that we were afraid or weak. In a press conference on Thanksgiving, our efforts were rewarded when Roland Bergheer, the spokesman for the Americans, told the press that the question of Iraq's invasion of Kuwait was bigger than any of them and that if it took an American counterattack to defeat the Iraqis, he was willing to sacrifice his life for the greater good. Defiance was the hallmark of our approach, and Roland expressed it perfectly.

By August 17, Saddam's fiction that hostages were mere "guests" was laid to rest when the Iraqis announced that they were going to hold the nationals from any countries threatening Iraq until the threats ceased. At the same time, Saddam still tried to promote the idea that he was a benevolent host who cared about the welfare of those in his custody. In one notorious television appearance a few days later, "Uncle Saddam" was seen asking a seven-year-old British boy, Stuart Lockwood, if he had had his milk that day. The scared look on Stuart's face, and his parents' equally frightened expressions, chilled viewers worldwide.

I met with the Egyptian ambassador at his home the day after the Lockwood incident. He was very concerned about the welfare of the four million Egyptian nationals working in Iraq. As the ambassador and I were comparing notes, he mentioned that the international community needed to ratchet up its propaganda against what Saddam was doing. He commented that a statue of Saddam, the first of its kind, had recently been erected in the Arab Knight Square in Baghdad, replacing a statue of an Arab warrior on horseback. At the same time, Iraqi police had gone to businesses around the country that were named Arab Knight and had told them to change their name, since "there is only one Arab knight in Iraq, and you are not it." So the local Arab Knight dry cleaning establishments or fast food outlets were now all called something else. Since Saddam clearly wanted to be recognized as *The* Arab Knight, the Egyptian continued, perhaps we ought to point out that true Arab knights do not hide behind the skirts of women or behind little children.

I thought this was a great idea and later in the evening mentioned it to Dan Rather, who was leaving the following morning for Amman. He liked the idea and agreed that he should wait until he left Iraq to file the story. While he was among America's most respected news anchors, his reputation might not be enough to protect him against Saddam's petulant wrath. In fact, a British journalist had been executed just a few months before on trumped-up espionage charges.

I was told later that Rather filed the story from Amman, Jordan, on August 22, shortly after his arrival there. Some days after that British Prime Minister Margaret Thatcher repeated on the floor of the House of Commons the insult that Saddam was hiding behind the skirts of women. On August 28, the Iraqi government announced that women and children would be free to leave. While we could not absolutely confirm that our campaign to humiliate Saddam was responsible for this decision, we were sure that our general strategy of confrontation had contributed to it.

I was also in the midst of sensitive negotiations with the Iraqi foreign ministry on the status of our embassy in Kuwait. With the "annexation" of Kuwait on August 8, Iraq had insisted that all foreign embassies be closed and the diplomats and other foreigners moved to Baghdad. Ambassador Howell was housing almost 150 Americans within his embassy compound, many of whom were private citizens who could not benefit from diplomatic protection and accordingly were potential hostages. In a meeting with Hamdun around the middle of August, I had "hypothetically" asked what guarantees the Iraqis might provide to our citizens should we decide to scale down our presence in Kuwait. I was ahead of Washington's thinking, uncomfortably so, as Skip Gnehm told me in a later conversation, reproaching me for having broached the subject while Washington was still deciding what its position should be. However, within a few days, I received instructions to go back to the foreign ministry and raise the subject again, only this time not in the hypothetical.

On August 17, I met with Tariq Aziz and asked him what we could expect in terms of treatment of our people if we were to reduce our presence in Kuwait. Tariq replied that Iraq would honor all of its obligations under both the Geneva and Vienna Conventions; these cover the rights of people to travel out of war zones and not be held against their will without reason. I specifically asked if he was telling me that the Americans who left Kuwait could be assured that they would be permitted to travel all the way out of the region. Aziz repeated his guarantees that the international treaties would be respected.

I dutifully reported back to Washington, recommending that Americans be moved from Kuwait as soon as possible. For all the hardships we were suffering in Baghdad, they were nothing compared to what Americans in Kuwait were enduring. The nightly threats to overrun the embassy compound had ceased, but there was limited electricity and the compound's food and water supplies were running low. Nat sent in his own analysis, in which he expressed his skepticism about Tariq Aziz's integrity. I seem to recall something along the lines of "he is a lying son of a bitch," but I imagine that Nat was more elegant in his characterization. I sent an additional message to Washington, seconding Nat's assessment of Aziz, but noted that even if the Iraqis did renege on their commitment, life in Baghdad was less dangerous than in Kuwait. Diplomats in Baghdad could circulate freely, and food and water were abundant. They were not threatened by the military or subjected to the hardships being experienced in Kuwait. All in all, they would, in my judgment, be better off in Baghdad than Kuwait City.

I was later told that the decision went to President Bush. I am not surprised, since, from my later experience at the National Security Council, I know presidents are intensely interested in the welfare of American citizens in harm's way. And in all of my communications with President Bush both during and after the Gulf War, he was always most concerned with the human consequences of his actions. In the event, he decided in my favor and ordered the drawdown of the embassy in Kuwait, leaving Nat and a skeleton crew to keep the flag flying and to support those who could not leave because of fear of being taken hostage.

The Iraqis were not going to be satisfied with even this minimal remaining presence in Kuwait, but making them happy was not our priority. Besides, we didn't accept their premise that Kuwait was no longer a sovereign state, no longer entitled to its own diplomatic representatives. The priority of the American government was to get as many of its citizens as possible out of danger. However, any continuing diplomatic presence in Kuwait was soon going to be an issue with the Iraqis.

A convoy of dozens of cars and more than 120 Americans left Kuwait City on the morning of August 23, their early departure predictably delayed by officious Iraqi military officers, despite the assurances of cooperation we had received. It wended its way up to Baghdad, led by one of our political officers who had traveled to Kuwait to serve as the liaison with Iraqi authorities. Meanwhile, in Baghdad, we were making arrangements to feed and house the travelers at the now empty Marine House for what would be a brief respite before we sent them on their way, north to Turkey.

We anticipated that they would be with us for dinner and a night's rest, so sandwiches were made, soft drinks cooled, and mattresses spread throughout the house. With preparations complete, we waitied. And waited. And waited. Finally, at about three A.M. on the morning of the 24th, the convoy pulled in to our embassy compound, twenty hours after they had begun their trip from Kuwait. Once again I had underestimated the time involved in travel by convoy. I had been on edge since eight the previous evening, but—at last—they had arrived. I was so pleased to see them that I ran down from my office, clipboard in hand, and ran right into the biggest man I had seen since Rosie Grier quit playing defensive tackle for the Los Angeles Rams. His name was Vern Nored, and he was a civilian employee of the Defense Department. He was unhappy, to say the least; and when he saw my clipboard, he assumed I was the general services officer, responsible for his care and feeding. He let me know in no uncertain terms of his displeasure at the hardships he and the others had endured the previous day. It took me a while to get him calmed down, and after he realized who I was and everything we had tried to do to get them to safety, he was mightily embarrassed at his conduct.

We became great friends and he really grew in my esteem a few weeks later when he took on his dream job as escort officer for Muhammad Ali during the charismatic champ's visit to Baghdad. At the time of our first meeting, I was just happy not to have been crushed in his massive grip. Our intrepid local staff moved everybody to their sleeping quarters, and Melvin Ang, the embassy consul, took their passports to secure the necessary exit visas before we sent them on their way the following morning

At 6:00 A.M., Ang showed up at the Baghdad immigration office with the 120 passports to obtain the exit visas, only to be refused. The double-cross Nat Howell warned of had taken place. I stormed to the foreign ministry and was told that the Americans who had come up from Kuwait would not be permitted to leave until the embassy in Kuwait had been closed, in line with Iraq's demand. Since Kuwait was no longer a sovereign country, I was told there was no justification for diplomatic representation there and that those Americans who had been accredited there would no longer benefit from diplomatic protections and immunities. I was furious and went looking for Tariq Aziz. He was not in the building, but his deputy chief of protocol took my message for Aziz stating that he lied to me when he had promised that his government would abide by its international obligations. The protocol official suggested that perhaps "liar" was not the best choice of terms for a diplomat, so I substituted "prevaricator" for liar, turned on my heel, and stomped out. A couple of days later, I crossed paths with the protocol official again. He was all smiles as he took me aside to whisper that he had passed my message to Aziz. I never did learn whether he had quoted me calling the foreign minister a liar or a prevaricator.

Our Kuwait colleagues were naturally very disappointed. We tried to ease their frustration with a cookout at the Marine House that evening, complete with swimming and volleyball. The nine of us accredited to Baghdad were now overwhelmed by 120 people who did not want to be with us and who had been staring at the barrel end of Iraqi guns for the previous three weeks. Their loyalty was to their comrades in Kuwait, not to our mission in Baghdad. Our task would be to turn this dispirited bunch into effective officers in our embassy, not because we needed them but because we could not permit them to just sit around and fume.

But first things first. We had not given up on getting at least the women and children out, and within a day we had arranged for the departure of all the women and children under eighteen. Males eighteen and above could not leave. So the caravan loaded up again— only this time, because of Iraqi intransigence, the women would have to drive themselves unaccompanied by their husbands. On August 27 they headed off north to Turkey, a difficult eighteen hours away, escorted by one of our political officers. Just like our previous evacuees, the family members proved to be tough and resilient as they faced the tribulations of their journey.

For the rest, our challenge was to put them to work in our small mission and give them something meaningful to do, so that they could be assets—rather than additional burdens. Their senior member was an economics officer by the name of Emil Skoden. Emil was level-headed, thoughtful, and a quiet leader. He was on good terms with the sixty-three remaining men from Kuwait and had been accepted by them as their chief. It was vital, if we were to succeed in the management of the new combined organization, that the loyalty of my new colleagues be transferred to our operation. The means to that end was through Emil; so together we mapped out a plan to make maximum use of everyone.

I made it clear that my objective was to see that their stay in Baghdad was as brief as I could possibly make it. I would continue working to secure their release. In the meantime, Emil would put his people to work and would serve as their conduit to me when necessary. Emil became my deputy and, by so doing, brought the Kuwait contingent into the fold with me. In one early talk with him, I described our "in your face strategy." He nodded knowingly and offered, "I'm from the public playgrounds of Chicago. I know exactly what you're talking about. It is how I grew up." He was a slight man, so it was hard for me to imagine him confronting toughs on the streets of Chicago. But toughness could not be assessed merely from appearance, and Emil Skoden proved to be as tough as they come.

Once, when I commented that the good news was that at least we had been trained throughout our careers for just such a situation, where our decisions had a big impact on global events, he responded, with refreshing humor, "Of course, the bad news is that we are in charge, and what the hell are we going to do?" He and I had an easy relationship that helped to encourage the best performance from everybody working with us. He was the one indispensable person in our operation, the perfect Mr. Inside to my Mr. Outside. He and I could not have achieved even a fraction of our successes without him.

The Marines who had come up from Kuwait were reconstituted as a new Baghdad detachment. We needed supplies and food for the population at the ambassador's residence and for our new arrivals, so we set up a veritable office of scavenger affairs, leaving them to procure everything we needed. This system was so effective that by the time we left in January 1991, we estimated that we had enough supplies to support 150 people for close to a year. Our scavengers located the thieves' markets in Baghdad that were reselling goods looted from Kuwait, and eventually were even able to recoup some items stolen from American houses in Kuwait. Purchases were by wholesale lot, so whatever was in a pile of goods was exactly what we got, even if we did not need it all. One such lot contained several cases of Japanese sake. It came in handy later when we learned that a former Japanese prime minister was coming to Baghdad to negotiate the release of his country's hostages. I sent the cases to the Japanese ambassador and made a friend for life.

Another office was established to maintain contact with the

hostages, whose number was now up to around 125. We published a weekly newsletter with innocuous information like football scores, and created a pen-pal program where every hostage had an embassy officer trying to communicate with him, as well as between him and his family. Weekly, we would deliver big boxes of letters to the Iraqi foreign ministry to be forwarded to the hostages. We never knew if they reached them, but we never stopped trying. These tasks also provided our stranded colleagues with something meaningful to do. They responded with consummate dedication, treating the names on the letters as family members, so concerned did they become about their charges.

Perhaps our most successful office was the one we created to monitor the movement of the hostages. We had learned that they were routinely being moved from one strategic site to another inside Iraq. As some were released they brought purloined letters from others to us, so that after a while we were able to identify some fifty-five sites that were being used around the country. We sent this information to Pentagon planners for their use.

As it turned out, Saddam had unwittingly shown us, by where he put the hostages, which locations were most important to him. I was gratified when several months later, on the first night of Desert Storm, long after the hostages had been released, many of those sites were ones hit by American bombs.

When the Iraqi government announced on August 28, 1990 that foreign women and children could leave, we launched another operation to evacuate those Americans who were now permitted to leave. Since the Iraqis had banned the flying of Western aircraft into Iraq or Kuwait, we were forced to charter planes from Iraqi Air. For the next several weeks, we flew close to a dozen evacuation flights from Baghdad down to Kuwait City, to load up Americans first, then anybody else who could leave, until the plane was full. We would then bring them back to Baghdad for exit visas and finally onward by air to safety in Amman.

The first flight contained several American wives of Kuwaiti nationals who were trying to leave with their children. However, the children were considered under Iraqi law to carry the nationality of their father, so when they arrived in Baghdad they were not permitted back on the plane to continue to Jordan. The mothers, who were American citizens, could go, but we were told the children would have to stay. When it became apparent that the Iraqi authorities really intended to separate the children from their mothers, I immediately confronted the senior Iraqi immigration official. I stepped into his office at the airport and insisted that he contact the foreign ministry at once.

When I had Nizar on the line, I told him, in controlled fury, "Your president did not permit the release of women and children because he cares about them but rather because he hoped to gain a public relations benefit from the gesture. CNN, CBS, NBC, and ABC have cameras set up just outside the immigration area. If all the American wives and their children, irrespective of the nationality of the children, are not permitted on the plane when it departs in half an hour, I have every intention of stepping in front of those cameras to describe how you have cruelly separated mothers from their young children. I don't think Saddam will be pleased with that publicity."

I hung up and settled back in the small windowless room to smoke the biggest cigar I had, with the Iraqi immigration official no more than a couple of feet across the desk from me. I was determined that he would get no satisfaction from his efforts to split up families and that his smug countenance would be obscured by a heavy cloud of smoke as I puffed away steadily. In Saddam's Iraq, there were four symbols of machismo: the ubiquitous pistol on the hip, the moustache, Ray-Ban aviator sunglasses, and big cigars. This official may have had his pistol and his moustache, but I had my cigar.

Twenty-five minutes later the phone rang, and after a few seconds, the official passed it through the thick haze to me as he raced out the door to execute the order he had just received. While the sunglasses masked his eyes, there was no mistaking the tension in the alacrity with which he moved. Whatever order had been given had come from the top. I put the receiver to my ear and Nizar informed me that the women and their children were all free to leave.

After the plane was off the ground and the wheels were up, I stepped in front of the microphones to announce that the first of our evacuation flights had been successfully completed. We did not have a full manifest of passengers or nationalities (the press was a stickler for those kinds of details), but I was pleased to confirm that the Iraqis had honored their word and had facilitated the exit visa process and other formalities. A corollary to "in your face" was a conscious decision to be gracious in victory and not to rub more salt in their wounds. It was enough that American women and their Kuwaiti offspring were on the plane. There was no need to gloat about the brinksmanship behind closed doors in the immigration official's office.

September was a blur of activity as we ran two or three flights a week out of Kuwait, filled with women, children, and men of nationalities not subject to Iraqi hostage-taking. Every flight had its own set of problems, and the Iraqis found new and ingenious ways to harass evacuees, tactics that we continually fought to preempt.

One flight contained a number of Kuwaiti mothers of American children. The Iraqis again invoked the rule that Kuwaitis, who were now deemed Iraqis after the annexation of Kuwait, could not travel and removed them from the aircraft; according to Iraqi law, the children could leave, but not their mothers. There was nothing I could do for them at this point. My responsibility was to the Americans, but I could not urge mothers to let their children fly out while they remained in Baghdad.

One such family had a Palestinian father accompanying his Kuwaiti wife and children born in America. He was enraged at what was happening and accosted me in the airport while I was in the middle of my own argument with the immigration authorities. He shouted in my ear that if I couldn't get his family on the plane, he was going to call Yasser Arafat. The humor in the idea that the head of the Palestinian Liberation Organization, who had thrown in his lot with Saddam over the invasion of Kuwait, was going to have some influence on how we ran our evacuation flights stopped me in mid-sentence.

As I laughed ruefully, the man then threatened to commit suicide. I turned back to my own argument and suggested to him that he do what he had to do. What I meant, of course was that he call Arafat if he thought that might help. A colleague later told me that the timing of my comment right after his suicide threat made it sound like I was encouraging the man to take his own life. Fortunately, he did not take my suggestion. And if he called Arafat, it did not affect the outcome. That family and others in the same straits were not permitted to travel, though they were not taken hostage and were able to move about the city freely for the remainder of their stay until the borders were reopened.

There was a law of diminishing returns at play in the evacuation flights. After an initial surge, fewer and fewer Americans came forward to be evacuated. Our flights, now running about once a week, would routinely return from Kuwait with just a few Americans on them, but filled with people of other nationalities. We ended up evacuating citizens from all over the world, from Filipino maids to Libyan businessmen, in addition to almost 1,900 American citizens stranded in Kuwait. Our approach was: if there is a seat, put a person in it. In the end, when the evacuation flights came to a close in mid-December, we were confident that every American who wanted to leave and could leave had done so. There were a number of Americans married to Iraqis who had taken Iraqi citizenship and therefore were subject to Iraqi travel restrictions. Most had been in Baghdad since the 1950s and had every intention of staying with their families.

There were also a few child custody cases where Iraqi men, divorced from American women, had returned to Iraq with their offspring. These were heartbreaking, since, short of kidnapping the children, there was nothing we could do other than to encourage, cajole, and pressure the fathers to do the right thing and let their children escape to safety. From back in the United States we received plaintive pleas from the mothers, and in Iraq encountered the steely determination of the fathers and their families to have the children remain with them.

September marked the beginning of the "celebrity statesmen tour" by prominent personalities who traveled to Baghdad in violation of U.N. and American sanctions to meet with Saddam and helped create an illusion of legitimacy for the dictator. They would be photographed sitting attentively next to him, would make some inane antiwar comments to the camera and, as a reward, Saddam would bestow a few hostages on them, enabling them to claim that they had been on an errand of mercy. American visitors included former Attorney General Ramsey Clark, former Texas Governor John Connally, and an already ill Muhammad Ali. Former British Prime Minister Edward Heath, German Prime Minister Willy Brandt, and Yousef Ibrahim (the former Cat Stevens) also came.

We were of two views regarding these visits. For the most part, they were well intentioned but misguided. Officially, we discouraged Americans from coming to Baghdad. It was a violation of American law and international sanctions, and it was dangerous, as Saddam had clearly demonstrated his penchant for taking hostages. At the same time, we applauded each new release as we continued to press for the safe departure of all Americans. We concluded that we would be as supportive as possible; after all, even if the visitors were in technical violation of American law, they were our citizens and, as such, were legitimate beneficiaries of whatever consular support we could provide.

We also tried to take advantage of the visits to secure the release of those hostages whom we knew suffered from medical problems. We prepared priority lists of hostages for release, with health and age our top two criteria, and forwarded them to the foreign ministry. Often, the hostages high on our list were released. Other times, hostages who happened to be incarcerated at sites near the capital were brought in and handed over to the visitors. We encouraged the family members of all hostages to make us aware of any medical problems, which we then transmitted to the foreign ministry as justification for early release. Eventually, we had a medical reason to justify the early release of virtually every hostage.

The first of our celebrity visitors was the inimitable Reverend Jesse Jackson, who arrived at the end of August, ostensibly to make a television program. I had first met Jesse in the Congo, several years previously. He was well known for his skill at upstaging events, and I had seen him do this in Brazzaville. His arrival there had coincided with President Sassou Nguesso's National Day reception. Jackson was whisked directly from the airport to the reception, where within a few minutes he managed to turn the event into a party for him rather than for the country. As a bemused Sassou stood by, Jackson carried on as if the gathering was in his honor, a welcome befitting his stature as a son of Africa.

The joke about Jackson was that the most dangerous place ever to be was between Jackson and a camera or a microphone. For all that, however, he was extraordinarily effective in Baghdad and later in Kuwait City, as he refused to take no for an answer and used some of his civil disobedience techniques, honed in the American Civil Rights movement, to confront the Iraqi army in Kuwait and secure the release of twenty sick and injured Americans from our embassy compound there. He also provided considerable comfort to our besieged embassy staff in Kuwait City. It was a task ideally suited to Jackson's larger-than-life public persona, and he deserved considerable credit for being willing to put himself in danger by directly confronting Iraqi troops to secure the release of the sick Americans.

By now, the Iraqis had cut off all water and electricity to our embassy compound in Kuwait. Our diplomats and their American citizen charges were reduced to the most spartan living conditions— rationing water and subsisting on canned tuna, while enduring 120-degree temperatures every day without air conditioning or even fans. They rose to the occasion, planting "freedom" gardens, digging a well, and never missing an opportunity to defy their Iraqi tormentors just the other side of the fence. They were not going to cower in the face of the Iraqis' threatening behavior any more than we were going to in Baghdad.

Chapter Seven

A Noose for a Necktie

A<small>T THE AMBASSADOR'S RESIDENCE IN</small> B<small>AGHDAD</small>, about a ten-minute drive from the embassy compound, a loose structure and organization emerged from within the community of forty American men now ensconced there. We called them our guests, to distinguish them from the hostages Saddam was holding and from our Kuwait diplomatic colleagues. Since these men were not diplomats, they were subject to being seized by the Iraqis and so for the most part were restricted to the residence except when traveling to the embassy in a diplomatic vehicle. The guests designated liaison officers with the embassy and with the ever-inquisitive press. They assigned tasks to each other to ensure that the facilities were properly maintained, and worked well together to keep spirits up through planned activities at the residence, such as movie nights and periodic barbeques to which embassy staff was invited.

I encouraged them to be as self-sufficient as possible, though we remained attentive to potential problems. As could be expected, there were some medical issues, particularly since a large segment of this population was older. A couple of men were taking antidepressant medication, and when it ran out, we were faced with some problems. But in general, morale and behavior were very good.

With every new arrival of the press, whose ranks turned over about every ten days, we would receive videotapes of movies and football games that were immediately sent to the residence. We also benefited from a steady supply of cigars. In fact, before Dan Rather left, he came to see me and asked what shortages we might be experiencing as a consequence of the sanctions. I polled our embassy officials and learned that the only thing we thought we might run out of was cigars. Every new group of journalists from then until my departure in January brought a box of cigars to us. I had never smoked such quality, then or since.

Inevitably, some of our guests went stir-crazy and were imprudent. Some left the compound and were picked up by the Iraqis; others plotted their escape across the desert into Jordan. I tried to discourage such dangerous actions, but I could not and would not stand in the way of those who were determined to try to escape. We arranged for our embassy in Jordan to send us maps of the border region and some compasses to help those determined to leave to find their way. We also stationed an embassy team on the Jordanian side of the border, with the permission of the Jordanian government, to receive them if they managed to make their way across the lightly guarded frontier.

One particular band of escapees bribed taxi drivers to drive them to within several miles of the border and then struck out on foot across the desert in the middle of the night. To our delight, we learned the next day that they had executed their plan perfectly and made it out. Over the next several weeks, a couple of other groups also escaped in the same way.

The sixty-three of our diplomatic colleagues from Kuwait, who were reassigned by the State Department to "temporary duty" (TDY) in Baghdad for the duration of their enforced stay, lived at the Marine House and in other embassy houses and apartments on the same side of the river as the embassy. The TDY'ers benefited from their status as diplomats and could move freely about the city, though they still could not leave the country.

My own schedule remained chaotic. I continued to reside in my own home, twenty minutes across the river from the embassy compound and ten from the ambassador's residence. I stayed there expressly so that there would be one officer on the same side of the river as the government ministries in case the bridges across the river were closed for whatever reason. For the few hours a day when I was not at work or at meetings, it was important to me to be in familiar surroundings with my music, my books, and my artwork.

I used the ambassador's fully armored car, even when the air conditioning failed, which it did often, and the hermetically sealed interior became as hot as the desert outside. My driver was an intensely loyal and brave Egyptian named Said, who remained with me day and night, refusing to be relieved so long as I was awake. He moved in with me and slept little more than I did over the next five months. Day or night, the car was ready for whatever foray I might have to make. We always traveled with the American flag flying from the bumper. It was one way of showing that we were not afraid. In fact, I knew that if something was going to happen to me, it would be only on the orders of the government and that I would not be in any position to resist or even defend myself. Throughout the crisis, ordinary Iraqis remained friendly and hospitable, often waving as my car passed.

Three shifts a day manned the task force at the State Department in Washington, D.C., rotating at eight in the morning, four in the afternoon, and midnight Washington time—or three in the afternoon, eleven at night, and seven in the morning Baghdad time. The senior officer of each shift of the task force expected to be briefed by me when he came on, meaning that most days I was in my office at the embassy by 6:30 A.M. and did not leave for home until after 11:30 at night. After the morning briefing with Washington, the embassy military attaché would brief me on American troop movements into the

Gulf and the state of military planning. This was followed by a general staff meeting in Baghdad, at which we reviewed the status of all of our programs and prepared for the daily off-the-record press briefing.

One particularly memorable staff meeting was interrupted almost as soon as we assembled when I was called out to speak with the task force. When I picked up the phone, the voice on the other end said flatly, "The balloon is going up." I replied to the voice that he was going to have to be more explicit, so he added, "The Iraqis have launched a missile, and, according to our estimates, it will land in either Tel Aviv or Haifa. If that happens, we will launch a counterattack and hit Iraq with everything we have."

I returned to the meeting and informed the participants. After a moment of stunned silence, we shifted focus to immediate security concerns and began to plan to move everybody to the ambassador's compound, well away from the embassy, which would be manned with only a skeleton crew in the event the Iraqis decided to retaliate against us. We sent one officer up to the roof to check wind direction, because we feared that an air attack would target suspected chemical and biological weapons sites, unleashing deadly winds that could drift toward us. We did not have gas masks or protective suits, so there was little we could have done anyway, but we were more than a bit curious.

Just as we were about to break up to take the actions we had outlined, I was called to the phone again. This time the voice told me, "False alarm. The missile landed well within Iraqi territory. It was just a test to calibrate their navigational system." I conveyed the reprieve to a very relieved team, who had been described by somebody arriving late to the meeting as the most ashen-faced group of people he had ever seen. I later joked that the lesson of that morning was to always bring a second pair of underwear to the office, just in case.

At 9:30 A.M. most mornings, the embassy press attaché, Steve Thibault, would usher the international press into the office for a half hour of questions. We tried to be as candid as possible, although the briefings were off the record, as Steve reminded the press every morning when he went over the ground rules. We tried to develop a theme every day and encouraged reporting on issues that were actually worrying us. We were not above putting our best interpretation on a story, and we rarely missed an opportunity to stick it to the Iraqis or embarrass them if we could.

One of these briefings took place on September 20, 1990. The Iraqis had circulated a diplomatic note to all embassies directing them to register citizens in their care with the appropriate authorities. Capital punishment was threatened for those who failed to comply, the implication being that even diplomatic personnel could be subject to this decree. However, registration could be accomplished only by personal appearance at the appropriate office, and our experience had been that Americans appearing were taken hostage. It was clearly a way for the Iraqis to replenish their stock of hostages. The choice, theoretically, was either to turn over Americans or to defy the note and risk execution.

I thought this was a tailor-made opportunity to confront the authorities over their increasingly draconian measures. I decided to give copies of the note to the press attending the briefing that morning, and then, to underscore the threat of execution, I asked the Marine security guard to fashion a hangman's noose for me to wear. I wanted to make the point that faced with the choice of sacrificing Americans under my protection or suffering capital punishment, my response to Saddam was "if he wants to execute me for keeping Americans from being taken hostage, I will bring my own fucking rope," as I told the reporters that morning.

Like all of our press briefings, this one was off the record, so news of my less-than-fashionable necktie wasn't intended to be made public. Unfortunately, either Thibault neglected to set the ground rules that morning, or else one of the journalists decided that the story was just too good to pass up and violated the agreement. By noon, the story had been so distorted in the retelling that French news announced that the Iraqis intended to hang the American chargé d'affaires by sundown.

Not surprisingly, the Iraqis were furious, and Tariq Aziz convoked a meeting of the entire diplomatic corps for that evening. Even though most of the hundred or so heads of embassies attended the meeting, it was essentially a showdown between Aziz and me. With what I'd done now widely known, I wasn't going to back down, so I played my hand as aggressively as I could. We sat at opposite ends of a long table. Tariq lit a cigar. I did as well. He asserted that the diplomatic note was not intended to require compliance by embassies. I jumped in and asked, "Then why was it sent as a diplomatic note?" Such notes generally set forth government procedures on various issues and required compliance from the diplomatic corps.

Tariq said that the Iraqis had no intention of executing diplomats. I responded, "Then why did they refer to capital punishment in the note?" The meeting broke up inconclusively. Tariq had tried to embarrass me in front of my diplomatic colleagues, but I was having none of it. My charges were my fellow citizens, not other diplomats. The next day, we received another diplomatic note from the Iraqi foreign ministry, withdrawing the previous note. Once again, we had stood up to the Iraqis and forced them to back down from a malicious demand.

The morning press briefing would often break up with several of the journalists staying behind to ask one last question, or if they were newly arrived, to get one of my business cards. One day I asked a journalist why he needed yet another card since his news organization must have had at least ten in their offices. He replied without hesitation that the press betting was that I was not going to survive, and he thought the card might prove valuable someday. I handed him a card, after autographing it for him.

After the press cleared out, we would work on our daily tasks, from planning evacuation flights to scheduling meetings with foreign ministry officials or other diplomats. I regularly sought out my foreign counterparts to keep them up to date on what we were doing and also to exchange information. One of my most amusing exchanges was with the Austrian ambassador. One morning, he asked if he could drop by and see me. I offered that since he was an ambassador and I a mere chargé, I would be pleased to call on him. But it was important to him that he call on me, and so he showed up within a few minutes.

A historian by training, he referred to Neville Chamberlain's infamous meeting with Hitler—also an Austrian by birth—at Munich in September 1938, and urged as strongly as possible that we remain tough and not yield to appeasement tendencies being expressed in other capitals. I was gratified by his comments, since we had been subjected to a number of slights from some of our Western colleagues for our hard-line position, and I conveyed his sentiments to Washington. Several years later, he told me that when he had been introduced to President Bush after the end of the Gulf War, the president commented to him how much he had appreciated his remarks as relayed by me.

The British ambassador, Harold "Hooky" Walker, in particular, was critical of our aggressive approach. Our strained relations stemmed from our embassy decision early on to offer Americans safe haven to keep them out of Saddam's clutches. British citizens were subject to the same threats as Americans, and when they saw what we had done, they demanded that their ambassador offer the same support. Unfortunately, the British embassy did not have the resources that we did, so when they finally invited their citizens to stay on their embassy compound, they had to turn to us for refrigerators, stoves, and other equipment to help furnish their improvised quarters.

In dealing with the Iraqis, the British always believed they had the best approach, favoring a more traditional quiet diplomacy. At one point, Hooky snobbishly remarked to me that we reminded him of a bunch of cowboys sitting on the stoop of our ranch house with our rifles across our chests, waiting for the Indians to come over the horizon and attack us. Since a similar image of the Alamo had occurred to me more than once, I thanked him for the compliment. His deputy was more philosophical about our plight. In one of our exchanges, he noted, "When in our careers will we ever again be reasonably well paid to be as obnoxious as we like?" He was right; we were not going to achieve results by acting as if this was a popularity contest. I was convinced then and am convinced now that we would never have succeeded in saving Americans if we had relied on traditional diplomacy. Saddam respected only strength. Diplomatic niceties were viewed by him as signs of weakness to be pocketed, with the supplicant then walked all over. A serial violator of international law and treaties could not be coddled.

After briefing the task force coordinator who came on duty in Washington at 8:00 A.M., or 3:00 P.M. Baghdad time, I would go home for lunch and a brief rest. On most afternoons, around five o'clock, I would attend a daily meeting of the European Union ambassadors as an observer. I would share what we were doing and invite them to support us. Since their rules required not just consultation with their own governments but also a consensus within the community, they were ill equipped to act in a timely matter. Sometimes they would follow our lead ten days later, but we could not count on their solidarity with us.

Some European ambassadors could be infuriating. In early October, the German ambassador to Iraq hosted a reception to celebrate the momentous occasion of Germany's reunification at the end of the Cold War. Attending the event was the erstwhile East German colleague, who'd served as ambassador to Kuwait. The East German joked with me that he was no doubt the only diplomat in the history of our profession to lose not just the country to which he had been accredited, Kuwait, but also the country from which he had been sent, East Germany. His gallows humor in the face of not just a difficult present but also an uncertain future upon his return to a newly united Germany, was impressive. After all, however well he may have performed in Kuwait, the only thing that was guaranteed when he arrived back in his country was that he would be out of a job.

The reception was extremely well attended by Iraqi officials, and they hung on every word the representative of the reunified Germany had to say. The German ambassador, a sometimes difficult colleague, offered a longwinded toast extolling the virtues of national unity after forty-five years of separation. I thought as I listened that however splendidly the speech might play in Berlin, it was totally inappropriate in the context of the current crisis. Here Iraq claimed it was uniting with Kuwait to correct a historic error, that is, the separation of the two countries earlier in the century. I do not know if our host had any idea what effect his comments might have on the Iraqis, but the effect was so predictable that he certainly should have known better. Within hours the Iraqis were citing German unification as the precedent and justification for their own actions in Kuwait.

On another occasion, the same German ambassador invited his fellow ambassadors from Britain, France, and Japan, plus myself, to meet with him. He proudly announced that he had just arranged with the Iraqis to provide safe passage for all of our respective citizens still in Kuwait. I asked him if the safe passage was out of Iraq and to safety, and he responded that it was only to Baghdad, after which they would be taken into custody by the Iraqis and dispersed to the "strategic sites." I gritted my teeth and coldly thanked him for his efforts, saying I would relay his offer to Washington. I was pretty damn sure, though, that there was no way President Bush was going to take any action that would add to the number of Americans being held in Iraq by Saddam. I was right. Secretary Baker sent our ambassador to Germany, the venerable Vernon Walters, to meet with the German foreign minister, Hans-Dietrich Genscher, to register our disdain for the plan, which soon was abandoned.

At seven every evening, I met with the Turkish, French, British, and Soviet deputy chiefs of mission. They were my closest colleagues and the persons best informed and most directly involved in the situation. Our meetings were informal and candid exchanges among friends. Though our approaches were dictated by our governments, we also understood that each of us was playing a different role in this drama. Ours was to be the most belligerent, the Soviets' to be the most accommodating, the French to be both. The Turks were soft in rhetoric but firmly behind the American position.

It was the one opportunity of the day to relax with friends, among whom I had worked over the past two years. We would trade information and views and bring each other up to date on what our respective governments were thinking and doing, all informally over pasta and cold beer. These became cherished interludes, which frequently became quite personal as we talked about the impact of the crisis on our families and friends at home. I would mention the infrequent conversations I had with my twins, Joe and Sabrina, now twelve. They were of an age where it was awkward to talk with Dad so far away. Our phone calls were punctuated by long silences and careful avoidance of their worries about my safety, though Susan relayed how scared they were for me. They understood I was in a dangerous predicament.

I would return to the embassy every night for one last briefing with the Washington task force at eleven o'clock before finally going home for the night. Once home, I would unwind with a steady diet of movies, football tapes, and the British program *Yes, Minister*, the story of a hapless politician hopelessly outmaneuvered by his clever professional staff. My taste in movies during these months tended toward gratuitous violence—I probably watched *Die Hard* a dozen times. I could relate to its hero, trying to avoid getting killed while being responsible for saving people. The bruising contact in the football games reflected what I often wanted to do to certain Iraqis. *Yes, Minister* was a hysterical look at governmental bureaucracy; for all the support we received from Washington, sometimes we felt like we were dealing with similar bumbling ourselves as the static organization back home tried to cope with a fast-moving situation. This made the British comedy all the more enjoyable and funny during my off hours.

At one in the morning, I usually tuned in to the BBC World Service on radio, which every night offered superb analyses of the situation from some of the world's leading experts on the Middle East. Finally, at one-thirty I would hit the sack.

I could never sleep the entire night, or what was left of it, however, consumed as I was with figuring out how to outfox the Iraqis. We had made progress on the margins—some of our most vulnerable hostages had been released—but every time we thought we had discovered a loophole in the hostage policy, Saddam would cinch it closed. I would get out of bed at least once during the night and pace the floors of my house, wondering what else we might do to achieve some leverage in a situation where the adversary had all the guns and all the power. I had never paced like this before. It was a new phenomenon, but one that I learned I shared with others who under pressure found it a helpful way to gather one's thoughts. At 6:00 A.M., the cycle would begin anew.

In early November, in bed for a couple of days with a cold and flu, I opened Henry Kissinger's book, *The White House Years*, the memoir of his years as national security adviser in the Nixon administration. In it, he recounted meeting Anwar Sadat in 1973 and coming away from the meeting convinced that there would be no new Middle East war, only to have hostilities break out a mere matter of weeks later in what the Israeli's called the *Yom Kippur* War. I remember thinking that if Kissinger could be fooled, surely I could be, too. It was reassuring to know that better minds than mine had been confounded by their Arab interlocutors.

As we approached Thanksgiving, my embassy colleagues and I decided that the holiday provided us with a perfect backdrop for reminding Americans that there were still hostages in Iraq and that the embassy was working around the clock to obtain their release. I pitched a proposal to Washington that included an early morning visit to the Iraqi foreign ministry with diplomatic notes prepared by Emil and our ad hoc consular section, demanding the release on health grounds of each of the hostages—a separate note for each of the almost 120 hostages. This would be followed by a press conference in which I would, for once, answer questions on the record. Later, I would give the press an opportunity to film the preparations for the Thanksgiving meal at my house. The spokesman for our American guests would also speak with the journalists that afternoon.

The proposal was met with a curious silence from Washington, even after two follow-up calls. I finally pressed the task force chief for an answer. "Nobody is going to tell you not to do it," he said, "but with the president traveling to Saudi Arabia to have Thanksgiving with the troops, the White House press office is concerned that you might step on the president's story. That said, if you insist, feel free to go ahead. Just so you are aware of the concerns here." The message was clear: proceed at your own risk. I thought about it for a while and asked myself, even if I were to step on the president's message, something I could not imagine happening—after all, he was the president and I was just Joe Wilson—what could Washington do to show its displeasure? Send me to Baghdad? On the other hand, the hostage message needed to be hammered home, and what better time to do it? I decided to take my chances.

The program went as scripted, including camera shots of turkey being served and our American guests' spokesman, Roland Bergheer, delivering a stirringly patriotic statement about how the liberation of Kuwait was more important than the lives of the Americans stuck in Iraq. Later, as I was tucking into my own holiday dinner with a few friends, very satisfied with the way the day had gone, the doorbell rang. It was CNN correspondent Richard Roth at the door with his camera crew and the news that the Iraqis had brought some American hostages to Baghdad for a government-provided Thanksgiving dinner, complete with CNN cameras to record it. The dinner had taken place less than a mile from my house. Did I have a reaction? Roth asked.

You bet, I said, and launched into a rant about the barbaric and sadistic nature of a regime that would parade hostages before the cameras as a propaganda tool while denying them access to their country's embassy or consular officials. Roth thanked me and went on his way. A couple of days after this, a cable arrived "from President Bush to chargé d'affaires Joe Wilson." He wrote: "I recently saw you on CNN saying what you thought of Saddam's latest attempt to derive political gain out of understandable concern here for the hostages. I could not have said it better. It is relatively easy to speak out from the safety and comfort of Washington; what you are doing day in and day out under the most trying conditions is truly inspiring. Keep fighting the good fight; you and your stalwart colleagues are always in our thoughts and prayers."

When I called Richard Haass, the senior director at the National Security Council, to thank him for drafting such a nice message, he told me that the president had drafted it himself. All of us at the embassy were gratified, all the more in knowing that at least the president was not concerned that we might have distracted people from his message. I had a copy of the cable made and sent over to Richard Roth with the personal note that he was at least as responsible as I was, since he had provided the means through which I had delivered the message. I understand he still has the cable in his office. I do too.

A week after Thanksgiving, on November 27, the Senate Armed Services Committee convened to debate a resolution to give the president the authority he needed to wage war to liberate Kuwait. The most notable of the witnesses, from our perspective in Baghdad, was retired Admiral William J. Crowe, President Bush's former chairman of the Joint Chiefs of Staff. He testified on November 28 that "we should give sanctions a fair chance before we discard them . . . If, in fact, the sanctions will work in twelve to eighteen months instead of six months, a trade-off of avoiding war, with its attendant sacrifices and uncertainties, would in my estimation be more than worth it."

The reaction in Baghdad was electric. Here was one of President Bush's former senior military officers breaking with his commander in chief. The Iraqis immediately began to voice doubt that the American military would allow the president to make war.

On substance, Crowe was flat wrong. We had sent an analysis of the effects of sanctions to Washington several weeks earlier. We had concluded that the sanctions were having a deleterious effect on Saddam's war machine, but that they would not in and of themselves drive him out of Kuwait, not in a decade or even longer. While we had seen ample evidence of the lack of spare parts, fuel additives, and spare tires for military equipment, it was clear that the sanctions would affect the economy and infrastructure only gradually and incrementally. The Iraqi economy, we argued, was not a fragile house of cards that would just collapse from one day to the next. On the contrary, it would grind down over time.

One year, the people might be driving Chevrolets, several years later Volkswagens, later still riding donkeys or bicycles. It would be a decade at least, we estimated, before the Iraqi infrastructure would be so run-down that Saddam might have to face the decision to withdraw from Kuwait in order to get out from under the sanctions. By that time, he would have looted the Kuwait treasury, found ways around the sanctions, and repopulated Kuwait with Iraqis so as to rig any vote on the future of the country. Sanctions would make the war easier, we believed, but not unnecessary, as long as our goal was to liberate Kuwait.

As the congressional debate in Washington opened, we had made considerable progress on securing the release of the remaining American hostages. The increasing pressure of war had made the Iraqis more amenable to some arrangement to release them, perhaps in exchange for American concessions. But we were not in the concession business. We argued instead that unless the Iraqis wanted war over the mistreatment of American citizens, they ought to see it in their interest to release all Americans in their custody. When Admiral Crowe made his ill-considered statement, Iraqi willingness to discuss the issue with us abruptly ceased for several days: the Iraqis had concluded that they might just as well hold out a bit longer to see if they could extract a better deal for the hostages.

I had remained in regular contact with my friends Al Gore and Tom Foley, now Speaker of the House, since the invasion. Gore had been the first person outside the State Department to be in touch with me. Though he had been in the midst of his Senate reelection campaign, he took time out of his schedule to reach out to me and offer his support. It was a gesture I have never forgotten. He also asked me to keep him informed about the situation as it evolved. I telephoned him, and later Foley, regularly throughout the crisis, from an open line in my office, hopeful that Iraqi intelligence was listening in on my tough talk with two of my country's elected leaders. I wanted Saddam to know that the United States was deadly serious about the liberation of Kuwait and was willing to use force if necessary.

During the Senate debate on whether to authorize the president to use force, I phoned Gore's office, but he was on the Senate floor. I offered to call back, but his aide insisted on patching me through to the Senate Democrats' cloakroom. The senator came off the floor and questioned me intensely for twenty minutes about whether sanctions alone could get Saddam out of Kuwait. I didn't know it at the time, but it was the very day of the vote on the war resolution, and Gore would be one of the few Democrats to vote with President Bush. It

pained me during the 2000 presidential election campaign to see
former Senator Alan Simpson accuse Al of being "Prime Time Al"
because of the timing of the speech announcing his support of the
president. This was the same Alan Simpson who had been practically
on bended knee before Saddam in April 1990, reassuring the Iraqi
dictator that he had a press problem and not a policy problem. It was
an outrage that a decade later he had the nerve to be critical of the one
senator who had really taken the time to listen to an analysis from the
field and factor that in to his decision on what most senators agreed
was one of the most momentous votes of their careers.

Our efforts on behalf of the hostages, as useless as they seemed
right after the Crowe testimony, did not flag. In addition to daily notes
to the foreign ministry on behalf of specific cases, and quiet meetings
with Hamdun to see what we might do on behalf of some of the sicker
hostages, I also worked with some thoughtful members of the international press. My goal was to bring some focus to bear on the argument that holding on to the hostages was not in Saddam's interest,
unless he wanted to go to war over that issue rather than over his continued occupation of Kuwait.

I met over lunch one day with an Arab journalist who had considerable influence in the region. To her I reiterated that President
Bush had clearly already concluded that, given the size of the war
being contemplated, the loss of a couple of hundred American civilians was acceptable, even if lamentable. Saddam was therefore
deluding himself if he thought he could prevent war by keeping
hostages. And the other side of the coin was that Saddam needed to
understand that should something happen to the hostages, either
accidentally or as a consequence of mistreatment, American anger
might be such that the president would be forced to go to war to
avenge that mistreatment. It was important that the region's leaders
comprehend what the consequences might be if something went
wrong with the hostages. If Saddam did not want to risk war over

hostages, he should just let them go. They were not an asset to him, but rather a grave liability.

In late November, about ten days after that lunch, we received a copy of the minutes from a meeting between our ambassador to Algeria, Chris Ross, and Algerian Foreign Minister Sid Ahmed Ghozali, in which the minister expressed his concern that Saddam did not understand the risk he ran by continuing to hold the hostages. His analysis was precisely the one I had shared with the Arab journalist. I was certain that my contact had been speaking to other Arab leaders, and I saw that the thesis was gaining some traction. It would soon get back to Saddam from Arab interlocutors.

It did not matter how many times I told the Iraqis the risks they ran—they expected *me* to say it. But when a fellow Arab said the same thing, it would have far greater impact.

We did not have to wait long, only until King Hussein of Jordan and Yasser Arafat traveled to Baghdad in early December to meet with Saddam. According to a report we received from our ambassador in Amman, Roger Harrison, Hussein raised the issue of the hostages with Saddam and laid out the same case against continuing to hold them. The Arab journalist with whom I'd lunched was also a personal friend of King Hussein and had obviously shared our discussion with him.

That meeting with the king and Arafat was the real clincher. Saddam, who had just invited the wives of the hostages to return to Baghdad to see their husbands, announced on December 6 that Iraq's defenses were now strong enough to withstand an American offensive, so the hostages could now go home. We were elated and went back into the charter aircraft business. In addition to evacuating the remaining hostages, we ended up flying their wives out for the second time at government expense, even though they had come back to Baghdad over our strong objections.

On December 13, I was able to go out to the airport and greet Ambassador Nat Howell and his remaining troops as they transited

Baghdad on the last charter we flew from Kuwait. They would be home for Christmas, as would the TDY'ers who had been stranded with us since August and who had performed such valuable service. They had comported themselves in the finest traditions of our foreign service, with dignity and tenacity in the face of considerable hardship. They made all of us in the embassy proud. The few of us who remained in Baghdad would miss them, but we were delighted that the number of Americans in danger had dropped from close to two hundred to fewer than ten.

While the hostage issue and the safe evacuation of all Americans had been the primary responsibility of our embassy, we also regularly provided to Washington our analysis of the situation in Baghdad. This included recommendations on what we might do further to pressure Saddam to withdraw peacefully from Kuwait, although at the same time we remained steadfast in our view that only the credible threat of force could possibly convince Saddam to retreat. We reported on everything from the impact of sanctions, to the Iraqi reaction to the buildup of American forces in the Gulf, as well as the reaction in Baghdad to the inflammatory rhetoric coming out of Washington. After the departure of the hostages, the guests, and even our TDY'ers from Kuwait, we were down to six Americans—all with but one goal, which was to ensure that both sides understood the gravity of the situation and would avoid needlessly going to war if possible. I did believe, however, that there were some "fig leaves" that we could offer Saddam that would not compromise our hard-line and fully justified position but that might allow him a face-saving way to withdraw. My thinking involved four such fig leaves that could be subtly suggested to him. If he chose to grab one, so much the better; if not, we had lost nothing.

The four ideas were: survival of his army if it departed Kuwait peacefully; a reduction of the heated rhetoric, including the references to Saddam as a Hitler-like figure; a commitment to work with

Iraq and Kuwait on the legitimate issues of concern to Saddam; and finally, a rededication to working toward a lasting solution to the Arab/Israeli peace process—not because Saddam had tried to link the two but because it was the right thing to do.

Saddam's effort to claim he had invaded Kuwait in order to liberate Palestine had been one of the most cynical of all of his ploys, but that did not mean that we should ignore one of the major irritants in the region.

I was not the only one thinking along these lines, and was gratified to read that in a number of television appearances during the month of December, senior administration officials let drop remarks that hinted at each of the four fig leaves. As soon as I would receive the transcript of such an interview that an administration official had given to American media, I would scour it for useful statements and pass them on to Nizar Hamdun to share with the rest of his government. The Iraqi embassy in Washington had long since ceased to be a credible conduit of information from Washington to Baghdad, so we had become the sole source of official information from Washington for the Iraqis.

As much as I continued to hope for a peaceful solution, however, it was clear to me that we were on a collision course for war.

However rational the August 2 invasion might have been from the Iraqi perspective, Saddam had miscalculated every step of the way since November 8, when President Bush had announced that he was sending the U.S. Army's Seventh Corps from Germany to the Gulf to prepare to roll back the invasion. The Seventh Corps was a big, heavy military machine made to roll over an enemy. The president would not commit the corps unless he was serious. Moreover, what Saddam failed to understand was that we would not have moved forces from the European theater if we were not comfortable that the Soviets would not meddle in Europe in our absence. Saddam always assumed that the Soviets would save him; he was wrong on that, as on so many other things. Despite two visits to Baghdad by Yevgeny Primakov, then the

Soviet envoy, selected to mediate because of his longstanding personal relationship with Saddam, it was clear that Moscow understood that its long-term interests lay with the United States, not with Iraq.

Shortly after the invasion, I had suggested to Washington that we should try to find ways to drive a wedge between Saddam and his military command by convincing the latter that if a war were to take place, it would not be set-piece trench warfare—as the Iran–Iraq war had been—but a fast-moving conflict with all the awesome firepower that the United States could bring to bear. I proposed a video be made showing what we could do from land, sea, and air; everything from cruise missiles hitting sites hundreds of miles apart to tanks rolling over sand dunes while their turrets turned to hit targets that could not even be seen.

I wanted the Iraqi high command to lie awake at night knowing that their troops were going to be utterly decimated. Our Special Operations Commanding General Wayne Downing liked the idea and produced the video, a copy of which he later gave me. Unfortunately, as he later told me, the State Department held up the distribution until December because of concerns that it was too "bellicose." I couldn't believe it. We had close to 500,000 troops in the Gulf primed and ready to attack, and we were squeamish about a video designed to give Saddam's high command second thoughts. By the time it was finally distributed, it was too late to do any good. The stage was set.

Throughout the month of December, I also worked on the proposal put forth by President Bush that we "go the extra mile for peace" by holding meetings between Secretary of State James Baker and Tariq Aziz in Washington and in Baghdad. The Iraqis again miscalculated, taking what was essentially an ultimatum as an invitation to debate. By the time we arrived at agreement, the two meetings in the respective capitals had been collapsed into one in Geneva, scheduled for early January 1991.

By the middle of December, the beating of the war drums in Washington actually left the Iraqis thinking that we really were not going to attack. One well-informed journalist for the London *Sunday Times* reported to me: "The Iraqis have concluded that you are bluffing. If you were serious, you wouldn't keep beating your chests. You would let your actions speak for you."

I took that to heart and relayed her thoughts to Washington, recommending that we tone down our threats. I remember the cable as being appropriately polite; but Larry Grahl, who hand-carried my message to Secretary Baker, later told me, "I thought you had lost your mind, telling the president and the secretary in effect to shut up." Then, a couple of days later, when he realized the U.S. government had gone silent, "I concluded you were brilliant," Grahl said. It was, of course, the British journalist who had had the brilliant idea, but soon the benefit was nullified, as every pundit and member of Congress had jumped on the chattering bandwagon, and silence was not maintained.

At the embassy, it was not clear if Washington was going to withdraw the six of us before the war, or even if the Iraqis would allow us to leave if we tried. That was fine with me. I had every intention of remaining as long as necessary to provide diplomatic support, whatever the circumstances that unfolded. I received a message from Washington advising that there would be military means at the ready—to extract us—in the event Saddam tried to prevent us from departing, when and if a decision on our removal was made. We would drive into the desert to the east of Baghdad, near the Iranian border, where a helicopter and a contingent of Special Operations forces would be standing by to whisk us to safety. My reply was that close to a hundred other diplomatic missions were depending on us to tell them when the time had come to leave. I was not going to betray their confidence by sneaking out under the cover of darkness without letting them know, unless personally ordered to do so by the president. That reaction ended the discussion and, I understand, the serious planning. I wanted to leave by the front door or not leave at all.

The Baker–Aziz meeting finally took place in Geneva on January 9, 1991. Secretary Baker later told me that he asked Aziz four times for assurances that Iraq would permit the remaining American diplomats to leave if the U.S. decided to suspend our diplomatic representation. Each time Aziz demurred, saying only that he had to refer the question to "higher authority." "When I left that meeting, I did not know if we were going to get you out or not," Baker said.

On January 9, I received a call from Nizar Hamdun confirming that "higher authority" had agreed not to prevent our departure if we decided to go. When I informed Washington, I was instructed to buy economy-class tickets to Amman for the remaining six of us and told that we should make our way home from there as best we could. Since the Jordanians had announced that in the event of the outbreak of hostilities they would close their airport, and since there were already more than three hundred Americans waiting for flights in Amman, this struck me as a particularly unhelpful idea. Did the State Department intend for us to be stuck in Jordan throughout the war? I countered with the suggestion that we should charter the lone Iraqi Air 747, fly to Amman and pick up as many of the three hundred Americans stranded there as possible, then fly everybody to Germany to meet commercial flights back to the States. The department relented, and we compromised on chartering the smaller Iraqi Air 727 to fly directly to Germany, bypassing Amman but at least moving us completely out of the region.

Our indefatigable general services officer, Jeanette Pena, who had been the embassy's logistical genius from the beginning, organized the final charter flight for January 12. We invited the American press to join us, noting that when we left, there would be no embassy to turn to for support. Only two journalists took us up on the offer, both of whom had been caught behind the lines when the American embassy was evacuated in Saigon in 1974 and who had no intention of reliving the experience. I also informed all the remaining diplomatic missions in Baghdad of our decision and offered seats on our plane, on a space-available basis, to those who wanted to leave with us.

On the afternoon of January 11, I delivered to Nizar the diplomatic note that suspended our diplomatic relations and turned over our mission to the Polish embassy, which would act as our protecting power. Tariq Aziz declined to receive me, perhaps still sore at being called a liar. Nizar and I had a brief and melancholy exchange in his private office, with CNN on the television behind us, the first time I had been in that office and seen CNN since August. Looking at the screen, it was apparent to us both that there was no longer any way to avoid war. I told him I took no joy in having to close the embassy but that I hoped the time might come when I could return to be part of an effort to rebuild our relations.

On January 12, I lowered the flag over the embassy, folded it, and tucked it under my arm before driving to the airport. I also said farewell to the Iraqi staff we were leaving behind. It was probably the most difficult thing I have ever had to do. They had been unfailingly loyal to us, even as they came under tremendous pressure from the authorities, and from their own families, to quit their jobs. Now I had to leave them to fend for themselves. The last hugs all around left me flat and emotionally drained, wondering what would become of these brave and decent souls.

Getting on the airplane, I was elated that our ordeal was finally over, and buoyed by the gratitude of the diplomats from other nations who had taken us up on our offer of seats on the flight. And yet, I was saddened that our efforts had ended as they did, without Saddam's peaceful withdrawal from Kuwait. I had done everything in my power to avoid war, and Saddam could never claim that he did not understand the consequences of continuing to occupy his neighbor after the January 15, 1991, deadline established by the U.N. But that did little to ease the deep foreboding I felt on the eve of the coming war.

After a night in Frankfurt, we arrived in Washington late in the evening of January 13, a Sunday night, to a warm reception from families and colleagues. The shock of being in Washington and no longer in the pressure cooker of Baghdad, as well as the jet lag, kept me awake most of the night. Early on the morning of the fourteenth, not knowing what to do with myself, I strolled from my Dupont Circle apartment down to the State Department twenty minutes away, thinking that I would have a leisurely morning, chatting with colleagues and thanking the task force for all the hard work they had done.

When I arrived at the office of Iraqi Affairs at the opening of the business day, I was surprised to learn that the White House had already telephoned with an invitation to a one o'clock meeting with President Bush. Assistant Secretary John Kelly took Jeanette and me to the White House, where we were met by the chief of protocol, Ambassador Joseph Verner Reed, who escorted us in to meet the president of the United States.

As the door to the Oval Office from the Roosevelt Room opened, President Bush was standing there to greet me. He shook my hand warmly, and I said to him, "We never personally spoke during my time in Baghdad, but I felt from the very beginning that we were on the same wavelength." He replied, "You're absolutely right," and turned to introduce me to the others in the office, his war cabinet: Vice President Quayle, Secretary of State Baker, National Security Adviser Scowcroft, CIA Director Webster, Chief of Staff Sununu, and several staff people.

I have no memory of the president's introduction, but John Kelly told me later that he said, "Gentlemen, let me introduce you to true American heroes."

We then shook hands all around. The press came in, took a lot of pictures, and left. After they were ushered out, the door was closed and the briefing began. Peppered first with questions from the president, then the others, I responded as well as I could. I described the fear and the fatalism in the streets and markets in Baghdad and the continuing hostility of the regime. For the first fifteen minutes of the meeting, I was devoid of any emotional feeling whatsoever, utterly unconscious of the trappings of power in the Oval Office and the level of the group I was addressing. A mixture of jet lag, culture shock, and sheer exhaustion had overwhelmed my nervous system.

Finally, I took a second to look around the room and woke up. After all, Jim Baker was sitting beside me on the sofa; the president was seated in a chair to my right, in front of the fireplace. Across the room, sitting next to the desk, was Brent Scowcroft taking notes on a legal-size yellow pad. It looked to me like he was writing down everything I said. My first conscious thought, since the moment I had been introduced to President Bush, occurred when I looked at Scowcroft and his legal pad.

"Who would have ever thought," I said to myself, "that this ex-hippie-surfer from California would someday find himself in the Oval Office with the president of the United States and his war cabinet, with the president's national security adviser, a retired three-star general, serving as note taker?" Then I got nervous, and it was suddenly crystal-clear to me just where I was and whom I was with.

Just as the butterflies in my stomach started to take over, my fearless colleague Jeanette took over and carried the ball for us both. She described to our attentive audience what it was like to live in prewar Baghdad, with an openly hostile regime monitoring every move and putting obstacles in the way of everything she needed to do to keep the embassy functioning. She was affable, articulate, and funny as she offered vignettes from our daily lives. All too soon, Secretary Baker looked at his watch, the signal that the meeting was over.

Walking out of the Oval Office, the president's personal aide took me aside to invite me to the White House living quarters to meet Mrs. Bush. I was delighted. We walked over to the residence, and she came outside in a wheelchair with one leg propped up—she had recently been in a sledding accident. She reached up and gave me a warm hug. To be hugged by Barbara Bush is an experience not to be missed, and I was savoring it when a shadow hovered over us. Still in her embrace, I looked around to find the president right behind me. He had caught me hugging his wife.

For the next fifteen minutes, the three of us talked about Baghdad, its citizens, and the emotions they would be feeling on the eve of war. The president asked all the questions one would hope to hear from one's leader. He expressed real concern and compassion. It was clear to me that he truly felt the weight of the decisions he had been obliged to take.

Thirty-six hours later, the United States launched Operation Desert Storm. I watched CNN nonstop for the next several days, my stomach turning with the images of bombs exploding in Baghdad and the Iraqi antiaircraft batteries firing aimlessly in the air. I felt no joy in the fact that we had to go to war to achieve our objectives. However justified—and in my judgment Desert Storm was fully justified—the consequences of military assault on the people of Iraq could not be ignored. War is the bluntest of all weapons in our national security repertoire. The decision to use it is an awesome one. President Bush understood that, as did his senior advisers. So did I.

Chapter Eight
Watching the War from a Distance

T HE TRIUMPHANT COVERAGE OF DESERT STORM in the American media gave me no satisfaction whatsoever. After all the efforts my colleagues and I had made to convince Saddam to withdraw peacefully from Kuwait, I was left with a profound sense of sadness and failure as I stared at the televised images of the bombing of Baghdad.

I had been tougher than anybody in Baghdad, offering no quarter to avoid the war other than the withdrawal of Iraqi troops from every inch of Kuwaiti territory. It was the only position, I felt, that gave us even a glimmer of a chance to avoid war, while also liberating Kuwait, our highest priority. Saddam was never going to leave unless he calculated that the costs of staying were far greater than the costs of leaving. Diplomatic efforts would succeed only if they were supported by the credible threat of force. And in order for the threat to be credible, we had to show we were prepared to use it. Accordingly, the one American the Iraqis saw every day in Baghdad—me—had to be utterly convincing when he warned that the only outcome that could possibly avert war was total withdrawal.

Even though I understood intellectually that Saddam had brought about the international coalition's military action by his own miscalculations and brutality, it did not make it any easier for me to watch

Baghdad in flames after nightly bombings. I wondered about all the friends, colleagues, and Iraqi employees left behind. I assumed that Nizar Hamdun was probably the first casualty. With televised pictures of me leaving with the American flag tucked under my arm, I thought that Saddam would probably blame Nizar, the architect of U.S.–Iraq relations since his time in Washington in the mid-1980s as ambassador.

Nizar did survive, but I later learned that another friend of ours at the embassy, a sophisticated woman who owned a popular art gallery frequented by the expatriate community, went mad when she learned that a second son had been killed in the recent fighting. She had lost her first son in the Iran–Iraq war and now the second in Kuwait. It was too much for her, and according to reports, she was reduced to incomprehensible muttering and wandering forlornly through her now-filthy shop.

My feelings were very confused. During the day, while I was in restaurants or walking on the streets of Washington, people often would recognize me and congratulate me for my efforts in Baghdad. Colleagues in the State Department told me how much they had feared I was going to be killed and how much they admired the way I had managed the crisis. At night I would be glued to the television, disconsolate at what I thought was the failure of diplomacy, and my own efforts.

My personal life, meanwhile, was in a shambles. Since my French wife had left Baghdad in the first evacuation convoy, we had not seen each other and had only rarely spoken in the intervening five months. The separation and the stress had damaged what had always been a shaky marriage. I was totally exhausted and felt like an alien in my own country. The change from the high-pressure environment in Baghdad to the placid sidelines in Washington was a real letdown. There was no longer anything I could do to try to affect the outcome of events.

In the first few days of the war, I helped by making bomb-damage assessments, sitting in the Pentagon basement and looking at satellite photos to determine what we had struck in Baghdad. I was invited to appear on *Larry King Live* and *Sixty Minutes,* but I declined both invitations, as I did all other requests for interviews. I had said everything I had to say about Desert Shield while in Baghdad. The war spoke for itself. The drama had shifted from the attempt to affect Iraq's actions through diplomatic leverage to the means of weapons and force. I had been a public figure only because that was what the situation required, and I longed to return to anonymity.

Finally, I escaped to St. Croix in the Virgin Islands for a long vacation, swimming and skin-diving in the Caribbean and relaxing to the fiery sunsets and the soft breezes wafting through the palm trees. After a couple of weeks decompressing, I realized that the war and its consequences were out of my hands and that I bore no responsibility for the consequences of Saddam Hussein's belligerent stupidity. Sitting on the white sand beaches looking out on the multicolored sea, darkening to aquamarine, cobalt, and finally midnight blue far from the shore, I came to the realization that I was lucky to be alive, as my colleagues had told me, and should be grateful for that. In fact, after having concluded on August 8 that I probably would not survive the experience, every day that followed had been an unexpected gift. I still feel that way thirteen years later. It is liberating and puts everything into perspective.

The war itself resulted in many fewer American deaths and casualties than had been feared. Far from the 50,000 wounded the armed forces had planned for, fewer than 750 Americans died or were injured, including 121 deaths in noncombat incidents. After thirty days of incessant B-52 bombing of Iraqi positions, the coalition ground campaign took only one hundred hours to liberate Kuwait and drive the Iraqi forces back across their border. The pictures of Kuwaitis reclaiming their country were compelling. Their nightmare was at least partially over. We could take great satisfaction in the superb performance of our military, and we could celebrate the validation of the principle that countries will not get away with invading and conquering their smaller neighbors as a way to resolve their mutual problems. The Iraqi invasion of Kuwait was a brazen case of armed robbery, pure and simple.

The war also established the blueprint for the post–Cold War New World Order. For the first time since the Korean War, the world had engaged in a conflict sanctioned by international law. In the aftermath of the fall of the Berlin Wall, America's foreign policy establishment understood that the next generation's war would not be of the World War II variety, with huge mobilizations of national assets and a fight for survival among the major powers; it would instead consist of small, bloody conflicts that would best be dealt with by a coalition of the willing operating under the mandate of the United Nations.

Our challenge would be to ensure that the United States did not become the world's policeman, a costly and enervating task, but rather used our power to mobilize coalitions and share costs and responsibilities. In my mind, Desert Shield and Storm were case studies of how to manage both the diplomacy and the military aspects of an international crisis. We were successful in obtaining international financing to cover most of the costs of the war, we were successful in putting together a coalition force with troops from more than twenty nations, and we were successful in obtaining an international legal mandate to conduct the war. It was, in every way, an international effort driven by American political will and diplomatic leadership. Even as I lamented the need to resort to military action to achieve our goals, I was proud to have been part of the team that executed the policy and the war.

We expelled Saddam from Kuwait, but we did not remove him from power or take the battle all the way to Baghdad. Although I was no longer involved in the issue—I was still in the Caribbean when General Schwarzkopf negotiated the cease-fire with the Iraqi generals at Safwan in southern Iraq—the question I am still asked most frequently about this period is, why had we not done so?

As satisfying as it would have been to go on to Baghdad in 1991, there were many reasons to stop where and when we did. The goal that had been agreed upon within the international community was Saddam's expulsion from Kuwait. There was no legal authority to proceed further. Since the concept of the New World Order depended on international agreement and material support as we faced these smaller conflicts together, it was vital to establish from the outset the parameters for action and then adhere to them. Admittedly, stopping at Kuwait's border and leaving Saddam in power was not the ideal outcome, given the brutality of his regime. But international approval for his removal by force was never going to be achieved.

Quite naturally, governments are wary about approving the overthrow of other governments, however vile they might be. The principle of noninterference in the internal affairs of a sovereign nation has always been one of the pillars of the international community and was actually one of the principles that invalidated Saddam's claim of sovereignty over Kuwait. In order to attract more nations to the cause of liberating Kuwait, it had been necessary to narrow the objective to one that a large bloc of countries would support. The more limited the objectives, the broader the coalition of nations who agreed to support them. Had the objectives been broader, fewer nations would have stepped up to support the effort.

Additionally, if we had crossed into Iraq and moved on toward Baghdad, much Arab suspicion of our motives would have been confirmed, and the support we had enjoyed in Arab countries would have evaporated with each mile we pushed deeper into Iraqi territory. Intellectually, many Arabs understood the need to repel Saddam's aggression but feared that the United States would use the invasion of Kuwait to invade and occupy their lands for other reasons. Their chief concern was that all we wanted was to get our hands on their oil.

The credibility that we later enjoyed—which permitted us to make subsequent progress on Middle East peace at the Madrid Conference in October 1991, and through the Oslo process, launched in September 1993—was directly related to our having honored our promises and not exceeded the mandate from the international community.

Moreover, proceeding to Baghdad would have meant largely going alone, as our Arab partners would surely have deserted the coalition at that point, as might have the Soviets, Chinese, French, and others. It would have guaranteed that there would never again be a U.N. consensus on use of force to combat a violation of its charter. The New World Order would have been stillborn as an operating principle.

The last days of the liberation of Kuwait included the devastating destruction of many Iraqi forces along the so-called Highway of Death. The Iraqis were fleeing Kuwait when we hit their retreating troops in an awesome display of firepower. Pictures of this encounter gave the impression of a massacre. Such pictures might well have become the norm had we pursued the Iraqi army up the Tigris and Euphrates valleys, and would have turned international opinion against us quickly. What had been the nobly undertaken liberation of a small country would have come to be seen as an ugly moment when retreating troops were shot in the back. That is not the way Americans like to think of their country waging war.

The road to Baghdad might have been swift, though we had not planned or equipped our forces to make the trek. But it might also have been arduous and deadly for American troops. Iraqis had fought fiercely against Iranian invaders, and while we brought far more force and professionalism to war-making, a rear-guard guerrilla war in the cities could well have thwarted our drive to rout the regime.

However simple or difficult the invasion, occupying Iraq would have been a different proposition altogether. We would have inherited all the problems of governing a difficult nation without the global, or even American, political will to do so. And we might not have easily found Saddam. Every day in Iraq would have been a drain on our resources, stripped of the coalition support that had propelled the liberation of Kuwait. It was a scenario replete with potential nightmares.

Finally, there were also those who argued that the overthrow of Saddam would have left a void into which Iraq's neighbors, especially

Iran, would have stepped. An Iranian-dominated Iraq would have threatened the oil-rich Gulf States to the south with their large Shia populations.

None of the conditions that made the decision not to drive on to Baghdad in 1991 the correct call changed in the years following, right up to the second Gulf War in 2003.

Saddam was the ultimate survivor. He truly believed in *"L'état, c'est moi,"* and to prove he was the supreme being, he was willing to sacrifice tens of thousands of his citizens in the fruitless prosecution of a war he could not possibly win militarily. With impunity, he regularly tortured and systematically killed anyone who dared to challenge him and any ethnic group that rebelled against his rule. Because he equated himself with Iraq, and the machinery of state was so totally identified with him, as long as he survived he believed that Iraq survived, no matter how many of his fellow citizens had to die. It was that sense of personal privilege and right that drove the ruthless crushing of the Shiite and Kurdish rebellions in the aftermath of the Gulf War. The Shia and Kurds sensed that the tyrant was vulnerable and, encouraged by a statement from President Bush, launched an assault on Saddam.

"There is another way for the bloodshed to stop," Bush announced, "and that is for the Iraqi military and the Iraq people to take matters in their own hands, to force Saddam Hussein, the dictator, to step aside, and to comply with United Nations resolutions and then rejoin the family of peace-loving nations."

Unfortunately for the rebels, they did not realize that, despite all the casualties suffered in Kuwait, the Iraqi army was still strong enough to put down domestic disturbances, and, largely Sunni, it remained loyal to the regime. The rebellions were doomed when Schwarzkopf failed to prohibit Iraqi military use of helicopters, and later when the administration declined to provide military support to the insurgents.

* * *

In the spring of 1992, President Bush nominated me to serve as his ambassador to two African countries, the Gabonese Republic and the Democratic Republic of São Tomé and Príncipe. My nomination would require Senate confirmation, the first time any of my diplomatic appointments had required me to undergo this congressional ritual. At my hearings, I appeared with several other nominees for African posts, all of us to be questioned by Senator Paul Simon, Democratic senator from Illinois and chairman of the Africa subcommittee of the Senate Foreign Relations Committee (SFRC), and Republican Senator Nancy Kassebaum from Kansas.

My colleagues at the hearing included nominees to South Africa and Ghana, far more important to American national interests than the countries I was slated for. While Saddam's abuse of the human rights of Iraqi citizens had always been a grave issue for the U.S. government and for anyone in the Foreign Service posted in Iraq, I had every reason to believe that my fellow foreign service officers would get the tough questions and I would breeze through unscathed. Senators generally focus on the future and not the past.

The hearing took place in the committee's formal chamber, with the senators sitting high on the dais behind a carved wooden front, looking down on us in the well. Despite the warm welcome and the positive tone of the senators, the setting was intimidating, even for somebody who within the last year had been through the experiences I'd had in Baghdad.

On my way into the hearing room, I ran into Peter Galbraith, still a senior staffer to Senator Claiborne Pell, with whom I exchanged pleasantries. I was mildly surprised when a half hour later, just as the senators turned to question me, the door behind Simon opened and Galbraith appeared. He handed Senator Simon a sheet of paper, which I realized pertained to my session when Simon looked down at me and said, "Mr. Wilson, now I'd like to ask you a few questions about your previous job." A few turned out to be fourteen, designed to produce responses from me that could be potentially embarrassing for Secretary of State Baker. The questions were clearly designed to establish the fact that the embassy in Baghdad had advised the State Department that Saddam Hussein was engaged in the systematic abuse of the human rights of its citizens. This was trigger language for cutting off U.S. financial assistance to Iraq through the Agricultural Commodity Credit Program, but the implication was that the State Department, in its turn, had failed to act.

Simon was kind enough to ask me only two or three of Galbraith's questions before he stopped and suggested that I provide written responses for the record to the rest of them. I asked the State Department to help me prepare the responses and was told that since these were questions for *me*, I had to answer them myself. They were not *for* me, of course, but *through* me to the administration, and the unwillingness to assist in the preparation of responses struck me as short-sighted and unwise, given the leading nature of the inquiry.

I went ahead and submitted my responses, drawing extensively on our human rights reports for the three years of my tenure in Baghdad. The human rights report is a study of the human rights practices of foreign countries; it is mandated by Congress and submitted annually. My answers emphasized that, yes, Saddam systematically killed and tortured people, and that the embassy had discharged its responsibilities in a timely fashion, reporting to Congress through the annual report. Congress had received all the information it needed to assess whether Iraq had engaged in such egregious behavior as to warrant sanction.

Thus, I lobbed the ball back into Congress's court.

I was confirmed at the end of June and sworn in as ambassador in a private ceremony at our consulate in Marseilles, where I was on vacation at the time President Bush signed my orders.

After more than fifteen years in the Foreign Service, I was thrilled to be selected to serve as an ambassador, and excited to return to the continent where my career had begun.

Chapter Nine
All in a Diplomat's Life— from Gabon to Albania

I

N AUGUST 1992, I ARRIVED IN LIBREVILLE, the capital of Gabon, as the newly minted ambassador, one of the youngest ever appointed from the career ranks. As honored as I was, it was not lost on me that surviving Baghdad had catapulted me to the head of the ambassadorial line. And if I forgot, my friends in the Foreign Service were quick to remind me what a great career move it had been to be in Iraq during a war. The solicitous concern that I might not survive the experience had given way to good-natured kidding about the career benefits of having lived through it after all.

Gabon is best known internationally as the site of the leper hospital and mission of Nobel Peace Prize winner Albert Schweitzer, in Lamberene. The country sits astride the equator on the west coast of Africa. On the north side of the equator, water goes down the drains counterclockwise; on the south side, clockwise, and on the equator itself, straight down, a phenomenon easily tested by driving just an hour from Libreville. A mere flush of a toilet would tell you which hemisphere you were in—that is, if you could find a proper flush toilet in the lightly populated nation. Gabon has only about a million people in a country the size of Colorado. It has a long coastline along gentle seas and is heavily forested. The climate is tropical, hot, and very humid. Clothes were wet and clinging within minutes of stepping outside. The two seasons are hot and dry and hot and wet, with monsoons dumping huge amounts of water on the country and flooding the streets of Libreville regularly during the rainy season.

Libreville is built on an estuary that serves as the country's principal port, and with a population of over 400,000 people, it is far and away the largest and most important city. The country's wealth comes from its oil production, from logging of its forests, and from some mining. But as a Gabonese once told me, "We live in paradise. If I want food, I put a line in one of our rivers or in the ocean and catch a fish within minutes, or I go into the forest and hunt or trap one of the many species that inhabit it. If I want to drink, I cut into a palm tree and let the juice that drains from it ferment for three days and I have a potent brew. I have no need of elaborate housing in the tropics, and little need of clothes. I don't need to work hard to survive, so why should I?"

Unlike those West Africans who have a long history of trade between and among tribes, Gabonese are from hunting and gathering groups, among whom contact was always difficult, owing to the dense forests. It was not until the opening of the forests to commercial logging during the colonial period in the nineteenth century that the various tribal groups living in what would become Gabon began to know each other. In fact, according to tribal lore, the first marriage between a Fang from the north along the border with Cameroon and a Myene from the southern coast did not take place until 1954, and was still widely spoken about by members of both tribes when I began my tenure in the country.

I first learned about this infamous marriage from a Fang woman at a dinner. She related the tale and concluded with the comment, "We did not understand how one of our sons could marry a woman from a tribe known to be immoral and lazy." She believed that the Myene had been spoiled by more frequent and intimate contact with Euro-

pean colonists, and that a Myene woman would have been less motivated and unable to toil in the fields as well as the tougher Fang ladies.

A couple of weeks later, my dinner partner was a Myene woman
who recounted a similar story. She explained to me that the Myene
were appalled that one of their young ladies could possibly want to
marry into a tribe suspected of practicing cannibalism. "Eaters of
men," she derisively called the Fang.

Listening to these opposite versions of the same event—the
marriage—which had taken place the same year that the Supreme
Court of the United States finally acted to integrate American schools
in the *Brown vs. Board of Education* decision, it struck me that we were
not alone in finding it a lengthy process to overcome blind prejudice.

My orders read that I would serve concomitantly as ambassador
to São Tomé and Príncipe, as well—but without additional compensation, they spelled out—giving me responsibility for American relations with a second African nation, in addition to Gabon.

São Tomé and Príncipe is a single sovereign state that comprises
two main islands and four islets about 120 miles off the coast of Gabon
in the Atlantic Ocean. The islands lie on an alignment of once-active
volcanoes with rugged landscapes, with dense forests, dramatic mountains including volcanic plugs that look like spires rising from the valley
floors, and crystalline coves perfect for snorkeling and skin-diving. The
smallest country in Africa, the population totals about 120,000 people,
with 6,000 of them living on the tiny island of Príncipe.

I only visited Príncipe once—by helicopter, landing in the middle
of the town's soccer field on a rainy day. It was just the second time in
local memory that a helicopter had landed on the island, a moment
that was not to be missed by local residents, the vast majority of
whom swarmed to the field to look at and touch the strange flying
machine that had descended upon them. After my tour of the small
island, I returned to find muddy hand- and footprints all over the
fuselage from those who had touched the machine. Moving them

away before departure was a chore, since there was no understanding of the force or power of the helicopter among a population that was barely familiar with automobiles. Once the craft was fired up and the noisy props were turning, the locals scattered and we were able to lift off. For people who had no experience with such modern vehicles, and who had no television and only intermittent electricity, it was quite an event.

São Tomé and Príncipe was discovered by the Portuguese in the fifteenth century. Over the next three hundred years, African workers were imported, mostly from the Portuguese colonies of Angola and Cape Verde, to labor on the cacao plantations. Cacao beans, the raw material for chocolate, was the big cash crop for several centuries, and the plantation system generated an elaborate social structure. The Portuguese landowners built hospitals, schools, and housing to meet the needs of their indentured farm laborers. By the end of the nineteenth century, São Tomé cacao was the most highly prized and most expensive on the London commodity exchange.

However, early in the twentieth century, a British inquiry had been launched into allegations of slave labor in the São Tomé plantations. By the time the inquiry was completed several years later, the commercial center for cacao had shifted north to Ghana, yielding a fortune for the Ghanaian economy and striking a blow to São Tomé's economy, from which it has yet to recover.

Because of the composition of São Tomé's population, imported from off-island, the traditional African village and tribal structure was not there to provide a safety net in hard times. The society was totally dependent on the plantation owners; when their enterprises failed, there was nothing to turn to. Subsistence farming was unknown on the island, and with no villages to return to and no tribal support to fall back on, workers and their families simply continued to squat on the derelict plantations and eke out an existence with international assistance.

It was the poorest country I had ever visited. People had only rags for clothing, and the telltale signs of malnutrition—bloated stomachs and discolored hair—were everywhere. Yet, for all the hardship they faced daily, crime and violence were very low. The people managed to live peaceably enough, unlike many other countries on the continent where conflict is rampant. As then-President Miguel Trovoada told me, "We understand the need not to resort to violence, because we all have to live here. We have no place to go, surrounded by ocean as we are."

São Tomé and Príncipe became independent from Portugal in July 1975 and was ruled as a one-party state by the longtime leftist leader of the nationalist independence movement, Manuel Pinto Da Costa, until 1991, when the nation's first multiparty elections were held. Miguel Trovoada, who had figured prominently in São Tomé's independence movement in the '60s and '70s, lost out in the internal political struggles that accompanied independence. However, after years in exile in Libreville and Paris, he returned to triumph in the presidential elections of 1991. His election marked one of the first instances of an African country moving successfully from a dictatorship to a democracy.

The Portuguese, as the former colonial power, attempted to maintain their primacy as São Tomé's privileged partner, but the French were aggressively competing for influence. Among other efforts the French were pursuing was the intention to convince São Tomé to adopt the French-backed CFA currency and become part of the CFA monetary zone, a grouping of French Central African countries, all of whom used it. The Portuguese resisted the currency transfer as strenously as they could and were increasingly hostile and resentful of the French encroachment.

One night, at a dinner I attended at the residence of the Portuguese ambassador, on a hill overlooking the city of São Tomé and the bay, this ordinarily extremely courteous and polite man could not contain himself any longer. Over coffee, he began berating the French for what he considered their heavy-handed approach. His attack soon became personal as he singled out the French aid director, who happened to be the brother of the French ambassador to Gabon. The ambassador and his brother were from Corsica, the Portuguese ambassador explained. "We have had experience with Corsicans," he told me, alluding to that most famous of Corsicans, Napoleon Bonaparte, "and we kept him from taking our country then; and, by God, we will keep these Corsicans from taking over our territory here."

The following day, I had lunch with the French aid director to discuss French development programs on the islands. After a typically excellent meal, he leaned back in his chair, lit a strong Gauloise cigarette, and snidely commented: "The Portuguese have this long history with São Tomé, but, frankly, they're just no longer up to the task of providing what's necessary for the country and its people. They should stop fighting history and let us get on with the job." I left, amused by the intensity of the feelings between the two men, stuck on a small island and waging a battle—that nobody in their respective capitals cared about—over influence in one of the world's poorest countries. The relationship between the two men deteriorated to the point where they refused to speak to each other, even refused to attend the same events. Their petty conflicts and bristly egos seemed straight out of a Graham Greene novel.

São Tomé proved to be fertile ground for embassy activities in several important ways. It provided a perfect posting for Peace Corps volunteers, for one. We opened a Peace Corps office and brought about twenty-five volunteers to the islands to work on health, education, and environment projects. The Peace Corps is an ambassador's dream because of the volunteers' impact on the lives of the people in villages where Americans otherwise are rarely seen. Volunteers are the human face of our country and consistently represent our values superbly.

São Tomé also provided us with a perfect location for setting up a Voice of America transmitter station. The United States government long had broadcast to Africa from a relay station located in Monrovia, Liberia. After civil war and chronic instability afflicted that country, we were obliged to move our operations elsewhere. We invested almost $60 million developing and building a station in São Tomé to handle the Voice of America programming. The location was ideal. Broadcasting across the water to the continent gave us far greater range than we had anticipated. The water magnified the radio waves coming across, to the point that we found ourselves in pitched battle with the Vatican's own Africa radio station, as our signal overwhelmed theirs in many countries. Instead of the Holy Father, people heard American pop music, making the Vatican very unhappy. The radio project was so large that the United States became the single largest employer in São Tomé, dwarfing the efforts of the squabbling French and Portuguese.

By contrast to São Tomé, Gabon remained firmly in the French camp, and the French were not going to let anything threaten their position. Gabon, with its oil, gold, and minerals, was a cash cow for the French. Moreover, the Gabonese were inveterate Francophiles. In fact, Gabon had been the only colony that voted to remain part of France in a referendum prior to independence in 1960.

Gabon's oil had long wedded her to the French petroleum company Elf, which was still a French state-run company in the early nineties. (Considering the corrupt entanglement of French and African elections, when suitcases of money might flow north and south across two continents, which I had first observed in the Congo, I was not surprised when Elf's Gabon operations were later implicated in a major financial and political scandal that reached high into the governments of both countries.)

Elf Gabon had established a very tight relationship, an inextricable mix of politics and business, with the republic's president, Omar Bongo. Elf was interwoven in most aspects of life in Gabon. Its money fueled both the economy and the politics of the country, as it did in neighboring Congo.

The French ambassador to Gabon, Louis Dominici, had been there for twelve years when I arrived. Ambassadors from France generally served in Gabon for many years, reflecting the importance of their assignments there as the power behind the throne. Bongo had been personally selected for the presidency by Charles de Gaulle in 1968, and successive French presidents had supported his hold on power. He was their man.

Bongo was also one of the ablest politicians I had known in Africa, and as adept in using the French for his advantage as they were in using him. His personal relations with the French political establishment were legendary, fueled, no doubt, in part by monetary largess but also by a generation of friendship and personal relations. After the return of Jacques Chirac's party to power in the French legislative elections of 1995, I was sitting with Bongo in his ornate presidential office one day overlooking the estuary when he invited me over to his desk, a couple of steps up on a landing. Behind the desk were two doors. Rumor had it that one was an escape route down some hidden corridors to safety, and the other was to a bedroom where he either napped or bedded willing maidens. He was not called the father of his country for nothing.

But this day, he wanted to show me a letter he had sent to his friend "Jacques." After rummaging through a pile of papers, he found the document he was looking for and proudly showed me how he had recommended to Chirac whom he should put in the cabinet of the new French government. "Twelve of those I suggested are now ministers," he announced with satisfaction. Such was the relationship between the two countries.

Bongo was a Bateke tribesman from Franceville, in the Gabonese interior, east of the great forests in a savannah zone. He grew up in Brazzaville in the Congo, which was then the capital of the French Central African colonies. He was recognized early on as being very bright, and the French groomed him from a young age for advanced responsibilities. He moved into positions in the French-run bureaucracy and after Gabon's independence was promoted up the ranks of Gabonese political positions, becoming vice president in 1967. After the death of Gabon's first president, Leon Mba, in 1968, Bongo became president. He was then thirty-three years old. In the decades that followed, he was elected three more times, and would soon be running again.

In his younger days, Bongo had a keen eye for women and an insatiable yen for champagne. His parties at the presidential palace were legendary. He would have all the doors to the palace locked so that none of his guests could leave before he did, which was usually not before three or four o'clock in the morning. This practice proved to be something of an imposition on the stodgy diplomatic set, which generally retires early. One of my predecessors as American ambassador offered me a valuable tip: there was a bathroom on the ground floor with a window that opened up onto the palace garden and was big enough to climb through and escape. He told me about it conspiratorially, as if he had used it many times.

During my tenure, Bongo's parties still ran late, but the doors were no longer locked. As a matter of principle and protocol, though, I would stay until the president left. Most of the other diplomats would leave early, so I was usually among the last of the guests Bongo would see as the party broke up. That helped solidify my reputation as someone who enjoyed the Gabonese and Bongo himself. It helped advance American interests in Gabon, and it drove the French nuts. Frankly, I enjoyed Bongo's parties because they provided an opportunity to socialize with the Gabonese, and I did enjoy him—tremendously.

Bongo and I talked regularly. When I first arrived, we focused principally on bringing more American investment to the petroleum sector in Gabon. We also worked together on the upcoming African, African-American Summit to be convened in Libreville in the middle of 1994. The African, African-American Summit was the brainchild of Philadelphia clergyman and civil rights leader Leon Sullivan, who was best known for having set up guidelines for American companies doing business in South Africa during apartheid. The Sullivan Principles, as they were known, called on corporate America to include social responsibility and human rights in its labor policies by promoting equal opportunity and equal treatment in any country that was discriminating against the majority of its own population. The Sullivan Principles provided a compromise between the absolutist camp that wanted America to disinvest completely in South Africa and the pragmatist camp that wanted to divorce business from politics and human rights.

A larger-than-life man with unbounded self-confidence, Sullivan was a tireless advocate of U.S.–Africa relations. I had first come into contact with his organization in Togo fifteen years earlier and admired his commitment, energy, and creativity. He was a spellbinding orator who could take an audience on a real journey with his use of language. His stem-winding sermons were not to be missed, as once he got on a roll, his orations would be punctuated with regular "amens," "hallelujahs," and exhortations of "praise the Lord" from his rapt listeners.

Once, while I was attending a subsequent summit in Harare, Zimbabwe, I was listening to Leon with an old friend of mine, who'd been an early member of Sullivan's international team. He turned to me and said, "I came just for this. I have a lot to do at home, but I couldn't not come to be with him here, since, after all, without him I would still be on the mean streets of Philadelphia, or dead." That said it all about the tremendous impact of Leon Sullivan on people's lives.

When he came to Libreville for the summit, Sullivan brought with him the luminaries of the American Civil Rights movement, as well as close to 1,200 African-Americans. Many of them were business-people, but most were from African-American churches throughout the United States, visiting Africa for the first time. They were full of goodwill, and thrilled to have a chance to see a part of the continent from which their ancestors had been forcibly removed.

I invited them to attend a reception at the ambassador's residence, and it turned out to be one of the most moving evenings of my life. After having welcomed my guests in a formal receiving line, I wandered among them, making small talk. My stroll eventually took me back to the house, where I stood in the dining room and looked over the balcony into the living room several steps below. In one corner was Coretta Scott King, chatting with Cicely Tyson and Dorothy Height. A bit further along the wall, the head of the Southern Christian Leadership Conference, Reverend Joseph Lowery, was trading jokes with former Secretary of Health and Human Services Louis Sullivan, former U.N. Ambassador Andrew Young, and Jesse Jackson. Some of the most distinguished leaders of perhaps the most important movement since American independence were gathered in my living room.

Assistant Secretary for African Affairs George Moose also attended the summit, lending an even greater American government show of support to the proceedings. There were also eleven African presidents and delegations from many other countries headed by senior ministers. I used the occasion to invite Bongo to my home for a private dinner with Moose on the eve of the opening of the conference. To my surprise and delight, he accepted. Having him in was quite a production, as I soon learned.

The chief of state's visit was preceded by security to check the house and grounds to make sure he'd be safe, protocol to make sure everyone would be seated properly, food tasters to make sure that nobody was going to poison him, and other precautions. No detail could be overlooked, but it was well worth it. Bongo told Moose that it marked the first time in more than twenty-six years in power that he had dined at the residence of an ambassador—from any country. In his toast, Bongo said that he had come not solely to meet the assistant secretary but also "because Wilson and I get along just fine; we have this good working relationship and we are friends."

Our relationship was beginning to bear fruit. American oil companies had shown a renewed interest in Gabon. The International Foundation for Electoral Systems (IFES) had been invited to work with the Gabonese on the planning of the upcoming presidential elections, scheduled for December 1993. Things were moving forward quickly, and this was making French Ambassador Dominici nervous. I spoke French fluently and had been in French-speaking Africa for a long time, so I was not intimidated either by the language or by French attitudes. For his part, Dominici saw our presence as a zero-sum game; he acted as if the U.S. could only make positive progress at the expense of French interests. And he was not going to stand by meekly while inroads were being made in one of the few remaining crown jewels of France's African empire.

At the same time, several other formerly French Central African countries were going through presidential elections. In Cameroon and the Central African Republic, the United States had activist ambassadors committed to seeing that the electoral process was free, fair, and transparent. This meant that the French government's hand-picked candidate did not get a free pass to the palace. In Cameroon, my former boss from Burundi, Frances Cook, was now the ambassador. She was giving the French fits, as it looked like the Anglophone candidate in that bilingual nation might wind up defeating the long-serving President Biya. In the Central African Republic, another colleague of mine, Dan Simpson, to the consternation of the host government, had made himself so popular with the political opposition that when he left the country, the streets were lined with supporters cheering him on his way. Even in Congo, where elections had already resulted in the departure of the French favorite, Sassou Nguesso, his successor, Pascal Lissouba, was actively working against the interests of Elf.

Elections in Gabon came about later than in the neighboring countries, so by the time the Gabonese started planning to hold one, people wondered if Bongo would be able to hold on. The opposition was well organized and had already shown an ability to disrupt things in a series of riots in Libreville and the oil capital along the coast, Port-Gentil.

Apart from the perceived threats to their commercial interests in Africa, which they would defend enthusiastically even though they represented only three percent of France's overall foreign trade, the problem for the French lay in their concern that democratization leads to instability.

It is a legitimate concern, for while the French may embrace democracy as a concept, they do not want to further undermine the fragile security situation in many of the countries where they have important interests. The French have large expatriate populations living in many of these countries who would be endangered by civil unrest. When these societies collapse into strife, the troubles generate refugees, who then cross borders, destabilizing neighboring French-speaking countries; many of the frightened and displaced people may end up in France itself. France also has to deploy troops in the event of instability, as they ultimately did in the Central African Republic and several years later in the Côte d'Ivoire.

The United States, by contrast, has very little at stake in Africa and, as a consequence, has always been more tolerant of disruptions that can occur in the transition to a more open political system. Our efforts might be more successful if we showed more patience and deeper understanding of the consequences of too-rapid change, while at the same time the French would do well to recognize the necessity of replacing dictatorships with more representative governments.

In Gabon, I tried to avoid being associated with any one political faction. From the beginning, I told President Bongo, the French ambassador, and anyone else who would listen that the United States didn't care who won or lost the elections, so long as the process was legitimate and all Gabonese had the opportunity to exercise the franchise.

In the run-up to the election, I began a practice not previously tried in Gabon: I had noticed that there was little social contact among the various political leaders and that in fact they often hardly knew each other. To remedy this, I hosted quarterly dinners attended by the heads of each of the Gabonese political parties—there were twelve of them—to give the leaders a chance to actually talk to each other outside the formal setting of the National Assembly. Parties were either ethnically or geographically based, and there had never been a mechanism for bringing them together informally. I told Bongo what I intended to do, since I knew it would get back to him anyway. Having been informed ahead of time, he would have no reason to be suspicious of my motives.

At the dinners themselves, I would set up three tables with an American at each table. The remaining guests were Gabonese of different political persuasions. I would open the evening with just one ground rule, that there would be no physical violence, pointing out that I was bigger than all of them. That got a laugh and people would begin to relax.

As the evening progressed, the party leaders would open up to each other in new ways. There would inevitably be some time spent talking politics, since that was the one thing they all had in common; then the rest of the evening would be a smorgasbord of interesting topics ranging from discussions about the key role of "magic forests" in specific regions to what the art and sculpture from different parts of the country represented. Magic forests bordered many villages, and were off-limits lest the wandering villagers wanted to risk death at the hands of the spirits who inhabited them. Most carved masks and sculptures were used as fetishes to ward off the evil spirits in traditional and animist ceremonies. I learned all of this, plus much about traditional tribal law and customs. Although the evenings inevitably began stiffly, as they went on the politicians began to relax in the comfortable social setting and learned from each other. They took great delight in comparing their experiences and trading stories.

Unfortunately, the closer we got to the elections, the more paranoid Bongo and his senior political advisors became, as they feared that they might actually be defeated. Dominici decided to capitalize on the concerns in the palace to weaken the relationship between Bongo and me and to reassert French primacy. He not only used his own close relationship with Bongo to undermine me, but he also cleverly planted articles in the Gabonese press to accuse me of actively supporting the opposition, just as his counterparts in the Central African Republic and Cameroon had done to my American colleagues.

Dominici even went after me quite personally, no doubt in the hope of having me expelled from the country. In November 1993, he invited me to breakfast. His house was down next to the beach; mine was up on the hill. Over croissants and strong French coffee, Dominici came to the point. He repeated charges in the local press that an opposition radio station broadcasting hate messages urging Gabonese to attack French citizens was financed and supported by the United States. He said his nationals were increasingly fearful for their security and he urged me to forcefully pressure the station to cease its threatening broadcasts.

In responding to Dominici, I reiterated what I had said quite publicly to Gabonese officials and to the local press: The United States neither financed nor supported the radio station in any way; that we deplored the hate messages as much as the French themselves; and that we told the station's operators of our disapproval at every opportunity.

Moreover, as I had also stated publicly, we did not support the opposition, any more than we supported the incumbent. Our position was clear: we wanted a process that was honest and fair, whoever won or lost.

Dominici observed that whatever the outcome, the constitution permitted only one more term for Bongo. I took his comment to mean that the United States should simply turn a blind eye to Bongo's potential reelection and not worry about a transition to more democratic governance until the completion of his next seven-year term. While it was clear to me that Dominici was warning me off of supporting the opposition, I accepted that his concern about his nationals was genuine. However, Dominici also wrote a report to Paris, later cited in the French weekly magazine *L'Événement du Jeudi,* in which he misrepresented my comments, claiming that I had admitted America was providing support for the incendiary radio station in question.

I must admit that in some respects our own naiveté in dealing with Francophone Africa played into the hands of those who would fear the worst from the U.S. For example, the National Democratic Institute (NDI), a Democratic party foundation dedicated to assisting foreign countries in their democratization efforts, had at one point offered to provide assistance to the Gabonese government as they organized their election procedures. NDI undertook a study to determine whether the system the Gabonese had put in place offered a reasonable chance for free, fair, and transparent elections. If NDI assessed that it had, then it was prepared to send observers to watch the election and ultimately certify it. For a third-world country new to the democracy business, certification of elections by international bodies was important for the credibility of their fledgling process.

Unfortunately, the NDI mission was ill-fated from the start. The team leader for the study was an earnest young man who looked as if he was too young to have voted even once in our own American elections. He might have been twenty-three, but he looked fourteen. When I escorted him to meet with Bongo and the party barons, I felt as if I was feeding chum to a school of sharks.

Politics in Gabon, like most places, is blood sport. It is all about power, not about such niceties as fair outcomes. Who wins is on top, who doesn't is cast out, whether the process is fair or not. NDI was all about creating fairness, but systems that advocate fairness are inevitably trumped by winner-take-all politics unless there is real power behind the former. Unfortunately, this young NDI rep just did not have enough heft to make an impact. Bongo was political down to his very fingertips; neither his friends nor his enemies would dispute that. He knows the Gabonese inside and out, and he knows what to do to get their vote. With all of his experience and his savvy, he was not going to be deterred by this all-American lad.

In addition to the problems stemming from the NDI staffer's lack of seniority, no sooner was the NDI report prepared than it was sabotaged: somebody in the NDI office had leaked an unedited draft to the Gabonese. Among other inappropriate things, it referred to the five-foot, four-inch Bongo as "diminutive" and commented on his "high heel shoes," as if the stature and footwear of the chief of state had any relevance in a report designed to determine whether conditions were propitious for a legitimate election process. The report also described the head of the constitutional court, which is the body that counts and certifies election returns, as Bongo's wife. The head of the court was, in fact, a very accomplished jurist, and although she once may have been a paramour of the president, she was definitely not his wife, as everybody in Gabon knew.

The leaked draft NDI report reinforced the worst fears of the Gabonese about American motives and added fuel to the fire the French were trying to build outside our gates. It confirmed that the Americans obviously wanted Bongo out of office; the French raged, and they held Joe Wilson—who, after all, had escorted the NDI representative in to see Bongo—responsible.

Clearly NDI had disqualified itself and would not be permitted to return to Gabon. Despite this, at the embassy we still wanted to ensure that we had some presence during the electoral process. We were determined to do what we could to stave off what we feared would be the great temptation among all parties to cheat. Before the election, NDI was replaced by the oldest American nongovernmental organization dedicated to promoting relations between the United States and Africa, the Africa-American Institute, which provided a new report and new election observers.

There were three main candidates contesting the election: a Fang candidate from the north, which comprises about 40 to 45 percent of the country's population; Bongo, who represented the southern tribes, about 35 percent of the population; and the candidate of the Myene, along the Gabonese coast. The Myene, who made up close to 20 percent of the electorate, held the swing vote. In the first round of the elections, it was expected that the Myene would mostly vote for their own candidate. The other 80 percent would be nearly equally split, most people figured, with Bongo leading slightly. If no candidate received more than 50 percent of the vote in the first round, the top two vote-getters would go to a second round to determine the new president. The French feared that if Bongo did not win in the first round, the Myene vote would go to his opponent in the second round.

At 11:30 P.M., late on election night, the chief justice of the constitutional court announced that 51.17 percent of the vote had been cast for Omar Bongo. The French and Bongo had decided to short-circuit the process, and he had been reelected in the first round. It was clear to me that the French had decided they could not afford the cost of a second round, either politically or even financially, clearly not wanting to spend any more than necessary on a process the outcome of which had already been rigged. One way or another, Bongo was going to remain president, so why go to the additional expense of a second round if you could simply impose your will after the first? The cynicism was stunning.

The opposition reacted swiftly and violently. Their supporters rioted in the streets, trashing and burning property, overturning cars, particularly those of foreigners, and roughing up the occupants. My residence was located in an opposition stronghold; for months, they had launched their peaceful demonstrations from in front of my house to ensure that I witnessed and reported on them. The post-election demonstrations turned violent and several people were killed, including two just in front of my residence.

Despite the violence, the opposition had no quarrel with me or with Americans. Nor were they attacking known American cars. To better protect ourselves while moving about Libreville I issued small American flags to all Americans to put on their windshields so rioters could identify us. In fact, when the rioters saw the flags, not only would they leave us alone but they often applauded.

That tactic offended Dominici, who complained to Bongo. When the president asked me about the charge, I pointed out that my first concern was the safety and security of the American citizens on Gabonese soil, a concern I was sure he shared. I then told him that if Dominici was worried about his own citizens, Bongo should feel free to tell him that I had plenty of flags left and would be pleased to loan them to him to distribute to his French nationals for their own protection. We shared a laugh at the thought of the French driving around with American flags on their windshields.

Unfortunately, the Gabonese government's response to the riots was aggressive and foolish: the minister of defense, a Bongo cousin, had deployed troops and artillery around that irritant, the opposition radio station, and the leading opposition candidate's house. After a night of heavy shelling, the two structures had been leveled. I strongly protested to Bongo, telling him that if he wanted to close down the radio station or arrest the opposition leader, the proper way to do the job was to send his minister of justice or his attorney general, not the army. "Arrest them if laws have been broken," I said, "don't destroy them."

In the midst of the riots, I awoke one morning to find that the whites of my eyes and my face had turned orange. I had hepatitis A, contracted in São Tomé when I ate undercooked seafood. I had to be evacuated to Paris. Fortunately, the streets had begun to calm down. The press, however, had a field day attacking me as the de facto head of the opposition fomenting the disturbances, now fleeing the country in fear.

I flew to Paris and spent ten days in the hospital and in an apartment recovering. As I was getting off the plane on my return, a young Gabonese steward approached me and handed me a note written on the back of an immigration form. It read: "Speaking for myself and most probably for more than a few, thank you very much for what you are doing for democracy and human rights in Gabon. God bless you." It was one of the most meaningful compliments I have ever received, coming from the heart of a regular citizen, and I keep it still, framed in a place of honor on my desk.

Once back in Libreville, I immediately called on Bongo and brought along a couple of the most egregious newspaper articles so I could confront him with the coverage in what amounted to the state-sanctioned press. I told him that if he wanted to martyr the American ambassador in articles like the ones I had in front of me, that was fine. But he also needed to understand that by so doing he poisoned our relationship, at the same time making me a hero with my own government, able to see through the lies. After reminding him of the times we had spent together, including meals in each other's homes, I said he should know that much of what had been said was patently false and unacceptable among friends. I told him that he had been badly served by his advisers if he believed the lies about me and the United States they were feeding him. This clearing of the air was successful. The articles stopped, and within days a key adviser at the palace had been replaced.

At the Gabonese National Day celebration in August 1994, four months after that meeting with Bongo, I attended the banquet hosted by the president and his wife. At least a thousand Gabonese, the entire political class, were there that evening. Between the main course and dessert, during a lull in the general conversation—so that everyone in the huge room had to notice—Bongo signaled someone on his staff over to the head table and whispered in his ear. As people turned to watch, the man slowly walked around the presidential table and through the guests over to me.

He leaned down and said, "The president would like to see you outside." By this time, all eyes were clapped on us as I followed the messenger back around the banquet hall to the door just behind the president's table that led to an expansive terrace overlooking the estuary.

As I headed outside, I could see Bongo get up to join me. For the next several minutes, Bongo engaged me in small talk before we made our way back into the banquet hall together. He returned to his table and I to mine, but the point had been made and was lost on nobody in the room. The hatchet had been buried.

It was a masterful piece of political theatre, worthy of Machiavelli: attitudes toward the United States and toward me underwent a tectonic shift. Relations between the two of us and, by extension, our two countries were back on track. There were no more negative articles in the press for the remainder of my stay in Gabon. In fact, on the eve of my departure, my journalistic nemesis there, the editor of the government-run newspaper, published a most flattering portrait and interview, noting that I had been decorated with one of the country's highest honors.

My third year in Gabon, after the dramatic tête-à-tête in the presidential gardens, was smooth sailing. Omar Bongo and I worked closely together on the never-ending Angolan peace process, which had become stalled. Despite the withdrawal of foreign forces after Chester Crocker's mediation more than five years earlier, the Angolans were still in the midst of a bloody civil war that seemed to defy solution.

Bongo and I also worked together to pressure President Obiang, of neighboring Equatorial Guinea, to cease his abysmal human rights violations. In the midst of a crackdown on those who opposed his dictatorship, Obiang traveled to Libreville to seek Bongo's counsel. The morning of his arrival, I received a call from one of Bongo's senior advisers, asking if I had any issues I thought the president should raise with his Equatorial Guinean counterpart.

I had plenty of them, I said, most of them dealing with human rights abuses, and I would be delighted to come to President Bongo's office to discuss them directly if he wished. Ten minutes later, the adviser called again, this time to relay an invitation from Bongo for me to speak directly with Obiang when he arrived.

We had an able ambassador, John Bennett, in Malabo, the island capital of Equatorial Guinea, so I hesitated, saying I would have to have permission for any substantive meeting with a president from a country where I was not the ambassador. After receiving approval from the State Department, I agreed to a brief meeting to support the protests that my colleague regularly made to Obiang's government about arbitrary arrests and routine beatings of prisoners. I declined an invitation to dine with the two presidents, pointing out that protesting to Obiang was one thing, breaking bread with him quite another.

Bongo was not to be refused, however, and within minutes I was called again by the military general in charge of presidential protocol. His message was brusque and to the point: I was to be at the president's private home at 8:00 P.M. and I would be dining with the two presidents. Yes, sir.

That evening, the three of us and a junior member of my staff, Greg Thome, met on a patio beside the president's swimming pool. For forty-five minutes before dinner, Bongo and I verbally attacked Obiang for his human rights practices. Bongo was as stern as I was, much to my surprise. He told Obiang, in no uncertain terms, what he needed to do to move the political process in his country through the crisis in which it was then mired. "Appoint a national unity government," Bongo urged. "Bring the opposition into the fold, give them experience in governing and make them stakeholders in the future."

It was vintage Bongo. He had long practice in inclusion as a means of disarming his opposition and ultimately co-opting, another form of dividing and conquering. He was all for democracy, as long as he remained in the presidential palace, above challenge. As we made our way into dinner, he winked at me, pleased with the way the discussion had gone.

Regrettably, Obiang did not heed Bongo's advice, which even came with a healthy dose of financial support. It took Bongo a long time to forgive Obiang. He referred to it often when we met, inevitably shaking his head in disappointment.

Later at dinner, I sat next to Obiang's foreign minister, who railed against Ambassador Bennett. The chief complaint was that John liked to jog through the red-light district in Malabo in the middle of the night, wearing shorts with a pistol tucked in the waistband. While the minister feigned worry about John's security, his comments were clearly designed to smear him. I did not rise to the bait. I told the minister that it sounded rather dangerous to me. After all, what would happen to poor John if the gun went off?

In the middle of 1995, Bongo became mired in something of a sex scandal. He patronized a tailor out of Paris, an Italian named Francesco Smalto, whose high-class clientele included many of the elite in Africa and the Middle East. When Smalto's tailors traveled to measure their clients, they brought more than swatches of fabric with them. Smalto also provided expensive European call girls to his customers.

French authorities had broken up Smalto's prostitution ring in the mid-1990s and were prosecuting. Bongo's name figured most prominently, something he considered to be a racist attack because a number of prominent Arab and North African leaders were implicated as clients as well, though not as publicly. "They go after me because I am a black African," he told me.

When the news of the scandal broke, I immediately called Bongo at home to tell him how sorry I was, as a friend, that this sort of gossip was being given such prominent play in the French newspapers. (It never hurt to get in a dig at the French.) The whole affair, I pointed out to him the next day, gave him good reason hereafter to buy his suits from the United States instead of from disreputable Parisian tailors. Bongo, by then, had recovered his good humor and observed that anybody who knew him understood that he did not like blondes. "Brunettes, oui, blondes, non." Actually, most people who knew him knew that he liked women, period.

By the end of my tour in the middle of 1995, we had had a big impact on Gabon's human rights practices, respect for the rule of law, and despite the fact that the presidential elections had not gone as well as we would have liked, political life in Libreville was lively and even combative, including direct and often vicious criticism of the president and his government.

We had also made considerable progress in creating opportunities for American investors. We were never going to supplant the French, but commercial competition was a good thing—for us, for the Gabonese, and, frankly, for the French themselves. Their interests were too often blinded by the political necessity of pandering to parochial monopolistic interests, which had the result of harming their relationships with countries such as the United States. The Gabonese benefited from having more trade partners, and additional American investment gave us real reason to care about the future of the country and our relations with it.

After the elections, *L'Événement du Jeudi* reported that French President Mitterrand's senior adviser on Africa, Bruno Delaye, and our embassy Africa-watcher in Paris had met to discuss the Dominici allegation and that Delaye was reassured we were not involved with the radio station.

Mitterrand had long taken a keen interest in African affairs: he viewed Africa rather like a fiefdom and worried about American inroads. Still, our Africa-watcher had a good relationship with Delaye, and when the two of them had compared the different versions of the same meeting, Delaye realized that his ambassador had misstated the facts. *L'Événement du Jeudi*, later reported that Dominici traveled to Paris several months after the elections in Gabon to meet with Delaye, only to find himself accused, essentially, of lying. Shortly thereafter, in April 1994, Louis Dominici, the self-described *"grand ambassadeur,"* received his onward assignment. After a dozen years in Gabon, a plum posting for senior French diplomats, he was dispatched to Tirana, Albania.

I could not have been more pleased, after all the dirty tricks Dominici had played at my expense. I called Washington to report the welcome news and spoke slowly so the French intelligence services that routinely tapped our telephone lines would transcribe every word and, I hoped, share them with Dominici. After all, I did so want him to know how pleased I was that he was being sent to a country with which the United States and much of the Western world had had no diplomatic relationship for close to forty years.

Over the years, I have noticed that most people outside the diplomatic trade think of ambassadors as genteel and urbane government functionaries. But, in fact, we are capable of being extremely protective of our national and personal interests, fierce when we see them under threat, and savoring of victory when we best a rival in another embassy. In short, we are as human as the next guy.

I left Africa doubting that I would ever return to live there again. I had no intention of remaining in the Foreign Service any longer than necessary to qualify for my retirement, which was just a few years off. There were other things I wanted to do in life, and I had already accomplished far more than I had ever expected I would in my diplomatic career. For the remaining years before my retirement,

I was going to look for new and different experiences. I had done
my time in embassies, in jobs from the lowest of the low to the
highest. I had been in hot wars and I had fought the Cold War where
that war was hot, in Africa, and where the adversary often spoke
French, not Russian. I had the diplomatic scars on my back to show
for it. But at least I had never been posted to Tirana, Albania, not
yet anyway.

Chapter Ten
Diplomats and Generals

AMBASSADORIAL TOURS ARE LIMITED to three years except on rare occasions, and as much as I might have wanted to stay in Libreville for another year or two, my time there was drawing to a close. It was a pity, as I would have enjoyed more time among the Gabonese, especially because they had finally accepted me into their world.

A reserved people, the Gabonese are wary of foreigners and somewhat aloof. Therefore, my last year there was a breakthrough, as Gabonese from all social and political strata—for whom it is a highly unusual sign of friendship to invite a foreigner into their homes—frequently invited me into theirs. I found myself at weddings, funerals, and intimate gatherings, dining on traditional Gabonese food, and meeting family and friends. It was a welcome conclusion to a fascinating experience with a society that was in the throes of a transition from the traditional to the modern and from a tribal political structure, with its chiefs, to a more representative system including governmental checks and balances.

For all the problems and the irregularities in the presidential election of 1993, which the French had shuttered prematurely, the Gabonese had made considerable progress. Omar Bongo was largely benign in his despotism, tolerating opposition, criticism, and even satire that was quite insulting. There was enough liquidity in the political system from the oil revenues to grease the process and ensure that the fights did not spill out into the streets, except at election time. Bongo was a master at co-opting his opposition—his principal presidential opponent, whose home had been leveled by artillery shells in 1993, was elected, with Bongo's tacit support, as the mayor of Libreville less than two years later.

Since the United States Congress passed the Goldwater-Nichols Defense Reorganization Act in 1986, the American military has been organized into two sorts of commands, regional and functional, resulting in closer cooperation among the services and delegation of considerable authority to the commanders in chief (CINC) of the commands. The European Command, created in the aftermath of World War II to defend Western Europe from attack by the Warsaw Pact countries, is the granddaddy of these commands. The CINC of European Command also serves as the NATO supreme commander, a position first held by General Dwight D. Eisenhower from 1951 until he ran for president the following year.

Each of the five geographic CINCs has a political adviser, normally appointed from among the ranks of former ambassadors. The European Command (EUCOM) is also responsible for U.S. military relations with ninety-three countries from eastern Europe to South Africa, including southern Europe and stretching as far east as Israel. The political adviser position was a good fit for my background and experience, and I was keenly interested in it. I had long been involved in the role of the military in the conduct of our diplomacy, not just from experiences in the Angolan peace process and the Gulf War, but also because few embassies in Africa are assigned military attachés and therefore must manage the military programs on their own. Typically, these programs include training for foreign soldiers, both in Africa and at military bases in the United States; exercises with American troops in the country; and sales of arms and equipment. I had been responsible for these activities in Burundi and in the Congo and had enjoyed the interaction with our armed services.

I had found that the young men and women who commit themselves to taking up arms to defend our country merit all the support and plaudits that we can possibly bestow on them. They are dedicated, well-trained, responsible individuals who work well in teams and larger organizational units. The leadership has improved steadily over the years, and the cohesion and unity of purpose has made for a military force that is lethal when deployed.

Watching the actions of the U.S. military from the embassy in Baghdad as our troops deployed from Europe to fight the first Gulf War, I found their presence reassuring, as I had to remain tough with the Iraqis. (It is always easier to be tough when you have a big gun right behind you.) I also had visited their headquarters in Stuttgart several times over the years for meetings and was fascinated by the breadth of responsibilities and by the nature of the military enterprise. I applied for the political adviser position, and after a telephone interview with the deputy commander in chief (DCINC), Air Force four-star General Jim Jamerson, I was selected.

I arrived at the headquarters of the European Command just outside Stuttgart, Germany, in September 1995, no longer a sitting ambassador but still with the title, along with the protocol rank of a three-star general as the senior civilian officer in the command. The CINC, who is also the NATO commander, normally resides in Mons, Belgium, where he manages the international command. His deputy, Jamerson, resided in Stuttgart, and had day-to-day charge of the command when Joulwan was not present.

Joulwan was one of the army's most experienced "warrior diplomats," brimming with command presence and a master of the evocative sound bite. "One team, one fight" was his motto for a military action,

"One team, one mission" for less violent activities. He was gregarious but somewhat imperious, and could be quite demanding. He was also driven, his airplane as much an office and a residence as his headquarters in Mons. He was always in transit, moving among centers of military activity and capitals in Europe and Washington.

Having served two combat tours in Vietnam, he was part of the generation that rebuilt the army after the divisive Southeast Asian war. He had spent a large part of his career in Europe and was the first NATO commander ever to have served at every level in the alliance. He was serving in Germany when the Berlin Wall was built, and again when it came down. His previous Washington assignments had included a stint as deputy chief of staff to Alexander Haig at the White House in the days of Watergate, so he was familiar with the political wars waged on the banks of the Potomac. For all of General Joulwan's military bravura, he was an effective leader and motivator, and he made great leaps in forging operating relationships with international and nongovernmental organizations that would become important as we deployed international troops into Bosnia and, later, Kosovo.

Jim Jamerson, his deputy, was the perfect foil for Joulwan's hard-charging and sometimes prickly personality. A southerner from North Carolina, he masked a sharp intellect and penchant for excellence beneath a relaxed, self-effacing exterior and good ol' boy drawl. He was unfailingly supportive of his troops, had the patience of Job, and kept all the elements in the command moving in the same direction, not an easy task in an organization that includes officers from each of the four branches of the armed forces.

The "joint" command, as it is called, is an outgrowth of the Goldwater-Nichols Act's goal of integrating the military leadership of the services to produce more operational coordination and, by extension, more effective war-making. The results were evident as early as the first Gulf War. Jim had spent a number of years working in joint commands

Mallorca, Spain, 1966. I'm sixteen years old, sitting on the wall in front of our home with the Mediterranean Sea in the background. My parents were journalists who covered cultural topics in Europe for the King Features Syndicate, the *San Francisco Chronicle* and the *International Herald Tribune*.

My first diplomatic position was from 1976 to 1978 in Niger, the desert country in West Africa. This posting launched my lifelong love affair with the whole continent—its peoples, its magnificent landscapes, and its abundant wildlife. On this and the following four pages are photographs from that time in my life.

A baboon in a tree in W Park, Niger. The park takes its name from the bends in the Niger River which runs through it.

African antelope in W Park. The park is bordered by Niger, Benin, and Burkina Faso (then known as Upper Volta).

A Tuareg nomad, majestic on his camel as he observes the campsite that my wife Susan and I had made in the countryside between Niger's capital Niamey and its northern city, Agadez.

Two Nigerien women, as elegant and proud as they are poor.

The mosque in Agadez is a fascinating structure that dates back to the sixteenth century. It is constructed of adobe and timber.

A Nigerien man butchering a sheep for mechouis, the Nigerien version of a communal barbecue.

Nigerien children playing by an adobe wall. Children are ubiquitous in this high-birth-rate country and, like kids everywhere, curious about foreigners.

I'm grinning after a great day of hiking in W Park.

Giraffe in game park in Kenya, 1977.

Unlike Niger, Burundi has deep forests. I saw this Burundian man walking in one in 1984.

For Joe Wilson, a great friend and co-worker; Thanks for a job well done.

In 1985 I worked as a Congressional Fellow on agricultural issues in Al Gore's office. I found him a down-to-earth representative for the people. In 1990 I spoke with him from Baghdad while he took a break in the Senate cloakroom and solicited my views during the debate on the use-of-force resolution prior to the launching of Desert Storm. I told him that I did not believe sanctions alone would drive Saddam from Kuwait.

Majority Whip Tom Foley was my other boss during my Congressional Fellowship. Here, on the floor of the House of Representatives on July 4, 1986, Tom opened the doors of the House chamber and hosted Joe and Sabrina, my twins, then seven, after we had watched Independence Day fireworks from the balcony of the Capitol.

Paris, 1986. Even though I've never had a chance to serve there, I always love to visit the City of Light.

The Champs Élysées, July 14, 1987. My twins, Joe and Sabrina, wanted a better view of the Bastille Day parade. A father can only indulge his children.

Senator Richard Shelby (seen here holding hands with Saddam Hussein) and Senator Arlen Spector, December 1988. To my right is Nancy Johnson, the embassy political officer. To Senator Spector's left are two senate staffers. The senators came to see whether there was a possible positive role for Saddam to play in the Middle East Peace Process. They were ultimately disappointed.

On August 6, 1990, four days after Iraq invaded Kuwait, I met with Saddam Hussein. He wanted to find out if he could keep Kuwait in exchange for oil at a cheap price. I told him to get out of Kuwait immediately.

Saddam's business card was sent to me with pictures from our August 6 meeting. It was a strange courtesy from a ruthless dictator's government. The card reads "Saddam Hussein, President of the Republic of Iraq."

The Oval Office, January 14, 1991. Just back from Baghdad, meeting my commander-in-chief. He welcomed me with kind words and gratifying praise.

1-30-91

THE PRESIDENT

Dear Joe —
Both Barbara & I appreciated your note of Jan 25. Even more we appreciate your service to your country *and* your courageous leadership when you were in Baghdad.
Good Luck.
Many Thanks.
Gg Bush

When I received this personal note from President George H. W. Bush, I was honored that with everything else he had to deal with then he took the time to write me. It was in character for a thoughtful man.

The Rose Garden, the White House, Washington, January 14 1991. Thirty-six hours before the launching of Desert Storm, President Bush is asking me the most humane of questions about Baghdad and the Iraqi people, exactly the questions I would want a president to ponder before a war.

To Joe Wilson —
With Respect & Best Wishes
Gg Bush

To Joe Wilson with deep appreciation for your outstanding service to the nation—and with warmest personal regards Jim Baker

The Oval Office, January 14, 1991. Secretary of State James Baker and I are talking about how I felt finally being out of Baghdad, something he had worried would never happen. I'm pretty happy—and so is he, judging from his smile.

[above left] A year after President Bush appointed me Ambassador to Gabon and Sâo Tomé and Príncipe in 1992, Joe and Sabrina came to visit me there. Here we're at the home of President Miguel Trovoada. [above right] In the jungles of Gabon, the bridges across the swift rivers are often made of vines and rope woven together.

After presenting my letters of credentials to the president of Gabon, Omar Bongo, in the capital, Libreville, the two of us engaged in a brief chat.

I am with Jesse Jackson and Leon Sullivan at my residence in Libreville, Gabon, in 1993, during a reception for the participants in the African African-American Summit. Many of the most important figures of the Civil Rights movement came for the summit, where Sullivan, one of the greatest orators of his generation, gave a spellbinding address.

To Joe Wilson,
    With Best Wishes   Bill Clinton

The Oval Office, 1997, meeting President Clinton for the first
time, as Sandy Berger looks on. Al Gore helped break the ice at
this first meeting. In the background are Tom Pickering, the
under secretary of state for political affairs (left, facing camera),
and Leon Fuerth, the vice president's national security adviser.

The Oval Office, 1997. I am briefing President Clinton for a
meeting with the Malian president, Alpha Oumar Konare, while
Susan Rice, the assistant secretary of state for Africa, and Jim
Steinberg, the deputy national security adviser look on. Sandy
Berger, the national security adviser is checking his notes. In the
background near the windows, Leon Fuerth and Strobe Talbott
(right), deputy secretary of state, are chatting.

A personal note from President Clinton,
written the day his impeachment trial
opened in the Senate. Judging by the last
sentence about Africa, he probably would
have liked to be as far away from
Washington as possible at that moment.

I am talking with Denis Sassou Nguesso, president of the
Congo, and two of his government ministers at a luncheon in
Washington, D.C., in 2002.

I am sitting with Senegalese President Abdou Diouf, in Dakar in
2000. He is telling the local press, out of camera shot, that he cred-
ited me with bringing the president of the United States to Africa.

I am making a point to Tim Russert during my appearance on *Meet the Press,* October 5, 2003. Earlier, on July 6, I had defended my *New York Times* article "What I Didn't Find in Africa" on the NBC show when Andrea Mitchell was the guest host. The second time I was defending myself and my wife. The second picture [below], of Tim and me, commemorates the later event.

To Joe Wilson — Thanks for sharing your views on MTP! Tim Russert

As an early observance of Halloween, a month before the holiday, a clever cartoonist satirized the outing of my wife. It provided one of the humorous moments during this period. (By permission of Mike Luckovich and Creators Syndicate, Inc.)

and was adept at integrating the separate parts into a coherent package. He was adored by the people who worked for him—in two years, I never heard anything other than effusive praise and affection directed toward him—and he enjoyed the confidence of his peers. He was often called upon to mediate disputes and personality conflicts between Joulwan and some of his component commanders—all very forceful personalities. Jim would listen politely while the officers were venting and inevitably send them on their way feeling better about their relations with the CINC.

I lived on the base in Stuttgart, in senior officer housing on "Geriatric Row," so named by the younger staff because only generals and senior colonels lived there. White hair and wrinkles were a prerequisite. For somebody like me, who had spent most of his adult life living with foreigners, living in an enclave with several thousand Americans was a new and different experience. There was the post supermarket, the PX, a bowling alley, and a pizza joint, as well as a high school and gym and all the usual amenities of a small town. The Germans—after all, we were in Germany—were on the other side of the fence, but you could spend your entire tour inside the enclave without ever venturing beyond it if you chose. To leave and return, senior officers had a laminated card tucked in the sun visor of their cars with their rank in stars printed on it. On approach to the guard post, you would pull down the visor, alerting the soldier standing watch of your rank. He would see the stars and snap to attention, waving the officer through with a salute. My old college friend Bob Moore, who had been with me in the hospital when my first wife, Susan, had been so near death in 1979, came to visit and found that respect to be the most impressive testament of anything I had yet accomplished in my career.

Since the command was responsible for so many countries, most of the senior officers were on the road a lot, myself included. The first trip I made with Jamerson was to Turkey and northern Iraq in the fall of 1995 to review Operation Provide Comfort, the U.S.-U.K.-Turkish action to defend the Kurds against potential Iraqi attacks and to enforce the no-fly zone in northern Iraq.

Our air force planes flew out of a base in Incirlik, Turkey, near Adana, in the south-central part of the country. The cooperation of the Turks was essential to the success of the mission, and it was not won easily. Careful management of our relations with this secular Muslim country was essential at every level of the command and the embassy. We traveled there often and had the Turkish general staff to our headquarters many times.

After meetings at the air force base in Incirlik, we continued on to the Iraqi town of Zakho, just across the border, to see our Special Forces who were based there to support the Kurds. Jim had set up Operation Provide Comfort just after the Gulf War, when the Kurds were fleeing Saddam's crushing counterattack against their rebellion, and became the mission's first commander. He was greeted on his return by the Kurdish fighters, called the Peshmerga, who were working with our troops, like a long-lost family member. The American general who had done so much to protect and defend the Kurds when they were under attack had returned, accompanied by the American diplomat who had gone head-to-head with Saddam in Baghdad half a decade before. It was a veritable reunion.

I knew that within hours, Saddam would be informed that Jim and I were back in his country, and I hoped it made him uneasy.

Zakho is a dusty market town, inhabited largely by Kurds, on the plain just to the north of the mountains that form the heartland of the Kurdish region in northern Iraq. It benefits from the trade that has flowed back and forth across the border for millennia. Markets were full of goods of all sorts, and the townspeople appeared prosperous. This was not surprising, since they controlled one of the principal routes for supplies going from Turkey to Baghdad and for the oil being sent north across the border in the hundreds of tanker trucks that snaked up the principal north–south artery from the oilfields near Kirkuk. Sanctions against Iraq had translated into premiums to be paid to border guards who would look the other way.

We spent a day in meetings and touring with the troops before returning to our base in Incirlik for the night, helicoptering and later flying in the back of a cargo plane over sparsely populated southern Turkey. The next day was spent in tough negotiations with the Turkish general staff. The Turks were uncomfortable with our aggressive enforcement actions against Iraq. The rules of engagement for American pilots allowed them to take retaliatory action whenever Iraqi radar locked on to their planes, even if the Iraqis did not actually fire on them. This was excessive, argued the Turkish military, sensitive to repercussions later as a consequence of bombs dropped on Iraq from planes launched from Turkish territory. We would leave Turkey someday, but Turkey would always have to live next door to Iraq.

In a toast at the dinner to close our discussions, General Cevik Bir, the Turkish deputy chief of staff, pointed out how Turkey was in a tough neighborhood, surrounded by hostile countries. Among all its neighbors, he said, Turkey's relations with Iraq were the best. My initial reaction to Bir's comments was that Turkey's diplomats and politicians needed to work harder in the region if Iraq was truly their best friend among all their neighbors.

Bir's point, however, was that our hard-line position was complicating Turkey's relations with a country that it did not believe posed a significant threat to it. Left unsaid were revenues lost to Turkey because of the sanctions, as well as Turkish concerns that our protection of the Kurds would lead to a resurgence of Kurdish independence ambitions that might spread to Turkey's own Kurdish population and further fuel the terrorism that had afflicted southern Turkey for years.

Throughout the two years I was at European Command, our relations with the Turkish military needed constant attention. Jim

Jamerson was on the phone several times a week with the U.S. ambassador to Turkey, Marc Grossman, working on the most trivial details. American complaints of Turkish interference with operations in Incirlik never ceased. For all that, however, Provide Comfort, which was later renamed Operation Northern Watch, continued to function up to the second Gulf War in 2003, interdicting Iraqi use of its own airspace and regularly destroying antiaircraft batteries when their crews made the mistake of turning on their radar.

Shortly thereafter, in January 1996, Jim and I made our first voyage to Africa together. This was Jim's first time south of the Sahara desert. One of our stops was Luanda, Angola. The United States was still trying to broker a peace agreement in the continuing Angolan civil war and had begun working with the United Nations and its representative in Luanda, former Malian Foreign Minister Alioune Blondin Beye. We went to Luanda to support a renewed effort at confidence building between the government and the rebel movement, UNITA. Madeleine Albright, the U.S. ambassador to the United Nations, and J. Brian Atwood, the USAID director, had already been there to work on diplomatic and assistance-related issues. Our task was to meet with the Angolan military and defense establishment. Accompanying us on the trip was the State Department's deputy assistant secretary of state for Africa, Ambassador Bill Twaddell, an old friend who had served in several African posts, including Mozambique, Mauritania, and Liberia.

As soon as we arrived, we also met with the U.S. ambassador to Angola, Don Steinberg, who had spent several tours in Africa before his assignment in Angola, and with President Clinton's special envoy to the Angolan peace process, wizened veteran diplomat Ambassador Paul Hare. Hare, white-haired, wrinkled, and always in threadbare clothes with a cigarette dangling from his lips, was the perfect choice to be the itinerant ambassador to the process. He was utterly without pretension and displayed both the patience needed to deal with the recalcitrant parties and a mastery of understatement when negotiating with the huge egos of the protagonists. Paul had been a close adviser to Chester Crocker in the eighties and had gone on to serve as ambassador to Zambia. While in Zambia, he had been one of Crocker's emissaries to the Angolans at the same time our embassy was working on the issue from Brazzaville, Congo, in 1987. We also crossed paths later when he was serving as a deputy assistant secretary for the Middle East and I was in Baghdad.

Twaddell, Hare, Steinberg, and I were able to give General Jamerson a thorough and candid briefing on the state of the ongoing hostilities, a decade after I had first become involved in the negotiations to get South Africa and Cuba out of the middle of the war. In short, in Luanda Jamerson was surrounded by experienced people who had devoted large chunks of their careers to representing American interests in Africa and, more specifically, to the resolution of the intractable Angolan war. Despite all of our efforts over three decades, the war just would not be over until the death of Jonas Savimbi, as he was never going to make peace with the Angolan government. However attractive the rest of the terms offered to him, unless he was going to be president of the country, he would not be satisfied. Whatever peace deal was negotiated, he was sure to break it, sure to find another sponsor who'd trade diamonds for guns.

Our 1996 stop in Luanda coincided with a delicate moment in the negotiations. The Angolans had tiptoed up to a rapprochement in the early nineties, culminating in a 1992 election that included candidates from Savimbi's UNITA movement. Immediately after the elections, however, in which UNITA fared poorly, violence broke out again and Savimbi fled back to the bush, from which he relaunched the civil war. After protracted negotiations, a tentative agreement had been reached to try again to integrate UNITA into the political process. Several senior officials from the movement's political arm took up residence in Luanda in late 1995, even as the war continued to rage in the countryside. They were very nervous about their security, and their concerns were probably justified.

After the failed elections in 1992, several UNITA officials had been killed in government attacks inside the capital. When we met with them, their only concern was for their personal safety; political agendas were secondary. Over the next two years, so much progress would be made in Luanda that those concerns would fade and be replaced by discussions about how to manage a filibuster and, as a member of the minority, how to block the majority from imposing its will on the whole country. But in our meetings on this first trip with Jamerson, we spent most of our time listening to pleas for bodyguards and for concrete assurances from the government that they would not kill those few UNITA politicos who had been designated by Savimbi to live among the enemy.

Jamerson was a quick study and had mastered the issues before confronting the foreign generals. His meetings with them were extraordinarily positive. This was no small feat, since the Angolan senior military suffered from an excess of hubris gained not from battlefield prowess but rather, like Savimbi, from its involvement in the illicit diamond trade. Profits from this activity had both enriched and corrupted them to the point that any cessation of the war might well dry up this lucrative revenue stream and would therefore be opposed. War had become good business for those who were waging it—on both sides.

On the return flight north, we stopped in Abidjan, Cote d'Ivoire, to refuel, and took the occasion to meet with one of our most senior ambassadors, Lannon Walker, who was a legend in our little world. Brilliant, articulate, and headstrong, his swashbuckling style was a throwback to a different era, and he often landed in trouble with a State Department that had become more and more bureaucratic over the course of his many years of service.

That did not lead to any change in his style, however, as he

assumed that he could prevail in any altercation with the bureaucracy—
and he generally did. A colleague had once affectionately described
Lannon as a snake-oil salesman, able to sell ice boxes to Eskimos. He
spoke as much with his hands as with his mouth, gesturing repeatedly
to punctuate the complex pictures he would draw with his words. He
was seductively engaging and as meticulous about his personal
appearance as he was flamboyant, sporting an Errol Flynn mustache.
With his French artist wife, he cut quite a figure, so Bill Twaddell and
I thought it was a good idea to brief Jamerson on the personage he
was about to meet.

Lannon lived up to our billing of him, wooing Jim with his tales
and his analysis of the situation in Cote d'Ivoire. In less than half an
hour, he had pitched several training and equipment programs he
wanted EUCOM to undertake immediately. It was a vintage performance; by the time we got back on our airplane, less than two hours
later, Jim's head was swimming. But he was laughing heartily. He
turned to Bill and me and said simply: "You fellas sure had him
pegged." It was the big breakthrough. Jim had spent a week in sub-
Saharan Africa, had met some of the Foreign Service's most distinguished Africanists, and now had conveyed with a brief remark that
since there was much to be done by the command in Africa, he was
willing to trust those of us who had spent so much of our careers on
the continent.

It was a timely recognition of the importance of the continent to
the command. We deployed troops there several times in the next two
years on training exercises, to evacuate foreigners from Sierra Leone
and the Central African Republic, and to protect our embassy in
Liberia. The command developed new ways of working with African
national militaries, as well as encouraging them to work together in a
set of newly conceived training events.

Traditionally, the joint training of American and African troops
was conducted bilaterally. It was generally successful but was limited

to just the two countries. On one occasion, Jim and I were visiting our troops on maneuvers with Malian forces. A U.S. Army master sergeant told us that coming to Mali was the highlight of his outfit's training because of the chance they had to live and work for a while in such a hospitable country. He mentioned, however, they had also enjoyed a real professional benefit. "We deployed last year to Haiti," he told Jamerson, "and one day on patrol we came around a corner and ran into these troops from Mali who we recognized immediately from our having trained together the previous spring. That relationship carried over to the deployment, and we found that we were able to integrate seamlessly because of that earlier training together. Too bad we couldn't do that with every military we had to coordinate with there."

That one comment gave Jim a new insight. If training with African militaries made later deployments with them easier, then we should train more often with them, and we should encourage them to train jointly with one another, as well as with the U.S., in multilateral exercises. We called our new effort the Flintlock program and began to plan for future exercises.

At about the same time, Washington, and especially the dynamic senior director for Africa at the National Security Council, Susan Rice, was launching what came to be called the African Crisis Response Initiative (ACRI). In the aftermath of the genocide in Rwanda in 1994, the world groped for a mechanism to respond to such tragic situations before they could spin so badly out of control. Rwanda is a tiny nation in the mountains of central Africa, next door to Burundi and with the same Hutu and Tutsi ethnic mix (85 percent and 14 percent). As in Burundi, the two tribes have engaged in horrific bloodletting periodically over the years. In 1994, the increasingly beleaguered president of Rwanda, Juvenal Habyarimana, was assassinated when his airplane was shot down as it was landing at the capital's airport. The assassination touched off a round of brutal killings that consumed 800,000 human beings, many of them women and children, within four months.

The ACRI was designed to develop a cadre of African forces to respond more quickly to such crises, without the delay inherent in raising troops under the U.N. flag. The new Flintlock military exercise program dovetailed perfectly with what Washington was promoting in Africa and among countries like France that have historic ties on the continent. We were able to complement diplomatic efforts designed to foster support for the new program with concrete activities that benefited African militaries. We traveled throughout Africa, enlisting partners in this new initiative, and were largely successful after overcoming initial concerns about our motives.

Jamerson and I also made several visits to New York to meet with the U.N. Peacekeeping Operation, as we sought to harmonize what the U.S. was doing with what the U.N. had already accomplished. Our objective was to shape an initiative that reflected and satisfied the U.N. and ourselves, avoiding, as much as possible, duplication and inefficiency. Above all, my colleagues and I wanted to ensure that the programs and procedures in our initiative were technically and philosophically consistent with those that the U.N. Peacekeeping Operation might apply on their entry into a crisis.

The potential benefits of this program were clear. The U.S. military would be able to mobilize willing partners more quickly in the event of a crisis, and those forces would be better trained and more quickly able to operate together as a combined force. Pressure on the United States to provide all the troops in these dangerous situations would ease as we could enlist others to put their boots on the ground and our commitment could be limited to our areas of particular expertise: logistical support, command and control, and intelligence.

By the time I left EUCOM in 1997, Jim had succeeded in making Africa a key priority for the command. He did so partly out of necessity, because of the frequent emergency interventions that were required, but also because he realized that the time had long since passed for the unique focus of the command to be the defense of the Fulda Gap, the land corridor that is the shortest route from East Germany to the Rhine. The Berlin Wall had fallen seven years earlier; future threats and activities would emanate from elsewhere, and the command needed to be much smarter about the rest of its theater of concern.

When I first arrived in Stuttgart, the Africa planning office had been a small, dispirited, and demoralized graveyard for military officers. When I left, they were stars, traveling with General Jamerson every couple of months to different parts of African and coming up with innovative plans and new programs that they were able to brief directly to John Shalikashvili, the chairman of the Joint Chiefs of Staff, and to the secretary of defense, William Perry. When Jamerson and I were not traveling to Africa ourselves, other senior generals went, as Africa became the place everybody wanted to go. General Joe Ralston, the vice chairman of the Joint Chiefs, put it best when he called Jim "The King of Africa."

Part and parcel of working with the Africans was engaging their traditional partners in Europe. At the time, France was moving to reintegrate itself into the NATO military command from which it had withdrawn some thirty years earlier when Charles de Gaulle was president. De Gaulle's insistence on being independent of both the United States and the USSR at the height of the Cold War, while consistent with France's explicit objective of leveraging its influence over larger powers, was seen as an act of betrayal of the Western alliance. Accordingly, when France wanted back into NATO, there was considerable suspicion about its motives and resistance to many of its demands for command roles within the military command. Jim and I felt that there were areas in which we could benefit by closer collaboration outside NATO's area of responsibilities, so we traveled to Paris to explore new avenues of cooperation with our French counterparts.

After a successful set of meetings, including a wonderful lunch at the home of the head of the French armed forces, air force General Jean-Philippe Douin, looking out on the Eiffel Tower, I was deputized to pursue discussions on how we might deepen our contacts, develop new intelligence-sharing procedures, and undertake some planning exercises together. After years in the Foreign Service, still pining for a Parisian assignment following that near-miss in 1988 when I was instead assigned to Iraq, I was delighted to finally have a chance to be in Paris for my work, even if I wasn't actually living there. I traveled there regularly with a military team while we put mechanisms into place that would serve us well in Africa, where the French had bases and a long history of involvement. We hoped that our successful efforts together in Africa might ease the tension in other areas, such as France's reintegration into NATO.

Generally, professional military officers of different nationalities relate to each other very well, and it was no different with the French. They shared with the American officer corps a sense of professional fraternity that transcended political differences. They were task-oriented and operated on pragmatic principles comparable to those of U.S. officers. On the other hand, many professionals in the French ministry of foreign affairs, just as in the U.S. State Department, seemed to relish an atmosphere of intrigue, even though it bred petty jealousies and pointless rivalries. Then there was the plain speech of the military people I was working with; it differed significantly in style from the diplomatic politesse I was accustomed to hearing. Despite my own two decades in diplomacy, I found it considerably easier to deal with the French military than with the French foreign ministry. The French generals, for their part, came to have confidence in me, certainly not because I came out of the diplomatic caste but because I spoke good French and had served many years in a number of French-speaking African countries.

The mechanisms we had jointly put into place started bearing fruit immediately, when the Zairian war broke out, bringing longtime rebel figure Laurent Kabila to power in May 1997. For thirty years, Kabila had been operating out of the hills of eastern Zaire, near Lake Tanganyika and the Burundi border. He was noted mostly for gold smuggling and other illegal activities that financed his quest to overthrow Zaire's long-serving dictator, Mobutu Sese Seko. Kabila had been responsible for the kidnapping of several American primate researchers from Jane Goodall's Tanzanian game reserve in the early seventies. Rwandan Vice President Paul Kagame, the real power in his country, now took Kabila under his wing and used him as an instrument to depose Mobuto.

Kagame, a member of the minority Tutsi tribe, had commanded the rebel force that finally defeated the Hutu government in 1994. Since Tutsis number only 14 percent of the population to the Hutus' 85 percent, he installed a Hutu as a figurehead president while he ran the government and the military from his vice president post. In the aftermath of the 1994 genocide, a flood of Rwandan refugees fled to neighboring Zaire, living in camps close to the Zaire–Rwanda border. There were regular cross-border shellings and attacks into Rwanda from the area near the refugee camps, and Kagame accused Mobuto of using the refugee camps to destabilize his regime.

Jim and I met with Kagame in early 1996, after first visiting an old school building that had served as a genocide execution site, an hour outside of Rwanda's capital, Kigali. The Rwandans had exhumed the bodies of the 25,000 people who had perished there, and we walked among the lime-covered corpses to bear witness to the carnage. The stench was only partly cut by the lime, and the violent deaths the victims had suffered were evident in the wounds we could see on the bodies—severed limbs, bullet holes in skulls. When we met after our mournful tour of the schoolyard, he made it clear to us that he would no longer tolerate the cross-border attacks from those who had earlier committed atrocities. If the U.N., under whose auspices the refugee camps existed, did not move the camps further into Zaire and away from his border, he would do so himself. Several months later, he did just that, and more, using Kabila as his instrument and supporting him with Rwandan forces and advisors, as Kabila swept across Zaire, a vast country the size of the United States east of the Mississippi. The offensive also led to the Rwandans destroying the refugee camps and driving tens of thousands of refugees deeper into the forests of eastern Zaire, to an almost-certain death.

At EUCOM we quickly mobilized security assets to monitor these events and began to plan a military operation to stabilize the situation. We activated the new liason and joint planning arrangements we had put in place with the French, which allowed us to share not just the conclusions our analysts had reached on the numbers of refugees involved but also the way we had reached those conclusions. Though we still had serious differences over how many refugees were at risk, we had narrowed them down, even as French and American politicians continued to squabble publicly.

In late November, the command hosted a planning conference for the purposes of assembling a coalition of the willing, under the command of a Canadian general, to deploy a force into eastern Zaire. The goal was to stabilize the situation and stop the violence that was devastating the refugee population, by now dispersed into the forests and reduced to foraging for food and shelter, at the mercy of the local hostile population. The military planning was straightforward. Our command had already set up a number of forward bases in eastern Africa to facilitate the flow of troops in the event a decision were made to deploy them. The questions that remained were about who would provide troops and what tasks each force would undertake. Our ACRI program was already bearing fruit, as a number of African militaries were present at the conference and expressed a desire to participate.

The international politics were much more problematic. There was no consensus at the United Nations on how to proceed. There were several different factions fighting in eastern Zaire, and it was impossible to negotiate a cease-fire that would permit the international force to enter peacefully; they were probably going to have to fight their way into position and defend their presence against hostile indigenous forces. Moreover, the presence of an international force would have an impact on Kagame's and Kabila's war against Mobutu. Some, including the United States, wanted Mobutu out after more than thirty years of dictatorship that had ruined his country; others, the French included, feared that his military overthrow would lead to even greater instability in the region, and opposed the Rwandan armed forces for the inflammatory role they were playing in the conflict. Intelligence analysts worried that nations in eastern Africa were moving to dismember Zaire and reap the spoils from its resource-rich carcass.

In the end, the political differences and security concerns doomed the deployment, and tens of thousands of refugees perished while the fighters who were based among the refugees in the camps slipped out to fight in the conflicts that continued to convulse the region. Our inability to prevent the killing was more proof of the need for the international community to develop new streamlined means to react to these human catastrophes, means such as the ACRI. While the planning conference itself marked a milestone for the command—the first time a multilateral meeting had been convened to prepare for a mission in Africa—as good as the planning was, we never received the political authority to act, and thousands more perished.

Before he left EUCOM, a year after I did, Jim Jamerson had visited almost every country on the continent, broken new ground, and worked to increase contact and cooperation with African militaries in anticipation of the operations we would inevitably be mounting with many of them.

Chapter Eleven
U.S. Peacekeeping in Bosnia

THE MOST SIGNIFICANT DEPLOYMENT of American armed forces during my tenure in Stuttgart was into Bosnia, to stabilize that former Yugoslavian state after years of bloodshed and "ethnic cleansing" at the direction of the Serbs in Belgrade. After four years of stonewalling and thwarting the efforts of the United Nations, including the humiliation of U.N. peacekeepers, in 1995 Serbian President Milosevic finally agreed to the Dayton peace plan brokered by veteran American diplomat Richard Holbrooke. The parties—Milosevic, along with Alijia Izetbegovic of Bosnia and Franjo Tudjman of Croatia—agreed that an international force would serve as peacekeepers, drawn from NATO member states and other Central and Eastern European countries that agreed to serve under NATO command. The United States provided 20,000 of the approximately 45,000 troops. EUCOM retained responsibility for the American contingent until the troops arrived at the base NATO had established in Tuzla, Bosnia, after which they were turned over to the nato commander. Practically, that meant that EUCOM was responsible for the training of the troops and the logistics of moving them and 300,000 tons of armaments and supplies through several countries before finally arriving in Bosnia. The diplomacy and negotiation of agreements with the countries to permit the transit of our troops and

equipment was a complicated effort that fell to me and my EUCOM colleagues. Each country—Austria, Croatia, the Czech Republic, France,
Germany, Italy, Hungary, Slovakia, Slovenia, and Switzerland—had
its own laws and rules and regulations, and they were often very different from each other; yet each set of national laws had to be honored
in this unprecedented move across Central Europe and into the frag-
mented Balkans by NATO troops.

The command put together a team, led by me, to travel to the capitals of most of the countries on the force's route. We had an airplane
dedicated to our use and a team of colonels, lieutenant colonels, and
majors to explain what we were going to do, and how we were going
to do it, for civilian and military authorities in the countries that U.S.
forces would be transiting.

The American officers and I were received by top officials in all
the countries we visited. I met personally with the American ambassadors in each country before meeting with the host governments;
representatives from our embassies were always present at those briefings. After our initial trips, we would send experts in each of the areas
of concern to the countries to resolve whatever problems might still
exist and to sign Status of Forces agreements that governed everything related to the journey the soldiers were about to make across
their lands: illnesses and injuries to soldiers in transit, carrying of
sidearms in countries that forbade it, and soldier misconduct were all
among the issues that needed close attention. We traveled by airplane
several days a week, often to two capitals in the same day, returning
late each evening to Stuttgart to debrief our generals and to organize
the follow-up trips with the experts, logisticians, doctors, and lawyers
to nail down the agreements. We also invited each country to send a
liaison officer to our logistical headquarters to coordinate all aspects
of the transit through their country.

There were vastly different reactions to our briefings from the
countries we visited. In Belgrade, the head of the former Yugoslavia's

defense forces, General Momcilo Perisic, a nervous chain smoker, used the occasion to launch a diatribe against the West, "with whom we have been allied in every major war," for having supposedly betrayed that historic friendship. He then stomped out, bringing a briefing that had not yet begun to a screeching halt. We looked around the conference table at Yugoslav analysts who could not mask their disappointment at the early end to the briefing that would have provided them with a treasure trove of intelligence about our plans— innocuous plans as far as we were concerned, but otherwise unavailable to them.

After I reported this encounter to General Joulwan, he traveled to Belgrade himself, strode right past the welcoming Perisic to meet directly with Milosevic, to reinforce our commitment to a successful operation that would brook no Serbian interference.

The Croatians claimed to be worried about environmental damage that might be created by our moving through their country, a crass attempt to extort funds for road repair. In Prague, Czech Republic, the official in charge was the same man who had managed the logistics of the "Velvet Divorce" in 1993, when the republic separated from Slovakia. He was delighted with what we were planning and asked only that we provide advance notice before the transit of the first train so that the Czechs could welcome our arrival with appropriate fanfare. In a classic instance of Murphy's Law, the first train arrived forty-eight hours before it was scheduled, disrupting all the plans for a brass band and confetti reception.

By contrast, just across the border, in Bratislava, Slovakia, the government was much more ambivalent about the American effort, and was reluctant to permit any transit across its territory for fear of criticism by the sitting government's energized opposition, with a consequent domestic backlash. While we were ultimately able to resolve the differences, the negotiations were protracted and difficult, for reasons that appeared insignificant to us. Of course, we had not grown up on propaganda that defending the nation and the people against the NATO hordes was the highest national priority, lest they attack and pillage and rape across the countryside. An enemy they had grown up fearing was about to transit their country and set up on their eastern front.

The Swiss courted our command assiduously, to encourage a shipment to transit the Alpine country. They were in the midst of redefining their cherished neutrality in the post–Cold War world and wanted to demonstrate to their citizenry that participation in an internationally sanctioned peacekeeping and humanitarian operation did not compromise their long-standing principles. They met with us on every possible occasion and even sent their defense chief to our headquarters in Stuttgart to lobby us. We were amenable and wanted to be supportive, but there was a significant logistic hurdle. In a comic scenario that reminded me a bit of children playing with toys, we learned that trains passing through mountainous Switzerland are obliged to travel through tunnels, most of which are too small to accommodate large and bulky items like tanks or armored personnel carriers. In the end, the U.S. Army configured a special load that met the specifications for Swiss tunnels, and we sent it on its way through the Alps, happy we could satisfy the request.

Other nations besides the former Yugoslavia also used our visits to air their grievances. When we visited Rome, the Italian chief of defense asked me to step away from the briefing our officers were providing and join him in his offices. Anticipating a cup of delicious cappuccino, I gladly mounted the worn marble stairs to his high-ceilinged office overlooking one of Rome's busiest and noisiest streets. We sat, and as I sipped, the general launched into a recitation of every complaint the Italians had against the American military, dating back to when we were allies for the last two years of World War II.

The coffee was so delicious, I did not have the heart to tell him that in fact we had been enemies throughout most of that war. When I called Joulwan to report on the meeting, he was not at all surprised.

He knew the speech, having heard it himself every time he met with his Italian counterpart. He made a note to stop in Rome to schmooze with the Italians once again.

The command also strove to develop close relations with many nongovernmental organizations prior to the deployment. General Joulwan understood that when the military first arrived in Bosnia, it would be required to handle all activities, civilian as well as military. These included humanitarian relief, food distribution, and medical support for the civilian population in Bosnia, in addition to the core responsibility of separating the belligerents and securing the peace. In his briefing presentation, he was fond of showing one particular slide that communicated his vision of the relationship between the militaries and the NGOs.

On one side of the image was a big *M* for military, and a little *C* for civilian. On the other side the letters were reversed, a little *M* and a big *C*. Joulwan knew that the military was responsible for everything during the stabilization phase of the operation. The instability made it impossible for civilian and nongovernmental organizations to take on the tasks for which they were constituted, at least until order was established. This meant that there would be a big military component at the outset, and a very limited civilian responsibility. As peace and security returned, the military role—the big *M*—would shrink, and civilian NGOs—the little *C*—would take on additional tasks until such time as the military was out of the humanitarian relief and development business altogether. It made sense. As peace was restored, the military could sideline activities that weren't usually part of its core mission and focus on what it does best.

In the fall of 1995, we traveled to Geneva to meet with Mrs. Sadako Ogata, the U.N. high commissioner for refugees, to establish a liaison office that would manage the relationship between the military and the relief community. Joulwan had done the same thing in the spring of 1994 during the genocide in Rwanda, and the system he had established had worked well. Not surprisingly, the military and the NGO community view the world from vastly different perspectives. Many in the humanitarian relief business are viscerally antiwar, for one thing. Their work often takes them into conflict zones, and they see firsthand the effects of war on civilian populations. The military often finds the work of the NGOs a distraction. A good part of the mutual suspicion is due as well to the lack of contact between the two communities. Joulwan understood that there were legitimate roles for each to play and gave early attention to fostering cooperation between the two. It paid off.

Through a series of planning sessions and other meetings, the friction was eased as relationships were developed. Once our troops and the civilian relief workers realized that they shared many of the same objectives, and that working together made achieving those objectives easier, much of the mutual antipathy disappeared.

After our efforts at developing closer cooperation with the French began producing results, including the joint planning for eastern Zaire, we also undertook evacuations of foreigners caught up in the conflicts in the Central African Republic and Sierra Leone. Next, Jim Jamerson decided we should branch out and try to create the same relationships with other European militaries. The mechanism for coordination within Europe was NATO, but there was no similar entity to coordinate operations outside of the alliance's backyard. Jim and I traveled to London to meet with the British and visited their newly created Joint Command, and to Brussels to meet with the Belgians and with the fledgling European Defense Force office.

These new relationships were put to the test when, in May 1997, Laurent Kabila's forces finally surrounded Kinshasa, Zaire, preparatory to invading the capital and driving Mobutu out. Our fear was that the upcoming battle would result in anarchy in the capital of four million, generating panicked refugees trying to flee across the wide and dangerously swift Congo River that separated Kinshasa from Brazzaville,

Congo, on the northern bank. We worked with the British, French, and Belgians, deploying forces from all four countries to Libreville, Gabon, and Brazzaville, in the event we would be required to move into Kinshasa to prevent chaos.

In the end, Mobutu willingly went into exile and Kinshasa fell to the rebels without violence, so we did not need to send in the troops we had readied. It was, nonetheless, an excellent example of how American civilian and military leadership could work with our counterparts in other governments and militaries to anticipate a crisis, plan a productive approach together, and ultimately deploy and operate jointly. We were now cooperating closely at the military and diplomatic level, even as there were disputes among our political masters.

In May 1997, I was offered a position on the staff of President Clinton's National Security Council as the senior director for African Affairs. It was an offer I could not refuse, and despite the great satisfaction of serving at EUCOM and the great respect I had for the men and women who serve in the United States armed forces, I prepared to return to Washington. Before I left, I was honored with the Defense Department's Distinguished Service award, one of that department's most senior decorations. The citation read, in part: "Ambassador Wilson's strategic vision and diplomatic talents significantly contributed to the United States' defense policy and goals in Central and Eastern Europe and in Africa. His efforts were instrumental in the smooth transit of soldiers and equipment in support of the Implementation Forces in Bosnia. He aggressively pursued new political–military initiatives in Africa by articulating and revising command goals and objectives. . . . Ambassador Wilson's foresight and skill unequivocally bolstered USEUCOM's sphere of influence in the European theater." It was signed by William S. Cohen, the secretary of defense.

It was extraordinarily gratifying to have my contributions recognized by the military, an institution I had come to admire so much, even though I had never served in uniform.

At dinner with Jim Jamerson on the eve of my departure, he commented that if historians ever wrote about the command, they would have to acknowledge that the previous two years had marked a fundamental shift in the direction of the command, with the military bureaucracy increasingly focusing on new threats as those in the heart of Europe receded. He believed we could take great pride in our contributions. Of course, he added wryly, we would have to be the ones writing the history for that story to be told, and it seemed highly unlikely either of us would ever do so. I chuckled too, so unlikely did it seem that I would be writing a book within a few years.

In many ways, African conflicts propelled the European Command into the political realities of the late twentieth century. Integral to our security agenda were peacekeeping and peacemaking operations, critical interventions in small but bloody conflicts before they could spill across borders to affect other countries. They pointed to the need for greater military cooperation among allies, friends, and potential coalition partners.

The Bosnian peacekeeping operation offered numerous lessons. As in African crises, a coalition of forces limited American exposure and spread responsibility among many parties for the outcome. Coordination with civilian relief organizations before the deployment helped to minimize confusion and disruption to affected populations; occupation casualties were directly proportionate to the numbers of troops deployed; the more troops on the ground, the fewer the casualties. It is true that today the American military can project lethal force farther and faster than ever in history, and that as a consequence, the practice of taking territory has changed. But holding on to that territory is still dangerous, all the more so if we are undermanned. The most important assets in the U.S. armed forces are the men and women in uniform defending our nation. Not to provide them with the best protection we can is derelict, and a breach of trust.

Finally, the lesson of all the deployments we undertook was that peacekeeping is a beneficial activity, not just for civilian populations but also for American forces. The alternative is war and the death and destruction that all too often victimize civilian communities. The cost in human suffering and economic deprivation can be devastating, the scars long-lasting. It should not be such a difficult decision to engage in conflict-resolution activities, so long as we work to minimize the risk to our troops and are also able to involve forces from other countries.

The shared vision of George Joulwan and Jim Jamerson succeeded in realigning the European Command to a direction relevant to the threats and opportunities we faced in the aftermath of the Cold War. The command acquired a new flexibility and assumed a new dimension that included engagement and nontraditional military activities. The mid-1990s were a defining moment for the command, and it was a thrill to be part of it. It meant traveling from Estonia in the north to South Africa in the south, to Israel and Turkey in the east and Ireland in the west, and to most countries in between, as Jim and I spent close to 70 percent of our time on the road. We became dear friends, sharing an airplane, hotels, and many cigars at the end of our long days. We came to spend even weekends together playing golf. There could have been no better way to learn about the philosophy and practice of military leadership and no more cherished friend to learn from.

Chapter Twelve
Coming Home for Good

I N JUNE OF 1997, I arrived back in Washington to take my new job directing the African Affairs desk at the National Security Council. It would be my first assignment in the city since 1978. I had spent only three years of the previous twenty-one in the nation's capital, and eighteen months of that had been in training or on my 1985 Congressional Fellowship. I was not an expert in the bureaucratic politics that dominate Washington policy making, nor was I politically well connected at the working level despite knowing Vice President Al Gore, one of my sponsors during the fellowship. I had only once met the national security adviser, Sandy Berger, and that was when he interviewed me for the post, and I had not yet met Bill Clinton. (While I generally voted for the Democratic candidate for president, President Bush had received my vote in the 1992 election that brought Clinton into office. Not surprisingly, my votes generally reflected the political agenda most important to me: foreign policy and national security.)

I was introduced to President Clinton when I was called in to the Oval Office to participate in a meeting in advance of a visit by the president of Mali, Alpha Oumar Konare. Sandy Berger, who clearly did not know my career well, did the honors, referring to me as the former ambassador to Ghana rather than Gabon. It did not matter, as I knew he had a lot on his mind, but as he was fumbling my career history, Gore strode in, listened for the briefest of instants, and interrupted, saying to the president: "But the most important job Joe ever had was on my staff in the Senate." That settled it for Clinton; he smiled and welcomed me. Once again, Al Gore had reached out to me and shown a personal touch.

Bill Clinton was an imposing figure who had clearly grown into the office and into his international responsibilities. He was legendary for his ability to do several things at once, keeping different thoughts and issues at the forefront of his mind simultaneously. While I was briefing him for his meeting with the president of Mali—hardly the center of Washington's foreign policy universe—I stood in front of his desk while he was seated behind it. As I looked down at him, describing Mali, President Konare, and the points my office wanted Clinton to make in their meeting, Clinton was working a crossword puzzle. It was disconcerting and added to my own nervousness at being in his presence—you never get over the butterflies the first time in the Oval Office with a president you have just met. The power of the office and, by extension, of the person occupying it is intimidating.

But when his African guest entered, Clinton was brilliant. He demonstrated an understanding of Mali and a keen interest in his visitor and the issues being raised; it was a virtuoso performance. I decided then and there to take up crossword puzzles!

My move back to Washington coincided with the return to D.C. of a woman named Valerie Plame. I had first met her several months earlier at a reception in Washington I was attending with General Jim Jamerson at the residence of the Turkish ambassador. We were there to accept an award from the American Turkish Council, on behalf of the American troops of the European Command who were working in close collaboration with their Turkish counterparts in Iraq and Bosnia. I had been circulating, talking to friends from the State Department, when I looked up and saw across the room this willowy blonde, resembling a young Grace Kelly. She looked at me, and I immediately thought that I knew her from somewhere, so I smiled. She smiled broadly back and began to move toward me. At that instant, my world went into slow motion as I watched her approach. Suddenly I saw nobody else in a throng that must have numbered two hundred people, and I heard nothing as a silence seemed to fall over the room.

It was only when she was practically right next to me, and held out her hand to shake mine, that I realized we had never met. But by then it was too late: I was hopelessly smitten. The French call it a *coup de foudre* (a thunderclap); we call it love at first sight. I turned away from the friends who were watching my behavior with amusement and made Valerie the sole object of my attention. We spent the rest of the evening at the reception in conversation, and later over coffee, getting to know each other. She described herself as an energy executive living in Brussels, and I told her about my background. She later told me that she had called a lawyer friend the next day and asked her to run a Lexis-Nexis™ computer search on me, since my stories were so unbelievable that she wanted to verify I really was who I claimed to be. After all, how many times does a complete stranger regale you with stories about shaking hands with Saddam Hussein? It was a line she had not heard before. As she put it later, "A lady cannot be too careful."

The following night was the awards banquet, and I waited restlessly for Valerie to arrive so that I could have another chance to at least say hello and look for signs as to whether I had made a good impression. She arrived late and gravitated directly to me. Out of the corner of my eye, I could see people hovering nearby, trying to find a way to jump into our conversation and bask in her incandescent glow, but she effectively discouraged any interruption, focusing all of her attention on me. Finally, we had to split up to go to our respective tables, but not before exchanging business cards.

As Jim Jamerson and I slipped out of the dinner a couple of

hours later to return to Stuttgart, I made sure I passed by Valerie's table to say good-bye and tell her how much I had enjoyed meeting her. Unfortunately, she was in the ladies' room and I could not wait, so I wondered all night long on the plane to Stuttgart whether I would ever see her again.

I need not have worried, as a couple of days later I received an E-mail addressed to "Mr. Ambassador." My assumption when I read the note was that she was being polite to somebody she thought might be interesting as a friend or mentor, but who was of little romantic interest to her. The age difference between us was almost fourteen years, and she was an up-and-coming international executive and unmarried to boot. On the other hand, I was a soon-to-be-twice-divorced career government official on the downward slope of my career.

Nonetheless, I invited Valerie to dinner the next time I was in Brussels and found, to my great surprise, that she was interested in me, despite my rather poor track record in the marriage department, which included not yet having brought my second marriage to an official close. "Ladies don't date married men," she announced firmly as I tried to hold her hand.

By the time we each got back to Washington five months later, we were hooked on each other. My divorce, delayed because I was never in one place long enough to complete the process, was finally moving forward, and Valerie and I were becoming closer all the time.

She had by now taken me into her confidence. It was important to her, if we were going to move to another stage in our relationship, that she be honest about what she did. She told me what was permissible, under the circumstances, since I had the requisite clearances. She worried about my reaction, though she had not really needed to. I had been involved with national security for a long time and I had great respect for all my colleagues working to make our world a safer place.

When she told me about what she did, my only question was: "Is your real name Valerie? That brought a laugh and reassured her.

Soon after our return to Washington, we decided to move in together in an apartment in the Watergate apartment building. She went to work at her headquarters and I to the ornate, Napoleon III–style Old Executive Office Building (OEOB) right next to the West Wing of the White House.

The Office of African Affairs at the National Security Council serves as the coordinator of U.S. government policy to Africa, bringing together all the agencies with interests and programs on the continent to ensure that each one is taking positions consistent with the president's views. The State Department has the lead on the conduct of relations with the nations of Africa, but a number of other departments are engaged as well. As can be expected, there are often differences in approach. Policies are often controversial within an administration, and program objectives in different cabinet departments may occasionally clash with one another.

An early example occurred over Sudan. The United States had closed its embassy in Khartoum in 1996, amid fears of an attack on our personnel there and broader concerns about Sudanese support for terrorism. At that time, I was still at the European Command and watched as we positioned a ship full of Marines in the Mediterranean off the Egyptian coast as a precaution. In mid-1997, a consensus emerged at the State Department that the American Embassy should be reopened. Ambassador Thomas Pickering, State's under secretary for political affairs, made the case that embassies are tools by which the U.S. government advances its own interests, not a political bauble to be offered or withheld depending on a foreign regime's behavior. He believed that even if our influence was limited, we needed a presence in Khartoum to monitor events and trends in that difficult country. State's position was that the embassies belonged to them, and therefore they could be reopened at the discretion of the secretary of state, Madeleine Albright.

When we go to great lengths to isolate a foreign regime, we often end up isolating ourselves too. It is hard to exert influence if you are not on the scene. While I personally agreed with Tom's point of view, the NSC was opposed. An interagency committee chaired by the NSC counterterrorism office had recommended the withdrawal, taking into account past terrorist acts launched from Sudanese territory, such as the attempted assassination of Egyptian President Hosni Mubarak at a summit meeting in Addis Ababa, Ethiopia, in June 1995, and the harboring of international terrorists, including one named Osama bin Laden until 1996, as well as suspected threats against American interests. Accordingly, reopening the embassy would require an affirmative decision by the same committee that had closed it.

The dispute pitted me against Pickering, who had been the U.N. ambassador and a big supporter of mine when I had been in Baghdad and later, as well as against my former boss in Iraq, Ambassador April Glaspie, now the State Department director for East African Affairs. At the end of my second week with the NSC, the issue came to a head as State decided to circumvent the NSC, unilaterally moving to reopen the embassy.

The decision was communicated to Congress and leaked to the press, but nobody called me. Once I had learned about it from John Prendergast, my NSC colleague responsible for East Africa, we agreed that we could not permit the reopening of the embassy until those who were responsible for tracking and thwarting terrorists had offered their recommendation. It was not so much a policy disagreement as a question of process—and, most of all, it concerned the safety of the Americans who were going to be sent back into Khartoum. We swung into action and moved the issue up to Sandy Berger. Before the weekend was over, the decision to reopen had been rolled back. Diplomats would not be sent back to Khartoum until there was a broader review, one that included security and terrorism analyses.

It was a major embarrassment for State, particularly for Tom and April, when the press wrote about the reversal of their decision by the NSC. Susan Rice, my predecessor at the NSC and soon to be the assistant secretary of state for Africa, called to praise me as a "bureaucratic Samurai." She was at home on maternity leave and awaiting confirmation in her new post when the effort to reopen the embassy was launched. Even though she wasn't confirmed yet, she fully supported the NSC position. There had been a deliberate effort to implement the action before she could block it.

I was unenthusiastic about blocking State, both because I was not yet seasoned in such bureaucratic infighting involving friends and because I agreed with the premise that embassies are established and maintained in America's own interests. But as a veteran of the State Department who knew the protagonists in this dispute very well, I was offended that anyone would try to take advantage of my rookie status at the NSC, which I judged was one of the elements in play. I was accustomed to serving at embassies where a premium was put on coordination and communication, not on circumvention. It was a rude awakening to a new corporate culture where the tactics were less collegial.

After the dust had settled several weeks later, I called Pickering and suggested he resubmit the question to the NSC, promising to support the reopening unless there was credible intelligence that it would be too risky for our diplomats, but the State Department decided not to press the point. Susan Rice was adamantly opposed to any contact with the Sudanese and refused even to meet with Sudan's ambassador to the United States. Now that she was in place, it would have been difficult to overcome her objections.

The Clinton administration's approach to Africa was one that was easy for a veteran Africanist like me to support. President Clinton and his foreign policy team worked assiduously to give African issues a higher priority in our foreign policy constellation. While administrations of both parties expressed keen interest in African affairs, Africa had always been a low appropriations priority and a political punching bag. For years, as the chairman of the Senate Foreign Relations Committee, Senator Jesse Helms railed against foreign aid budgets, often comparing aid funding in Africa to "pouring money down a rat hole." Yet without aid, these countries' fragile economies were doomed to fail.

In the absence of congressional support for aid, President Clinton set out to encourage the private sector to become engaged and to invest in the development of Africa as a means of stimulating growth. Secretary of Commerce Ron Brown, before his death in a tragic airplane crash in Croatia in 1996, made it clear that the United States would aggressively support American companies investing in Africa. In mid-1995, Brown had traveled to Senegal and announced that the United States would no longer concede the African market to the continent's former colonial powers. In doing so, he inaugurated a new strategy and approach to the United States' economic relationship with Africa, which would advance American commercial interests through an invigorated emphasis on trade and investment. Even if it worried the French, Brown's declaration was a refreshing recommitment to Africa. No longer would the continent and its growing problems be shunted to the bottom of the deck.

Democratic Congressmen Jim McDermott and Charlie Rangel teamed with Republican Phil Crane to introduce a bill called the African Growth and Opportunity Act, spearheaded by congressional staffer Mike Williams, a dedicated advocate of improved relations with Africa. It was designed to complement, not supplant, traditional aid programs by providing increased access to American markets for African nations willing to engage in economic and political reform. The greater the reform, the more access. At the same time, it proposed incentives to American firms to invest in African economies. It was the perfect vehicle for the administration to demonstrate that the new approach to Africa was about more than just speech making, and we jumped aboard to support it fully. Not surprisingly, the probusiness tilt also attracted considerable Republican support.

Despite Senator Helms's contempt for them, United States Agency for International Development (USAID) programs in Africa had been useful, even if reform of many of their practices was overdue. For more than three decades, Africa had experienced a steady economic decline, mitigated in part only by the efforts of the international community, USAID, and the Peace Corps.

For example, in 1976, when I first went to Niger, conventional wisdom had it that people living in the Sahel region of West Africa would not be able to survive to the end of the century, that they would be forced by the relentless advance of the Sahara Desert to move south into neighboring, more hospitable regions. Yet over the past twenty-five years, they have beaten the dire predictions. While not wealthy, they continue to occupy the land, and their agricultural production has grown enough to at least meet the growth in population. Programs for agricultural development, distribution systems, economic infrastructure, and health care have enabled Africa's first postcolonial generation to defy conventional wisdom and the crude Helmsian metaphor. Much of that success was directly attributable to the efforts of AID programs and U.S. collaboration with other donor nations.

It was in America's strategic interest to have a strong presence in Africa. The 1996 National Security Strategy Statement clearly articulated our concerns about threats posed by failing states as breeding grounds for international terrorism. It was incumbent on us to defend ourselves against threats that might emanate from failed nation-states, and to engage with other governments to eliminate both the threats and the underlying conditions that provide the impetus for them. The same National Security Strategy Statement also addressed itself to the problems of organized crime on the continent and to the scourge of diseases like AIDS that respect no borders. HIV/AIDS had been of concern to those of us serving in Africa since the early eighties. I was then in Burundi and watched several of my Burundian friends die of the disease. Unlike in the United States, AIDS in Africa was mostly transmitted through heterosexual sex and therefore was not stigmatized as a "gay" plague, as many conservatives in the United States thought of it. The prevalence of other sexually transmitted diseases facilitated its spread throughout the continent, first among high-risk populations like prostitutes and their clients, then to the broader population. Programs to address its spread through the continent were high on our agenda, although the competition with other programs for resources was great.

On the positive side, we wanted to redouble our efforts to support economic reform and foster a more robust commercial relationship with Africa, building on the successes we had seen in some African nations. Africa is a landmass large enough to accommodate all of the United States and Western Europe, with a good piece of Southeast Asia and Australia tossed in, and is home to enormous reserves of natural resources—metals, minerals, oil, timber—that have yet to be exploited to the benefit of the local populations. Oil reserves off its west coast alone, for example, provide an attractive alternative to dependence on the Arabian Gulf. With a population of 700,000 people, the challenge is to take a region that has been a consumer of global government resources for forty years and turn it into a contributor to global wealth. In the Clinton administration, we were committed to awakening the economic development of this slumbering giant that comprises the largest world population still on the outside looking in at the phenomena of globalization.

This is an enormous undertaking, with 90 percent of the indigenous population still subsistence farmers and most of the remaining 10 percent working in small-business activities or in government. At the time independence began taking hold about forty years ago, African governments, largely in reaction to the colonial experience, made poor public policy choices. Instead of pursuing market-based economic policies, the first generation of independent African leaders by and large adopted socialist centralized planning solutions, and the anemic results were predictable. Bureaucracies that responded to their own agendas rather than to the needs of the people have engendered stagnant or declining economies ever since.

There had been some exceptions: Côte d'Ivoire, Gabon, and Kenya all had resisted the socialist solution and had economies that performed well, until corruption and sclerotic regimes undermined performance. In recent years, Ghana, Uganda, and Botswana were examples of both political stability and economic growth. Mozambique had surprised everybody with its resurgence after a bloody civil war, and South Africa, under the steady hand of Nelson Mandela, had survived a wrenching transition with a minimal amount of dislocation. It was incumbent on the entire international community to build on these islands of progress and to assist other governments to replicate them.

One of our early challenges was to formulate an approach to the new government of Laurent Kabila, the rebel who had driven Mobutu Sese Seko from power in Zaire. Now ensconced in Kinshasa, and having changed the name of his country to the Democratic Republic of the Congo, Kabila was always going to be a problem. He had evolved little from the days when he holed up in the mountains of Eastern Congo, smuggling, kidnapping, and eking out a high-wayman's living. Fate, in the name of Rwandan Vice President Paul Kagame, landed him in the president's palace, though he was uniquely unqualified for the challenges of a country brought to its knees by the kleptocracy of his predecessor. It was immediately clear to all of us that any progress in the Congo would have to be *despite* Kabila, who was more interested in the perquisites of power than in the responsibilities of office.

We simply could not overlook either the geostrategic location of the Congo in Central Africa or the consequences, for a population of 47,000,000 people, should the nation fall into even greater chaos. AID came up with an ingenious approach to deliver assistance to the people of the Congo while keeping Kabila at bay. Creating a number of hubs in the provinces rather than centralizing the operation in Kinshasa, AID stayed out of the capital altogether and delivered assistance within the respective provinces. Our efforts to move quickly, however, were being hindered by Kabila's defiance of United Nations attempts to investigate allegations of ethnic cleansing and genocide committed by his troops on their march to Kinshasa. The U.S. Congress worried that we would be rewarding another terrible dictator with our aid. The administration agreed that the U.N. should vigorously pursue all allegations of genocide, but we did not want to tie the delivery of much-needed assistance for the long-suffering population to Kabila's compliance. The plan developed by AID allowed us to do both. The NSC shepherded interagency agreement on the plan, and we met almost weekly to hammer out agreement on the approach—not all agencies agreed this one was best—and then to follow its progress and adapt it as necessary. It was very satisfying to watch my fellow public servants work day and night to relieve the tragedy of war, dictatorship, and deprivation in a country so far away from ours.

The Angolan civil war, still being waged after nearly thirty years, occupied my attention once again. The U.N. secretary general's special representative for Angola, Blondin Beye, came frequently to Washington, and we worked together to try to bring pressure on all sides to end the conflict. UNITA and Jonas Savimbi retained some residual support among conservatives in Washington, who continued to see the government in Luanda as communist, and UNITA as pro-Western and democratic, even though Savimbi himself had been trained by Chinese communists. In the administration, however, we did gain support for U.N. sanctions on UNITA, prohibiting trade with it in diamonds, weapons, and spare parts for its military, and restricting the travel of its leadership.

Beye, a former Malian foreign minister, was a tremendous force in the U.N.'s efforts. I marveled at the strength of his commitment, even as his efforts had been frustrated time and time again by the belligerents. He worked closely with Paul Hare, Jim Jamerson, and, of course, Don Steinberg, still our ambassador in Luanda. I saw Beye every time he came to Washington, including the last time, in early June 1998. We met in my office, and after our discussions, I reminded him about his habit of saying a little prayer every time his airplane took off or landed. I had traveled with him several times while I served in Libreville, Gabon, as we were trying to put together a meeting of the high commands of the two Angolan militaries. He would inevitably break off all conversation to pray just before takeoff and touchdown, and once we were safe, he would return to the subject at hand, missing nary a beat. I thanked him now for all the prayers he had uttered on my behalf. Three weeks later, I was crushed when he perished in a plane crash en route from Togo to Côte d'Ivoire. Africa had lost one of its finest public servants, a leader capable of envisioning a truly inspirational future.

By the late 1990s, the insurgency had become so entangled with the person of Savimbi that there was little to justify the ongoing conflict, other than his ambition to rule from Luanda. But we continued trying to bring pressure to bear, in the hope that UNITA could be transformed from a rebel guerrilla movement into a legitimate political party. As it became increasingly clear that Savimbi was the impediment to any resolution, the U.S., Russia, and Portugal—constituting the troika partnership that worked together to implement and monitor the peace process known as the Lusaka protocol—along with the U.N. and its special representative, all agreed that we needed more sanctions against Savimbi.

New sanctions were proposed in the spring of 1998, but, curiously, the State Department did not initially support them, and it was leaked that the United States might actually oppose them. The analysis may well have been that additional sanctions would be of limited effect—after all, Savimbi had proven that he was adept at circumventing them—or even counterproductive at a time when there was still faint hope that Savimbi could be cajoled into finally playing a positive role in the peace process.

The veto threat, when the Angolan government learned of it, served to reinforce its paranoia about American intentions, as the leadership feared that we still harbored the insidious notion of installing Savimbi in power. I strongly believed that enhanced sanctions on UNITA, as supported by the troika and by Beye, were important to pursue. Savimbi's time had long since passed. He had little international legitimacy, and while he was still dangerous, it was clear that over time he would be defeated. I also worried about the implications of the U.S. threatening to veto a resolution that our partners in the peace process had recommended, whatever the merits of the State Department's concern. The entire process would be undermined by such an action.

I shared these concerns with Tom Pickering informally after a meeting at the White House, as we were walking out of the West Wing. He had not known about the leaked threat and was incensed, uttering a colorful obscenity. The U.S. did not in the end veto the sanctions resolution, but the leak itself poisoned our relations with the Angolan government for several months and damaged our credibility as a mediator. When I left government in 1998, the war, which had begun before I even began my diplomatic career two and a half decades earlier, was still ravaging that once-prosperous nation. It would take several more years and the killing of Savimbi by the Angolan army in February 2002 before the war would finally wind down.

Problems brewing in West Africa were equally disturbing. Nigeria was in the firm clutches of Sani Abacha, a corrupt and brutal general who helped himself to hundreds of millions of dollars and capriciously imprisoned his political opponents. Ken Saro-Wiwa, a prominent activist, was one who had died in police custody. Olusegun Obasanjo, an internationally respected former president languished in jail. Abacha was a classic thug, but there was little we could do—imposing sanctions on the oil sector in Nigeria, for example—without the support of the international community, and that support was not forthcoming.

We endlessly debated the possibility of unilateral sanctions, which would have had limited impact and only given Abacha an external enemy to rail against. I also worried that sanctions would make it more difficult for us to work on the other national security issues presented by Nigeria, such as international criminal activities like money laundering and narco-trafficking. Others took the position best articulated by Jesse Jackson, then President Clinton's special envoy for Africa, that we needed to be on the "moral side of history." But in June of 1998 Abacha died a suspicious death—reputedly poisoned while in the company of two prostitutes—so we were spared the need to take action. In the aftermath, Nigerian politics moved quickly and we were positioned to play a positive role. Obasanjo emerged from jail and was re-elected president in the subsequesnt elections in 1999.

Meanwhile, Liberia was in the hands of Charles Taylor, a vicious warlord who refused to be defeated and finally won a rigged election over an exhausted opposition. Next door, in Sierra Leone, the Revolutionary United Front (RUF), led by Foday Sankoh, with no apparent political agenda, terrorized the general population in the most despicable ways, cutting off the legs and arms of innocent citizens, small children and women included, as well as mutilating his opponents. A reign of terror had settled over that country.

In Côte d'Ivoire, the efforts of President Henri Konan Bedie to thwart the electoral process would lead to his overthrow and civil war in the country.

Africa has long been known to Americans only as a source of terrible violence, poverty, and disease, with pockets of dramatic game parks for well-off safari seekers and wildlife preserves for tourists. Though it is a continent containing fifty-three states, it is often referred to by the geographically illiterate as a "country" and described by many with no experience as "hopeless." It is a poor continent to be sure, and many of its nations find themselves in the throes of violent upheaval, consistent with the inability of the central governments to ensure security throughout their countries. But that is not the whole story.

Though there may be civil wars in ten countries at any one time, there are also thirty-seven states south of the Sahara in various stages of national evolution, striving to master the politics and economics of multi-tribal geographic entities, while living within borders inherited from colonial powers that bear little relationship to traditional tribal lands or any commonality of interests. A journey across this huge continent, with its great natural diversity, would take a traveler from ocean to ocean, through tropical forests and grassy plains with abundant herds of wildlife, to the top of snow-capped mountains, across barren deserts and some of the swiftest rivers on the planet. On the way, he would encounter peoples from a wide range of cultures and backgrounds, speaking hundreds of different languages, and pass through small villages where daily life is largely unchanged after hundreds of years. From there he might go on to sprawling urban areas with skyscrapers, traffic jams, and a mix of national and international cultural influences. In short, a visitor would be bombarded by myriad new sensations, smells, and tastes, and would be forever changed by the experience.

And through it all, a common thread of humanity would be discerned, with the continent's inhabitants eternally striving despite the obstacles that history and human foibles continue to pose. Africa has to be seen, touched, tasted, heard, and smelled to be believed. President Clinton understood that, and since he had never been there, he wanted very much to go and experience it all for himself, all the more so after First Lady Hillary Rodham Clinton had made her own trip in 1997.

Time is the most precious asset in a president's possession, and it is jealously guarded, parceled out minute by minute to competing interests. The responsibility falls to those around the president to determine what he should do, whom he should see, and how much time he should spend on each task and each visitor.

Early in January 1998, I was in my office on the third floor of the OEOB, with its high ceilings and, windows looking out into an inner courtyard, its historic grandeur diminished by the need to carve the original space into two rooms to accommodate a growing staff in our cramped quarters. The phone rang. It was a call from President Clinton's schedulers.

The caller informed me that the president could commit to traveling to Africa for the last two weeks in March for certain, or alternatively he might be able to travel there during two weeks in August, depending on other priorities. In making our decision, the scheduler said, we should take into account that it normally takes six months to plan a presidential trip. The bottom line was that if we could put together the most significant trip a president of the United States had ever made to the most logistically challenging continent on Earth in just ten weeks, then the dates were ours. Otherwise, we could take the twenty-six weeks usually required for the preparation of such a trip and hope that nothing else came along to bump the trip off the president's calendar.

While we had known that a presidential trip to Africa was a possibility, and had been actively pushing him to make one, the length of time President Clinton was prepared to spend there surprised us greatly—and the little time for organizing the enterprise was daunting.

Nonetheless, my three intrepid directors were unanimous in their recommendation that we take the March date and work day and night to make the trip a success. I was not surprised. The NSC was, at the best of times, a highly charged organization requiring long hours and intense effort from those who work there. It was not for the faint of heart. This presidential trip was the chance of a lifetime for professionals working on Africa, and we were not going to even think of letting it get lost in the mix of other priorities eight months down the road. We informed a skeptical Sandy Berger and the scheduler that we would be ready to go by the March date and had no need to wait until August.

We had barely ten weeks to prepare a trip that would take the president and his entourage to six countries in an eleven-day period. Only once since the founding of our republic had a president of the United States set foot on sub-Saharan African territory with the express purpose of visiting with African leaders: in 1977, Jimmy Carter had visited Liberia and Nigeria on his around-the-world tour of emerging nations. Other than that, Franklin Roosevelt had once stopped in Liberia en route to Morocco, and George H. W. Bush had traveled to Somalia to visit U.S. troops at the end of his administration. This would be a history-making trip with profound impact on the continent, and there was no precedent for it, either logistically or from a policy perspective. We would be breaking new ground—and in a hurry.

The first challenge we faced was deciding which countries to select for the president to visit and determining the dates we were going to be there. Naturally, every African ambassador called to plead on behalf of his country: just a stopover, a night, a meal, an airport refueling, anything at all to commemorate the historic friendship between his nation and our own.

The Malian ambassador, Chiek Oumar Diarrah, had a particularly good case to make. His president, Alpha Oumar Konare, had already been received by President Clinton, at which time they had established quite a good rapport. The Malians were eager for the United States to show support for Konare's efforts to bring democracy to their country, long a military dictatorship before the elections that had swept him to power. Diarrah and I had been friends since we were together in Brazzaville, Congo, where he was a professor at the local university. I had known him through Seydou Badian, the Malian adviser to Congolese President Sassou Nguesso, when we were working on Angolan issues in 1987. Diarrah was an expert on African issues, and I frequently consulted with him and welcomed his understanding of the nuances of African politics.

I could not, however, recommend that the president travel to Bamako, Mali's capital, as much as I would have liked to. There were so many countries, and our time was so limited, that those who had already basked in the glow of the American president were eliminated from the list, with the sole exception of Nelson Mandela.

South Africa was to be the centerpiece of our trip, the one non-negotiable stop. President Clinton had tremendous affection for Mandela and deep respect for the fight he had led for several decades, many of them spent in a jail cell on Robben Island just off of Cape Town. Mandela's generosity toward his erstwhile captors and his successful steering of South Africa from a racist apartheid regime to majority rule, without the destructive violence that it was widely feared would attend such an upheaval, was one of history's great feats. To see Mandela cheered by white South Africans at least as loudly as by his own fellow blacks gave the world hope for the future of that once-divided land.

The first date to fix, therefore, was South Africa, and my office arranged for the president to call Mandela on a Saturday morning in mid-January 1998, barely a week since we had locked in the March time frame. Barely a week—but what a week it had been. Just two days after confirming that the trip was a "go," as we were madly scrambling to organize ourselves, we looked up at the television screen in our office to see a breathless-seeming Sam Donaldson. "If he's not telling the truth, I think his presidency could be numbered in days, not weeks," he exclaimed. The story of course was the president's dalliance with a White House intern, who turned out to be Monica Lewinsky. For the next several days, as we held meetings and debated the itinerary and the themes we wanted to stress, we were wondered if the trip would go forward, and whether, if it did, it would be with Bill Clinton as president or, perhaps, with a newly sworn in Al Gore. The press frenzy drowned out all other public discussion, and Washington took on the atmosphere of tabloid central as the pressures mounted to drive the president from the city, preferably tarred and feathered.

When my deputy, Robin Sanders, and I walked into the Oval Office the Saturday morning of the call to Mandela, we had no idea what to expect. Would the president be undone by his personal travails, resembling a shell of his normally larger-than-life self? Robin, an elegant lady with extensive experience in Africa, was hobbled, having badly sprained her ankle in a fall, and was using crutches to limp around.

As we entered, the president stood to greet us and immediately asked about Robin's injury. That thoughtfulness, I saw both then and later, was the hallmark of Bill Clinton's relations with those he came into contact with. He was in a subdued mood but seemed none the worse for wear and made absolutely no mention of his personal problems. His legendary talent for compartmentalization was evident in our small talk while waiting for the telephone connection with Nelson Mandela.

Robin and I sat on a couch in the Oval Office and the president was at his desk when the call came through. The speaker phone was on, and the president had only three points to make: I want to come to South Africa, when is a good time, and I look forward to seeing you. That was it. We were there in case Mandela had some questions for the president that we could easily answer for him.

The president started to make his points but was interrupted by a passionate Mandela, who made the first mention of Monicagate, exclaiming, "What the press is doing to you is terrible," and going on to proclaim all of Africa's love for the entire Clinton family. For the next several minutes, every time Clinton began to speak, Mandela returned to this refrain. Robin and I looked everywhere except at the president as we became increasingly uncomfortable. I looked down at my shoes and the blue rug, up at the molding where the ceiling met the walls, noting how tightly it followed the curve of the wall. I studied the decorations, the busts, the artwork, the knicknacks.

Finally, I looked over at the president, who by this time was resigned to having to listen to his friend's well-intentioned but embarrassing expressions of sympathy and support. His elbow was on the desk, phone cradled in his hand against his ear as he leaned heavily on his arm, fatalistically waiting for the opportunity to make his points and end the conversation. He was patient and unfailingly polite, but the experience was excruciating for us, and it must have been at least uncomfortable for him.

He finally nailed down the date with Mandela and was able to bring the conversation to a close. I jumped up and Robin struggled with her crutches as we said well-done to the president and started to ease out of the Oval Office. But Clinton came around the desk and, in a half-blocking move, stopped us with a simple, "This is going to be a good trip, isn't it?" That was all it took for Robin and me to shift gears and launch into a twenty-minute discussion about the wonders of Africa, sharing our respective experiences. Sitting back at his desk while we stood in front of it, Clinton told us how he had read about Africa as a teenager and had always longed to travel there.

He was excited about the prospect of the trip, his pleasure leading Robin and me to forget all about the awkward telephone conversation. Since then, I have often wondered whether the president consciously wanted us to go on our way thinking about Africa, and not about

Monica. If so, he succeeded—but then again, so did we. We had just spent twenty minutes alone with the most powerful man in the world, sharing with him our impressions of the continent we each loved and leaving him even more enthusiastic about what we planned. We were able to take his mind off the budding scandal just as much as he did ours. I walked out of the Oval Office absolutely convinced that Bill Clinton would still be the president in March and that we would be flying off with him, aboard Air Force One, to the continent where I had always left part of myself.

Chapter Thirteen
Taking President Clinton to Africa

THE PLANNING OF PRESIDENT CLINTON'S TRIP to Africa involved several different offices in the White House and throughout the government, most of which my colleagues and I at the Africa Bureau of the National Security Council (NSC) usually had little contact with. Fortunately, the offices were staffed with people for whom planning presidential trips was a way of life. They knew what they were doing, even if much of it was new to me. Advance teams were dispatched to the short list of countries under consideration to determine whether they could accommodate an invasion of at least six hundred people, a traveling horde that includes the full delegation and staff plus security, logistics, and communications. Possible events were discussed, and sites for speeches and conferences scouted. Negotiations were undertaken with host governments to ensure that common views existed about what we may want the two presidents to discuss and to accomplish. The Secret Service looked hard at the security implications of everything being planned and had the telling vote in one of the most important decisions we had to make about the itinerary.

I tried to use all the management techniques I had learned over the years, especially from my time in Baghdad with my colleague, Emil Skoden, and with General Jim Jamerson in Stuttgart. In working with both, I had seen just how valuable teamwork can be and the importance of obtaining full participation from all parties. In addition to sound management, it was imperative, if we were going to meet the deadline of mid-March, that as much authority be delegated as possible. Fortunately, the White House is a place where every employee is dedicated and highly motivated, and my office was no exception. Robin Sanders, my deputy, also in charge of Central Africa; John Prendergast, responsible for East Africa; and Erica Barks-Ruggles, the West and Southern African director, epitomized public service at its best. John referred to the three of them as the "pack mules," because I could just keep loading more and more responsibility and tasks on their backs, and they would find a way to carry out each mission. We would gather in our office every morning, argue about where we should go and what we should do, continue to argue throughout the day, and finally settle all the issues midway through the night and then return the following morning to start all over again. Emotions were high, as the directors had their favorite countries and issues, the domestic constituencies had theirs, and the interest groups theirs as well. Everything had to be negotiated, and sometimes renegotiated.

We were bombarded with more good ideas, and some bad ones, than we knew what to do with, both from within and from people we had never seen or heard of before. Jesse Jackson pitched the president to go to Zimbabwe and meet with President Robert Mugabe, for example, and even though Mugabe was, and always had been, an unacceptable dictator, we still had to beat that suggestion back. It fell to me to tell the president directly that it was not a good idea. Despite the mythology surrounding Mugabe in some circles as a liberation leader and an agrarian reformer, he was just another authoritarian driving his great country into the ground.

We narrowed the debate early by establishing criteria consistent with what we wanted to achieve. Our overarching theme for the trip was Africa in all its glory, as a counterbalance to the calamities regularly broadcast on television and headlined in newspapers. Therefore, we looked first at countries that had engaged in significant political reform and had managed to incorporate market solutions to drive economic growth. Second, we knew that we could not ignore the conflicts that affected large swaths of the continent, and in fact I did not want us to give that short shrift. There was no political gain for the president to travel to Rwanda. But there was every policy reason to try to hammer home the point that the international community had to react faster and better in the future than it had in that country so damaged by genocide in 1994. So "conflict resolution" was a second theme.

We also emphasized the importance of education, health (especially the HIV/AIDS crisis), human rights and post-conflict reconciliation, and environmental issues. One thing we hoped to do, too, was visit a country that faced these issues and was not English-speaking, so as not to be accused of slighting a large portion of the continent's people. The itinerary was thus whittled down to Ghana, Uganda, Rwanda, South Africa, Botswana, and Senegal, where French is spoken. While in Uganda, President Clinton was to cochair, with President Museveni, a regional summit of seven Central and East African leaders to discuss the arc of conflict that afflicted countries from Angola and Congo in the west, up through Burundi and Rwanda, to Sudan.

As we developed our plans, the keepers of the president's time began to push back, asking why we needed eleven days and couldn't we scale the trip back to three countries in four days? Our colleagues managing North Africa and the Middle East lobbied for a stop in Tunisia or Morocco. After all, since the president was in the neighborhood, how much time would that add to the schedule? We had wonderful allies in Hillary Clinton and her staff, led by Melanne Verveer, and, of course, the president himself, who must have been looking forward to getting out of Washington and the distractions of the Starr inquisition and our original eleven-day itinerary was still intact.

Perhaps the biggest debate in my office was over the stop in Uganda instead of one in Ethiopia, the headquarters of the Organization of African Unity. Both countries merited attention, but Uganda had made exemplary progress in bringing down HIV/AIDS infection rates. We wanted to showcase that success. I traveled to Addis Ababa, the Ethiopian capital, a week before the president's trip, ostensibly to give a speech but really to convey to Meles Zenawi, the prime minister, that the decision to bypass Addis was not political but a concession to the reality that the president could not do everything in the time allotted, and he was looking forward to seeing Prime Minister Meles in Uganda at the summit on Central African conflict.

Rwanda posed a special problem for us, owing to the security situation there in the aftermath of the 1994 war. The Secret Service was very nervous since it had been the shooting down of the former Rwandan president's airplane as it was landing in Kigali that had precipitated the 1994 genocide there. We had a series of meetings with the head of the presidential detail to answer all of his questions, reassuring him that the situation was stable enough for the president to travel there, and stressing that the policy implications made the stop worth the effort if there were not specific security objections. The Secret Service did their own assessment with that in mind, and they concluded that the stop could be made. Rwanda had made the itinerary.

While my directors and I were working flat-out to put all the pieces together, we also decided to use the trip as an opportunity to bring in the broader community of U.S. interests with a major stake in the continent and ask them to help us identify the goals we should focus on. This was the first time the White House had conducted such an outreach program before a presidential trip, but we felt that since it was such a rare event, we should actively engage groups that long had been supportive of a more active U.S. government approach to Africa. We covered a series of roundtable discussions, often grouping together constituencies with little in common, putting representatives from business together with nongovernmental organizations, for example. Locked in a room for three hours, discussing all of their distinct hopes for a successful presidential trip, the representatives would leave the meetings realizing that they shared many of the same objectives. The events helped to dispel mutual suspicion and antipathy among the groups, leading in the aftermath to several efforts to work cooperatively. The roundtables proved to be a highly useful source of information and ideas for the president, and after the trip, many of the participants were gratified to see their contributions reflected in what he had said and done while traveling through Africa.

All too soon, the time came to brief the president, Mrs. Clinton, who was also going on the trip, and senior cabinet and White House officials. The briefing was held in the Cabinet Room, and, in another first, I insisted that my three directors—Sanders, Prendergast, and Barks-Ruggles, who had shouldered so much of the work—accompany me so that they could brief the president themselves on the specific countries they were looking after, following an overview I would provide. Normally, only the national security adviser and the senior director, me in this case, would conduct the briefing, but each of my deputies deserved to bask in the glow of the president's positive reaction to all the planning they had done. The smiles on their faces and the spring in their step, even though we were all exhausted, told me that the decision had been the right one. They deserved the accolades, and I was delighted that they were able to receive them directly from the president.

On the night of March 22, 1998, we boarded Air Force One, knowing that we had done all we could to make the trip a success but still wondering what lay ahead. The excellent briefing books we carried had been prepared by our colleagues at the State Department, under the watchful eye and sharp editorial pencil of Susan Rice. Our embassies had been gearing up for weeks, and with great expectancy, millions of Africans awaited the arrival of the American president. I could not help but be nervous. The trip had attracted naysayers even before we left, many of whom were the usual anti-Clintonites, never missing a chance to criticize him. They argued that the trip was all show and no substance.

Unquestionably, there was *some* show. After all, an announced objective was to beam back to the American people a different picture of Africa than the one they usually saw, and we were not going to be able to do that without generating positive visual images of the land and its people. We wanted Americans to see the president with ordinary African families as well as heads of state, with survivors of genocide as well as the new breed of business entrepreneurs. Only through making Africa vividly real to Americans would they understand why the policies that we wanted to implement, including the African Growth and Opportunity Act, known informally as the African Trade Bill, deserved their support.

After an all-night flight, we touched down in Accra, Ghana, where the president was to make his opening speech and showcase the Peace Corps' thirty-plus years of presence there. I was particularly worried about this first stop. What President Clinton said here would set the tone for the entire trip, and for the coverage of it back home. The White House advance staff had resisted the Ghanaian government's entreaties that his speech be held in the huge Independence Square; they feared that the vast space would not be full and that it would look like their boss was speaking to a half-capacity audience. They could not believe Bill Clinton would draw the half million people it would take to fill the square. I finally intervened when the two sides appeared deadlocked. I had been in Africa a long time and had seen visits of leaders from French President Mitterrand to Muhammar Qhadafi. I was absolutely convinced that the excitement surrounding this historic visit of an American president, as well as President Clinton's own infectious charisma, would bring out huge crowds.

I went out on a limb and guaranteed the advance staff that Independence Square would be full. Reckless, perhaps, I thought as we landed, but my doubts soon faded. The streets from the airport into the capital were jammed with people cheering our motorcade. I was in a car with Jesse Jackson, for whom the welcome was only slightly less enthusiastic than for the president himself. There were at least 500,000 people on the sidewalks as we snaked through the city. Given the festive atmosphere, it was clear they would soon join the others already at the square.

The welcome in Ghana and the president's speech did indeed set the tone for the trip. President Jerry Rawlings draped President Clinton in the colorful kente cloth for which Ghana is famous, and the American president addressed the largest audience he had ever faced, a sea of African faces all across the square. The enthusiasm was indeed infectious; by the time we returned to the plane for the night flight across the continent to Uganda, all doubts had been erased. The continent had welcomed the president with the warmth and enthusiasm for which it was famous, and American news cameras had recorded it all.

In Uganda, the president visited a school to underscore our support for girls' education, and an AIDS clinic to support Uganda's efforts. Then we made our way to Rwanda to meet with genocide survivors before returning to Kampala to conduct the summit of Central African leaders.

The stop in Kigali, the capital of Rwanda, was not without controversy in the administration. There were those who felt that the president had nothing to gain by revisiting a painful experience where the international response to a horrible bloodletting had been ineffectual and unacceptable. President Clinton felt differently: it was important to make the gesture, not as an apology, as some congressional critics later complained, but as a commitment to a better future. We could not ignore the instability that continued to threaten to engulf Central Africa, and there could be no more appropriate place to address it than in Rwanda. We wanted the president to have the opportunity to meet with survivors of the genocide—not simply to hear the litanies of suffering they had endured during the massacres, and the grievous losses they had experienced, though we did not shy away from that—but to showcase how they had put their lives back together in the aftermath of the tragedy, that they had resumed coexisting even among neighbors who may have killed their sisters, brothers, parents, sons, daughters.

The draft of the president's upcoming speech was closely reviewed en route to Kigali and generated a spirited discussion about how far he should go toward saying "never again" on the question of genocide. Sandy Berger, Susan Rice, and I were summoned to Clinton's office on Air Force One to go over, line by line, what had been written. The discussion over what he should say became animated, with Sandy urging caution about committing the U.S. to something we might not be able to achieve, and Susan and me arguing that he should seize the occasion to challenge his and future administrations to come up with a rapid response plan that would address similar crisis situations before 800,000 people perished in another bloodletting somewhere.

We were still going at it when, much to our surprise, the plane landed. None of us, the president included, had even buckled up our safety belts. We were excused as he prepared for the arrival ceremony without knowing what the president was finally going to say.

After meeting with dozens of survivors of the genocide—many of whom had been forced to watch or listen as their loved ones were butchered by neighbors—President Clinton walked from the meeting site, adjacent to the landing strip, to the airport terminal in deep and somber conversation with his hosts, the all-powerful vice president, Paul Kagame, and the figurehead president, Pasteur Bizimungu. Clearly moved by what he had just witnessed and the stories he had heard, Clinton stepped up to the podium and began speaking. Suddenly I realized that the words I was hearing were not the words we had written. The president had discarded his text, and was speaking from the heart, after his affecting encounters with those who had survived. It was so wrenching that when I looked around the audience, the usually stoic Rwandans were reacting with strong emotion. Among our own delegation there were few dry eyes. It was the most moving speech I had ever heard.

Having walked among piles of dead bodies myself in Rwanda just a few years previously, I knew that we had to do better, and that was what my president was committing us to. We could not promise to prevent all acts of genocide, but we could make sure we improved our response prior to a catastrophe. He could not commit the United States government to "never again" countenance a genocide, but he got as close to it as he possibly could when he said: "Genocide can occur anywhere. It is not an African phenomenon. We must have global vigilance. And never again must we be shy in the face of the evidence." His speech soared with hope for the future, even as he sadly acknowledged our failure to react to the tragedy as it was occurring until after so many had been killed. He adopted the cadence of a Southern preacher, almost singing to the audience. It was poetry.

When he had concluded, I rose and moved into the holding room just behind the stage from where the president had spoken. A minute or so later, Clinton came in. Just the two of us were there together— no Secret Service people, no staff, no one else—and the president, with tears in his eyes, walked up to me and asked, "Did I do okay?" I was barely able to speak, the lump in my own throat was so big, but I managed to blurt out, "Yes, just fine," when he put his arms around me in a warm hug. We separated, the Secret Service came in, and the tableau dissolved seconds later. To this day it remains one of the most stirring moments of my life. My president got it, pure and simple.

Our next stop was Entebbe, Uganda, where we held the Central

African summit, which included several leaders whose countries we didn't have time to visit on the trip. Discussions there focused on conflict resolution and post-conflict reconstruction and reconciliation, and gave rise to the Great Lakes Justice Initiative, with a mandate to repair a region damaged by years of horrible violence from successive civil wars.

In South Africa, President Clinton clearly wanted to render homage to Nelson Mandela. We visited Cape Town, where the two leaders paid a visit to the prison cell on Robben Island where Mandela had been imprisoned for so many years. Mandela is one of those rare individuals for whom a lifetime of struggle and adversity has left an aura of serenity and quiet self-confidence. In Mandela's case this translates into plain talk sprinkled with humor. In the press conference after the meeting of the two presidents, Mandela made plain his differences with the United States over policies toward leaders who had supported him during his time in prison, notably Qhadafi and Castro. Clinton could only listen. Mandela, because he was Mandela, could say whatever he wanted without arousing the anger of the United States.

In Soweto, near Johannesburg, the president attended church services and then met with a number of groups of human rights activists. We had two policy objectives that we wanted to address with the South Africa stop: commitment to the development of civil society, and support for increased investment and trade between the U.S. and Africa. In Johannesburg, we opened the Ron Brown Commercial Center to support the latter goal.

The morning of our departure for our next stop, Botswana, I glanced in the mirror and was startled to see that half of my face was paralyzed. I could not move the right side of my mouth or nose, or my right eyebrow. Assuming either a spider bite or a stroke, I could not find evidence of a bite. As I thought about it, I was glad that only my face was paralyzed. If it was a stroke, I had gotten off lightly, though Valerie might think twice about marrying a man with only half a smile.

When I saw the president on Air Force One, he knew immediately what I had—Bell's palsy, an inflammation of the nerves on one side of the face. He took the time to tell me about friends of his who had been afflicted with it and what they had done to get over it. It is treatable with anti-inflammatory medication and, if caught early, can clear up within months. It was difficult to eat soup or smoke cigars, but there was not much I could do about that. Bill Clinton's kind attention helped me realize that however weird I might feel and appear, it would eventually go away once I got help for the condition. Fortunately, traveling with the president meant traveling with his doctor as well, and within hours I was taking the appropriate medication.

Botswana provided the president's road show with two superb opportunities to show off Africa in a favorable light. The first was the peaceful transfer of power from a democratically elected president to his vice president and successor. In other words, the president was there to celebrate democracy. The second came a day later when we visited Moana Game Park in Kasane, along the Chobe River in the north of the country, and used that setting to talk about environmental issues. We had all agreed that the president could not come to Africa without visiting one of the famous game reserves. Its wildlife is one of Africa's gifts to the world. The president so enjoyed his afternoon there that he returned the next morning, delighted with the parade of elephants, lions, hippos, giraffes, and various species of antelope that inhabit the preserve on the sandy plain along the banks of the river. When he returned to share his thoughts with his audience, he spoke passionately about the environment in Africa, about its fragility and about the need for conservancy and good stewardship to protect its future.

By then, we were about halfway through the trip, so the visit to Chobe gave everyone a bit of a break. But not me. When the president went to Moana, Jim Jamerson, who had accompanied us as the military representative on the trip, and I flew from Botswana to Angola to meet with Angolan President Jose Eduardo Dos Santos. It was yet another effort to try to move the peace process forward. On arrival in

Luanda, I made a televised statement to the Angolan people on behalf of President Clinton. We followed that with meetings with Dos Santos and his key advisors and returned to the plane in the afternoon to fly back to Botswana.

Before we boarded, Angolan radio asked for one last interview, which I was pleased to accommodate. We went into a private room with a television on. I looked at the screen and saw myself delivering the statement made when I arrived. Because of the Bell's palsy, I looked for all the world like a gangster from a B movie talking out of one side of my mouth. I was comforted in knowing that only a few Angolans had probably ever seen Edward G. Robinson in his cinematic heyday.

Our last stop on the trip was Senegal, which we had selected as the Francophone country because, under the exemplary leadership of President Abdou Diouf, it had long been functioning effectively as a moderate democracy, even though Diouf's party had been in power since independence twenty-eight years before. Senegal offered other accomplishments as well. We observed a USAID women-in-development project, which was helping to effect the empowerment of Senegalese women. We reviewed a military exercise that had been organized by the European Command with Senegalese troops—an event that allowed the president to promote the African Crisis Response Initiative (ACRI), which Susan Rice, Jim Jamerson, and I had worked on for the past several years.

To underscore the cultural and historical ties that bound the United States to Africa, the president visited Goree Island, where a building that had once housed slaves has been turned into a museum and shrine to those Africans who passed through its door of no return to be taken to America as slaves. On this occasion, the president again delivered another moving and heartfelt speech, introducing all the African Americans accompanying him on the trip, from Susan Rice to his secretary, Betty Currie.

His acknowledgement of cabinet officers like Secretary of Transportation Rodney Slater and Secretary of Labor Alexis Herman, and the numerous other African Americans with him, enabled the president to make the point that no matter how humble our origins—and no origin could be more humble than that of a slave in America 150 years ago—we could still aspire to, and achieve, positions of great political importance. The president then exhorted the Senegalese and all Africans to take pride in the accomplishments of their cousins despite the humble beginnings that their ancestors experienced in America.

The big news in the American press out of Senegal, however, was not the president's eloquence at Goree Island; instead, it was his response to the latest development in the legal cases that continued to preoccupy the press in America. The Paula Jones harassment suit had been thrown out of court on April 1, and somebody from the press contingent accompanying us had espied the president celebrating, playing some bongo drums—or so they reported. While the reporting did nothing to dampen enthusiasm in Senegal for the president's stop, it clearly detracted from the message we were trying to convey to our fellow citizens back home.

At one point on Goree Island, President Diouf, whom I had known for several years, turned to his wife and asked if she had been introduced to me. She had and told him so, but he continued: "It is thanks to Ambassador Wilson that the president of the United States came to Africa, and, in particular, that President Clinton is here in Senegal with us." I listened to his compliment and thought to myself that it couldn't get much better than this, when a highly respected African head of state gives you the credit for bringing the president of the United States to his continent and his country. For me, there could have been no better ending to the president's African trip on which my team and I had worked so hard. We returned to Washington, D.C., that night exhausted—and exhilarated.

The next day, Valerie and I were married at the District Building, Washington's City Hall, with her parents as our witnesses. Paralyzed face and all, it had been a hell of a couple of weeks.

Chapter Fourteen
Private Citizen

PRIVATE CITIZEN: THAT WAS MY NEW TITLE, a status I hadn't experienced during twenty-three years as an officer in the United States diplomatic corps. Getting married to Valerie hadn't been the only change in my life. I had risen about as high as I could in the Foreign Service and decided it was time to retire and try something else in life while I was still young enough to make the transition. I spent the period from July 1998 until early 2002 relishing my new life outside of officialdom. I opened a "boutique" consulting business to help American and international companies invest in Africa. Risk assessment, project development, and strategic management in foreign environments were my focus, as I wanted to take the lessons of my foreign service years and put them to use managing businesses in an international setting. With Africa still in everyone's thoughts after President Clinton's trip, and with the subsequent passage of the African Trade Bill, there was much to do. My list of clients was small, as I did not want to overextend myself while learning the ropes, but my geographical reach extended into Africa, Western Europe, and Turkey. The breadth of companies and sectors was already fascinating for me. I had become involved in gold mining in West Africa—including in Niger, which was just opening up some fields—as well as telecommunications and the petroleum sector. Oil from Africa was emerging as an alternative to oil from the Persian Gulf, with new discoveries in Angola and Equatorial Guinea fueling a surge in interest.

In May 1998, one month after Valerie and I were married, we moved into a new home. We had been looking at houses since our return from Europe the previous summer, taking every Sunday and as many Saturday afternoons as I could get away from the NSC to look at neighborhoods and houses for sale. We knew that we wanted to live in Washington itself and to have a view, if possible. There are not many areas within the district that fit that bill, but after months of searching, in February we found a house under construction that matched our criteria. To get inside, we had to inch our way carefully down an unpaved muddy drive and clamber up a half-built stairway that opened onto the kitchen. I pulled Valerie up, and we looked out through the floor-to-ceiling windows at a view of the Potomac River, the Washington Monument and Lincoln Memorial, and the skyline of Rosslyn, Virginia, across the river. It was perfect, and I wanted to make an offer on the spot. Valerie, ever the prudent one, was concerned about the cost, so we hesitated for a couple of weeks, until my brother, Will, a real estate broker visiting from San Clemente, California, showed her how it would actually cost us less per month after taxes than renting our apartment in the Watergate.

Before we found our perfect home, there had been just two issues to resolve. The first involved our life together. As Valerie put it, she hadn't wanted to push me into getting married if I wasn't ready, but she did want me to understand that if she was going to make such a large investment with me, she was damn well going to sign on the dotted line as Valerie Wilson, or not at all. That was an easy one. There had never been a question in my mind of whether we were going to marry, just when. We had known from the beginning that we were meant for each other. The purchase of the house gave us a reason to do it sooner rather than later. We had married on April 3, the day after my return from the president's trip to Africa, and a month later we signed the final sales document for our new home. It had been quite a year since we returned from Europe, and it didn't look likely to slacken off.

The other question we discussed before getting married was about children. Valerie and I had also discussed this before we married. She wanted a child, but because I already had two grown children—my twins, Sabrina and Joe, who were now in college—she was uncertain about my willingness to do it all over again. Would I be amenable to one more? she asked. H'mm, the choice seemed to be between long, kid-free vacations at ski resorts or on Caribbean beaches, and the full-time job of parenthood. Looking at my soon-to-be-wife, though, I found it hard to refuse her anything. She was the most loving and positive and best-organized person I had ever known, and was destined to make as wonderful a mother as a wife. I figured that one new addition would not substantially change our lives. One kid, one backpack, one stroller—it ought to be a piece of cake.

In January 2000, Valerie did the improbable, giving birth to my second set of twins, Trevor and Samantha.

When Valerie became pregnant, all of my friends, most of them just a pregnancy away from being grandparents, feigned wanting to congratulate me, but I knew they were really saying to themselves: "Better you than me." But they were wrong about that. Trevor and Samantha have enriched our lives enormously. Day by day they change, and every day their wonder, antics, joys, and discovery bring smiles to our faces. When the controversies surrounding my piece in the *New York Times* and the subsequent disclosure of Valerie's employment broke, their innocence, their complete dependence on us—not as envoy and operative but as parents—kept it all in perspective. Our knowledge that what's truly meaningful lies in their future, far more than in our past, has meant a lot to us. The way they keep growing, the way they wake up every morning giggling and looking for new ways to get into mischief, makes it easier to abide, or even ignore, life's upsets.

After childbirth, Valerie suffered a bout of postpartum depression (PPD), an insidious hormonal imbalance that is widely acknowledged in the medical community but plays no part in routine after-birth examinations. New mothers are rarely asked how they are responding emotionally to new additions to the family. So, unless they raise the issue of psychological malaise, PPD goes undiagnosed. Fortunately for us, Valerie is self-confident enough and knows herself well enough that when she was not feeling like herself, she reached out and got the help she needed rather than let the condition fester. In her case, medication rebalanced her hormones within a few months and she was soon back to being her old optimistic self.

My older son, Joe, favors the phrase "relentlessly cheerful" to describe her. And it is true. She can find the good in every person and in every situation. Even in the midst of dealing with the anxieties and fears that can accompany PPD, she vowed to help others cope with its debilitating effects. She became a founding member of a Washington, D.C., foundation created to encourage the medical profession to pay attention to the condition and to help new mothers cope with it.

My record of voting for winning candidates is embarrassingly poor, but that has never dampened my enthusiasm for participating in the election of our leaders. Having lived in dictatorships around the world, from the latter years of Franco's Spain in the mid-1960s to Saddam's Iraq and throughout Africa, I know from long experience that participation in our vibrant democracy is a privilege to be cherished and celebrated, not an annoyance to be ignored. The very success of the system depends on as many Americans as possible becoming engaged in the political process.

I am happy donating money to candidates—of either party—in whom I sense the potential for good leadership, and chose to make a contribution to the Bush campaign before the 2000 South Carolina primary. John McCain—despite all of his laudable military and government service to our country, including years as a prisoner of war in Vietnam—simply did not seem to me to be the best Republican candidate. Bush's rhetoric of compassionate conservatism appealed to me. It sounded as if he would revitalize the approach to foreign policy which I served under in the first Bush administration, and that struck me as a much more measured and prudent alternative to anything that McCain had to offer. I could live, I decided, with a second Bush administration in which the son's principles and polices mirrored his father's. I was also no doubt influenced by my deep respect for the father and for many of his advisers with whom I had worked a decade before.

After Bush's poor showing in New Hampshire, he moved on to South Carolina, where his campaign adopted some despicable tactics to defeat McCain. While Bush masqueraded as his affable self, promising to change the tone in Washington and restore honor and dignity to the White House, his underlings started spreading malicious rumors that McCain's wife was a drug addict and that they had a black baby. In fact, his wife had reportedly become dependent on pain pills she had been taking for a medical condition many years before. And, yes, the McCains did have an adopted child. But whose business was it that Mrs. McCain had suffered health problems? And what difference did it make that a child being raised by the McCains came from a different ethnic group than their own? How scared was the Bush campaign after their drubbing in the New Hampshire primary, and how low would they stoop to smear a candidate who dared challenge what the campaign regarded as Bush's right to the nomination? I should have learned more than I did from watching that experience, for similar tactics would later be employed to try to destroy me.

I probably would not have voted for the Republican nominee in any case, since social issues are also important to me and my views here put me firmly in the camp of the Democratic Party. But the

Bush campaign tactics in the South Carolina Republican primary represented the worst in American political discourse and should have been repudiated by the candidate. Campaigns rooted in the exploitation of people's fears, prejudices, and hatreds prevent us from identifying and electing our most capable leaders.

Soon after the South Carolina primary, I made a contribution to the Gore campaign and joined the foreign policy group advising him, meeting with them on a regular basis. Our role was not to stump for the candidate but to shape the positions that the vice president would articulate and to answer questions that came from the electorate or the press. Foreign policy was not a high priority—it rarely is, even in national campaigns—so we were not overworked. Anyway, Al was so steeped in national security matters, with his years as senator and vice president, that our contributions to his effort only supported what he already stood for rather than broke any new policy ground.

As I came to discover, this is not unusual. A campaign is as much an extended exercise in logistics as it is a showcase for new ideas. The candidate has a basic stump speech, which varies somewhat from audience to audience, but which seeks mostly to energize supporters and attract new ones. Position papers and the occasional substantive speech are used to highlight differences with competitors and to make sweeping promises, usually without many gritty details. Broad goals rather than fine points are the norm. The policy committees, such as the one I served on, provide guidance on specific issues, but their work remains mostly in the background.

The busiest people on any campaign, with the exception of the candidate, are the ones who move him from place to place and those who try to keep him "on message." The latter are the gatekeepers through which new ideas and policy proposals have to pass. American campaigns emphasize the image, character, and personality of the candidate far more than they do positions or even experience. New ideas are assessed not for their policy import but for their political impact, and the candidate naturally becomes far more scripted and less spontaneous than he might otherwise have been.

The Al Gore I accompanied to town meetings throughout Tennessee in 1985 was relaxed, humorous, and approachable, but the Al Gore in the debates and in front of the cameras during the 2000 presidential campaign came across as distant, impersonal, even arrogant to some. As a consequence, a public servant who had devoted his adult life to his country, from service in Vietnam to the vice presidency, found himself out of a job in January 2001. I have often wondered if Al wouldn't have done better if he'd been left more to his own instincts. The one time when he seemed to actually relax, other than in his concession speech after the Supreme Court ruling that made George W. Bush president, was after his Democratic primary debate with Bill Bradley at the Apollo Theater in Harlem. In a post-debate interview, he was energized, funny, and human, a far cry from the Al Gore of the debates with Bush that were so wickedly satirized on *Saturday Night Live.*

The Florida debacle and the questionable intervention of the Supreme Court left me with a bad taste, not for the incoming president but for a process that had diminished our democracy, including people gathering across from the vice president's residence in Washington and chanting "Get out of Cheney's house now." An Angolan friend of mine remarked: "One candidate loses the popular vote by over 500,000 ballots, but his brother is governor of the one state where the outcome is too close to call. The effort to count the ballots is disrupted by the Washington staffs of elected representatives from the candidate's party, and the court that ultimately adjudicates the outcome is made up largely by people appointed by the candidate's father. Sounds a lot like an election in Africa."

The 2000 election was the first I had spent in the United States since 1980, and I was stunned by the personal animus I saw among partisans of both parties. In my career, I had worked with both Republicans and Democrats and found that while we often disagreed on approaches, we shared many of the same basic objectives. I liked to think that the exchange of ideas enriched the policy outcome. Foreign policy had generally operated within well-defined parameters. The international structure developed since the end of World War II had served our national interests well. We were the world's preeminent political, economic, and military power, a position attained not simply by the growth of our military prowess but by the value of our ideas, the vitality of our culture, and the innovativeness of our economy. That success in and of itself blunted attempts to radically change direction. There was simply no reason to upset the system that had benefited us so much. Yet now there was no dialogue, just shouting, and the zealotry of ideologues. The divisions were profound and, at least in my areas of experience, unnecessary.

In retrospect, I was naïve in thinking that a mature democracy like ours would naturally embrace the rule of law and engage in polite discourse instead of the law of tooth and claw I had seen operate abroad. In this case, the shameless lust for power, and the genuine hatred among the right wing for Bill Clinton, just overwhelmed the Democrats. I was appalled by the gutter tactics of the out-of-state rabble that bullied public servants and intimidated them into stopping the recount of ballots in Miami-Dade County. I had railed against such conduct in flawed elections in Africa, and disliked it just as much in my own country.

Although I had voted for the candidate who ultimately lost the election, I assumed hopefully, and naïvely again, that once in office George W. Bush and his experienced team would curb the excesses of the extremists, and that the country would be in good hands. Valerie and I even attended a swank inauguration reception on Pennsylvania Avenue where we looked down on the president's parade route and celebrated with Bush supporters the peaceful transition of power that is the hallmark of our democracy.

One of my professional activities during this period led to a seat on the Defense subcommittee of the board of the American Turkish Council, a nonprofit organization dedicated to the promotion of U.S.-Turkish relations. Its chairman was retired General Brent Scowcroft, one of the most honorable men I have known in public life. He served as national security adviser under the first President Bush, as he had in the administration of President Ford. Pragmatic in outlook, Brent reflects the very best of traditional Republican foreign policy values. He is a committed internationalist who understands that American strength is enhanced through global cooperation and, like most military veterans, views war as a last resort to be used only in cases of absolute necessity and when all else has failed. In his mid-seventies, the general remains energetic and vigorous. While he has earned and certainly deserves his status as an icon of the foreign policy establishment and a true elder statesman, he remains as easygoing and unpretentious as one could imagine. Indeed, Scowcroft is the perfect gentleman, ever polite and always interested in the views of others. His one extravagance is a silver Mercedes convertible. Valerie has a not-so-secret crush on him—not for his car, but for his charm.

To my great pleasure, our work with the American Turkish Council threw us together from time to time. We fell into an easy relationship and would banter back and forth about the new administration and its predecessors. After board meetings or other events, we often Metroed back across town together. As the obsession with Iraq overtook many influential members of the Bush administration, our conversations turned frequently to the emerging debate on Iraq and the merits of the approach being advanced by the prowar crowd.

When the first airplane hit the World Trade Center that fateful morning, I was stuck in traffic on the Whitehurst Freeway, a mile-long stretch of highway that skirts Georgetown along the Potomac River. I could see the Kennedy Center, its modern lines squaring up at the soft bend in the river. Behind it the Washington Monument poked into the cloudless blue sky; the sticky humidity of barely a week before had disappeared. I was on my cell phone, talking with a friend, as cars around me eased forward only a few feet with every change of the traffic lights. He told me that an airplane had hit the north tower and that I should to turn on the television as soon as I arrived at work. He was describing what he was watching on TV when he suddenly cried out that a second plane had just hit the other tower. Clearly, terrorists had struck.

I arrived at my office, a block from the White House on Pennsylvania Avenue, and was talking to a colleague when the phone rang with the news that the Pentagon had also been hit. Then Valerie called from CIA headquarters; I told her that I would go home and get the kids into the house. They were with our nanny at a park down the street from where we lived, a park that lay right in the landing pattern for flights into Ronald Reagan Washington National Airport, across the Potomac River from the White House and downtown Washington. I closed the office and sent everybody home; nobody was going to get any work done this day. It was a good decision. Within ten minutes of leaving our building, the federal government closed, and the relatively empty streets that I had just navigated were clogged with vehicles fleeing the center of the city.

With three targets already hit, could the White House or the Capitol be next? Or, for that matter, could CIA headquarters be a target?

Heading home, I could see the white smoke pouring from the Pentagon across the river. I worried about my twins, now almost two years old. If it became necessary to shoot down a suspicious aircraft, I was certain we would do it. We would have no choice. I wanted my kids nowhere near the landmarks under a flight path. Fortunately, by the time I arrived at the park, National Airport had been closed to traffic. I got the kids and the nanny into the back of the car and raced home. While they fussed in the other room, I restlessly flipped from one TV channel to another, mesmerized by the enormity of the disaster. Phone lines were saturated, and it was impossible to get through to Valerie's parents in Pennsylvania, though I did manage to reassure my brother, in California, that we were safe.

Valerie arrived home about lunchtime. Throughout the afternoon we watched TV fixedly as the rumors of more planes en route to strategic sites and of bombs going off near the State Department made us wonder how extensive the attack was.

As the nightmare unfolded over the next few days, our neighborhood was remarkably calm. With all flights grounded, the familiar sounds of airplanes making their final turn down the river about a half mile from our house were eerily absent. The chirping of birds, usually drowned out by the drone of jet engines, was the only background noise—but to our ears it was joyless music. Smoke continued to rise from the wreckage of the Pentagon wing that had been hit, and day and night, the airwaves bore the raw emotions of a nation in mourning, a nation shocked at the loss of thousands of our fellow citizens and the assault on these important symbols in two of our greatest cities. The country was coming to grips with its new vulnerability after two centuries of seeming invincibility afforded by two oceans. As a people, we had to deal with this assault on our person, our property, and our innocence.

Valerie and I watched as our president made us proud with his trip to New York and with his eulogy at the National Cathedral. Knowing his father, I was particularly touched to see the former president reach over and pat the present one on the arm when he returned to his pew. That gesture epitomized perfectly the character, as I knew him, of this most human of presidents and of men. Later, we applauded as his son, the young president, stood in the rubble of the twin towers with his arm around a firefighter and a bullhorn to his mouth, defiantly promising to avenge the attack. President Bush comforted us all in a time of great emotional need. He had risen to the occasion and had shown the mettle that the situation demanded. He and his team had lived up to their billing as experienced and sober men ready to meet any challenge to our national security.

In the ensuing days, we later learned, before the airports reopened and the planes flew again, officials at the National Security Council meetings chaired by the president began to consider the range of actions that might be taken in response to the attack. According to Bob Woodward's book *Bush at War*, even as the Taliban regime in Afghanistan was coming into view as a legitimate target of our response on the afternoon of September 12, Secretary of Defense Rumsfeld had already raised the possibility of using the terrorist attacks as a pretext to overthrow the regime of Saddam Hussein: "Why shouldn't we go against Iraq, not just al Qaeda?" he asked. Rumsfeld was speaking not only for himself when he raised the question. His deputy, Paul C. Wolfowitz, was committed to a policy that would make Iraq a principal target for the first round in the war on terrorism, according to Woodward.

More recently, we have learned that the focus on Iraq began even earlier than the day after the terrorist attacks. The revelations in Ron Suskind's *The Price of Loyalty: George W. Bush, the White House, and the Education of Paul O'Neill* document that in the first National Security Council meeting of the Bush presidency, on January 30, 2001—more than seven months before 9/11—the administration made the decision that the ouster of Saddam Hussein would take center stage on the policy agenda, while at the same time they would disengage from mediation of the Israeli–Palestinian conflict.

In the book, O'Neill recalls the administration's early days this way: "From the start, we were building the case against Hussein and looking at how we could take him out and change Iraq into a new country. And, if we did that, it would solve everything. It was all about finding *a way to do it*. That was the tone of it. The President saying, 'Fine. Go find me a way to do this.' "

In that earlier NSC meeting, President Bush, remembering a heli-copter flight he'd made over Palestinian refugee camps with Ariel Sharon in 1998, said: "'Looked real bad down there. I don't see much we can do over there at this point. I think it's time to pull out of that situation.'" The recollections of O'Neill and other administration officials in Suskind's book shed much light on the unprecedented decision to reduce our efforts to mediate peace between Israel and its neighbors, even as the sit-uation began to spiral downward with the onset of the second intifada.

In the aftermath of 9/11, to the members of the president's inner circle, the focus of their counterattack was already destined to include Iraq, even if no ties were to be found between Saddam Hussein and Osama bin Laden's al Qaeda. Even as the administration was bril-liantly reacting to the attacks and preparing to destroy al Qaeda and its Taliban host, it was already becoming distracted from the war on terrorism to focus on the military invasion and conquest of Iraq. As Bob Woodward points out in his book, Paul Wolfowitz and fellow neoconservatives had long seen Saddam as the most dangerous threat to peace in the Middle East. The seeds of the new Iraq war had been sown in the first Gulf War in 1991 and grew in the frustration that Saddam had not been deposed then. The trigger that propelled the renewed effort to take him down was a monstrous national calamity not of Saddam's making, nor any immediate threat that Iraq posed to our national security. That a tragedy would be used to abuse the instruments of government, deceive the American people, and entangle us in a foreign adventure guaranteed to fail before we put the first sol-dier across the border is a travesty. It was also a strategic mistake of historic proportions.

Most analysts agreed that Saddam's hard line against Israel, his support for some of the region's most notorious characters, his stock-pile of chemical weapons, and his ambition to develop both biological and nuclear weapons had made him an enemy who could not be ignored. There was no question that his regime had regional ambitions, that it had weapons of mass destruction (WMD), and that it sought additional capability.

The Israelis did not ignore him. In 1981, they had perceived the Iraqi construction of a nuclear power facility as such a danger that they destroyed it in a precision air attack.

The United States had not ignored him either. In 1991, we had effectively destroyed his army, at the time estimated to be the fourth largest in the world.

The United Nations, under our leadership, had run a successful inspection regime for seven years, destroying more WMD than even the Gulf War coalition had, and also ferreting out the details of Saddam's nuclear program. (Yes, a defector had provided the key clue, but detective work usually depends on a break here and a break there; and, irrespective of how, the goal had been achieved.) The United States, the United Kingdom, and Turkey had successfully interdicted Iraqi control of most of its own airspace since 1991, and, of course, the sanctions had made key ingredients for a WMD program very difficult to obtain without detection. Even after the withdrawal of the inspectors in 1998, and the erosion of the international will to maintain sanctions on Iraq, Saddam was still contained. There was minimal threat to the region or to us so long as we remained vigilant.

In short, Saddam was hardly being ignored.

But Wolfowitz and his colleagues persisted in arguing that the only way to deal with the menace of Iraq was with invasive military action. For many years they had lobbied to build support in Congress, where Saddam—a notorious tyrant and serial sociopath, who started wars with impunity, gassed his own people, and engaged in some of the most dastardly human rights violations of the twentieth century—surely had no friends. His ongoing efforts to thwart the weapons inspectors, his clumsy attempt to assassinate former President Bush in Kuwait, and his unremitting hostility toward his neighbors and Israel made him anathema to all American leaders, of both parties. However, the United States does not invade a country simply because it has an evil leader; it only does so if that country poses a grave and gathering danger to our national security.

In 1998 Congress had passed—and President Clinton signed— the Iraq Liberation Act, which codified regime change and made available approximately $90 million per year to fund opposition activities. Even without such legislation, American administrations have long had regime-change policies in place toward countries whose leaders we did not like—Cuba, Libya, and Sudan, for instance. There had been a number of precedents for effecting regime change without resorting to war, including successful efforts during the Reagan administration in Poland and in the southern Africa countries of Namibia and South Africa.

Our military is the greatest in the world, but our society is not a marauding one that readily agrees to using our might on foreign adventures. The attack on September 11, 2001, was key for the prowar crowd because it provided a cataclysmic event the administration could use to frighten Americans into believing that Saddam Hussein was at the root of all their fears and that an offensive war against Iraq was the only remedy. It was not happenstance that large pluralities of Americans came to believe that Saddam had been responsible for 9/11 and that he had nuclear weapons. These were misconceptions fostered by administration officials who continually made misleading statements in a classic propaganda operation staged to fool all of the people in the some-of-the-time it took to go to war.

Before 9/11, regime change by invasion was still just a fringe part of the debate about how to handle Saddam Hussein. The Iraq Liberation Act was viewed mostly as a way to bring additional pressure to bear on him by activating other tools at America's disposal—funding of resistance efforts, subversion, and propaganda—and not as a call to commit American troops to war. As we know from the rapidly rising costs of the war that the Bush administration committed the country to ($150 billion as of February 2004), the $90 million annual appropriation in the 1998 act would barely have funded three days' meals for the conquering army, much less a full-scale war. Very few saw the act as presaging a military offensive. But one who did was Marine Corps General Anthony Zinni, the commander of U.S. armed forces responsible for the Gulf region, of Central Command (CENTCOM), from 1997 to 2000. As the bill made its way through Congress, he warned some senior members of his staff about its implications and said the bill was far more serious than skeptics believed. Zinni understood that this was no mere gesture but a rallying point for the prowar crowd. It was a preliminary stride toward invasion, not just another small step in the political campaign to undermine Saddam. He was, of course, right, but few were listening.

Well before the fires in the World Trade Center wreckage had stopped smoldering, neoconservatives were on their favored cable television shows calling on the administration to implement the thrust of the Iraq Liberation Act by going to war. The act's passage was cited as the bipartisan expression of the will of Congress that now, in the aftermath of the terrorist attacks, must be fully implemented. The drums of war against Iraq were being pounded. They would beat relentlessly for the next year and a half.

When Brent Scowcroft and I would talk about the strident tone of the neoconservatives, he was dismissive. "Right-wing nuts," he called them. I was more alarmed, but he reassured me that they did not enjoy senior administration support, even as their rhetoric reached fever pitch. "They will not win the policy," he would say. I listened and wanted to believe him. Occasionally, I'd gently tease him that the Republicans seemed to be straying off course. We were committing our future, I'd say, to a band of fanatics whose approach was the opposite of that pursued by the first President Bush, or articulated by candidate George W. Bush in his November 1999 foreign policy speech at the Reagan Library and in his debates with Al Gore.

Brent had worked with Vice President Cheney and with Secretary

Rumsfeld since the Ford administration. He had been part of the team that coined the phrase "New World Order" to encapsulate a vision of an interconnected global security system that fostered international cooperation to deal with threats to our common good. Surely, I thought, his sage counsel was being listened to in the White House.

In May 2002, several months after my trip to Niger, I participated in the annual conference of the American Turkish Council. One of the keynote speakers was Richard Perle, a resident scholar at the American Enterprise Institute and one of the most virulent of the neoconservative war advocates. In a seminal paper, written in 1996 for Israeli Prime Minister Benjamin Netanyahu entitled "A Clean Break: A New Security Strategy for the Realm," Perle and his coauthors argued for the redrawing of the political map of the Middle East to serve Israel's national security interests. The strategy included the overthrow of Saddam—"a laudable goal in its own right," remarked the paper—as well as the neutralization of Israel's other neighbors.

In his speech at the conference, Perle spoke openly of a coming war with Iraq. His words, laden with the fire and brimstone of the true zealot, troubled me deeply. In a symposium that I cochaired the same afternoon with the former Turkish military commander, Cevik Bir, I voiced my concerns.

It was the first time in more than a decade that I'd spoken publicly about Iraq. I had been out of government for four years. I was making a nice second career for myself by seeking out investment opportunities for select international clients. I did not need any notoriety that might result from stating my views publicly. Yet I was increasingly worried that only one point of view was being presented in a debate of paramount importance to any society, but particularly to a great democracy such as ours. No decision is more important than that to send a nation's sons and daughters to a foreign land in order to kill and perhaps die for their country. As a democracy, we are all participants in that decision. Not to speak out would amount to complicity in whatever decision was taken.

In my comments at the symposium, I argued that if we were prepared to entertain the possibility that in the coming year Iraq might be reduced to a chemical, biological, and nuclear wasteland, then we should march in lockstep to the martial music being played by Perle; if not, then we should think about alternatives to war. Bir, an experienced military man who had also served with the United Nations effort in Somalia, agreed, and, if anything, was even more strident than me in his opposition to military action. For the most part, the audience, largely American and Turkish businessmen, agreed with us. Perle, of course, had long since departed the meeting.

As I later discovered while debating the issue, the prowar advocates were little inclined to listen to the views of others. They had made up their minds long ago, and now it was a matter of ramming their agenda through the decision-making process.

By June 2002, it was clear that there were few forces willing to confront the neoconservative juggernaut. They had mastered the art of marketing their policy prescriptions and were aggressive and intimidating in debate. Their strategy, as I discovered, was to make an opening statement, interrupt the person making a different argument, and then filibuster to the end of a five-minute television segment. That domination of the available time, coupled with aggressively stated talking points and *ad hominem* attacks on the credibility and intelligence of their interlocutor, was designed to leave viewers with the impression these neocon experts were the only ones who knew what they were talking about. After a while, many of the genuine experts on the region, people who had spent their careers living and working in the Arab world, simply refused to subject themselves to such demeaning behavior and retired to the sidelines.

Up to that point, my own participation in the debate had been limited to my involvement at the American Turkish Council symposium and to some private discussions with former colleagues who had formed a small organization, the Alliance for American Leadership. Its mission was to bring together policy makers from previous, mostly Democratic, administrations to discuss the direction in which the country was headed. This group, mirroring the roiling emotions within the country, was divided on the question but generally supported the notion that we should use our military to take out Saddam. His horrible behavior had so soured American policy makers of both parties that the desire to see him removed overwhelmed serious discussion about whether he constituted a real threat to our national security. Nor did the Alliance ponder the potential unintended consequences of an ill-considered military action.

I tried to share my concerns about the difficulties we might face in getting to Baghdad and in occupying it once we got there, but it was to a mostly indifferent audience. The consensus was that opposing the administration was a losing cause. Politics trumped sound policy.

The head of the Alliance, former ambassador to Morocco, Marc Ginsberg, had frequently appeared as a pundit on various FOX news programs. Despite our different views, he arranged for me to make guest appearances on a couple of them over the summer of 2002. On those occasions, I pointed out that Iraq posed one legitimate national security threat to the United States, and that was from Saddam's weapons of mass destruction. A series of U.N. Security Council resolutions passed before and after the first Gulf War recognized that threat and had sought to deal with it through the intrusive inspections. That enforcement mechanism of inspections had collapsed when the international inspection teams were withdrawn in 1998 just prior to the Clinton administration's four-day "Desert Fox" cruise missile attacks on suspected WMD sites. They had not returned since.

International support, both for inspections and for the ongoing economic sanctions, had waned. Key members of the U.N. Security Council, notably the French and the Russians, were meanwhile actively seeking to normalize relations with Iraq, and it was clear that reinvigorating the international will to monitor Saddam's programs would be difficult. Kenneth Pollack, in his acclaimed book *The Threatening Storm*—the definitive case that to disarm Saddam we would have to militarily overthrow him—concluded that it would be all but impossible to regain an international consensus to coercively contain Saddam, and that it was too dangerous to ignore him.

Brent Scowcroft was becoming increasingly concerned that perhaps his earlier optimism had been misplaced. No longer certain that the administration would shun the neoconservative path, he wrote a piece that appeared in the *Wall Street Journal* on August 15, 2002. He warned of potential disaster if we tried to deal with Saddam militarily. Former Secretary of State James Baker III, too, was cautionary; he wrote in the *Washington Post* that whatever we decided had to be underpinned by an international consensus and coalition.

Former U.N. Ambassador Richard Holbrooke followed suit in another op-ed, and the debate was joined, albeit somewhat feebly, by other informed public officials who worried about the consequences of taking unilateral military action. While both Baker and Holbrooke entertained the possibility of a war for regime change, they each favored working with the international community, which virtually guaranteed that any U.N. resolution would surely stop short of authorizing the invasion of a member state, however deplorable. Meanwhile, I continued to grouse privately and to make occasional appearances on little-watched cable television outlets.

I made an early summer appearance on CNN's *American Morning* with Paula Zahn and repeated my point that we needed to be wary of a regime-change war as the best way to achieve the disarmament objective. Paula could not have been sweeter as she delivered a classic brush-off: "Thank you very much, Ambassador Wilson. That is one man's opinion." I heard nothing more from her producers for several weeks, as the pro–regime-change war rhetoric dominated the broadcast debate.

Friends of both political persuasions grew tired of my whining about the direction in which the policy was headed, prompting one, Anita Sharma, the talented director of the Conflict Resolution Program at the Woodrow Wilson International Center for Scholars in Washington, to suggest bluntly that if I didn't like the course the administration was pursuing, I should write an article laying out my alternative views. Do something about it or shut up! Enough complaining, she said; and she was right. It is never enough to just sit on the sidelines and kvetch. Democracy asks us, requires us, to be engaged with issues, to become involved and not to accede to the loudest voices without questioning them.

I wrote my first newspaper article for the *San Jose Mercury News* Perspective section on October 13, 2002, arguing that although the disarmament of Iraq was a legitimate international goal, the president would need a credible threat of force behind his diplomacy if he ever hoped to persuade Saddam to comply. However, I said, we had to be very careful about setting up regime change as our military objective. My personal experience with Saddam and his henchmen had persuaded me that he would engage in every dirty trick in the book if he believed that the goal of military action was to topple him. On the other hand, I added, he might value his personal survival more than his WMD, and not resist disarmament if he thought that might enable him to survive. The trick was to make clear to him that he was going to be disarmed one way or another; however, should he use WMD to defend himself against coalition actions, military or otherwise, or if he should use them against any of his neighbors or against Israel, that would be justification to destroy him and his regime. I made the point, furthermore, that this was not a question of war versus no war, but a choice between smart military action for the right reasons and a misguided war fought for dumb reasons.

I sent my article to Scowcroft, Baker, and the president's father out of courtesy, because in it I referred to the lessons learned in the diplomacy of the first Gulf War. In particular, I cited the Baker–Aziz meeting in Geneva in January 1991 and Secretary Baker's unmistakable message to Tariq Aziz: If Saddam did not withdraw his troops from Kuwait peacefully by January 15, then the coalition armed forces would drive Iraq's forces back across its border; should Saddam use WMD against our action, then Baker made it clear that we would destroy the regime, the implication being that we might even use nuclear weapons in response to a chemical attack. If Saddam had been considering using WMD, the tactic worked; he was deterred.

By contrast, I believed that the current regime-change rhetoric ensured that Saddam would use every weapon in his arsenal, for there was nothing to deter him from doing his worst. Offering a way out allowed at least the possibility that we would not provoke precisely what we were trying to avoid—a chemical, biological, and potentially nuclear war in the Arabian desert.

Brent called me when he received the article. He kindly asked if he could "take it over to the White House," only about two blocks from his downtown office. He said that he thought senior officials ought to read the views of somebody who actually had experience in Iraq and with Saddam's government. By this, I took him to mean that he intended to share it with the national security adviser, Dr. Condoleezza Rice, or her deputy, Stephen Hadley. Dr. Rice, a Scowcroft protégée, had been brought into the National Security Council during the first Bush administration. At the time of the first Gulf War, she had been in charge of Soviet Affairs. While we had never met during that period, I assumed that she knew who I was because of my frequent cables from Baghdad, especially since the U.S. was then working so closely with the Russians.

At that time, President Gorbachev had sent his special envoy, Yevgeny Primakov, to Baghdad twice to try to convince Saddam to quit Kuwait rather than suffer a military defeat. Primakov had emerged from his second meeting with Saddam saying that he had "been mildly encouraged by what he had not heard from the Iraqi dictator." What he had not heard was mistakenly interpreted as a hint that Saddam was showing some flexibility. ("Thin gruel, indeed," was the tart observation by Frank Wisner, U.S. ambassador to Egypt.) Surely Dr. Rice had to have followed these developments and the names of those reporting from the field. I had no misplaced desire for notoriety in this: even if she didn't recognize my name, my experiences in Baghdad were clearly described in the article.

Later, when the administration stumbled in its pronouncements after my *New York Times* op-ed column on July 6, I could not understand what Rice thought she was accomplishing by leaving interviewers with the impression that she had no idea who I was. Perhaps she has a poor memory, although I find that as improbable as her claim later that she had simply forgotten about the CIA memoranda dealing with the vital question of purported uranium sales from Niger to Iraq.

Several days after the call from General Scowcroft, I received a letter from former President Bush. It was a warm note, not unexpected in light of the many communications I had received from him over the years. My relationship with the former president, even though contact was infrequent, is one that I shall always cherish. His concern for me and for every other American citizen in harm's way during the first Gulf War, as well as the personal attention he afforded me when so many other demands were competing for his time, guarantees my unqualified personal affection. In the note, he said he "agreed with almost everything" I had written.

A few weeks later, I also received a letter from Secretary Baker, in which he kindly offered that "the administration seems to have taken your advice."

By the time I received Baker's letter, President Bush's rhetoric had undergone a decided shift, largely due to efforts of British Prime Minister Tony Blair to reframe the issue as one of disarmament. Gone from the president's public statements were references to regime change. Instead, he was making statements to the effect that either "he will disarm or we will disarm him." When later asked if the language represented a change in approach, senior officials scoffed at the notion. If Saddam disarmed, then the regime had by definition changed, they explained.

A number of Web sites that aggregate and distribute via E-mail important articles, such as Truthout.org, Buzzflash.com, Common-dreams.org, and Alternet.org, were evidently interested in mine, and their electronic distribution of it generated some new invitations for me to appear on television. I began to field calls from producers for pro-grams including *Hannity & Colmes* and *The O'Reilly Factor* on FOX and *Buchanan and Press* on MSNBC. A producer from Paula Zahn's show even called and invited me back.

I welcomed the opportunity to participate, because I honestly believed that insights I had drawn from my experience in Iraq would contribute to our understanding of the potential consequences of the war being contemplated. Disarmament was a legitimate objective to pursue, particularly as it had been supported by the international community on repeated occasions. I simply disagreed with the need to invade, conquer, and occupy Iraq in order to arrive at a high degree of confidence that it had been disarmed.

As to the other justifications for war, I stated on TV that Iraq's operational ties to international terrorism "with a global reach," to use the president's phrase, were debatable and, at a minimum, inconclu-sive. The suggestion that Saddam might give WMD to international ter-rorists was always specious. Director of the CIA George Tenet testified to Congress and advanced the widely accepted view, which I shared, that the only time Saddam might let go of his WMD would be in the final throes of a defeat, in a desperate attempt to inflict a posthumous last laugh on his enemies. Saddam was nothing if not a control freak; control of his WMD, if he still had them, the crown jewels of his rule, would be his highest priority. To contend that he would surrender that control to an unaccountable group of nihilistic terrorists had always been absurd.

Further justification for the invasion lay in the frequently asserted need to liberate and democratize the Iraqis after thirty years of tyranny that included, as we heard repeatedly, mass graves and barbaric human rights violations, including Saddam's use of chemical weapons. Who can forget the poignant sight of Secretary of State Colin Powell at the mass graves of Iraqi Kurds in Halabja in September 2003? But do we remember that the same Colin Powell was national security adviser in the first Bush administration when the gassing of those Kurds had occurred? It had long been legitimate to accuse Saddam of genocide against his own population; but previous administrations, notably those in office when he was committing the most egregious of his murderous activities, had never before seriously sought to punish his behavior. These violations of human rights had not elicited much opprobrium from the United States government, back when relations with Saddam had served as a useful counterweight in our dealings with Iran.

One mechanism to condemn the murderous aspects of Saddam's rule would have been to use the International Convention on Genocide, which provides legal underpinning for action against murderous regimes. While after the 2003 invasion the Bush administration would inveigh even more vociferously against his brutality, exercising the terms of the genocide treaty was never seriously discussed, either domestically or at the U.N., by an administration so averse to the multilateralism this would have required.

At the time of my first *Mercury News* piece, however, Congress was in the midst of its debate on a resolution that, if passed, would give the president broad powers to take action against Iraq, including military action if he deemed it necessary. The resolution enjoyed the broad support of the Republican Party, especially in the House of Representatives, where Majority Leader Tom DeLay guaranteed total discipline among his troops. In the Senate, the support was more considered, and certain changes were made in the resolution, though none that imposed significant restraint on the president. Democratic Senators Robert Byrd (with superb eloquence), Edward Kennedy, Carl Levin, and the chairman of the Foreign Relations Committee, Joe Biden, made a concerted effort to impose some limits on the "blank-check resolution," so called for the latitude it would give the president.

President Bush argued—disingenuously, as it turned out—that he needed the resolution not to go to war, but to be able to negotiate a strong disarmament resolution at the United Nations. Absent the threat of the U.S. going it alone, the president claimed that the U.N. would never reconstitute an intrusive inspections regime. Republicans increased the pressure on Democrats by making it clear that if they did not get their resolution language quickly, they would accuse Democrats of being soft on national security in the upcoming midterm elections. This was a killer charge in the aftermath of the World Trade Center and Pentagon attacks, even though it was unfair and untrue. In the end, both chambers submitted to the president's insistence that America's national security was at stake and passed the war resolution.

In a bitter irony, the Republicans ran a "soft on terrorism" campaign against Georgia Senator Max Cleland anyway. Senator Cleland—who had lost his two legs and an arm fighting for his country in Vietnam—tried to prevent the administration from using the Homeland Security Act as a vehicle for gutting traditional civil-service protections for federal workers under the new Homeland Security Department. For that, Cleland's Republican opponent ran attack ads that literally put him alongside Osama bin Laden. It was one of the most despicable Senate campaigns ever, and the Vietnam veteran lost his seat to a candidate who had never served in the military. It was shameful treatment of a true patriot.

On November 8, 2002, armed with his use-of-force resolution from Congress, the president's strategy paid off when the United Nations Security Council unanimously passed Resolution 1441. Iraq would be given one last chance to comply with all the previous resolutions and was required to submit an updated declaration of everything it had produced in the way of programs, weapons, missiles, precursors—essentially everything regarding its weapons of mass destruction—within thirty days, or face the consequences.

Even before the due date of the Iraqi declaration was reached, the hard-liners began declaring that anything Saddam delivered would, by definition, be a lie and that we should invade Iraq as soon after the deadline as possible. If the neoconservatives had been angry before the U.N. deal—and they were—they were truly furious afterward. The ink on the resolution was barely dry before they launched attacks on Colin Powell for having led the president down the wrong path, one in which he was placing his faith in what they said was a feckless international community.

Attacks on Hans Blix, the Swedish diplomat who headed the U.N. inspection effort, followed soon after. They turned very personal and came from a very senior level in the administration. Vice President Cheney claimed on several occasions that Blix and his International Atomic Energy Agency counterpart, Dr. Mohamed El Baradei, had been fooled by Saddam in the past and, by implication, would be again. Critics of the U.N. said the U.S. should never allow a bunch of foreigners to prevent the administration from doing everything in its power to defend the country in the war on terror. The message was clear: the war party would not be denied its fight by some meddlesome international bureaucrats, even if the WMD threat did not merit war and there were no clear links between

Saddam Hussein and Osama bin Laden. They simply would not accept any outcome but war.

With the deadline looming, chicken hawks, including Ken Adelman, James Woolsey, former director of the CIA, and Richard Perle, claimed that since Saddam would never declare all of his weapons, President Bush, to be credible, would have to act no more than a few days after the Iraqi declaration. The war would kick off before Christmas— if not by then, no later than mid-January, they solemnly intoned.

Reading from the neocons' script, no sooner had the declaration landed at the U.N. in New York than the administration proclaimed that it was full of holes. By December 19, the State Department had published a fact sheet with its version of Iraq's inconsistencies listed. I did not see the fact sheet at the time, but I learned later that the first iteration contained a reference to Iraqi attempts to buy uranium from Niger. The reference was apparently scrubbed soon after, and the Niger charge was removed—at least for a time. News reports after the fact suggested that the neoconservative mole in the State Department, John Bolton, the under secretary for Arms Control, had slipped the reference into the first version, but someone at State had caught the mistake and deleted it.

The first public reference to the uranium charge had been in a British white paper published in September 2002, three months before receipt of Iraq's weapons declaration. In it, the British asserted that Iraq had sought significant quantities of uranium from Africa. I had read the press reports on the white paper, and though I was mildly curious about which country in Africa the British were talking about, I did not inquire. After all, there are four African countries that produce uranium: Niger, where I had started my career; Gabon, where I had served as ambassador; and South Africa, where I had also worked. The fourth was Namibia, where I had not served. I thought it possible that the British were referring to South Africa, though that seemed unlikely, or perhaps Namibia.

I wouldn't learn for six months that the country referred to in the British claim was, in fact, Niger. At the State Department, the charge that Iraq had sought uranium there clearly had no credibility. But I would soon discover that ideologues there, and in other parts of the administration, were determined to keep pushing the lie about an Iraq–Niger uranium transaction, no matter how many times it would be refuted.

Chapter Fifteen
The Road to the Second Gulf War

FROM OCTOBER 2002, SHORTLY AFTER THE PUBLICATION of my first opinion piece, up to the beginning of the war in March 2003, my own contributions to the debate on Iraq continued, mostly on cable news broadcasts. I appeared three times on *Hannity & Colmes,* the FOX political talk show that resembles the old Morton Downey, Jr. show more than it does serious debate. Sean Hannity, easily one of the least interesting people I have ever spoken to, takes more interest in pushing an extremist right-wing agenda than in promoting an honest discussion of the issues. He also has no idea what he is talking about, at least on foreign policy, and does a great disservice to his audience. His tactic of making *ad hominem* attacks on the integrity and patriotism of those whose views he does not share may make for amusing entertainment, but it denigrates the serious discussion we should have before we send our military marching off to war. Fair and balanced it is not.

I accepted invitations to appear on *Hannity & Colmes,* and on the equally vapid *O'Reilly Factor,* because I thought those programs drew audiences that deserved to have the benefit of another point of view on which to base their political judgments. Issues of war and peace are so critical to the future of our country and our national security that they rate more than simply propagandistic treatment. War is not entertainment; it is serious business. So, like other concerned citizens, including former Maine Congressman Tom Andrews, the head of the Win Without War coalition, and Mike Farrell, the longtime Human Rights Watch activist and costar of TV's M*A*S*H, I laid out my case for tough disarmament on these shows.

To his credit, Bill O'Reilly was a polite interviewer and at least listened to the airing of all sides of the issue. Hannity, on the other hand, made his guests mere props for his political rants. On my final appearance on Hannity's show, he began the segment by implying that I was an appeaser and a Bush-hating Democrat, neither of which bore any relationship to my position on the war or to who I am. I responded forcefully, pointing out that his position as host did not allow him to spout lies about his guests. He went ballistic when I wouldn't let him interrupt me and threatened to cut off my microphone. I decided then that I wouldn't waste any more time on his program, as he clearly wasn't interested in providing his audience with any views other than his own.

For many years, I had known Edward (Ned) Walker, president of the Middle East Institute, a venerable Washington institution dedicated to fostering a deeper understanding of the region. Ned had been ambassador to Egypt and the United Arab Emirates (U.A.E.) and to Israel, as well as assistant secretary for Near Eastern Affairs. The institute he runs is refreshingly free of ideology and polemics and serves as a useful forum for views from all sides.

Walker and I crossed paths at a luncheon cohosted by the institute for a delegation from Jordan, which included many former members of the Jordanian government and advisers to the late King Hussein. They had come to Washington to plead the case for a more even-handed approach to the plight of the Palestinians in the Israeli-occupied territories. I brashly offered, with all respect, that if the delegation were to succeed, its members needed to understand that the American administration and the American people viewed the Arab–Israeli problem through the prism of terrorism. Given our own shock at the attacks on us, we naturally sided with others who themselves were victims of monstrous violence. The second intifada, Arafat's horrendous response to the failure to reach agreement in the negotiations brokered by the Clinton administration during its last days, had been a disaster, I said, that fed into the hands of extremists of all sides.

After lunch, the Middle East Institute's communications director, Maggie Mitchell, complimented me on the frankness of my comments and suggested that the institute name me an unpaid adjunct scholar and refer news outlets to me for any information or opinion they might require regarding the Middle East—Iraq, in particular. I was pleased to accept her offer.

The air waves were saturated with spokesmen from the neoconservative faction. They were continually popping up under different titles; one of their strategies had been to create a whole host of pseudo-foundations and nongovernmental organizations to give the public the impression that they enjoyed a groundswell of support far broader than was the case. Their marketing strategy was as good as the policy they were advocating was flawed. They would make assertions devoid of sense with total confidence, and utter known falsehoods as the gospel truth. A classic from their reperteroire: the supposed meeting in Prague of the suicide hijacker Mohammed Atta with an Iraqi intelligence officer, now knocked down by a number of intelligence services, including our own.

I had one such exchange with Ken Adelman, an acolyte of former U.N. Ambassador Jeanne Kirkpatrick, in the fall of 2002. He had not been in government for several years, until he was picked to serve on the unpaid but very influential Defense Policy Board, made famous by the presence of Richard Perle, its chairman for a time (he has since resigned from the group entirely). In my exchange with Adelman, he tried to ridicule my position on disarmament by saying that I did not have access to intelligence and therefore could not comment knowledgably on the subject. Given the trip I had taken to Niger February 2002, I could not help but chuckle to myself. However, I continued to push the point that our true national security concern was weapons of mass destruction in the arsenal of a rogue state like Iraq. I insisted that we focus our energies on meeting that threat, not allowing ourselves to be sidetracked by the seductive dream of regime change.

When I entered into a mini-debate with former Reagan defense official and arch neocon Frank Gaffney some weeks later, on another cable news program, I decided that I was not going to let myself be victimized by the usual neocon tactics. I let Frank have the first word and listened to him carefully. The host of the show asked me what I thought of what Frank had said, and I answered "Hogwash," then started my rebuttal. Predictably, Frank interrupted, or tried to. I told him he would have his chance after I had said my piece, and kept speaking over him till he shut up. I then filibustered till the end of the segment. As we went to commercial, I looked down at the screen to see Gaffney red-faced and sputtering. I thought to myself that here was somebody who was never likely to be a friend.

I had never believed that the "due date" for the Iraqi WMD declaration would be the go-to-war date. In fact, I continued to think there was some chance that the administration could achieve its disarmament objective peacefully and that war could be avoided. So did other moderates from both parties. After all, the declaration would serve as a baseline for the resumption of the intrusive inspection regime proposed in the resolution. It would take time to translate the declaration, and the logistics of remounting the inspection program would be daunting. Hiring inspectors, opening offices, obtaining cars and airplanes and helicopters, establishing liaison relationships with the

Iraqis and with the members of the security council, especially the United States—would all take time and energy. There remained, too, the question of whether we could go to war without at least a second consultation at the U.N.

Somehow, I was relatively optimistic. I felt that the president, supported by Congress, had done the right thing. Although I was uneasy with the very broad language of the congressional resolution, and with the implication that it gave the president the authority to go to war at his discretion without further congressional action, I wanted to take him at his word when he said that congressional authorization of a military strike "does not mean that military action is imminent or unavoidable. The resolution will tell the United Nations, and all nations, that America speaks with one voice and is determined to make the demands of the civilized world mean something," as reported in the *Los Angeles Times* on October 10.

There was no need to invade Iraq, at least not then, or in the near future, so long as an intrusive U.N. inspection program was achieving results; and even if we were at some point obliged to back the disarmament demands with force, that force could be directed at achieving the disarmament objective and not require the regime change so fervently lusted after by the neocons. I thought the president had successfully steered the U.S. and the U.N. back to the appropriate course. I pointed out in my appearances that the president had in fact proven the thesis of Kenneth Pollack's book wrong, that he had been hugely successful at obtaining the international support for coercive containment that Ken had eloquently argued would be impossible. The attacks of September 11, 2001, a forceful president, and a compliant Congress had given us exactly what was needed: the will to deal with the real threat posed by Saddam—WMD in the hands of a rogue state—and not the distracting targets of regime change and spurious links between al Qaeda and Saddam.

My optimism, however, was dampened as early as December 9

when I participated in a symposium at the Nixon Center in Washington, cochaired by former Secretary of Defense James Schlesinger and Ambassador L. Paul (Jerry) Bremer, a retired foreign service officer then best known as an expert on terrorism, and the center's director, Dimitri Simes. I listened as the other participants waxed eloquent about how we would reshape the Middle East with our invasion of Iraq. Also in attendance was conservative commentator Charles Krauthammer. He offered three reasons to justify the war that most of the participants saw as inevitable and desirable. Weapons of mass destruction was the one presented loudly and frequently to the public, Krauthammer said, but American credibility and the democratization of the Arab world were the other two—if largely understated—reasons. American credibility was at stake, claimed Krauthammer, because

> if for no other reason, having said what the president has said—starting with his "axis of evil" speech, the speech at West Point [in January 2002], and all the way through the year—he had consistently said that this state of affairs will not stand. If he doesn't follow through, I think there will be a tremendous collapse of everything we had achieved by the war in Afghanistan. That would be a great strategic setback. And it would have negative effects on the region, especially on the war on terrorism.

The democratization of the Arab world—Krauthammer's "third reason for the war in Iraq"—was, he said,

> what I would call "coming ashore." Our attitude to the Arab world has always been that we could be the "off-shore balancer" of last resort. We would pacify the regime by buying off the corrupt governments in Egypt

and Saudi Arabia. We would police and we would patrol offshore. This hands-off, offshore policy, I think, is over. Iraq will be the first act in the play of an America coming ashore in Arabia, trying to do what it did in Germany and Japan. I know the analogy is obviously a strained one but I think, historically, this is what the mission is. It's not just about weapons of mass destruction or American credibility. It's about reforming the Arab world. I think we don't know the answer to the question of whether the Arab–Islamic world is inherently allergic to democracy. The assumption is that it is—but I don't know if anyone can answer that question today. We haven't attempted it so far. The attempt will begin with Iraq. Afterwards, we are going to have empirical evidence; history will tell us whether this assumption was correct or not.

I was stunned by the unabashed ambition of this imperial project, by the willingness to countenance a major military engagement and lengthy occupation in order to "attempt" to reform the Arab world, to remake it to our liking. What hubris, to put American lives and treasure at stake in order to gain empirical evidence to test an assumption. Krauthammer concluded his remarks with a chilling comment that we needed to go to war soon, before the antiwar movement coalesced—in other words, before Americans woke up to the fact that this war was not at all about combating the publicly proclaimed grave and gathering danger posed by Saddam.

I could not restrain myself. When I spoke, I drew the analogy that the neoconservatives were to the president as were Napoleon's generals to the emperor as they sat around the table and listened to his plans on the eve of the march on Moscow. Schlesinger commented that he preferred to think of it as the night before the Battle of Austerlitz—which, Simes reminded us, led to that failed Russian campaign. I replied that since Schlesinger had always seemed to be something of an imperial figure, perhaps I should begin to refer to him as Mr. Bonaparte. The thin smile on the face of the former secretary of defense indicated that he was not amused. Neither was I.

Krauthammer remarked that he viewed the prospective war with Iraq as the night before D-day, the eve in June 1944 of the liberation of France and the defeat of Germany. If the advocates of the coming-ashore vision in the symposium had their way, we really were going to try to bring Jeffersonian democracy to the Arab world on the coattails of an American military conquest. We were going to be waging an imperial war, pure and simple.

I was not prepared to concede the necessity of the neoconservatives' war so long as there were alternatives. Retired Marine Corps General Anthony Zinni, who had been urging caution for months, wrote me in December 2002 with disgust that the debate was over and the decisions already made to launch an invasion. Despite the general's sobering analysis, I continued to speak out, along with an ever-shrinking number of others, including Tom Andrews, Mike Farrell, and Katrina van den Heuvel and David Corn from *The Nation* magazine. But we were a dwindling breed.

Over the 2002 Christmas holidays and most of January 2003, Congress was out of town, so there was no real focal point for those calling for the consideration of alternatives to the drive to war. The antiwar coalition, while well intentioned, was doomed to fail. It had organized itself too late and left itself too open to the ill-considered charges of appeasement from the ruthless right-wing war camp.

On January 28, 2003, President Bush spoke to the nation in the State of the Union address. It was arguably the most important speech he had yet made in his presidency. The country and the world listened—a world growing increasingly nervous that the United States, fresh from a quick military victory in Afghanistan, was about to go to war again. Quite apart from the now infamous sixteen words—"The British government has learned that Saddam Hussein recently sought significant quantities of uranium from Africa"—the speech was replete with other assertions that, to put it charitably, were questionable.

In perhaps the most striking moment of the evening, which regrettably received less attention from pundits and the press than the notorious sixteen words, the president stated that "throughout the twentieth century, small groups of men seized control of great nations, built armies and arsenals, and set out to dominate the weak and intimidate the world." What irony: this was a president who had come to power in a hotly disputed election in which he won fewer popular votes than his opponent. Now he was advocating an aggressive foreign policy born of a small band of zealots—a policy the precise opposite of the one he had championed as a candidate—who had callously seized the opportunity presented by the tragedy of a terrorist attack on our country to foist its dangerous ideas on the nation and the world.

But the sixteen words certainly piqued my curiosity. The following day, I called a colleague at the State Department and suggested to him that if the president had been speaking of Niger in his reference to Africa, then my report, along with the report of our ambassador on the scene, and that of the Marine Corps four-star general, had all been wrong. Or had the president misspoken? In that case, the record needed to be corrected.

My colleague replied simply that perhaps the president had been speaking about an African country other than Niger. I had no reason to doubt my informant—his access and knowledge were more current than mine—so I didn't pursue the matter. It was my business only if the president was referring to Niger. I later learned from Walter Kansteiner, assistant secretary for Africa at State, that he had not even seen the State of the Union speech to read it before it was given, and that Colin Powell himself had been given only a few hours to review it for accuracy.

Another statement from the State of the Union address gave me serious concern. For the previous few months, with the exception of a few ill-chosen remarks by Bush at political rallies during the midterm election campaign about how "Saddam tried to kill my dad," the president had adhered to his talking point that "Saddam will either disarm or we will disarm him." When asked whether that position represented a change from the regime-change rhetoric thrown about so freely the previous year, senior officials, including Colin Powell and the president himself, argued that disarmament effectively *was* regime change, even if Saddam remained in power.

I still agreed with this formulation. Otherwise, if Saddam concluded that all we wanted was his scalp, he would have no incentive to comply with the disarmament demand. We did not want to fight through whatever nefarious defenses he might be able to muster just so we could occupy Baghdad, which would present us with all the problems attendant to administering a restive population. Those of us who had been involved in the first Gulf War had concluded before Desert Storm that there was little to be gained, and much potentially lost, in invading Iraq and pushing all the way to Baghdad. That assessment still held in early 2003.

In *A World Transformed,* which President George H. W. Bush coauthored with Brent Scowcroft, and published in 1998, they explained it best:

> Trying to eliminate Saddam . . . would have incurred
> incalculable human and political costs. . . . We would
> have been forced to occupy Baghdad and, in effect, rule
> Iraq . . . there was no viable "exit strategy" we could

see, violating another of our principles. Furthermore, we had been consciously trying to set a pattern for handling aggression in the post–Cold War world. Going in and occupying Iraq, thus unilaterally exceeding the United Nations' mandate, would have destroyed the precedent of international response to aggression that we hoped to establish. Had we gone the invasion route, the United States could conceivably still be an occupying power in a bitterly hostile land.

Regrettably, as we have discovered, the instincts of the former president and his national security adviser were prescient.

But in his speech to the world, George W. Bush included a statement that could be interpreted by Saddam only as a direct personal threat. "Tonight I have a message for the brave and oppressed people of Iraq: Your enemy is not surrounding your country, your enemy is *ruling* your country. And the day he and his regime are removed from power will be the day of your liberation." Not simply promising the disarmament of Iraq as he had in his recent speeches, the president now stated outright his intention to rout Saddam from power, and to kill or capture him. It was an unwise thing to say. It made whatever strategy we adopted for Iraq that much more dangerous because it so blatantly telegraphed our next move and our ultimate goal.

A week after the State of the Union address, on February 5, 2003, Powell appeared before the U.N. Security Council and dramatically detailed the American case against Saddam—and the case for war. The next day, even many liberal pundits were persuaded by his theatrical performance. I had heard a different speech, however. So had a longtime colleague of mine, retired Colonel Pat Lang, a bona fide specialist in the region and a highly decorated senior intelligence official. He concluded from all the inferences and lack of specificity in

Powell's charges that there was simply no convincing case in the matter of weapons of mass destruction. Artists' renderings of trucks are not evidence. Satellite photos of buildings are not evidence. Cryptic recordings of conversations are not evidence.

But I heard something different still. Unlike Pat, what I heard Powell unwittingly say was that U.N. Security Council Resolution 1441 was working. After all, he and the president both made clear that the scientists responsible for doing the research and development of Iraq's WMD had either been secreted in neighboring countries, or else threatened with death if they cooperated with the inspectors. In either case, they were clearly not able to work on their programs. Others involved in the programs, we were told, were busy cleaning up suspected sites. If they were spending all their time cleaning, then they were not filling artillery shells with prohibited chemicals. U.N. inspectors had recently returned to Iraq and were roaming through Saddam's factories and palaces at will, Powell told us. We were watching everything Saddam's people did—flash to a satellite photo. We were listening to everything they said—cut to the audio recording of a conversation between two soldiers. The bottom line for people in the disarmament business is that disruption indicates a significant measure of success, and we were without doubt disrupting Saddam's programs. Thus, I concluded from Powell's speech that since 1441 was indeed working, there was no need to immediately undertake an extraordinarily high-risk, low-reward war.

Most newspapers and commentators were convinced otherwise. Headlines blared "Case Closed," lauding Powell for his compelling indictment. In retrospect, his performance was, as retired State Department intelligence analyst, Greg Thielman, put it, "a low point in his distinguished thirty-five-year career." For the previous two years, there had been a running debate on Powell in Washington. Some observers, myself included, felt that Powell was the one person standing in the way of the true believers and keeping them from completely taking over the government. Others had concluded that he was simply the kinder, gentler face of an extremist administration. After his speech at the U.N., I reluctantly moved to the second camp.

Powell utterly repudiated the carefully thought-out doctrine of force that has borne his own name since Desert Storm and failed the troops he had been privileged to lead for so many years. The Powell doctrine defined how and when to wield the blunt instrument of war; it laid out what conditions should be met prior to launching military action. It stated that military action should be used only as a last resort, and only if a clear risk to national security exists; that the force should be overwhelming and disproportionate to that of the adversary; that it should be used only if the general public stands in strong support of the campaign; and that an exit strategy has to have been devised.

In this case, war was not the last resort; there was no clear risk to our national security, and, as we know now at this writing in early 2004, there were no weapons of mass destruction and there never was a satisfactory exit strategy, only a precipitous cut-and-run approach geared to the presidential election calendar. Essentially, Powell took his lofty 82 percent national approval rating and threw it behind the neoconservative juggernaut.

The results were immediate. At speaking engagements over the several months previous to Powell's speech, I had noted in audiences considerable ambivalence about war with Iraq. There had been a slight bias in favor of the president's position, but it was not the strong support that the Powell doctrine insisted upon as a prerequisite. In fact, the support derived mostly from the residual anxieties of 9/11. It reflected the desire that our president succeed in his role as protector-in-chief. Boosting support, as well, was Americans' confusion over the nature of the threat, and particularly in the false impression administration officials had assiduously fostered that Saddam was somehow responsible for the terrorist attacks in New York and Washington. Yet it was Powell's credibility that finally put public opinion over the top.

Over and over again, I was told "Colin Powell wouldn't lie to us." After his speech and the press analysis of it, Americans were persuaded that the "last resort" of war now was the only course to take. Powell's support for invading Iraq with a pseudo-coalition was essential, and he deserves at least as much of the responsibility for the subsequent situation that we find ourselves in as anybody else in the administration, because, more than anyone else, it was his credibility and standing among the American people that tipped the scales.

In the wake of the increasingly bellicose rhetoric from the administration, and so-called experts, I began to speak openly about the hidden imperial agenda of the war proponents and to raise concerns about what a post-invasion Iraq might look like. Up to that point, my reason for being in the debate had been primarily to ensure that the fate of our troops be fully discussed before we sent them into battle. My agenda continued to grow, as I hoped to elucidate more fully the reasons, justified or not, that the administration was about to ask our sons and daughters in uniform to kill and die in our name.

In February, I had lunch with David Corn, the articulate and determined critic of the war. I had become acquainted with him when we kept bumping into each other in the "green room" at FOX. I shared with him my concerns about the imperial nature of the administration's drive to war, and he asked me to write an article for *The Nation*. He felt that my "establishment" credentials would lend credibility to the point of view espoused by the magazine—a point of view, I hasten to add, that, by and large, I had come to share. I agreed, and the piece, entitled "Republic or Empire," was published in mid-February. In it, I argued that we had, for the most part, already succeeded in our efforts to contain and disarm Saddam. Moreover, with new basing agreements for the U.S. military from Yemen to Afghanistan, we had established a dominant presence astride strategic oil reserves that would enable us to respond to crises in the region much more quickly and effectively in the future than we had ever been able to in the past. Thus, the conquest of

Iraq would not materially improve our influence from southern Asia to the Horn of Africa.

In President Bush's much-ballyhooed February 26 speech on democracy in the Middle East at the American Enterprise Institute, the home of the neoconservative leadership, he made his clearest statement yet about his vision for a future Iraq. He said:

> A new regime in Iraq would serve as a dramatic and inspiring example of freedom for other nations in the region.
>
> It is presumptuous and insulting to suggest that a whole region of the world—or the one-fifth of humanity that is Muslim—is somehow untouched by the most basic aspirations of life. Human cultures can be vastly different. Yet the human heart desires the same good things, everywhere on Earth. In our desire to be safe from brutal and bullying oppression, human beings are the same. In our desire to care for our children and give them a better life, we are the same. For these fundamental reasons, freedom and democracy will always and everywhere have greater appeal than the slogans of hatred and the tactics of terror.

With those words, the presidential seal of approval was stamped on a war to liberate an oppressed people and to redraw the political map of the Middle East. In the president's vision, the goal of American policy in the region was to foster Western-style democracy, thereby making it a safer place for us and for our friends in the Arab world. It was hard to disagree with the president that exporting democracy and freeing people from dictatorial regimes are laudable goals. But I also knew that that is not what we've structured the U.S. military to do for our country. Notwithstanding administration promises of a cakewalk in Iraq, I was concerned it would be enormously difficult, costly, and time-consuming to impose democracy there at the barrel of a gun, requiring, above all, a grateful and compliant population. If we didn't succeed, we would be forever blamed for the havoc we wrought in trying.

The publication of my article in *The Nation* led to a further series of appearances on more substantive news programs. On *NOW with Bill Moyers* on February 28, I was given a platform to more fully explain my unease with the administration's policy. I used my twenty minutes with Moyers to point out some of the pitfalls I saw in the president's vision of democratization as the panacea for our security concerns in the region. I told Bill:

> I've done democracy in Africa for twenty-five years. And I can tell you that doing democracy in the most benign environments is really tough sledding. And in a place like Iraq, where politics is a blood sport and where you have these clan, tribal, ethnic, and confessional cleavages, coming up with a democratic system that is pluralistic, functioning, and, as we like to say about democracies, not inclined to make war on other democracies, is going to be extraordinarily difficult.
>
> And let me just suggest a scenario. Assuming that you get the civic institutions and a thriving political culture in the first few iterations of presidential elections, you're going to have Candidate A, who is likely going to be a demagogue, and Candidate B, who is likely going to be a populist. That's what emerges from political discourse.
>
> Candidate A, Candidate B, the demagogue and the populist, are going to want to win elections for the presidency. And the way to win elections is to inflame the

passions of your population. The easy way for a dema-
gogue or a populist in the Middle East to inflame the
passion of the population is to define himself or herself
by their enemies.

And the great enemy in the Middle East is Israel
and its supplier, the United States. So it's hard to
believe, for me, that a thriving democracy, certainly
in the immediate and near-term and medium-term
future, is going to yield a successful presidential candidate who is going to be pro-Israel or pro-America.

On March 5, I participated in a *Nightline* town meeting debate
moderated by Ted Koppel, the title of which was "War in Iraq, Why
Now." James Woolsey, Senator John McCain, and Richard Land of
the Southern Baptist Convention debated Senator Carl Levin, the
Reverend Susan Thistlethwaite of the Chicago Theological Semi-
nary, and me. It was clear from the opening remarks that the other
side had thoroughly rehearsed what they were going to say. In fact,
the next day Randy Schoeneman, head of the Iraqi Liberation Foundation, told me that they had conducted a mock debate before the
town meeting. Our side certainly had not prepared. When we got to
the set, Carl Levin told me that he was going to emphasize the need
for multilateral as opposed to unilateral action. I replied that I was
going to stress the need for our actions to be related to the WMD threat
we all agreed we faced. Neither he nor I had met Ms. Thistlewaite
before; she proved to be a passionate and articulate voice, but we were
disadvantaged by our comparative lack of preparation.

It was an unpleasant evening from the beginning. Land reflected
the views of the one part of the American population that was gung-
ho for the war from the beginning. The Christian Right, with its lit-
eral interpretation of the Book of Revelation, had become
increasingly strident in promoting war in the Middle East as necessary

for the return of Jesus and the subsequent "rapture" promised on Judgment Day.

When I was making the point that we could achieve disarmament without resorting to occupation—not the best idea, given the potential for negative outcomes, I was about to say—John McCain interrupted me and likened my attitude to appeasement. I take great offense at having my patriotism questioned by anyone. John McCain's service to his country is unimpeachable but that does not give him a monopoly on loyalty, nor is it equatable with wisdom on national security issues.

McCain was ill-advised to echo the hard-right neoconservatives who were driving the war juggernaut. After all, who should know better than an officer-turned-POW, who so valiantly insisted that others be repatriated from the Hanoi Hilton before him, that the time to debate the serious issues of war and peace is before, not after, troops have been put in harm's way? He knew well what it would mean to send 130,000 soldiers to war without a clear mandate or exit strategy. Put simply, soldiers are unnecessarily exposed to lethal danger. To insist that that point be raised before our troops find themselves in that position is certainly not appeasement; it is an essential part of the national debate.

When I later noted that the democratization of Iraq would be a stiff challenge, Woolsey accused me of racism by twisting my words to suggest that I believed Arabs were not up to the task. He seemingly did not know, or want to acknowledge, that I had done democratization in the field on behalf of the U.S. for close to twenty years and was an ardent supporter of the work. Woolsey, on the other hand, had led the classic Washington-insider life. His accusation was an outrageously provocative insult and was seen as such by an audience made up of a number of African Americans, several of them members of the House of Representatives who had known me from my White House days managing Africa Affairs. The remark went over with a thud and was subsequently dropped from the standard set of neoconservative talking points spouted at me.

At the end of the evening, despite the vitriol hurled at us by the other side, Ted Koppel turned to McCain, Woolsey, and Land and said, "You have made some important points, gentlemen, but you have not made your case that war with Iraq now is necessary." If that had made us victors, it was a pyrrhic win. Unfortunately, of course, the one person whom we would have liked most to influence by our arguments—George W. Bush—was probably already asleep. But then, as he later told Brit Hume of FOX, he gets his information straight from his advisers rather than from newspapers and broadcast outlets.

After the debate, I waded into the audience and was warmly received by, among others, a small group of Iraqi Americans, who, for all their desire to see Saddam go, were concerned about the violence soon to be visited upon their country and their people. I was touched when they invited me to spend an evening with them at their center in Arlington, Virginia. We agreed to March 17, a few weeks later. The center was run by a Shia cleric but committed to Iraqis of all faiths, uniting them in their national identity rather than in religious affiliation. I took Valerie with me and was very pleased to have the opportunity to introduce my wife to people of the nationality among whom I had spent such a pivotal time of my life. This meeting took place, coincidentally, on the night that President Bush spoke to the nation and gave Saddam forty-eight hours to capitulate, thus making it clear that the U.S. was going to occupy Baghdad either peacefully or by force. The emotions in the social hall ran high. The die had been cast, war was at hand, and all we could do was pray for our troops and the innocent Iraqis who would surely suffer in the coming conflict. It was a poignant evening, and I was gratified to be spending it here, with Valerie, among people whose destiny my country was about to decide.

Two days later, America would be at war in the Gulf again.

Chapter Sixteen
What I Didn't Find in Africa

ON MARCH 7, 2003, the head of the International Atomic Energy Agency (IAEA), Dr. Mohamed El Baradei, told the U.N. Security Council that documents belatedly submitted by the administration relating to the purported sale of uranium from Niger to Iraq were not authentic. In fact, as one widely reported statement from his deputy, Jacques Baute in Vienna, pointed out, the forgeries were so obvious that a twenty-minute Google search would have exposed their flaws. The next day, a State Department spokesman was quoted as saying, "We fell for it."

I was astounded by the spokesman's comment. Within days after it made the news, I was on the set at CNN, waiting to do an interview, when David Ensor, a CNN national security reporter, happened by. He was looking at the story with an eye out for the perpetrators of the forgeries and asked me what I knew about the Niger uranium business. I told him that as far as I knew, the State Department spokesman had not spoken accurately.

I could have told him a lot more. I knew that in addition to my report, there were reports in the government files from our ambassador and from a Marine Corps general. I knew that at the State Department African Bureau, nobody in the management chain of command had *ever* believed there was anything to the story that a spokesman was now claiming they "fell for." I knew that even if the Nigerien military dictator, Mainassara Baré, assassinated in April 1999, had wanted to sell uranium to Iraq, the system did not lend itself to such circumvention. From the sixteen words on down, in short, the whole administration line was bogus, and I certainly wasn't the only one who knew it. As I sat there in the green room, I concluded that the U.S. government had to be held to account. It was unacceptable to lie about such an important issue.

I told Ensor that I would be helpful in his efforts to ferret out the truth, and offered to answer a question or two on the air and to provide leads to him. While I was not willing at that stage to disclose my own involvement, it was not a difficult decision to make, to point others in the right direction. The essential information—the forged documents—was already in the public domain; the State Department spokesman had purposely deceived the public in his response, or else he himself had been deceived. Whichever the case, in my mind it was essential that the record be corrected.

When I went on the air, the CNN newscaster, prompted by Ensor, asked me about the "We fell for it" line. I replied that if the U.S. government checked its files, it would, I believed, discover that it knew more about the case than the spokesman was letting on. I then added that either the spokesman was being disingenuous, or he was ill-informed. That statement apparently won me the attention of U.S. government officials. From a respected reporter close to the subsequent inquiry into the later disclosure of Valerie's status, I learned that a meeting right around the time of this particular CNN appearance led to the decision to produce a "workup" on me for the Office of the Vice President. It was not made clear to me whether Dick Cheney himself attended this meeting, although I was told that senior members of his staff and quite possibly other senior Republicans, including former Speaker of the House Newt Gingrich, were present and that Gingrich actively participated in a strategy session, the objective of which was to figure out how to discredit me.

I clearly remember a quite different White House response in January 1991, when I arrived home after the evacuation of the American embassy in Baghdad. To be greeted as a "true American hero" by President George H. W. Bush for the part I played throughout Operation Desert Shield, gratifying as it was, was not so heartening as the president's profound concern over the endangerment of thousands of Americans, coalition forces, and Iraqis in the imminent Desert Storm. Bush and I had spent twenty minutes together talking quietly about the upcoming conflict. The president's questions reflected his sense of awesome responsibility for the agonizing decisions he had been called upon to make. Indeed, all of our political leadership had grappled fully with the implications of going to war in the Gulf.

All the senators and representatives, Republicans and Democrats alike, who met with me in the days following my return from Baghdad explained to me, in excruciating detail, the extent to which they had plumbed the depths of their consciences before voting on the use-of-force authorization. I myself had fully supported the case for war. But it did not matter to me how our leaders voted regarding the use of force; what did matter was that they took the time to reflect on the enormity of their decision.

Reflection, conscience, concern, full consideration of the consequences—these qualities did *not* characterize the debate prior to the *second* Gulf War. All were superseded—and the congressional leaders of both parties were overwhelmed—by the superheated rhetoric of the administration and the neoconservatives that backed them up with their ubiquitous presence in the media and think-tanks. The looming midterm elections affected crucial decisions, as the administration made it clear that it would attack opponents for supposedly being soft on terrorism. There were some exceptions, notably Robert Byrd, who, after railing against the administration for its policy of pre-emption and its rush to invade Iraq, chastised his congressional colleagues for having abdicated their Constitutional responsibilities to declare war.

Senator Joe Biden and his Senate Foreign Relations Committee staff, headed by the very able Anthony Blinken, tried to constrain the White House by revising the language of the congressional resolution to authorize the use of force against Iraq, but that effort was short-circuited when the Democratic leadership essentially caved in. The combination of threats of defeat at the polls with presidential promises that the congressional resolution would provide him the ammunition he needed to negotiate a strong U.N. resolution on disarmament proved to be too much for careerist politicians.

The Democrats were extraordinarily conflicted about Iraq. It is important to remember the context of the moment. Americans were still reeling from the effects of 9/11. As the administration liked to repeat at every opportunity, our view of the world had changed as a consequence of the terror attacks. In 1998, Congress had passed the Iraq Liberation Act, which gave the policy to oust Saddam the force of law, while the United Nations had proven to be ineffective in its enforcement of existing resolutions. All along, Saddam had remained as intransigent as ever, and he continued to be so, even though he had been effectively contained and weakened by twelve years of sanctions, American military enforcement of no-fly zones, and swift counterattacks on air defense sites whenever the Iraqis turned their radar on our jets.

The escalation of Palestinian terrorist attacks on Israeli civilians after 9/11 and the retaliatory attacks by the Israelis contributed further to the sense of a world grown much more dangerous and threatening. When Saddam, in yet another act of stupidity, aligned himself with the Palestinian intifada by offering $25,000 to the families of Palestinian suicide bombers, he also gave the American war party a golden opportunity. Now, they could add his financing of Palestinian terrorism to their stock talking points.

But in fact the view of the world as seen by the president's closest advisers had not changed at all. For years, they had harbored an intense desire to go into Iraq and finish off Saddam. In the eighties Paul Wolfowitz had identified Saddam as the dictator every American should love to hate. Throughout the nineties, the demise of Saddam at the mighty hand of the American military became a rallying cry for the political Right.

The history of the first Gulf War was revised and rewritten in the pages of the neoconservative flagship publication *The Weekly Standard,* which persistently denigrated the clear diplomatic and military victory that the international community had achieved in driving Saddam from Kuwait. But we should not forget that war's signal accomplishments: extensive and tireless work that led to the international coalition; troops and funds assembled from scores of countries; a series of U.N. resolutions that legitimized military action under international law; the establishment of useful precedents for future engagements; and the patient and thoughtful debate in our own country over the use of force. The first Gulf War will go down in history as a model for the art of diplomacy and the practice of war in a crisis situation. The second Gulf War will not be so charitably reviewed.

In the early months of 2003, the leaders of the political Right held the megaphone, and they were bellowing into it to push for war. By the time we invaded Iraq, a majority of Americans believed that Saddam had been responsible for the attacks on our territory and that he already possessed nuclear weapons. "We cannot wait for the final proof—the smoking gun—that could come in the form of a mushroom cloud," the president warned us in his October 8, 2002, speech in Cincinnati, to make the case to the American people for the congressional resolution authorizing the use of force against Iraq.

The president and his senior advisers had used the "mushroom cloud" metaphor repeatedly over the months to pump up support for war. Now, with the IAEA's revelation that no negotiation for the Iraqi purchase of uranium from Niger had ever taken place, one key element underpinning the charge against Iraq was acknowledged to have been based on a fraud. The only other piece of information that the administration had marshaled as evidence of Saddam's nuclear intentions was a claim that aluminum tubes purchased by Iraq, but seized before they could reach their destination, were for centrifuges that could be used to enrich uranium and create fissile material. However, experts throughout the government, including at the Department of Energy, had concluded that the tubes were ill suited for that function. In fact, they matched the specifications for artillery rockets and were more likely to have been purchased for that purpose, as David Kay later concluded.

Aluminum tubes ill suited for enriching uranium that did not exist constituted a compound lie that badly undermined the argument that Iraq had posed a grave and gathering danger to the United States. It cut to the heart of the case for war. The casual fashion in which the administration subsequently dismissed the revelation that the uranium charge was false was inexcusable.

Somebody had allowed the president of the United States to proclaim as the truth a lie, and on an issue as momentous as our reason for going to war. To excuse the lie with "We fell for it"—which was another lie—was shameful.

Over the next several months, as journalists tried to get to the bottom of the story with my support, the administration continued to lie. For four months, from March until July, questions were parried or dismissed. Condoleezza Rice categorically denied that she or anyone else at senior levels in the White House knew that the received intelligence did not support the charge. Later, when finally forced to admit that the CIA had transmitted two memos and placed one telephone call to the National Security Council on the subject, she argued that the uranium charge was really just a small part of the nuclear weapons program indictment. Another lie. Had the charge been true, it would really have been the smoking gun to prove that Saddam had broken out of the box of containment into which the international community had effectively put him in 1991. That is why it was absolutely vital to determine the accuracy of the allegation.

The position of national security adviser was established after World War II to advise the president of the United States on strategic threats to the country; in other words, to keep count of nuclear weapons worldwide and to determine how to defend ourselves against any threat posed by them. In the post–Cold War period, most experts agreed that the single most serious threat we would face in the twenty-first century lay in weapons of mass destruction at the command of a rogue state or international terrorists. Accordingly, when it is suspected that a rogue state, such as Iraq, is seeking to develop a nuclear weapons program, a national security adviser of any administration and of any party would have no priority higher than that of finding the truth of the allegation. If it is found to be false, we can again breathe a bit easier and continue to maintain our vigilance. If it is found to be true, then we have reason to consider the whole range of possible actions, including war if necessary.

In the case of Iraq, it was known that the allegation was false, but the U.S. went to war anyway, after President Bush first deceived the nation and the world. Somebody else may have inserted the words into his speech, but the president uttered them.

Dr. Rice belatedly acknowledged that the National Security Council had been informed that the intelligence did not support the Niger–Iraq uranium charge, but that in the three months between the October speech in Cincinnati and the State of the Union address in January, "she forgot." How does somebody whose job it is to track nuclear weapon developments, especially in rogue states, receive such critical information and then proceed to forget it? This was not a grade school homework assignment. The short answer is that they don't forget, unless they are derelict. Regrettably, disingenuousness is another possibility. Condoleezza Rice may be many things, but she is hardly derelict.

The last straw came when Dr. Rice, in a June 8 appearance on *Meet the Press,* told Tim Russert: "Maybe somebody in the bowels of the Agency knew something about this, but nobody in my circles." That was a lie, and I knew it. She had to have known it as well.

The next day, I called a former government official who knew Dr. Rice and expressed my disgust at her continuing refusal to tell the truth. He replied that the interview had not been one of her finest moments. A call to a senior official in the administration elicited the suggestion that I might have to write the story myself. I took the remark to heart and called David Shipley, the editor of the op-ed page at the *New York Times.* He immediately offered me fifteen hundred words to tell my story.

Still, I hesitated, in the hope that pressure from journalists would force the hand of the administration. But two weeks after the Rice remark on *Meet the Press*, with my name now openly circulating among the press, it was clear that sooner or later my anonymity was going to be sacrificed on the altar of the story.

I learned that on Sunday, June 22, the London newspaper *The Independent* blared a headline across the top of the front page, just below a banner advertising Hollywood madam Heidi Fleiss's new book, that read "Retired American diplomat accuses British Ministers of being liars." I knew then that the story was spinning out of control and that I now had no choice but to write it myself.

A *Washington Post* reporter named Richard Leiby had earlier written about the hostages from the first Gulf War. After that article appeared, he had contacted me to let me know that all the former hostages he had interviewed had praised the efforts of the embassy in

Baghdad to care for them. "Whatever their feelings about the U.S. government, the Iraqis, or their own companies, they were uniformly complimentary about what you and your staff did to save their lives, and to a man they asked that I contact you and send you their warmest regards," he told me.

Now Rich wanted to profile me regarding my work during the first Gulf War. When he called, I told him that I'd welcome a profile, because an op-ed piece detailing my trip to Niger would be appearing in a Sunday edition of the *New York Times*. He knew about the trip, as his *Post* colleague Walter Pincus was one of the journalists I had spoken to on background in the months since the president's sixteen words. I thought that a separate article in the *Post* would complement my own piece by helping to establish who I was and what I had accomplished in my career. When Rich learned that my piece would be published in the *Times* on July 6, he offered to interview me immediately so the story could run the same day as the op-ed in the *Times*.

Rich came to our house the same evening and met Valerie in her guise as an energy consultant. He played with my naked twins (he also has twins) and watched my mother-in-law energetically helping us get the house ready for our annual Fourth of July party the next night. Despite the chaos, he managed to get the material he needed for the article, as well as a lot of additional material that he would later discover he could use for a piece on Valerie when her true employment became public knowledge.

On July 6, 2003, the *New York Times* published "What I Didn't Find in Africa." The night before, at about 10:30 P.M., the piece hit the *New York Times* Web site. At 10:32 P.M., I received a call from a *New York Post* reporter looking for a quote from me. At 10:34 P.M. a producer for *Meet the Press* called to invite me on the show the next morning to defend my article. To sweeten the offer, she told me that I would be leading off the program and would be followed by

Republican Senator John Warner and Democratic Senator Carl Levin, both of whom had just returned from Iraq. I agreed, took the phone off the hook, and went to bed.

The path to writing the op-ed piece had been straightforward in my own mind. My government had refused to address the fundamental question of how the lie regarding Saddam's supposed attempt to purchase African uranium had found its way into the State of the Union address. Time after time during the previous four months, from March to July, administration spokespeople had sloughed off the reality that the president of the United States had sent our country to war in order to defend us against the threat of the "mushroom cloud" when they knew, as I did, that at least one of the two "facts" underpinning the case was not a fact at all. It was disinformation. It had never occurred to me to keep quiet about this. Until the issue was addressed seriously, I felt obliged to keep raising it. In the end, when it became clear to me that my name was about to emerge in the public domain, I *had* to raise it, publicly and in my own words. I realized that my credibility would be called into question, and I was steeled for that. But, whatever one might say about me—and there is a lot—the truth remained: *There was never any evidence of Iraqi uranium purchases from Niger.*

Before I left for the NBC studios that Sunday morning, Valerie straightened my tie, brushed the lint off my suit, and reminded me, as only a wife could, that *Meet the Press* was not just the major leagues of news programs, it was the World Series. I needed to be at the top of my game.

With resolve I arrived at the NBC green room, where I waited with Senator Warner; David Broder, the venerable *Washington Post* political reporter; Elisabeth Bumiller from the *New York Times;* and the syndicated columnist Robert Novak. As Senator Warner and I walked onto the set, we discussed the crisis in Liberia and whether we should send American forces to restore order there.

Andrea Mitchell, sitting in for Tim Russert on that holiday weekend, opened the program with a discussion of my piece. I made two main points: first, that in a democracy the decision to send troops to war had to be based on commonly accepted facts; and second, that if the war had in fact been based on a trumped-up threat of weapons of mass destruction, should we in the future face a real WMD threat, it would be much more difficult to convince the world or even the American people of its actual seriousness.

My piece had now run in the *New York Times* and I had been profiled in the *Washington Post*. Senators Warner and Levin were supportive of my case and complimentary about my experience, while David Broder characterized the two points I had made as important. The positions I had taken were now part of the public discussion and my credibility, though sure to be attacked, had been vouched for.

Twenty-four hours later, the White House acknowledged that the sixteen words did "not rise to the level that we would put in a presidential speech." I honestly thought that my exposure in the matter would quickly fade, as the administration would now have to concentrate on the serious question of competence among the members of the president's staff. I told any interested friends and all inquisitive journalists that as my charges had been satisfactorily answered, I'd have nothing more to say. I honored obligations for interviews that I had previously accepted, but I declined any others in order to allow the waters I had roiled to still. I thought that surely the focus of the debate would now shift away from me. How naïve and mistaken I was on that score!

Astonishingly, when the administration officials finally did tell the truth, they quickly regretted it and began to backtrack. Almost as soon as the White House acknowledgement was announced, Walter Pincus told me he began to receive phone calls from members of the administration trying to take it back. One official told Walter that telling the truth "was the biggest mistake the administration had made."

On Monday evening, while the administration's mea culpa for their error was being circulated among the press, the president and his entourage set off for a trip to Africa. However, rather than simply getting the story behind them by finding and firing the person responsible for inserting the lie into the State of the Union address, they began trying to denigrate me.

Ari Fleisher, the president's press secretary, was planning to leave the White House after the current trip in order to set up his own communications shop to help corporations and CEOs deal with problems like the one his boss was currently experiencing. I am not sure his performance during his last week with the White House would have inspired anybody to hire him.

Within a day, Fleisher was putting a different spin on the situation and downplaying the importance of my report. At one briefing after another, he had something to say about me, and by doing so gave the journalists another news cycle to talk about the sixteen words rather than about the president's trip. Instead of containing the burgeoning press frenzy, Fleisher kept giving the story legs, so much so that it soon overwhelmed the president's agenda in Africa.

Fleisher stupidly attributed to me, for example, the official denials of the government of Niger. He spun: "Wouldn't any government deny it?" While I was not accepting television interviews, I was still deluged by the print press for my reactions to whatever Fleischer had said in each morning's press gaggle. He thus obliged me to point out to reporters that I had not spoken to the current Nigerien government, so there must be another report in U.S. hands. Of course, there were in fact *two* other reports: that of our ambassador to Niger, and that of a four-star Marine Corps General. Sorry, Ari.

I had been aware of both reports from the very beginning of my own involvement, of course, but had deliberately refrained from citing them in my piece, as I had wanted to limit my comments to my own personal experience.

By the third day of the president's trip to Africa, I was dismayed by the direction the White House was taking. Had I been the chief executive of this operation, as President Bush likes to say he is, I would have been furious that a member of my staff had inserted such an obviously false claim in the most important speech I might ever make. Simply sending Chief of Staff Andrew Card back to Washington from Senegal, the first African stop, with instructions to fire the offending staffer and to escort him off the White House premises prior to the president's return, would have stopped the story in its tracks.

Bush and the press corps could then have both focused on the purpose of the trip to Africa. Instead—and not for the first or certainly the last time—the president proved to be more loyal to his senior staff than they were to him—for, even though his administration had admitted error, his press secretary was floundering on Air Force One, lamely trying to turn the attention to me; while, back in Washington, right-wing hatchet men were being wheeled out to attack me. More ominously, plots were being hatched in the White House that would betray America's national security.

Clifford May was first off the mark, spewing uninformed vitriol in a piece in *National Review Online* blindly operating on the principle that facts, those pesky facts, just do not matter. May, a former Republican National Committee staffer, is president of an organization founded two days after 9/11, whose advisory boards include such likely suspects as Newt Gingrich, James Woolsey, Richard Perle, Charles Krauthammer, and Frank Gaffney. He suggested in a ridiculously argued article that I had told the truth because I was a partisan Democrat. Indeed. And if Democrats tell the truth, then what do Republicans do? In fact, if the president's staff had heeded my report, as well as the two others in their files, rather than the rubbish that produced the sixteen-word lie, the president would not have found it necessary to retract a portion of his speech.

No better argued was an opinion piece that appeared in the *Wall Street Journal* by former Secretary of Defense Caspar Weinberger, whose criticism was picked up by others. Weinberger took a sentence that I had inserted in my piece at the request of David Shipley merely to add some atmosphere—about drinking tea during my meetings in Niger—and made it the centerpiece of an attack, suggesting that supposedly I'd been excessively casual and dilatory in my approach to the mission. He charged that I'd had a less-than-stellar career, presumably because I had been ambassador only to two African countries and in charge of African affairs for President Clinton—which was to say that I'd not had an ambassadorship to a European capital like London or Bonn. Of course, Weinberger conveniently neglected to note that I had fulfilled my most recent mission for my government and brought the truth back from Niger. Moreover, he completely missed the larger point of my article, which asked how the president could be so poorly served by his staff—a staff that would allow a lie to appear in any remarks by him, but also to figure so significantly in such a crucial speech. Weinberger was not the most credible person to launch that particular counterattack, since, but for the grace of a pardon by the first President Bush, he might well have had to do jail time for how poorly he had served his president, Ronald Reagan, in the Iran–Contra affair.

It seemed that the motive for the attacks on me was to discourage anyone else from coming forward who had a critical story to tell. Prior to my *Times* piece, there had been a number of news stories quoting unnamed CIA analysts who cited pressure they felt at repeated visits to the Agency from the vice president, his chief of staff, Lewis Libby, and the ubiquitous Newt Gingrich. In essence, the message was: "If you pull a 'Wilson' on us, we will do worse to you." However offensive, there was a certain logic to it. If you have something to hide, one way to keep it secret is to threaten anyone who might expose it. But it was too late to silence me; I had already said all I had to say. Presumably though, they thought they could still silence others by attacking me.

On issues that entail national security, there are legitimate reasons for preserving secrecy. In my case, for example, I never mentioned my trip to Niger to anyone during the debate prior to the war, as it was a discreet mission with national security implications. Only after the documents regarding it became public and the administration began to misstate the facts of my findings in Niger did I speak out. At issue, for me, was not the purpose of the trip, or my findings; the issue was the lying on the part of the president's staff about its knowledge of those findings.

The decision of the president's people to come after me and make me an example arose from no concern over the emergence of secrets related to my mission—there weren't any—but rather from the worry that the pressure they had placed upon intelligence analysts, in order to manipulate data to conform their already determined political ends, would be exposed. From a journalist and a retired intelligence official, I heard of political appointees asking analysts the same question twenty, thirty times until the president's policy makers got the response that served their need, irrespective of the truth.

And when the warmongers discovered they could not browbeat the analysts, such as in the Niger uranium claim, they simply found a way around the objections of the intelligence community by attributing the allegation to the British white paper. Everybody in the intelligence-analysis world knew that the British claim was based on the same suspect reporting that our intelligence had rejected, but no matter. Greg Thielman, the State Department analyst, called it the rumor that would not go away, however many times it was knocked down. And when they were caught in their lie, they took the narrowest of legal explanations, such as when Donald Rumsfeld said in an interview, "Technically, the president was accurate," because he had cited the British as the source. Even though the United States spends approximately $30 billion a year on intelligence, much of it to ensure that the information provided to policy makers is as accurate as possible, our political leaders chose to reject the analysis of the intelligence community in favor of information that they knew to be untrue in order to scare the American people about the nature of the Iraqi threat.

The British, for their part, still maintain that independent intelligence sources substantiate their allegation, the details of which they claim they cannot share with us. But as the British know very well, article ten of UN Resolution 1441 calls on all member states to share information on prohibited nuclear programs with the International Atomic Energy Agency, something they have still not done in this case. So we are supposed to believe that the president's "technically accurate" sixteen words, based upon a piece of intelligence that our $30-billion-a-year intelligence operation had no opportunity to independently verify, is acceptable. Well, it isn't, and it isn't acceptable to threaten career public servants who challenge inappropriate behavior. But attempting to prop up the lie suited the objective of the administration.

I later learned from reporting in the *Washington Post* that it was also naked revenge that motivated the White House attacks on me. Somebody in the White House was incensed that I had dared to call a lie a lie—was furious at me rather than at the person who had put the lie in the speech. Spite is not a rational act. Nothing would change what had already been said; and, in any event, the White House had already admitted its error about the sixteen words. That a public servant charged with the stewardship of our national security would use his station in government to smear a perceived adversary purely for the sake of personal revenge struck me as a particularly egregious abuse of the public trust. I wanted a more rational cause.

Eventually I came to conclude that in all likelihood a combination of motives—to intimidate the intelligence community into silence and to fulfill some twisted sense of revenge—drove the attacks on me. This Bush administration clearly operates on the principle that it is acceptable, and indeed desirable, to shift the debate from the issue to the person, to divert attention from the facts, and to confuse rather than enlighten the American people. This administration knows no such thing as a fair fight; all that counts is who wins and who loses. Kicking an adversary in the political shins, pulling partisan hair, biting contrarian ankles—these are all acceptable. It was what they did to John McCain in South Carolina, and it was what some unnamed leakers in the White House tried to do to me after my article appeared on July 6, 2003.

The attacks were not worth worrying about, and they certainly didn't warrant my dignifying them with a response. All that week after the article appeared and the one following, I played as much golf as I possibly could, and refused requests for interviews and consciously avoided contact with the press, except to respond to the assertions coming from Ari Fleischer in Africa. On the golf course, it is considered bad form to allow a cell phone to ring. I had real reasons to observe that etiquette, apart from love of the game. The golf links provided a welcome refuge from the media feeding frenzy that was swirling around me.

Then came Bob Novak's article exposing Valerie. Here was the real wakeup call. It showed me how far, and where, the administration was willing and ready to push their attacks.

Chapter Seventeen
A Strange Encounter with Robert Novak

L ATE ON TUESDAY AFTERNOON, July 8, six days before Robert Novak's article about Valerie and me, a friend showed up at my office with a strange and disturbing tale. He had been walking down Pennsylvania Avenue toward my office near the White House when he came upon Novak, who, my friend assumed, was en route to the George Washington University auditorium for the daily taping of CNN's *Crossfire*. He asked Novak if he could walk a block or two with him, as they were headed in the same direction; Novak acquiesced. Striking up a conversation, my friend, without revealing that he knew me, asked Novak about the uranium controversy. It was a minor problem, Novak replied, and opined that the administration should have dealt with it weeks before. My friend then asked Novak what he thought about me, and Novak answered: "Wilson's an asshole. The CIA sent him. His wife, Valerie, works for the CIA. She's a weapons of mass destruction specialist. She sent him." At that point, my friend and Novak went their separate ways. My friend headed straight for my office a couple of blocks away.

Once he related this unsettling story to me, I asked him to immediately write down the details of the conversation and afterwards ushered him out of my office. Next, I contacted the head of the news division at CNN, Eason Jordan, Novak's titular boss, whom I had known for a number of years. It took several calls, but I finally tracked him down on his cell phone. I related to him the details of my friend's encounter with Novak and pointed out that whatever my wife might or might not be, it was the height of irresponsibility for Novak to share such information with an absolute stranger on a Washington street. I asked him to speak to Novak for me, but he demurred— he said he did not know him very well—and suggested that I speak to Novak myself. I arranged for him to have Novak call me and hung up.

Novak called the next morning, but I was out, and then so was he. We did not connect until the following day, July 10. He listened quietly as I repeated to him my friend's account of their conversation. I told him I couldn't imagine what had possessed him to blurt out to a complete stranger what he had thought he knew about my wife.

Novak apologized, and then asked if I would confirm what he had heard from a CIA source: that my wife worked at the Agency. I told him that I didn't answer questions about my wife. I told him that my story was not about my wife or even about me; it was about sixteen words in the State of the Union address.

I then read to him three sentences from a 1990 news story about the evacuation of Baghdad: "The chief American diplomat, Joe Wilson, shepherds his flock of some 800 known Americans like a village priest. At 4:30 Sunday morning, he was helping 55 wives and children of U.S. diplomats from Kuwait load themselves and their few remaining possessions on transport for the long haul on the desert to Jordan. He shows the stuff of heroism." The reporters who had written this, I pointed out, were Robert Novak and Rowland Evans. I suggested to Novak that he might want to check his files before writing about me. I also offered to send him all the articles I had written in the past year on policy toward Iraq so that he could educate himself on the positions I had taken. He would learn, if he took the time, that I was hardly antiwar, just anti–dumb war. Before I hung up, Novak apologized again for having spoken about Valerie to a complete stranger.

The following Monday, July 14, 2003, I read Novak's syndicated column in the *Washington Post*. The sixth paragraph of the ten-paragraph story leapt out at me: "Wilson never worked for the CIA, but his wife, Valerie Plame, is an Agency operative on weapons of mass destruction. Two senior administration officials told me Wilson's wife suggested sending him to Niger to investigate the Italian report."

When I showed it to Valerie, she was stoic in her manner but I could see she was crestfallen. Twenty years of loyal service down the drain, and for what, she asked after she had read it. What was Novak trying to say? What did blowing her cover have to do with the story? It was nothing but a hatchet job. She immediately began to prepare a checklist of things she needed to do to minimize the fallout to projects she was working on. Ever efficient, she jotted down reminders to mask the emotions swirling through her body. Finally, as the enormity of what Novak had done now settled on her, she sat in the corner and wondered aloud if she would still have any friends left after they found out that the person they knew was not her at all but a lie that she lived very convincingly.

Amid the welter of emotions I felt that morning, I tried to understand a particular element of Novak's story.

He cited not a CIA source, as he had indicated on the phone four days earlier, but rather two senior administration sources; I called him for a clarification. He asked if I was very displeased with the article, and I replied that I did not see what the mention of my wife had added to it but that the reason for my call was to question his sources. When we first spoke, he had cited to me a CIA source, yet his published story cited two senior administration sources. He replied: "I misspoke the first time we talked."

A couple of days before Novak's article was published, but after my friend's strange encounter with him, I had received a call from *Post* reporter Walter Pincus, who alerted me that "they are coming after you." Since I already knew what Novak had learned about Valerie, I was increasingly concerned over what else might be put out about her. I assumed, though, that the CIA would itself quash any article that made reference to Valerie. While not yet familiar with the specifics of the Intelligence Identities Protection Act, I knew that protection of the identity of agents in our clandestine service was the highest priority, and well understood by the experienced press corps in Washington. Novak had still been trolling for sources when we spoke on the telephone, so I assumed that he did not have the confirmations he would need from the CIA to publish the story. I told Valerie, who alerted the press liaison at the CIA, and we were left with the reasonable expectation that any reference to her would be dropped, since he would have no way of confirming the information—unless, of course, he got confirmations from another part of the government, such as the White House.

Quite apart from the matter of her employment, the assertion that Valerie had played any substantive role in the decision to ask me to go to Niger was false on the face of it. Anyone who knows anything about the government bureaucracy knows that public servants go to great lengths to avoid nepotism or any appearance of it. Family members are expressly forbidden from accepting employment that places them in any direct professional relationship, even once or twice removed. Absurd as these lengths may seem, a supervisor literally cannot even supervise the supervisor of the supervisor of another family member without high-level approval. Valerie could not have stood in the chain of command had she tried to. Dick Cheney might be able to find a way to appoint one of his daughters to a key decision-making position in the State Department's Middle East Bureau, as he did; but Valerie could not—and would not if she could—have had anything to do with the CIA decision to ask me to travel to Niamey.

The publication of the article marked a turning point in our lives. There was no possibility of Valerie recovering her former life. She would never be able to regain the anonymity and secrecy that her professional life had required; she would not be able to return to her discreet work on some of the most sensitive threats to our society in the foreseeable future, and perhaps ever.

I had many questions for Novak: What did the inclusion of Valerie's name add to his article? So what if she worked on intelligence related to weapons of mass destruction? There was nothing nefarious about that. All this had happened because Novak chose not to heed the entreaties of government officials to whom he spoke and who, by Novak's own admission, asked that he not publish her name or employment. While Novak has since downplayed the request of the CIA that he not publish her name, I wondered which part of 'NO' he didn't understand. Murray Waas, writing in the *American Prospect,* has a different take:

> Two government officials have told the FBI that conservative columnist Robert Novak was asked specifically not to publish the name of undercover CIA operative Valerie Plame in his now-famous July 14 newspaper column. The two officials told investigators they warned Novak that by naming Plame he might potentially jeopardize her ability to engage in covert work, stymie ongoing intelligence operations, and jeopardize sensitive overseas sources.

So what if she conveyed a request to me to come to the Agency to talk about Niger? She had played absolutely no part in the decision to send me there. Should an agency of the U.S. government not ask me about the uranium business in Niger, a subject that I knew well, just because my wife happened to work in the same suite of offices?

Lamely attempting to shirk responsibility, Novak claimed that the CIA no was "a soft no, not a hard no." On the wings of that ludicrous defense, he soared to new heights of journalistic irresponsibility. But Novak has long since demonstrated that he is not so much a scrupulous journalist as he is a confirmed purveyor of the right-wing party line, whether it's touting the truth or—as it all too often is, unfortunately—promoting the big lie. In this instance, in addition to buying into the big lie, Novak was slavishly doing the bidding of the cowards in the administration who had decided that the only way to discredit me was to betray national security. I will defend his First Amendment rights as a journalist, but I don't have to like what he did. In fact, watching Valerie's face fall as she realized that her life had been so irreparably altered, I felt that punching the man in the nose would not have been an unreasonable response.

I decided that I would not rise to Novak's bait or dignify his article with a published response, and that I would not speak about Valerie other than hypothetically. It was not up to me to confirm or deny her employment; it was up to the CIA. A few days later, *Newsday* reporter Timothy Phelps, whom I had met in Iraq twelve years earlier, informed me that he had heard from the CIA that what Novak had reported vis-à-vis Valerie's employment was not incorrect. I declined to be drawn into a confirmation even then.

The week was not without its drama, however. Even though I had been avoiding the press since the day after my article appeared in July, I had still been intently following the reporting about Novak's article in the media. Too intently. I was waking up in the middle of the night and pacing the floor, as I had during that critical period in Baghdad during Desert Shield. Back then, my mind would be going a thousand miles a minute, trying to gain an edge on the thugs in the Iraqi regime; now I was trying to predict what the thugs in my own government would do, so I'd be ready to react effectively to their next move. I would get up at 3:00 A.M., after only a few hours of sleep, and review press reports from around the world. In Britain, meanwhile, Prime Minister Tony Blair was under the gun for possibly having "sexed up" the case he had made on Iraq's weapons of mass destruction. In Australia, Prime Minister John Howard was subjected to similar hard questions as well; he would subsequently be censured for having deceived his parliament.

Howard and British Foreign Minister Jack Straw were both obliged to tell their press that they did not know Joe Wilson.

Four days after Novak's article appeared, Britain was convulsed by the suicide of a former weapons inspector named David Kelly, a longtime civil servant in the ministry of defense. Kelly had been a source for the BBC's exposé of the charge that the government had exaggerated the threat posed by Saddam. He had been under increasing pressure from the investigation and had apparently killed himself. I received several calls from friends wondering, first, whether it had in fact been a suicide; and, if not, was I watching my own security? They also wanted to know how I was bearing up under the pressure. I, too, wondered about Kelly's death and later told a BBC producer that I hoped the inquest into his death would be credible.

I was horrified that I could actually harbor suspicions—ones that were also being expressed by others—that a democratic government might actually do bodily harm to a political opponent. I laughed it off for my friends and pointed out that my golf handicap had gone down two strokes in the two and a half weeks of my enforced vacation. And I rationalized that in situations like the one in which I now found myself, it was important to be either so visible that your adversaries would be among the first to be blamed should anything out of the ordinary happen to you, or so invisible that nobody really knew who you were.

That same week, on Thursday, July 17, David Corn called to alert me that what Novak had done, or at least what the person who had leaked Valerie's name to him had done, was possibly a crime, in that it might represent a violation of the Intelligence Identities Protection Act of 1982. Corn then published a detailed explanation of the law to ensure that other journalists, as well as regular readers of *The Nation*, understood all the legalities involved.

Toward the end of that week, network producers and television correspondents were calling with rapidly mounting frequency. We had clearly entered a new phase. The questions were no longer about whether or not Valerie was CIA; rather, they sought to uncover some supposedly as-yet-unexplained link between the two of us and the trip to Niger.

Over the weekend, the calls became more insistent and more pointed. And the sources being cited by the reporters were consistently "White House officials or senior White House officials," so I could only conclude that the decision to push the story had been made at a high level in the administration. At that point, I knew that I would have to address the issue more publicly.

NBC's Andrea Mitchell, who had been guest-hosting *Meet the Press* when I'd been on the show two weeks earlier, reached me at home on the Sunday night after Novak's article appeared to ask for my reaction to "what White House sources were telling her about the real story being not the sixteen words but Wilson and his wife." I agreed to do an interview with her the following day in my office. Although I had planned not to appear on any television shows prior to Thursday, July 24, when I was scheduled to do *The Daily Show with Jon Stewart*, I felt I had no choice but to try to stop the White House from continuing to push this canard.

The principal question remained unanswered: Who had so badly served the president? Who Valerie was and what she did, or who I was and what I did, were merely the administration's means of obfuscating the real issue and confusing the public. The White House was trying to fling dust into the eyes of the press and public while descending into what a Republican staffer on the Hill later called a "slime-and-defend" mode.

On Monday morning, July 21, I sat down with Andrea and answered her questions. I was scrupulous in speaking about Valerie only hypothetically; I was careful to qualify my statements and to use the subjunctive: "If she were as Novak alleged, then. . . ." In response to Andrea's questions regarding statements made by White House officials about Valerie's professional life and its connection to me, I noted that the sources of the original leaks from the administration to Novak might have violated the law.

When the interview aired on the Monday evening news, NBC had systematically edited out every one of my qualifiers regarding Valerie's status, no doubt because of time constraints. They thus substantively changed the tenor of the interview and gave CIA lawyers cause to briefly consider whether or not I myself might have been in violation of the same law as the senior administration officials who had originally leaked the information about Valerie to Novak. I later called Andrea to request a copy of the full interview, so as to be able to defend myself, but NBC policy disallows providing transcripts of interviews in their unedited versions. I asked Andrea therefore to make sure that the full interview was preserved on tape in the event legal questions arose in the future. She agreed to do so.

That afternoon I received the call from Chris Matthews tersely informing me that Karl Rove had entered the fray with the comment that my wife was "fair game." To make a political point, to defend a political agenda, to blur the truth that one of the president's own staffers had scripted a lie into the president's mouth, one of the administration's most senior officials found it perfectly acceptable to push a story that exposed a national security asset. It was appalling.

The next morning I appeared on the *Today* show. Katie Couric was the interviewer. Unfortunately, I was on remote location, in Washington— my one chance to sit face-to-face with "America's sweetheart," and all I could see was the unblinking eye of the camera in front of me. At least the spot was televised live, so the hypotheticals that I used to qualify what I said about Valerie were not edited out. Again I made the point that the leak might well have been a violation of the law.

Although I received hundreds of phone calls from the national and international press in subsequent days, not once did I again hear a reporter cite White House sources in relation to that particular story. In the weeks ahead, the attacks from the White House reverted to more typical forms of character assassination.

*   *   *

At the same time that the White House was attempting to make me the subject of the news story, it still had to fend off the increasingly pointed interrogations as to who was responsible for the offending sixteen words. Although CIA director George Tenet had said—or had had to say—that the fault lay with him, it soon became clear that the problem had originated elsewhere. Attention shifted to the National Security Council, and it moved sequentially up the chain of command to Deputy National Security Adviser Stephen Hadley, who was one of those responsible for vetting Bush's State of the Union address. On July 22, Hadley acknowledged that he should have deleted the reference to Iraq's attempts to buy uranium, because months earlier, in two memos and a phone call from Tenet himself, the CIA had warned him that the claim was weak. All three of those warnings had been issued before the president's Cincinnati speech in early October. Hadley claimed that he had evidently failed to recall them three months later, in January. "The high standards the president set were not met," Hadley admitted.

Earlier, in a press briefing on July 11, Hadley's boss, Condoleezza Rice, had skirted the issue of the sixteen words by saying: "If there were doubts about the underlying intelligence to that National Intelligence Estimate (NIE), those doubts were not communicated to the president, the vice president, or to me." After Hadley admitted the existence of the memos and suddenly recalled the telephone call from Tenet, Rice had no choice but to own up to her own culpability in the matter. On July 30, in an interview with PBS correspondent Gwen Ifill, she grudgingly acknowledged her responsibility, but not before trying yet again to fob the blame off on Hadley, much as she had earlier tried to blame Tenet.

"What we learned later, and I did not know at the time, and certainly did not know until just before Steve Hadley went out to say what he said last week, was that the director had also sent over to the White House a set of clearance comments that explained why he wanted this out of the speech. I can tell you, I either didn't see the memo, or I don't remember seeing the memo." Gwen Ifill finally asked Rice directly: "Do you feel any personal failure or responsibility for not having seen this memo and flagged it to anybody else who was working on this speech?" Rice responded: "Well, I certainly feel personal responsibility for this entire episode. The president of the United States has every right to believe that what he is saying in his speeches is of [*sic*] the highest confidence of his staff."

It was now four months after Dr. El Baradei, the head of the International Atomic Energy Agency, had pronounced the Niger documents forgeries; three weeks after my *New York Times* piece made clear what I had not found in Niger; and two weeks after a senior official in the White House had blown the cover of a national security asset simply to discredit me—and the national security adviser was finally admitting the obvious: she was responsible. And the president once again demonstrated that he was more loyal to his senior staff than they had been to him: he rejected Hadley's offer to resign. Apparently, Rice did not even offer.

Dick Cheney, on the other hand, was characteristically unrepentant. In a speech he delivered to an amen chorus at the American Enterprise Institute on July 24, he classically demonstrated that the best defense is a good offense when he asked rhetorically: "How could any responsible leader have ignored the Iraqi threat?" It was of course the wrong question. No one doubted that Saddam had posed a threat. Rather, the question was, and had always been, whether that threat constituted such a grave and gathering danger that the conquest and occupation of Iraq was the only, or even the best, way to achieve the desired goal of disarmament.

On the same day that Cheney spoke, I addressed a decidedly different audience. I had been invited to appear on *The Daily Show with Jon Stewart* shortly after the *New York Times* ran my article, but had pushed the date back to the twenty-fourth in order to allow myself to gain some perspective on the situation. I'd had no idea then that over the next three weeks the story would take so many strange twists and unexpected turns—more than enough to keep it red-hot.

I traveled to New York early on July 24, as I had been invited to attend an editorial board meeting at *The Nation* offices that morning. David Corn, who jokingly called me an "establishment type," had been very kind to me over the past months, since before my February article in the magazine that had addressed some of the larger agendas of the neoconservatives. He and his magazine had also earned my admiration, even though it had never before been one of my regular reads. Corn and his boss, Katrina vanden Heuvel, had been tenacious and tough, publishing probing analyses of America's road to war in an attempt to bring some critical thinking to the decision-making process. They had appeared on every political talk show that would have them, and they were never less than fully prepared to debate any and every war promoter the other side set on them. Their intestinal fortitude in the face of volleys from the extreme Right was truly laudable. While they are far more critical of government than I am generally—being, as I am, an "establishment type"—they have been proven to be dead right about the extremist nature of this administration, and, I believe, have been properly cynical about its motives.

I walked into the cluttered boardroom at *The Nation*, and as I took my seat I heard somebody say, "We should give him a standing ovation." I was flattered to be so kindly received. In fact, I was taken aback. For all that Valerie and I had been through in the past several weeks, this was the first indication that we actually had a following, that other people out there were watching the events unfolding between us and the administration with more than the polite interest of a parlor game. There was real passion in the room. And anger. This was more than a family affair; a national audience was tuning in as the White House tried to hurt me by destroying my wife's career and life work.

After lunch, I taxied up to the *New York Times* through the July heat and humidity to meet David Shipley, editor of the op-ed page. A tropical drizzle rendered the Manhattan skyline dull and gray. I had never before been inside the *Times* building, known affectionately, I think, to the staff as the mother ship. David and I introduced ourselves when I stepped off the elevator and he escorted me to his office for a cup of coffee. En route, down a long windowless corridor with offices on either side, doors sporting the names of *Times* writers, we ran into veteran *Times*man Robert Semple. David explained that I was "the one who wrote the article on what he didn't find in Africa," and Semple, turning to me, said, "So you're the one who turned our paper around." The *Times* had been mired in the scandal surrounding Jayson Blair, the fraudulent journalist whose reporting had been questioned by a number of colleagues. The turmoil in the media about the *Times* had diminished in the past several weeks, but I had not imagined that anyone at the paper would attribute their improvement to me or to my piece. For the second time that day, I was struck by the extent of the reaction to me and the article outside the confines of Washington, D.C.

In David's office, his windows overlooking the neighborhood highrises with their brick façades and window air conditioners, I shared my surprise. I explained why for months I had hesitated to write the piece, and asked him if he had ever thought it would have such resonance. He noted that while he rarely knows whether an opinion piece is going to rouse people or not, my article did have one distinct advantage: it at long last attached a name to the allegation. Up to that point, the story had had no protagonist, just ubiquitous unnamed sources; but with my name, David said, it became the first criticism of the administration that really showed teeth. No longer could the White House communications office deflect criticism simply by stating repeatedly that the president had "moved on," thus indicating that the issue was supposed to be closed to further discussion. Now, with a name to drive the story, the press would be less willing to let it drop, I surmised.

And, of course, the attack on Valerie now added a whole new dimension. That a vicious act, one with the potential to place her and other innocent people in danger, had been undertaken by some unnamed senior official or officials at the White House lent an element of nefarious mystery to the tale. In and of itself, David noted, that should keep the journalists salivating—and correctly so, given the possibility that a crime had been committed by someone in the administration.

Somewhat awed by what I'd heard, I left the *Times* building. This was the widely read and highly regarded "paper of record," and despite its recent travails with a staffer who had systematically violated the ethics of the profession, it remained an authoritative voice and significant force in every national and international debate. It was clear from my conversation with David that the issue I had addressed, and the government's response to it, had raised many hackles. Whereas I had been satisfied with the admission that the sixteen words should not have been "put in a presidential speech," other concerned citizens wanted to know why the Congress and the American people had been lied to on an issue as important as committing their country to war.

As I had some time to kill, I walked from the *Times* building on West 43rd Street up to Comedy Central, a stroll of twenty or so Manhattan blocks. The rain had stopped, but the mugginess persisted. By the time I arrived at the Comedy Central studios, my shirt was wet under my suitcoat and I was looking a bit disheveled. I was reminded of the years I had spent in equatorial Africa, when a stroll of just a few minutes would leave me dripping. I would normally have left the jacket at home; after all, New York in August dished up weather barely to be endured in a polo shirt and chinos, let alone a gray suit and tie. But Valerie, always vigilant, pointed out that the people I'd be seeing in New York did not want to meet Joe Wilson, they wanted to meet "the ambassador," so I'd better dress like the ambassador. Great, I thought, *Brian* Wilson gets to dress in Hawaiian shirts and

Bermuda shorts because he's known as a Beach Boy, but *Joe* Wilson has to stick with the gray suit look.

Fortunately, the Jon Stewart Comedy Central building—yes, it is named after the *Daily Show* star—was equipped for comfort. I made my way to the door past the line of fans waiting for the day's show, introduced myself, and was escorted to a dressing room.

Jon's team made me feel extremely welcome. They pressed a clean shirt and tie for me, and touched up my suit—while I stretched out in a dressing room and took a nap. When Jon wandered into the area—I could hear him through the door, as he tried out some jokes on his team—I would have stepped out to say hello, but I was still in my boxer shorts.

I was more excited than I had been for any other television appearance I had yet made. This, after all, was not news; it was satire. I had of course given thought to what lessons from my experiences over the past eight months I wanted to impart to Jon's audience. The one that stood out most importantly for me that sultry afternoon in New York was that despite all the attacks, these recent weeks had reaffirmed for me what American democracy is all about. For I realized more surely than ever that holding our government accountable for its actions is not just a right protected under our constitution, but a civic duty as well.

Jon Stewart's show has an interesting viewership. Its young demographic, if not totally disaffected, tends not to participate in the political process in large numbers. Our hopes for a vibrant democracy require a broader participation than currently exists on the part of our entire population, and especially by younger citizens. Jon Stewart, with all of his humor, provides a way to reach that group. His spoofing of topical subjects leavens serious issues without trivializing them, and makes them less mystifying. And he is very, very funny.

I loved the show. The round of applause when I walked across the set, even if the audience was cued to provide it, left me unsure about what to do next. I was used to being seated and looking into a blank camera while I listened to a voice asking me questions through an earpiece. But this was a live audience cheering. I didn't know whether to ignore the applause or to wave; I think I did a little of both. I remember Jon coming around the couch and escorting me to my seat, but the next several minutes are a blur. Jon was so quick and so humorous that I found myself laughing heartily right along with the audience. At the end of the segment, he asked the producer if he could keep me on after the commercial break.

So we continued for another several minutes, which gave me a chance to share with Jon a form letter I had received from Dick Cheney asking me to be a cochairman of the Washington, D.C., campaign to reelect Bush–Cheney. I told Jon that with the receipt of that letter, I concluded that the administration had decided to let bygones be bygones. Jon took the letter, and I thought he was going to fall off his chair, he was laughing so hard. He showed the letter to the audience, then asked that a hat be passed to raise the one thousand dollars I needed to qualify for the distinction. Even as Republicans would later attack me for contributing to Democratic candidates, they were actively soliciting donations from me.

In the months that followed, one of the most frequent comments I heard from people around the country was, "I saw you on *The Daily Show*. You were great." It made me think that perhaps I had found a second career, playing straight man to a stand-up comic. More importantly, it validated my instincts that Americans are more widely interested in public affairs than we assume, but that they do not always get their information from traditional sources. I think political leaders of all stripes would be well-advised to reach out and explore every possible venue for talking to Americans.

By early August, I was still waiting for the CIA to refer the matter to the Justice Department for investigation. Progress toward that milestone under Attorney General John Ashcroft was unacceptably slow for a national security matter. A letter (pictured on facing page) from the CIA to Representative John Conyers, released February 2004,

Central Intelligence Agency

Washington, D.C. 20505

30 January 2004

The Honorable John Conyers, Jr.
Ranking Democratic Member
Committee on the Judiciary
House of Representatives
Washington, D.C. 20515

Dear Mr. Conyers:

Thank you for your letter of 29 September 2003 to the
Director of Central Intelligence (DCI) regarding any contacts
the Central Intelligence Agency (CIA) has had with the
Department of Justice (DoJ) to request an investigation into the
disclosure earlier that year of the identity of an employee
operating under cover. The DCI has asked me to respond to your
letter on his behalf.

Executive Order 12333 requires CIA to report to the
Attorney General "possible violations of criminal law." In
accordance with Executive Order 12333 on 24 July 2003, a CIA
attorney left a phone message for the Chief of the
Counterespionage Section of DoJ noting concern with recent
articles on this subject and stating that the CIA would forward
a written crimes report pending the outcome of a review of the
articles by subject matter experts. By letter dated 30 July
2003, the CIA reported to the Criminal Division of DoJ a
possible violation of criminal law concerning the unauthorized
disclosure of classified information. The letter also informed
DoJ that the CIA's Office of Security had opened an
investigation into this matter. This letter was sent again to
DoJ by facsimile on 5 September 2003.

By letter dated 16 September 2003, and in accordance with
standard practice in such matters, the CIA informed DoJ that the
Agency's investigation into this matter was complete, provided
DoJ a memorandum setting forth the results of that
investigation, and requested that the Federal Bureau of
Investigation (FBI) undertake a criminal investigation of this
matter. In a 29 September 2003 letter, DoJ advised that the
Counterespionage Section of DoJ had requested that the FBI
initiate an investigation of this matter.

I hope the information set forth in this letter provides
the assistance you were seeking.

Sincerely,

w⁻ George Tenem

for Stanley M. Moskowitz
Director of Congressional Affairs

shows clearly how hard the Agency had to push in July, August, and September before the Justice Department finally took up the case.

On January 30, 2004, the CIA's director of congressional affairs, Stanley M. Moskowitz, wrote in response to a request for information from Conyers that an attorney from the Agency first contacted the Counterespionage Section of the Department of Justice by phone on July 24, 2003, explaining that the CIA was beginning an investigation to determine if a violation of law had been committed. The Agency followed up by letter on July 30, stating their review indicated a crime may indeed have occurred; they re-sent that letter on September 5. On September 16, they sent another letter, stating that their review was complete, and requesting that the FBI initiate a criminal investigation. Finally, almost two weeks later, and nearly two and a half months after Novak's column had exposed Valerie, Justice belatedly advised the CIA that the FBI had begun an investigation. It seemed an extremely sluggish response by the Department of Justice. This, coupled with Ashcroft's refusal to recuse himself from the investigation once it finally began, left me, and many others, concerned about the ongoing damage to the national security under these lackadaisical conditions. It appeared that politics was winning out and that the administration was intent on sweeping the matter under the rug. As late as December 5, 2003, "a senior White House official" was quoted in the *Financial Times* gloating, "We have rolled the earthmovers in over this one."

I was invited in August to give a speech to ROAR (Retain Our American Rights), an activist organization in Los Angeles founded by Norman Lear, the legendary producer of such groundbreaking, socially responsible television sitcoms as *All in the Family, Mary Hartman, Mary Hartman,* and *All That Glitters.* I had corresponded with Norman after my appearance on *NOW with Bill Moyers* in February. I was only casually aware of Norman's civic activism in the years since his pioneering days in TV production, and to my chagrin I had not followed his efforts to resuscitate our democratic spirit by purchasing an early copy of the Declaration of Independence and touring it to communities around the country.

Norman met me at his guest house in Brentwood, and we immediately connected, quickly discovering that we are both older fathers of twins. His girls were eight at the time, while my younger set of twins was three and a half. We readily agreed that if parenting at an advanced age didn't kill you, it would keep you young. It certainly wasn't killing Norman. In terrific physical shape, he has all the experience of a worldly wise elder statesman and the indomitable passion of a college-age activist. While derided by the extreme Right as a liberal, Norman is fervently committed to democracy and the celebration of our diversity. He is also utterly opposed to the theocratic agenda of the religious Right. His longtime commitment to time-honored American democratic values and respect for the history that has made our country great are true inspirations to anyone who does not believe that our country's values are the sole property of television preachers.

We drove over to Beverly Hills to have lunch in a quiet café near Rodeo Drive. Joining us were his wife, Lyn, a gracious lady, easygoing companion, and dedicated partner; Mary Leonard, an ebullient interior decorator and political junkie; and the inimitable Warren Beatty, who breezed in late. Here I was, a middle-aged, moderate ex-bureaucrat, in the midst of some of the most committed progressives in Hollywood, that den of iniquity continually being smeared by right-wingers. All four of them were interesting, engaged, and well-informed students of American politics. I found myself impressed by their thoughtfulness, their enthusiasm, and their infectious optimism. What a welcome change from the politics of fear emanating from the president, the vice president, and their senior staff in Washington.

At that evening's ROAR event, I was introduced by Arianna Huffington. I asked for her to do so, not simply because her journey from Newt Gingrich's knee to Norman Lear's living room was itself such an unusual tale, but because I had found in her writings of the past few years such engrossing social commentary. Having just announced her candidacy for governor of California in the recall election, she was flush from the adrenaline that such a decision generates. It was an electric evening. The West Coast activists were hungry for news from Washington, and after a month of vexing controversy I was delighted to be so unconditionally welcomed by a community in my home state.

The following day was filled with interviews and speeches that had been organized by Robert Greenwald, the cofounder of Artists for Winning Without War, then producing the documentary *Uncovered*. One audience that I addressed was made up largely of religiously affiliated social workers who had been in Latin America for the previous three decades. If they had developed there an abiding dislike of the CIA, which they blamed for every disruptive occurrence from the suicide of Chilean President Salvador Allende to the support of the death squads in El Salvador's civil war, they had finally found something they hated more than CIA officers themselves, and that was a government that would so callously expose one of them. It was striking how offended they were by Valerie's outing, and it was proof that even those who saw themselves as implacable foes of the CIA were shocked at what the government had done to her.

In my interview with Greenwald that afternoon, I told my tale for his documentary and then spent the evening at a reception at his home on the beach. Present were leading progressives and liberals from Southern California, there to support Alternet, the Internet-based news site. I found myself surrounded by activists such as Tom Hayden, one-time defendant in the '60s' notorious Chicago Seven trial, and the leaders of Code Pink, a women's antiwar movement.

Overnight, Valerie and I had become symbols for the progressive Left. Or, rather, we had become examples of a broader, more general unease with the direction in which the administration was leading the country. Our case classically illustrated the lengths to which big government would go to crush its adversaries. We had become the human faces that people could identify with in the larger, increasingly unsettling political story of the Iraq war.

I had spent years living in dictatorships abroad and knew from personal experience what happened to people who dared to criticize their governments in such regimes. In Saddam's world, friends of mine, including senior Iraqi officials, would routinely be called in for questioning just for talking with me. In Africa, an editor friend of mine in Burundi would routinely find himself harassed if a particular article displeased the president; and in Gabon, the opposition presidential candidate had his home shelled by the Gabonese army after a particularly nasty election campaign designed to move the country from authoritarian rule to democracy. In the United States, though, our system thrives only when people participate in it. The differences were huge between what Valerie and I had endured and what critics suffered in other countries. But it was reassuring nonetheless to realize firsthand that in California and New York City we had gained so much support. Strength in numbers is important when facing a hostile government hell-bent on limiting the rights and freedoms of its citizens in the name of national security. I was delighted to be embraced by so many fine American citizens, who were as concerned as I was about—and were participating in—the future of our country.

Chapter Eighteen
Frog-Marching

FOR THE BETTER PART OF JULY, I had been sidetracked by the fallout from my piece in the *New York Times,* and from Robert Novak's article alleging that Valerie was a CIA operative. No longer were people interested in my views on the other two debates that were then raging in Washington, which I characterized as "how did we get into this mess" and "how do we get out of it." Instead, all anybody wanted to know was if I really was a partisan hack as alleged by the Republicans, and who had leaked my wife's name to the press. I didn't want to dignify the first charge by commenting on it, though I was unwilling to become a punching bag, and so hit back when necessary; meanwhile, I was still trying to quell public discussion of the latter topic, when possible, or at least reserve it for the realm of the hypothetical.

After appearing on the *Daily Show,* I was invited on CNN's *Late Edition* with Wolf Blitzer, for Sunday, August 3. I followed a spirited discussion between Senators Trent Lott and Evan Bayh about the situation on the ground in Iraq and what the U.S. should be doing there to create more stability.

I had met Senator Lott several times during the previous year in CNN and FOX green rooms and found him to be affable, even if our views on a number of issues were diametrically opposed. I remembered meeting him when he was the House of Representatives minority whip and Tom Foley was his Democratic counterpart. Their conversations were characterized by humor and congeniality. Rough partisan edges had not been in evidence then, and despite whatever differences we might have had, they were not in evidence now. Senator Lott was a courtly Southern gentleman. In fact, listening to him talk with Wolf, I discovered that we shared many of the same concerns regarding the situation in Iraq. I told him so as we changed positions on the set, laughing when he allowed that it wouldn't be in either of our interests to be seen in agreement on any subject right now. For Republicans, I was radioactive.

Wolf was kind enough to expand his line of questioning to include more than queries about Valerie. He asked me about the ongoing search for weapons of mass destruction being led by Dr. David Kay, a former U.N. inspector and then an aide to CIA Director George Tenet. I replied:

> I've had confidence that we would find weapons of mass destruction, and weapons of mass destruction programs, from the very beginning of the run-up to the war in Iraq. 687, the initial U.N. resolution dealing with weapons of mass destruction, demanded compliance; and it had, as its objective, disarmament. We have not yet achieved disarmament, so it was perfectly appropriate to continue to try and gather together the international consensus to disarm Saddam and his programs.
>
> I think we'll find chemical weapons. I think we'll find biological precursors that may or may not have been weaponized. And I think we will find a continuing interest in nuclear weapons. The question really is whether it met the threshold test of imminent threat

to our own national security, or even the test of grave
and gathering danger.

Many months later, I must now admit that I was mistaken about
the discovery of WMD. But then I never premised a preemptive war on
the fervent certainty that they would be found, nor had I argued that
a preemptive war was necessary to achieve the objective. On the other
hand, Kay has since resigned as head of the CIA's Iraqi Survey Group
and concluded that there never were weapons to be found, nullifying
one of the administration's prime justifications for the invasion of
Iraq. The intrusive inspections actually had been working.

By the next day, August 4, Deputy Secretary of Defense Paul Wolfowitz was quoting me in an interview, noting that "Even Joe Wilson
agrees that we will find weapons of mass destruction." Suddenly,
senior officials were reacting to things that I said. Not surprisingly,
Wolfowitz selectively used my words to bolster his point without
noting my assessment that the threat posed by such programs as there
may have been had not constituted a grave and gathering danger and
had not merited the military response we had executed.

That Tuesday, the *Wall Street Journal* editorial page took a
whack at me too. They charged that I was moving the goalposts by
saying that the threat posed by Saddam's weapons programs did not
meet the "imminent threat test." The *Journal* argued that the president had never mentioned "imminent threat" in his comments, and
that no senior administration officials had either. While the *Journal*
may have been technically correct that the president had not uttered
those exact words, he walked right up to the phrase when, on
November 23, 2002, he said, "The world is also uniting to answer the
unique and urgent threat posed by Iraq, whose dictator has already
used weapons of mass destruction to kill thousands." His staff and
administration allies, of course, had been less concerned about split-
ting hairs as they promoted the invasion.

The *Journal* also conveniently ignored the second part of my statement that the threat had not even met the test of grave and gathering danger, the administration's own watered-down justification for preemptive war. The administration and its supporters were the ones moving the goalposts. I had always said that the presence of a WMD threat was worthy of an international response, despite their efforts to claim otherwise about my statements.

The insistence by the *Journal* and senior administration officials that they had never said Saddam posed an imminent threat led to a contest sponsored by Josh Marshall, the author of one of the most compulsively readable weblogs ("blogs") on the Internet, Talkingpointsmemo.com. In the best tradition of Internet community, Josh's contest elicited from his readers statements by administration officials and their confederates spoken before the war that contradicted their best efforts at postwar spin. Josh wrote that not only did the administration blur the distinction between imminent threat and grave and gathering danger, it actually equated the two, dangerously lowering the bar for future action. Among the more notable of the five hundred submissions:

> Richard Perle: "As long as Saddam is there, with everything we know about Saddam, as long as he possesses the weapons that we know he possesses, there is a threat, and I believe it's imminent because he could choose at any time to take an action we all very much hope he won't take."
>
> Dan Bartlett, the president's communications director, in response to the following question from Wolf Blitzer: "Is [Saddam] an imminent threat to U.S. interests, either in that part of the world or to Americans right here at home?" Bartlett: "Well, of course he is."
>
> Ari Fleischer, the president's spokesman, in response

to the following question from a reporter a month after the war: "Well, we went to war, didn't we, to find these— because we said that these weapons were a direct and imminent threat to the United States? Isn't that true?" Fleischer: "Absolutely."

President Bush himself, from his October 7, 2002, speech in Cincinnati, Ohio: "Iraq could decide on any given day to provide a biological or chemical weapon to a terrorist group or individual terrorists. Alliance with terrorists could allow the Iraqi regime to attack America without leaving any fingerprints. . . . Facing clear evidence of peril, we cannot wait for the final proof—the smoking gun—that could come in the form of a mushroom cloud."

The point I had been making on *Late Edition* was that while we needed to be aggressive in disarming Saddam, the threat to our national security posed by those weapons never merited the invasion–conquest–occupation war scenario that the administration had chosen to wage.

When Wolfowitz selectively quoted me to support his war, that was a misrepresentation of my position; when the *Journal* accused me of moving the goalposts, that, too, was a misrepresentation of my position. I remembered that in Washington, your status is derivative of the status of your enemies. With Wolfowitz and the *Wall Street Journal* declared as adversaries, my status was clearly higher than it had been when I was at the National Security Council and only State Department desk officers had differed with me.

The week after my trip to Los Angeles, I traveled to Seattle to participate in a town meeting hosted by Democratic Congressman Jay Inslee, to discuss the use or misuse of intelligence in the run-up to the war. When he invited me, he said that he expected about 150 people to attend and that it would take a couple of hours. Though he could not offer a speaker's fee, and would have to use his own frequent-flyer miles to cover my economy-class ticket, he did promise a golf game afterwards, an offer too tempting to refuse.

I arrived in Seattle on August 20. Though I had lived nearby in the 1970s, in Sequim on the Olympic Peninsula, and had taken my Foreign Service oral exam in Seattle, I had only been back to the city twice in the intervening quarter century. The approach by air was as spectacular as I remembered. It was a clear day, not a cloud in the sky, as we flew over and around the Cascade Mountain range. Few sights are as majestic as the craggy peaks of Mount Rainier with broad Mount Olympus of the Olympic Mountains in the background on the western horizon. We swooped down and landed at Sea-Tac Airport, and I was soon on the ferry to Whidbey Island across Puget Sound, watching the Seattle Seahawks' new football stadium fade into the distance.

The next day, we learned that the town meeting had attracted an overwhelming response. Instead of 150 people, there would be more than 1,100 attendees. The auditorium at the high school would only handle 600, so they had put closed-circuit televisions in neighboring classrooms for the considerable overflow. I would be on a panel with retired Admiral Bill Center and Brewster Denny, the retired dean of the School of Public Affairs at the University of Washington, whom I had first met close to thirty years earlier when I was looking at graduate schools. I looked forward to reintroducing myself to Dean Denny and telling the audience that I owed my entire career to the fact that to get in to his graduate program, I had been obliged to demonstrate a commitment to public service. That requirement had led me to take the Foreign Service exam, and my diplomatic career was soon underway.

In the morning, Congressman Inslee and I were interviewed on the local FOX station and CNNfn, the financial news network. I used the latter appearance to state publicly something I had been pondering for a while—that Secretary of Defense Rumsfeld and most of his senior staff should be fired for having so badly managed the reconstruction effort in Iraq. I said it was unconscionable that we had performed so poorly on the restoration of public safety and the provision of such basic services as electricity and potable water. These were two essential prerequisites for winning the peace, and we had so miserably failed that the motives of those responsible had to be suspect. Was failure an acceptable outcome to them, even if it was a certainty that failure would lead to sustained instability and, quite possibly, the Balkanization of Iraq?

Arriving at the high school late in the morning on a Thursday, we watched as people streamed into the auditorium. We went first to the overflow rooms, so as not to deny any of those who had come to see us the opportunity to ask questions. The reception was warm and enthusiastic. It was uplifting to be among so many Americans who would take time from their daily schedules to listen to a discussion of war and peace and the policies that led to our precipitous occupation of Baghdad.

As we made our way to the stage from the rear of the auditorium, people noticed our entry and began applauding. Soon the audience was on its feet giving the four of us a standing ovation. I said to myself: "Jay Inslee is a real popular guy. I'll bet most congressmen would give their eyeteeth for this kind of reception in their districts."

Once his guests were all seated, the congressman introduced us to his constituents. When he presented me, there was another huge round of applause and another standing ovation. I was overwhelmed and didn't know quite what to do, as it went on and on. I finally motioned for people to sit down, and as they did, I leaned into the microphone and said, "Bob Novak, eat your heart out." That caused an outburst of laughter and yet more applause.

There was palpable anger in the hall. People were clearly worried by what they saw happening in Washington, D.C., and Iraq.

There were some committed pacifists and left-wing activists among the participants but most were simply interested citizens, there to learn and share their concerns about the direction in which the administration was taking the country. Admiral Center was a balanced voice with an extensive military career behind him, and even he acknowledged that he had never believed the threat posed by Iraq's weapons necessitated a military response. "Personally, I didn't feel very threatened," Center said. "I don't think many Americans felt very threatened."

Brewster Denny offered the most trenchant observation when he commented on American unilateralism in the face of international opposition: "We gave the world the royal finger." The audience responded with resounding applause and loud condemnation of what the dean said was quite possibly the administration's violation of international law.

In the question-and-answer session, I was asked about the investigation into the leak. I hesitated and then offered that my intention was to support the investigation because, after all, "wouldn't it be fun to see Karl Rove frog-marched out of the White House in handcuffs? And I measure my words." The reaction of the audience was swift and loud. At the mention of Rove's name the catcalls and whistles rained down followed by applause at the thought of everyone's favorite ogre being frog-marched.

One afternoon after I had returned home to Washington, Valerie asked if I had used the phrase in one of my speeches. Of course I always shared general details of events I participated in, but I usually didn't get into the specifics of language, and I had not told her about "frog-marching" Karl Rove "in handcuffs." Somebody at her office had apparently seen the reference on the Internet and told her about it. She was not thrilled by my use of the term and thought I had gone too far. Perhaps she was right. She urged me to temper my words if I was asked about the statement. There did not seem to be much other interest in the comment for a couple of weeks, giving me time to reflect on what I would say when asked.

In mid-September, when awareness of the statement finally did reach the mainstream press, I went out of my way in several interviews to put it in context for reporters, freely acknowledging that perhaps I had been carried away by the spirit of the moment in Seattle. But I did not significantly alter the thrust of my accusation, which was that, at a minimum, Rove had engaged in unethical behavior—by pushing the disclosure of Valerie's status to *Hardball's* Chris Matthews—and had possibly committed a crime, for which he should be investigated. I explained to reporters, ultimately including Tim Russert on *Meet the Press,* that while I had no personal knowledge that Rove had been the original leaker or that he had authorized the leak, I was confident from what a respectable reporter had told me (I had not yet publicly identified Matthews as my source) that Rove had been retailing the Novak article, thereby giving the leak his approval. Furthermore, the CIA is an executive branch agency that reports to the president of the United States. Karl Rove is the top political adviser to the president. The act of exposing my wife was clearly a political act, designed to discredit me and discourage other critics of the administration from speaking out.

The political office of the White House would seem like a good place to start an investigation, I mused for the press. Whether or not Rove had committed a crime, most certainly he was guilty of crassly giving credence to a story that never should have been published in the first place. He had also lent the power of the White House to the despicable act of attacking a family member as a way to smear someone who differed with the administration over policy. Criminality or lawfulness aside, the fact remains that the standard of behavior of senior public servants ought to be higher than "barely legal." His conduct contradicted the president's oft-stated desire to change the tone in Washington and to restore honor and dignity to the White House. If the frog-march statement brought the harsh glare of public opinion down on him, so much the better. I would never apologize or draw back from that. Considering what I knew he had done, it was immaterial to me whether, when he was frog-marched out of the White House, he was in handcuffs or not, so long as the frog-marching took place.

On September 14, I published a second piece in the *San Jose Mercury News*, this one titled "Seeking Honesty in U.S. Policy." I had been driven to write by the blatantly revisionist rhetoric coming from the administration, as well as by the overly rosy picture of postwar Iraq being painted by the neoconservatives both inside and outside the government. I had been particularly struck by Paul Wolfowitz's advice to Congress that all we needed to succeed in a deteriorating situation was to project a little confidence. That was patently untrue and smacked of the irresponsible happy talk of the Vietnam era. I argued that Iraqi reconstruction was proceeding so poorly that a "more cynical reading of the agenda of certain Bush advisers could conclude that the Balkanization of Iraq was always an acceptable outcome, because Israel would then find itself surrounded by small Arab countries worried about each other instead of forming a solid bloc against Israel." I also took umbrage at a statement by Under Secretary of State for Disarmament John Bolton, who had said while in London that whether Saddam's government actually possessed weapons of mass destruction "isn't really the issue. The issue, I think, has been the capability that Iraq sought to have . . . WMD programs."

"In other words," I continued, "we're now supposed to believe that we went to war not because Saddam's arsenal of weapons of mass destruction threatened us, but because he had scientists on his payroll."

I concluded the article by calling on the administration to level with the American people and to redouble its efforts to ease tensions in the Israeli–Palestinian conflict. "That is the thorn that must be pulled from the side of the region. The road to peace in the

Middle East still goes through Jerusalem." What I'd written was so highly critical of the administration that when I asked Brent Scowcroft, to whom I had sent it, if he was also going to share this one with the White House, he laughed and said he was in enough trouble with the administration already.

A week later, Tom Andrews called and invited me to participate in promoting Win Without War's campaign to urge Congress not to approve the administration's $87 billion supplemental budget request for Iraq until the president fired many of his key advisers, including Donald Rumsfeld, and committed to a transfer of authority to the United Nations preparatory to a sovereign Iraqi government taking power. Tom had brought a welcome voice to the debate before the war. He was one of the few critics consistently willing to suffer the rants of the right-wing cable talk-show hosts and was unflappable in such encounters.

At the end of 2002, he had invited me to be a part of the coalition when it was created, and I had appeared at a press conference with members of the organization at its launch ceremony. However, I had formally dissociated myself from them, "before they dissociate themselves from me," as I said, because many of the members were pacifists who on principle were against military action at any time.

By this point in September 2003, however, following President Bush's nationally televised speech on September 7 announcing the request for the $87 billion, I was delighted to be part of their campaign. The administration had run roughshod over the Congress since the beginning of the debate on Iraq. The use-of-force resolution was only part of the deception. Secretary of Defense Rumsfeld and his deputy, Wolfowitz, had systematically refused to share with the oversight committees the anticipated costs of the operation we were now in the middle of, and of the reconstruction for which we were responsible. Both repeatedly spoke of how oil revenues from Iraq would be used to fund reconstruction, even as serious studies from respected think-tanks concluded that it would be close to a decade before oil profits would be available for anything other than rehabilitation and modernization of the industry and the fields themselves. In one particularly egregious statement, U.S. Agency for International Development (USAID) Director Andrew Natsios proclaimed to ABC's Ted Koppel that the administration would require no more than $1.7 billion for all reconstruction in Iraq. "No more, never," he had the audacity to tell Koppel and *Nightline*'s national television audience.

I concluded that the only way to have any impact on the administration was to hold it to account and to make demands *prior* to providing the money, not after. Who in Congress could forget that the resolution passed in October 2002 had been to strengthen the hand of the president in his dealings with the United Nations, not to go to war without international support? Bush himself said in his Cincinnati address to the nation on October 7, 2002, that congressional authorization of use of force "does not mean that military action is imminent or unavoidable. The resolution will tell the United Nations, and all nations, that America speaks with one voice and is determined to make the demands of the civilized world mean something." Yet to war we went, despite the opposition on constitutional grounds so eloquently set forth by Senator Robert Byrd. Money with no strings attached would only encourage further irresponsibility from the administration.

In their vigorous letter-writing and E-mail campaign, Win Without War was joined by Moveon.org, the Web site. Moveon.org, as I learned, was the brainchild of Wes Boyd and his wife, Joan Blades, two Silicon Valley entrepreneurs, created to mobilize public opinion on key issues. Their mission statement reads: "MoveOn is working to bring ordinary people back into politics. With a system that today revolves around big money and big media, most citizens are left out. When it becomes clear that our 'representatives' don't represent the public, the foundations of democracy are in peril. MoveOn is a catalyst for a new kind of grassroots involvement, supporting busy but concerned citizens in finding their political voice."

Since its founding, it had become a rallying point for Americans concerned that the public's voice had been lost in the debates on key issues facing our country. Moveon.org had been a key sponsor of Al Gore's foreign policy and security speeches in 2002, and was active in mobilizing grassroots support against the precipitous war track the administration had put the country on. It had been active in the debate before the war and in the early days of the presidential campaign for 2004, sponsoring an Internet primary among its members.

The final letter that participants were invited to sign opposing the $87 billion appropriation bill reads as follows:

AN OPEN LETTER FROM THE AMERICAN PEOPLE TO PRESIDENT BUSH AND MEMBERS OF CONGRESS:

End the Quagmire in Iraq: Change Course—Change the Team

The invasion and occupation of Iraq—in defiance of our international allies—has led our country into a quagmire.

From the outset, we have been deceived and manipulated:

- The president and his defense team warned of Iraq's massive arsenals of weapons of mass destruction. There were no such arsenals of weapons of mass destruction.
- We were told that Saddam Hussein would give such weapons to al Qaeda terrorists. There is no evidence of any significant link between Hussein and al Qaeda.
- We were told that getting rid of Hussein was in response to the 9/11 attacks. Hussein had nothing to do with 9/11 attacks.

- We were assured that American soldiers would be greeted with flowers and democracy would blossom in Iraq and throughout the Middle East. Nothing could be further from the truth.
- We were told that the war would strike a blow against terrorism. In fact the U.S. occupation is spawning new terrorists, galvanized by our presence and moving freely into this lawless, broken country.
- The U.S. occupation has left American soldiers unprepared and vulnerable, the country degenerating into chaos and the Iraqi people embittered and hostile. Now, the president is asking Congress for a staggering $87 billion blank check to fund more of the same.

We say not so fast—not without changing course and changing the team that failed our soldiers and led us into a quagmire. We call on Congress to condition any additional funding for U.S. policy in Iraq on:

1. The dismissal of the Bush administration team responsible for the quagmire in Iraq—starting with Defense Secretary Rumsfeld; and
2. Ending the U.S. military occupation of Iraq by immediately transferring full authority of the United Nations for the transition of the country to a truly representative government.

Our campaign against the $87 billion would not ultimately block the passage of the appropriations bill, but it would prove to be successful in many other ways. President Bush's speech to the nation requesting the funds shocked many Americans, for whom the enormous cost of the war now became a reality. Efforts in Congress to question the administration on the reconstruction effort revealed that there had been no plan for how to deal with the aftermath of the war in Iraq. The criticisms were pointed and vocal.

Americans were becoming alert to the enormous difficulties of the occupation, and their support for the administration was declining. It was now apparent that this was not the cakewalk we were promised and that the "liberated" Iraqis were not cheering from the rooftops, but rather shooting at American GIs from them.

Chapter Nineteen
A Criminal Investigation

I PURSUED THE CALL for the resignation of most of the senior officials at the Defense Department in an interview the evening of September 24, with Lou Dobbs on CNN. Lou had been a supporter of the war and such a vocal critic of what he considered France's intransigence at the U.N. that I had earlier made a joke about offering to send him a French Hermes tie for Christmas. He now gave me full rein to make my points, as controversial as they were, and did not challenge them in any way. I was struck by a real change in Lou's attitude, which I attributed to the scorn of someone whose trust has been betrayed. Lou, it seemed to me, was increasingly disillusioned with the Bush administration.

The Win Without War campaign was the ideal platform from which to focus on the failure of Secretary Rumsfeld and his senior advisers. He and his team had failed the troops, failed the president, and failed the American people, pure and simple.

With respect to the troops, I charged that he had neglected the lessons of other deployments of American forces in foreign lands, including Bosnia, on which I had worked during my tenure with the European Command. Rumsfeld had been intent on proving that American forces could move farther and faster and take territory with fewer troops because of our awesome firepower and our ability to attack simultaneously from the air and sea as well on land. The qualitative edge of our "joint" fighting was well known, and it had been demonstrated in Afghanistan and Iraq. However, Rumsfeld ignored the other equally important lesson—to hold territory and occupy it, you need more troops and heavier equipment; otherwise you lose more of that most precious resource, the American sons and daughters called upon to fight the war.

In any war, casualties are a regrettable by-product, but a key element of modern American warfare has always been force protection. That essential element was rejected by the Rumsfeld team, and as a consequence, American soldiers have been dying at a steady rate since the end of "major combat operations" was announced by President Bush with his inglorious landing on the aircraft carrier *Abraham Lincoln* on May 1, 2003. As of the end of February 2004, 549 American soldiers have died and more than 3,500 have been injured needlessly. As surely as Rumsfeld had failed the troops through last summer, when we first called for his resignation, his continuing failure has been demonstrable and unpardonable, yet he and his minions are still in office.

Every president has his own way of assimilating information. Ronald Reagan used to like his briefings on foreign leaders in videotape form so he could watch them like a television program. Bill Clinton was wont to engage in late-night bull sessions and was an inveterate reader of the editorial pages. On FOX, President Bush told Brit Hume that he relies on his advisers for news and information. We should not begrudge him that, though I admit unease at his lack of greater curiosity about current events. As citizens we do have every right, however, to insist that our president get the best information possible and, hence, that he hire and retain the best advisers available.

Tragically, Donald Rumsfeld and his team have consistently provided the worst advice and counsel imaginable, ranging from the secretary's own gratuitous and divisive comments pitting Old Europe against New Europe, to a reconstruction that was so ill-conceived and badly executed that it has jeopardized the president's ostensible vision of a democratic Iraq serving as a beacon for the rest of the Middle East. Rumsfeld and company have failed—and continue to fail—the president as Iraq slides inexorably into civil unrest, while we scramble out of the country as quickly as we can so the president's reelection campaign can trumpet the transfer of sovereignty on schedule.

But if the sovereignty we hand over is so fragile that unrest becomes full-blown civil war and interethnic violence rages, we will forever be blamed for having wreaked such havoc on the erstwhile caliphate of the Islamic world. And in that world, where the memory of the expulsion of the Moors from Spain in 1492 is still vivid, "forever" is a long time. It has been more than a distraction from the legitimate war against international terrorists; it has led to the creation of a second front abroad where previously there had been only one—Afghanistan. Over 130,000 American troops are in danger at any one time in Iraq, and with the rotation of troops in the spring and summer of 2004, fully 40 percent of them are either National Guard or Reserve forces. At a time when we must be vigilant against the possiblity of further attacks on our own soil, every call-up of National Guard or Reservists means that more of our first responders are over there instead of over here, where they should form our first line of homeland security. Rumsfeld and his ilk have failed the country.

In a subsequent appearance on CNN with Paula Zahn, I mentioned to Torie Clark, Rumsfeld's former press secretary, that I was on the warpath against her former boss, and she allowed that she did not think he was losing any sleep over my charges. In fact, it was really Congress, holding the government purse strings, whose attention the Win Without War campaign was trying to attract; but the administration had not shown any particular willingness to listen to our elected representatives any more than it listened to critics like me. In fact, many in Congress, Republicans included, balked at the portion of the money given outright for Iraqi reconstruction, instead of as a loan that might someday be repaid to the United States. The idea of American taxpayers underwriting Iraq's reconstruction while other countries were still being paid interest on loans to Saddam's regime grated, and President Bush was obliged to call James Baker back into service to travel to foreign capitals to lean on leaders to forgive debt owed by Iraq.

My involvement in the campaign to hold up the funding until some accountability could be guaranteed would end abruptly the following weekend. On late Friday afternoon, September 26, I received a call from an ABC producer covering the Justice Department. He told me that ABC had one source telling them that a criminal referral had just arrived at Justice from the CIA concerning the leak of Valerie's name. He was looking for a second source before broadcasting the news and wondered if I had heard anything about it.

I had not, and told him so.

The referral was not, however, a surprise. As soon as the leak occurred, the CIA began its own internal investigation as we now know from the Agency's letter to Congressman Conyers. Despite the presence of political partisans at Justice, Valerie and I always believed that career prosecutors in the department would seriously pursue the perpetrators of the leak. An officer had been exposed, an act that threatened many intelligence professionals; justice would be served, we believed and hoped.

By Saturday morning, MSNBC had gone public with the news, scooping ABC. The leaking of the referral to the press and its subsequent confirmation, by first Justice and then the White House, meant that the government had effectively confirmed Valerie's status as alleged by Novak. There was no longer any need to speak of her employment in the hypothetical.

The following day, Sunday, September 28, the *Washington Post* carried a lengthy article by Mike Allen and Dana Priest quoting a "senior administration official" who "said that before Novak's column ran, two top White House officials called at least six Washington journalists and disclosed the identity and occupation of Wilson's wife." The article continued: "They [the leakers] alleged that Wilson, who was not a CIA employee, was selected for the Niger mission partly because his wife had recommended him."

It was a stunning piece of reporting, especially considering that it featured the words of one administration official reproaching two of his or her colleagues on the record. As Allen and Priest put it, "It is rare for one Bush administration official to turn on another. Asked about the motive for describing the leaks, the senior official said the leaks were 'wrong and a huge miscalculation, because they were irrelevant and did nothing to diminish Wilson's credibility.' " Much as I was pleased to learn that there was at least one Bush official who believed the conduct of his colleagues was "wrong," I was disappointed to read that he or she evidently judged it so not because it was a betrayal of national security but because it was beside the point and had done nothing to damage my credibility. Would the leak have been okay if it had really impeached my character and sent me skittering into some dungeon reserved for critics of the Bush administration?

After having lived abroad for so many years, I had to marvel anew at what a strange town Washington, D.C., really is. The story of the unethical and perhaps illegal disclosure of Valerie's identity had been percolating for almost exactly ten weeks—from July 14 to September 28. Yet reporting on it had been sporadic. I knew of only four mainstream publications that ran stories durning this lengthy interlude (*Newsday, The Nation, Time,* and the *Baltimore Sun*). One reporter told a friend of mine that it was "yesterday's news." But this new article, perhaps because of its titillating details about senior administration officials "turn[ing] on one another," rocketed the story around the country, resulting in headlines from coast to coast. My education in the politics of truth had become a veritable seminar in the moral ambiguities of leaking. I wondered: When is a leaker a true whistleblower, risking his personal security to inform the citizenry and preserve the public's interest? When is a leaker a mendacious opportunist, out to advance the narrow interests of himself or his boss? When does a leaker become so appalled at the self-serving actions of his colleagues that he crosses the line to shine a light on them? Is there is a reliable way to distinguish among the many varieties of that genus peculiarly indigenous to Washington, the leaker?

The article gave me a lot to think about. Two officials calling six reporters indicated to me that there must have been a meeting to decide on the action to take, and that the information on Valerie must have been in their hands well before the appearance of my article on Sunday, July 6. I paused and considered a few questions: How did the two senior administration officials ever learn of her status? Had there been an immediate breach of security that allowed them even to learn she was an operative? Did the leakers learn of her status by someone's deliberate action, or inadvertently? Whatever the answers to these questions, I knew for certain that the initial disclosure of her status, whether deliberate or inadvertent, was the first damaging act, before the calls to all the journalists were placed.

Novak had already been in possession of the information on July 8 when he blurted it out to my friend, and a bare two days, from Sunday to Tuesday, just did not seem like enough time for word to have spread about Valerie's status, for the "senior administration officials" to have that meeting, and then make all those calls to the six reporters. With my increasingly public stance against the administration's war policy, including the articles I'd published in the *San Jose Mercury News, The Nation,* and the *Los Angeles Times*—and the statement I'd made on CNN in March, that they knew more about the Niger story than they were admitting—a plan to attack me had been formed well before this moment. It was cocked and ready to fire as soon as I crossed the trip wire and wrote about what I hadn't found in Niger. My *New York Times* op-ed piece had triggered the attack, but I was not the only target of it. Now my wife was in their sights, as well. What then happened was not a case of the loose lips of an overly ardent junior defender of the administration flapping to one reporter, but an organized smear campaign directed from the highest reaches of the White House.

A group of supposed public servants, collecting salaries paid by American taxpayers and charged with defending the national security of the country, had taken it upon itself to attack me by exposing the identity of a member of the CIA's clandestine service, who happened to be my wife. Revenge and intimidation had been deemed more important than America's national security for these coconspirators. And still the right wing directed their fire at me, and even at Valerie, instead of going after what were now *two* groups—those who were responsible for the sixteen words in the State of the Union address, and those who had leaked Valerie's identity.

The next several days went by in a blur. Suddenly every news organization wanted an interview with me. Camera crews were set up in my office and in the conference room nearby, and I was running from one to the other. Valerie had immediately decided in July, when her cover was irretrievably blown by Novak, that she was not going to speak to the press. She awakened daily to see her name on the front page above the fold in the nation's newspapers, with profiles containing quotes from acquaintances and family. While she would not talk to reporters, there was no stopping enterprising journalists from finding people who knew her. When friends and neighbors would call for advice, Valerie had none. Nobody had known what she did for a living except for her family, and they were not going to say anything. Her only hope was that the kindness that she has always shown others would be reflected in what they had to say about her, and it was. Rich Leiby, the *Washington Post* reporter, had met her and her parents when he came to the house to interview me in July, and was able to draw on that experience to write a complimentary profile about her. *Time* magazine included quotes from former colleagues about her prowess with an AK-47. All in all, the image was of a head-turning blonde toting twin three-year-olds on one hip while stealing and keeping secrets for her country.

For all the positive comments, however, Valerie's life was turned upside down. Nobody, not even me by her side, could comprehend what it must be like for somebody who has practiced discretion and lived her cover for years—like a character in a stage play where the curtain never comes down—to suddenly find herself a household name. She likened it, aptly, to an out-of-body experience, floating above the new reality, unable to do anything but watch helplessly while people who knew nothing about her speculated about what she really did.

One particularly obtuse Republican congressman from Georgia, Jack Kingston, suggested on CNN's *Crossfire* on September 29 that Valerie might have been a "glorified secretary." The sexist insult in that statement was not only to Valerie but also to secretaries and to women in general who may have benefited from the protection afforded by the Intelligence Identities Protection Act. But Valerie maintained her outward calm, going to work every day and trying to contribute as she always had.

Then there were others who were trying to characterize me as a Democratic activist or a publicity seeker. On television, Novak referred to me as a Clinton appointee when, in fact, I had been a career foreign service officer occupying a position on the National Security Council staff in the Clinton administration. It was not in and of itself a political position, and there were many career diplomats and military officers in similar jobs. He neglected to mention that my one political appointment, as ambassador, had been made by George H. W. Bush. Novak also overlooked the fact that he had once favorably described my service in Baghdad in a column, and, oddly, had quoted it in his July 14 piece that outed Valerie.

Robert Novak was truly without shame.

On September 30, while waiting in the CNBC green room to appear on *Capital Report,* I received a call from a friend alerting me that he had just seen the Republican National Committee chairman, Ed Gillespie, on CNN saying that I had contributed money to the Gore and Kerry campaigns. I wondered if there was something wrong or unpatriotic about my having done that. The point he was trying to make, I suppose, was that it was justifiable for a Republican administration to expose the identity of an undercover CIA officer, if she happened to have a husband who had contributed to Democratic campaigns. But what Gillespie failed to mention was that I had also contributed to the 2000 campaign of George W. Bush and to Orange County Republican Ed Royce several times.

As my friend and I were talking, Gillespie walked into the CNBC green room. I removed my cell phone earpiece and asked him if he was aware of my contributions to Republicans. He admitted that he did know of them. "They are part of the public record," he said. So he knew but had decided not to disclose all the information he had about them. I went on *Capital Report* a few minutes later and corrected the record, saying it was clear that the administration had mobilized party apparatchiks to attack me, falsely, on partisan grounds.

When Gillespie was later asked by *Vanity Fair* about his selective use of my campaign donation history, he disputed my account that he had done so, claiming he "referred to Wilson's contributions to Bush on the air." But not until I challenged him on it. The transcript of his interview with Judy Woodruff on CNN is clear:

Gillespie: "So I think that there's a lot more to play in here. There is a lot of politics. The fact is that Ambassador Wilson is not only a, you know—a former foreign service officer, former ambassador, he is himself a partisan Democrat who is a contributor and supporter of Senator Kerry's presidential campaign."

Later,

Gillespie: "What I've said is that Ambassador Wilson is clearly— has a partisan history here, as someone who supports John Kerry, who was just on your air talking about the problem here. This is a guy who's a maxed-out contributor to John Kerry. . . ."

There had been no mention of contributions to any Republican by me. He had tried to shift attention from what the administration had done to Valerie and me, and later lied to *Vanity Fair* about it.

Characterizing me as a left-wing partisan hack was ridiculous, anyway. Two of my most memorable career moments, the Angolan peace negotiations and the Gulf War, had occurred while I served in Republican administrations.

As the attacks on me gained steam, Chester Crocker, the assistant secretary for African Affairs for the entire Reagan administration, was kind enough to allow himself to be quoted in a couple of profiles on me (which he later told me had some of his fellow Republicans looking askance at him). In a voice mail he left me after one of the profiles appeared, he laughed heartily and asked, "Since when have you become a left-wing pinko partisan?"

In between television, radio, and newspaper interviews, photographers from *Time, Newsweek,* and *U.S. News and World Report* clamored for "photo shoots" for possible use on their covers. The *Time* photographer got to me early in the week and took pictures in my office for an hour one morning. When he had finished, I went back to my desk to find eighty-five missed phone calls on my cell phone alone. Meanwhile, my business voice-mail box also filled up every hour as the press became increasingly insistent. Everybody needed to talk to me immediately, and would make their pitch to our office executive assistant, sometimes sweetly, sometimes rudely, but always insistently.

I finally prioritized the return of phone calls to exclude the foreign press, on the grounds that this was an American issue and American issues are fought out at home, not from overseas. I would return phone calls from the press working on deadline, then friends, then others as time allowed. I tried to accommodate as many requests as I could, so as not to show any favoritism. The administration's disastrous foreign policy was an important issue; because of the attacks on my family, the megaphone had been passed to me, and I was determined to make my views heard—views that were far better informed than those of Novak or Gillespie.

It is axiomatic in Washington that you do not get out of one of these maelstroms without running the gauntlet posed by the heavyweights of the news shows, Ted Koppel at *Nightline,* Tim Russert at *Meet the Press,* and Bob Schieffer at *Face the Nation. Nightline* was first up.

Ted called the morning of Wednesday, October 1, and asked me to appear that same evening. I had known him from the first Gulf War, when he came to Baghdad and reported from the suite of executive offices at the embassy. We had occasionally spoken over the years since, and in January I had appeared on the *Nightline* town hall debate "Why War Now." I accepted his latest invitation. The interview consisted of Ted asking questions like a prosecutor cross-examining a witness. In a dry but determined manner, he prodded, pushed, and drew me out on a whole host of subjects related to my trip to Niger and to Valerie's situation. It was as serious and thoughtful as any interview I had yet participated in.

Tim Russert and Bob Schieffer each asked me to come on their shows the following Sunday, October 5. *Meet the Press* was taped early Sunday morning. I arrived and was on the set with Tim before Novak, who was scheduled to follow me on the show, arrived. Tim handed me *Time* magazine. There I was, in the center of the cover, arms folded, with Ashcroft, Rove, Bush, and Tenet in a circle around me. Tim looked at my left wrist and commented that the African bracelet I have worn for many years to remind me of a continent I love looked like a handcuff. He showed me how the bracelet was right next to Rove's tie and wondered if that was to remind the readers of my "frog-march in handcuffs" comment that had caused such a stir. The picture was like a Rorschach inkblot, Tim said.

Tim was as tough an interviewer as Ted Koppel, but, unlike Ted, he did not follow up many of his questions or probe further. He asked me about some of the peripheral stories being peddled by, among others, Novak, such as a book deal or personal political ambitions, which gave me an opportunity to address them. The latest line of attack was that I was a self-serving partisan and a potential office-seeker doing all this to plug a book.

As to the book, I had been talking to a publisher since mid-August at the suggestion of a radio talk-show host from California, Jon Elliot, and his friend, New York book publicist Barbara Monteiro, both of whom thought that I had a good story to tell. Several years earlier, I sat for an oral history for the State Department, and so already had pages of personal stories from my whole career. But I had never contemplated turning them into a book. Jon and Barbara insisted, and Barbara arranged for Philip Turner, then executive editor for Carroll & Graf Publishers, an imprint of the Avalon Publishing Group, to give me a call in early July. After some prodding from Philip, I produced a brief outline; to my surprise, he soon told me that Avalon wanted to "bid on the rights." I was happy to sell it for a modest advance, around $10,000, and a commitment to publication in the spring of 2004.

To work out the details, I turned to my neighbor Chris Wolf, who serves as Valerie's and my lawyer, and he recommended his cousin Audrey Wolf, a literary agent. I trusted Chris, so I called her, and though we had never met, I asked her to deal with the details and the contract. I knew nothing of the economics of book deals; but when she told me that my new notoriety would make for a larger advance if she let several publishers bid on it, I declined, because I had already made a gentleman's agreement with Philip. Next, Philip pushed me to let his colleagues market the international rights to the book at the annual Frankfurt Book Fair, which was coming up soon.

Wanting to avoid the appearance that I was trying to cash in on my notoriety, I refused and asked that he not even publicize our agreement for several weeks, until I had begun to fade from the headlines. There would be time, I argued, and if the story was a good one, foreign publishers would still want to acquire the rights, and American readers and people around the world would still want to read it. Philip and his colleagues were prepared to accept my decision.

However, Novak had somehow gotten wind that I had sought out an agent. Indeed, I had previously received a note from one who expressed interest in representing me, and perhaps Novak had spoken to that person. Not that any of this mattered a bit; on Saturday, October 4, Novak wrote an article that included a tidbit about me seeking an agent. Philip alerted me to it, and now that it was out in the public domain, as part of the ongoing attack on my character, I judged there was no longer any reason not to take the book proposal to Frankfurt. I told him full steam ahead. When the question came up on *Meet the Press,* I replied that I had every right to write a book if I wanted to— after all, this is America—and that I was considering hiring Novak as my publicist, since every time he opened his mouth about me, my value seemed to increase.

To the question of whether I intended to exploit my notoriety to run for political office, I told Tim that we live in the District of Columbia, which has no representation, and that in any event the goodwill we had felt, from across the political spectrum, accrued naturally to my wife, who had informed me that she would rather cut off her right arm than speak to the press, and refused to be photographed. As good an elected representative as I thought she would make, it would be difficult for her to run for office if she would not talk to reporters and refused to be photographed.

As to my own plans, I told Russert that I intended to use my fifteen minutes of notoriety to encourage people to participate in our democracy more fully. After all, one lesson I had gained from experience was that this is a great country where a citizen can speak up and make a difference. Despite the vociferousness of the attacks on me, they had been quite transparent in their political motivation and had done me minimal damage. Even the attack on my wife, though possibly criminal, was nothing compared to what I had seen happen to friends I had known in dictatorships around the world over the past two decades. I told Russert that I would work for the defeat of this administration, which had betrayed its own views as articulated by candidate Bush in the 2000 campaign. Humility, cooperation, multilateralism—all had been superseded by partisan arrogance and unilateral aggression.

As I was leaving the set of *Meet the Press,* Novak was escorted up to take my place in front of the cameras. Between the two of us stood a camera, and we could walk one way or the other around it. I waited till Novak committed himself and then moved the same way to force him to shake my hand, which he did. At that moment, I was reminded of an old African saying: "When the elephants fight, the grass gets trampled." In this fight, Novak was a rather insignificant blade of grass, willingly bent to the political agenda of others. To this day, I ask myself how his colleagues continue to tolerate him in their presence. Around Washington his critics call him Bob "NoFact" for his sloppy tabloid-gossipy articles that often stray far from the truth. Having long since prostituted himself to the Right as its uncritical shill, he offers little original insight.

I raced to the set of *Face the Nation*, about fifteen minutes away, to be interviewed live by Bob Schieffer. Following me on the show was Republican Senator Chuck Hagel from Nebraska, one of the most thoughtful members of the Senate, a Vietnam veteran, and a constructive critic of the war on Iraq whose views I largely shared. Facing the nation with him was Democratic Congresswoman Jane Harman from California, ranking member on the House Intelligence Committee, who left her daughter's wedding brunch to appear on the program. I was honored that she would take time from such an important family event to address issues of such importance to me personally, and to the whole country.

Before I went on, Senator Hagel and I shared a few minutes alone, during which he expressed his outrage at what the administration had done to Valerie. I mentioned my bewilderment that some Republicans, notably National Committee Chairman Ed Gillespie, were attempting to turn a possible crime against the country into a partisan issue, suggesting that it was okay to attack a wife to get at her husband, even though if the report I brought back from Niger had been heeded, the lie would have never been in the president's speech. Later, in his segment on the program, Senator Hagel made the point that what had happened to Valerie was not partisan and should not be treated as such.

Bob Schieffer managed to make news that morning. He asked me about our personal security. While we had not given it much thought in the time between the appearance of the Novak column in July and the news of the criminal referral at the end of September, the increasingly white-hot glare of the press the past week had begun to worry us.

We had assumed that on the day the Novak article appeared, every intelligence office in Washington, and probably all those around the world, were running Valerie's name through their files and databases. Foreign intelligence services would not attack us, but they might well threaten any contacts Valerie might have made in their countries, and they would certainly be eager to unearth operations she might have been involved in.

International terrorist organizations were a different story, however. There was a history of international terrorists attacking exposed officers. The station chiefs in Athens, Greece, and Beirut, Lebanon, after having been exposed by renegade CIA officer Philip Agee, had been assassinated; and in the U.S., there had been the instance of a terrorist sniper killing employees as they were driving into the CIA headquarters grounds at Langley, Virginia, in 1993.

But what *really* made us nervous was the possibility of harm from some deranged person in the U.S. who believed that the voices in his head emanated from the transmitter the CIA had installed in his teeth the last time he visited the dentist. That was the main reason we wanted to ensure that Valerie's face not be readily identifiable when she strode the sidewalks of Washington. On the other hand, just as other Americans are unwilling to let fears of terrorism stop them from boarding an airplane or going to a ball game, Valerie and I weren't going to stop living our lives, including being together in public from time to time.

Meanwhile, nobody from the White House, the Justice Department, the FBI, or even the CIA had reached out to offer us security; so, without specifying what we had done, I told Schieffer we had been obliged to take some measures ourselves.

After the Sunday rites of passage on television, I began cutting back such appearances. I had answered all the questions that were being asked and had nothing else to offer on the subject. It did not matter, as the Right renewed its attack: I was a publicity seeker. The president lied and the White House had attacked my wife, but I was a publicity seeker. Of course, if it was publicity I was after, my campaign was a flop. Prior to Novak's article, I was still known as the last American diplomat to have met with Saddam Hussein. Now I had become Mr. Valerie Plame. "Welcome to the Dennis Thatcher club," a husband of a well-known woman said to me, a reference to

British Prime Minister Margaret Thatcher's spouse. I limited myself to radio interviews, one with Don Imus and the other with Diane Rehm of National Public Radio. The interview with Ms. Rehm was a full hour, so I was able to discuss in considerable detail the issues surrounding the war, as well as my wife's case.

The press coverage was very positive toward Valerie and me. So was the outpouring of support from across the political spectrum, from Pat Buchanan on the right to Jesse Jackson on the left. Serious people understood what had happened. It was only a small cadre of right-wing zealots and the White House itself that continued trying to spin the story and make of it something it was not.

I was particularly offended when President Bush, asked about the leak on October 7, claimed, "I want to know the truth." However, eager to place the responsibility upon journalists rather than shoulder it himself, he added, "You tell me: How many sources have you had that's leaked information, that you've exposed or had been exposed?" He added, "Probably none," making it clear that his question had been only a rhetorical one. Bush capped off his comments that day with a statement that infuriated me, and many people whom I later heard from: "This is a large administration and there's a lot of senior officials. . . . I have no idea whether we'll find out who the leaker is, partially because, in all due respect to your profession, you do a very good job of protecting the leakers." His lack of genuine concern stunned and disappointed me.

More than four years earlier, on April 26, 1999, the president's father, not only a former president but also former Director of CIA, spoke at the ceremonial rededication of CIA headquarters in Langley, Virginia, which would be known henceforth as the George Bush Center for Intelligence. Referring to those who would expose clandestine officers, he said, "I have nothing but contempt and anger for those who betray the trust by exposing the name of our sources. They are, in my view, the most insidious of traitors." For his son to pretend he was a mere onlooker in his own administration was dishonorable.

Chapter Twenty
A Family Photo

D URING THE FIRST WEEK of October, soon after news of the investigation hit the press, White House Chief of Staff Andrew Card instructed two thousand White House employees to turn over any relevant documents to investigators. However, this was an absurdly broad net, as there were only a very small number of people in the administration whose responsibilities overlap the national security and the political arenas, the best pool of possible suspects in which to start looking. If the president really wanted to "come to the bottom of this," as he claimed to reporters on October 7, he could have acted like the strong chief executive he claims to be and brought his senior people into a room and demanded that they produce the leaker. Alas, he chose another course, one that reflects poorly on him and on the institution of the presidency he represents, and which undermines his broad claim about protecting national security.

Samuel Dash, the former senior Watergate counsel and one-time adviser on ethics to Whitewater Special Prosecutor Kenneth Starr, published an article in *Newsday* in late October arguing that the Patriot Act should be invoked:

> If, as now seems likely, top White House aides leaked
> the identity of an American undercover agent, they may

have committed an act of domestic terrorism as defined
by the dragnet language of the Patriot Act their boss
wanted so much to help him catch terrorists.

Section 802 of the act defines, in part, domestic terrorism as "acts dangerous to human life that are a violation of the criminal laws of the United States or of
any state" that "appear to be intended to intimidate or
coerce a civilian population."

Clearly, disclosing the identity of a CIA undercover
agent is an act dangerous to life—the lives of the agent
and her contacts abroad whom terrorists [*sic*] groups
can now trace—and a violation of the criminal laws of
the United States.

And what about the intent of those White House
officials in disclosing this classified information?
Surely, this mean-spirited action on their part was for
the purpose of intimidating the CIA agent's husband,
former Ambassador Joseph C. Wilson IV, who had
become a strong critic of the Bush administration's
Iraq policies. And not just Wilson. By showing their
willingness to make such a dangerous disclosure, the
White House officials involved were sending a message to all critics of the administration to beware that
they too can be destroyed if they persist. That
apparent intention "to intimidate or coerce a civilian
population"—in this case American citizens—also
meets the Patriot Act definition of domestic terrorism.

In fact, the exposure of a national security asset, regardless of who
it might be, is fundamentally different from a mere leak of information. The president was flat wrong to equate the two. Dash concluded
his article with an important recommendation:

The history of White House scandals teaches a primary lesson. Delay, obfuscation and cover-up only make the scandal worse and create a quagmire that harms the presidency. President Bush has only one option. He should use his power as president and his control over his aides to demand that the leakers come forward and he should kick them out of the White House.

He should make it unambiguously clear that he does not and will not tolerate this kind of conduct by anyone who works for him. It is not enough for him to condemn generally such leaks and leave it up to only the Justice Department to find the leakers. He must act on his own if he wants to keep the confidence of the people and move ahead with his presidency.

Equating what the White House had done to putting a loaded gun against the temple of a CIA operative, New York Senator Charles Schumer took the lead in calling for a special counsel, and he was ably supported by Senators Kennedy, Leahy, Rockefeller, and others on the Justice and Intelligence Committees. My two senators, inasmuch as I still think of myself as a Californian, Dianne Feinstein and Barbara Boxer, joined by Michigan Senator Debbie Stabenow and Louisiana Senator Mary Landrieu, pointed out the sexism demonstrable in the exposure of my wife's career, which was quite separate from my own activities. Former White House Counsel John Dean likened it to the ordering of a Mafia hit.

But rather than adopting a forthcoming stance, the administration pushed it off on the Justice Department and then tried hiding behind the investigation to avoid answering questions. They preferred circling the wagons.

* * *

On October 15, I was honored to receive from the Fertel Foundation and The Nation Institute the first Ron Ridenhour Award as truth teller of the year. Ron Ridenhour was a Vietnam veteran who had sent letters to the Pentagon and to several members of Congress alerting them to the massacre at My Lai in 1968. His report eventually came to the attention of *New York Times* reporter Seymour Hersh, who then broke the story. Ridenhour, the soldier-turned-whistleblower, went on to become an investigative journalist and died most unexpectedly at fifty-two in 1998. I had not known his story before, but I have come to hold him in the utmost respect for his sturdy commitment to the truth-telling mission that defined his life.

I had been selected for the award several weeks before the criminal referral launched the most recent press orgy, and had been looking forward to receiving the award at a luncheon with Valerie at my side. Despite all the attention the story was receiving, we agreed she would still attend this function. We were determined to keep living a normal life, and not seclude ourselves. The Fertel and *Nation* staff were assiduous about keeping the photographers out of the luncheon, and escorted Valerie in through a side entrance at the National Press Club building so that she'd not encounter the reporters who had attended the press conference beforehand. At the luncheon we had a gratifying experience with an audience of patriotic Americans prepared to stand up and fight for our rights and freedoms. I was overwhelmed by the commitment of everybody there. At our table was the truth teller of the twentieth century, Daniel Ellsberg, the man who leaked the Pentagon Papers in the Vietnam era, along with Deborah Scroggins, the author of *Emma's War*, a revelatory book on the Sudan civil war. The two were honored for their remarkable accomplishments. Seymour Hersh was also in attendance.

After Katrina vanden Heuvel, editor of *The Nation* magazine, afforded me a very kind and generous introduction, I stood before the audience and said that in the midst of people who had been activists all their lives, I felt like an unlikely recipient of such an award. I liked to play golf, not a pastime normally associated with earnest activists. I smoked big cigars, and I drove a Jaguar convertible instead of a hybrid. I liked my Hermes ties, and I had done nothing more than write a modest article titled, "What I Didn't Find in Africa." To be mentioned in the same breath as Dan Ellsberg, whose conscience had led him to make seven thousand pages of secret documents available to the public, was humbling. I would never have even considered doing what he had done.

That morning, I had written myself a reminder of the points I wanted to make. One was to acknowledge the terrible offense done to Valerie by her own government. I started to say: "To my wife Valerie, I cannot begin to tell you how sorry I am for what your government has done to you. If I could give you your anonymity back, I would do it in an instant." But I had to stop midway. For the first time since the beginning of this ordeal, I was overcome with emotion, not because of the often inane and frequently childish attacks on me but because of what my own government, for which I had worked most of my adult life, had done to my wife. I looked at Valerie as she wiped a couple of tears from her eyes, and I wondered whether I was going to be able to continue. Fortunately, the moment passed. I regained my composure. It seemed to me like an eternity had ticked by while I'd stifled my unexpected surge of sentiment. From the sympathetic response of the audience as they waited for me to continue, I judged the silence was neither too awkward nor as long as it had seemed to me.

Once I had composed myself, I concluded my remarks with a personal and heartfelt attack on the president himself. Noting that while I had tried to be scrupulous in attacking the policies and not the person in this matter, I said I was "frankly appalled at the apparent nonchalance shown by the president of the United States." Bush knows how he felt about Saddam's attempt to assassinate his dad, I said; he cited it at campaign rallies before the 2002 midterm elections as yet another reason to attack Iraq. And I felt the same way about attacks on my wife. I found the idea that I had to defend her against her own political leadership to be repugnant.

In the two weeks following the criminal referral to Justice, a number of profiles had been published about both Valerie and me by responsible reporters. I was grateful, because I thought it important to have some unbiased profiles published to counter the fantasies being concocted by people who knew nothing about either of us. The *New York Times* published what I considered the most accurate profile of me. Coverage in the *Washington Post* and *Time* magazine guaranteed that Valerie would forever be known for what she is: an adoring mother of twins and an active volunteer in a family health foundation dedicated to helping mothers suffering from postpartum depression, while working full time to make her country safer.

The sympathetic portrayals helped to silence those who would question her qualifications and dedication. Gone were the asinine "analyst or glorified secretary" comments. Regrettably, there still seemed to be far too much partisanship in the discussion. While Republicans who phoned me were, if anything, more outraged than Democrats, that fact did not surface in the public debate.

Valerie had been a pillar of strength and serenity throughout this huge upheaval in her life. She had not tried to influence my actions in any way, except when she urged me to tone down my frog-march comments—and even then, she suggested only that I temper my remarks as I saw fit, say by dropping the "handcuffs" from the charge. Yet her life had irrevocably changed. All of her friends and most of her family looked at her differently now. Some, including mere acquaintances, expressed surprise that they had not known her true occupation, to which she would invariably reply: "That's the point of cover, isn't it? That you not know."

She fended off questions related to her work with the simple comment: "These are not things I would talk about before you heard what I did for a living; I am certainly not going to discuss them now." I noticed that she now took particular care with her grooming before we went out. She had always looked gorgeous, but now she would run the comb through her hair just once more or give a last-minute touch-up to the gloss on her lip—little details here and there. I teased her about it one day on our way to a wedding. "Of course," she said. "Everybody is going to be looking at me, voyeuristically curious, and you can be damn sure I am going to look my best!" Ever pragmatic, she was not going to let the new situation faze her, even as she remained adamant about not being quoted or photographed in a way that could identify her.

After the Ridenhour award ceremony, it struck Valerie and me that we had been in the pressure cooker for quite a while without a break. We thought it might be a good idea to get away for a while. Norman and Lyn Lear had invited us to spend a weekend with them in Los Angeles, and we gratefully took them up on their kind offer, leaving our twins with their adoring grandparents. I arranged to deliver a couple of speeches out there, and Valerie could meanwhile relax with our new friends, who did everything possible on our arrival to make her feel welcome and comfortable. Valerie had joked that "things had to be tough if we were going to L.A. to relax," but it proved to be just the tonic we needed.

The Lear guesthouse, set on a hillside, looked down a canyon to the Pacific Ocean. We arrived late in the afternoon on a Thursday and watched the sun set from our balcony, the California blue sky surrendering to a starry night while the lights of the city twinkled below. The silence in the hills was a welcome change from the roar of airplanes flying low over our Washington home. I could see the stress melt from Valerie's face and the tension ebb from her shoulders; she was finally able to let go.

On Friday, I gave a speech at UCLA, did a number of interviews, and met with students to talk about the war and to urge them to become politically active. That evening, Valerie and I attended a small dinner in our honor at the Lears'. Guests included Warren Beatty and Annette Bening. During the cocktail hour, Valerie and Annette, the mother of four, struck up an easy conversation, comparing the joys and trials of bringing up children. All the guests were politically savvy, with much to offer to the national dialogue, and consummate professionals. In many ways, they had been interpreters of American society for well over a generation, and their considerable success in the entertainment industry had sprung from a keen sensitivity to the pulse of American life, which their work reflected and recreated as it became part of the popular culture. The great irony was that these talented and involved people are routinely lambasted by the Right for daring to utter their political opinions, while a serial groper like Arnold Schwarzenegger, a caricature of a comic-book figure, had just received the benediction of none other than that self-promoting paragon of morality—and admitted gambling addict—William Bennett, in his run for governor of my home state. The hypocrisy was breathtaking.

At dinner Valerie found herself seated between Norman Lear and Warren Beatty. She turned to Warren and, looking around the room, remarked, "My life is becoming more surreal every day." And indeed it was. Here we were in the midst of some of our best-known performing artists, and the person they wanted to see was Valerie, the stories they wanted to hear were ours. They wanted to support us as we traversed the white-hot glare of the media circus. Their outrage at what the Bush administration had done was as strong as ours.

The following day, while Valerie continued to take full advantage of the brief respite from her strange new life, relaxing and reading on the terrace, I participated in the first screening of Robert Greenwald's documentary *Uncovered*. The completed film was a devastating deconstruction of the Bush administration's case for war. It intercut the statements of senior administration officials with interviews featuring many experts on weapons of mass destruction, the war, and Iraq, myself included. The effect created was a stark juxtaposition of the administration's self-justifying rhetoric and the insistence by its critics that the case for war was based on selectively cited and manipulated intelligence.

The film's critique of Colin Powell's theatrics at the United Nations was particularly devastating. One came away from that segment feeling sorry for—and angry with—the general, who, after such a distinguished career in the service of his country, had been reduced to being the front man for a war promoted under false pretenses. In his February 5, 2003 presentation at the U.N., Powell began by flatly stating that disarmament was the purpose of U.N. Resolution 1441. Not the prevention of terrorism, not the boon of Iraqi liberation, but the achievement of disarmament—that was the goal to which the international community had unanimously agreed. How to achieve that goal was what stood at issue. Was 1441 working or not, and if not, how should the international community proceed to achieve the disarmament goal? These were the questions that should have been before the world body.

To those who work on disarmament issues, the answer would have been "yes," 1441 was working. The Iraqi bureaucracy was spending so much time and energy on U.N. inspection-related tasks that it could not have made any progress toward a WMD program, whether it wanted to or not. Resolution 1441 was proving effective, and Powell's U.N. speech had said as much. But he spun the facts to conclude the opposite.

Uncovered went unflinchingly further. It pointed out every instance in which the secretary's conclusions were simply not supported by the analysis, including one example that showed a plane spraying "simulated" anthrax—only, the plane had been destroyed in 1991. And yet, in the hysteria of the moment, the supposed evidence presented in Powell's speech was widely interpreted as "the smoking gun." Powell had turned his back on his eponymous doctrine, on the U.S. armed forces, and on the American people who had put their trust in him.

Valerie and I returned from Los Angeles refreshed and profoundly grateful for the friendship of thoughtful and tolerant Americans and fellow Californians. I had given speeches and interviews before hundreds of people, and it was clear that no one had been fooled by the attack campaign being waged against Valerie and me. Everyone understood that this was serious business, not just the petty politics of revenge driven by partisan sympathies.

Valerie went back to work, and I tried to focus on the most important of the debates raging on Iraq.

In September, I had written a third article for the *San Jose Mercury News,* this one calling on the administration to internationalize the reconstruction of Iraq, and to stop misleading the American people about the serious problems we faced created by our occupation of the country. I feared that our poor management of the reconstruction would ultimately, after a bitter civil war, result in the Balkanization of Iraq unless we managed to curb the insurgency, restore public safety, and give Iraqis hope that their future would be better than what they had known: thirty years of Baathist tyranny, destruction caused by three wars, including the shock and awe of the recent American campaign.

But all anybody wanted to hear from me was a status report on the investigation. In my notoriety as Mr. Valerie Plame, I had been effectively sidelined in the important discussion about how to proceed and succeed in Iraq.

Vanity Fair writer Vicky Ward had been calling me for some time about doing an interview. I was not initially enthusiastic, but she was persistent; the more I thought about it, though, the more I concluded it would be a good idea. Right-wing hacks were still trying to define me with their lies, though there were some exceptions. Tony Blankley, the editor of the right-wing *Washington Times,* owned by the Korean cult leader Sun Myung Moon, was among those on his side of the political spectrum to write that the attack on my wife was wrong.

Blankley had once been Newt Gingrich's press secretary and later became a pundit and conservative columnist. I had little in common with him and his politics, but I called to thank him for his article. I told him the accusation that I was some left-wing crank was simplistic and inaccurate, to which he responded frankly that the right wing was intent on turning me into a caricature of liberal partisanship. I thought that an article in *Vanity Fair* would be a good way for me to take a stab at defining myself, rather than letting the opposition try to have their way. Moreover, *Vanity Fair* had been the preferred vehicle for the entire national security team, from the president on down, to pose for a victory photo shoot in the Oval Office. Surely, if they could find a forum in the magazine, then so could I.

We asked Vicky to our house, where she joined Valerie's dearest friend and godmother to our children, Janet Angstat, and the whole family for dinner in our home. The next day, I sat for an interview with Vicky that lasted the whole afternoon. We had agreed that Valerie would not be interviewed for the piece, but that she would not discourage her friends or family from speaking to Vicky if they were comfortable doing so. One pleasantly warm and sunny October day, a crew came down to do the requisite photo shoot for the piece. On the spur of the moment, Valerie, who is such an important part of my life and so central to this story, agreed to be photographed with me, so long as she could not be readily identified. She had already been described as the beautiful blonde that she is, and her cover had long since been blown, so the only concern remaining was whether strangers would be able to use a photo to recognize her in public. With proper precautions taken, I saw no reason to deprive ourselves of the pleasure of being photographed together as the happily married couple that we are. She is my wife and the mother of two of my children. I am proud to be her husband, and I love to have her on my arm.

The resulting photos and article were terrific. I was not portrayed as a saint, far from it, but as what I am: a loyal citizen with experience in my field, who had served my country with distinction in Republican as well as Democratic administrations. Some journalists and people on the right wing were critical, asserting that the picture of Valerie, in which she was not recognizable, violated my statement on *Meet the Press* and that, in fact, by allowing herself to be photographed, she had blown her own cover. It was laughable to suggest that the clandestine nature of her work had ever translated into invisibility and showed the extent to which the ideologues simply did not understand the concept of "cover." Cover is living a lie, yet living it openly, in public.

I welcomed the reaction to the *Vanity Fair* piece. The rants against us from the radical Right generated interest in the article, and soon we had notes from around the country, most of them from people who normally don't even read *Vanity Fair*. The critics, including Rush Limbaugh before he checked himself into drug rehab, sputtered about the pictures without bothering to read the article. Had they bothered to do so, they might not have been so vocal about publicizing it.

Though I had never met John Kerry, I was asked by a couple of friends if I would be interested in being part of his foreign policy committee in spring 2003, as they began setting up Kerry's presidential campaign. During the first several months of a campaign, such committees are little more than talking shops, as the campaign then has only one goal: raising money. I had great respect for the senior adviser and chair of the committee, Rand Beers. He and I had been at the NSC together. A former Marine, a career public servant, and a distinguished professional in the counterterrorism business, he had resigned in March, five days before the invasion of Iraq, as special assistant to President Bush for combating terrorism. Although he was loathe to tell reporters that his resignation was tied directly to administration policies, he did say this to the *Washington Post* in June: "The administration wasn't matching its deeds to its words in the war on terrorism. They're making us less secure, not more secure. As an insider, I saw the things that weren't being done. And the longer I sat and watched, the more concerned I became, until I got up and walked out." In short, he was no partisan actor, but a thoughtful and committed expert on issues of national security.

I was soon invited to play a more visible role by publicly endorsing and campaigning for Kerry; I was delighted and proud to do both. It is not often that one is asked for an endorsement, and I was proud to offer it. I agreed to travel to Iowa, New Hampshire, and wherever else the campaign wanted to send me, to speak on the senator's behalf. In addition to his sterling record of leadership on issues of importance to me, he and I had a common experience: we had both spoken the truth to a hostile administration, and had suffered its wrath as a consequence. I had done so after my professional career in the Foreign Service had come to a close; Kerry, on the other hand, had confronted the Nixon administration at the beginning of his career when, recently returned from two highly decorated tours in Vietnam, he challenged the U.S. Senate on the validity of that war.

"How do you ask a man to be the last man to die in Vietnam? How do you ask a man to be the last man to die for a mistake?" he said to them, and thus earned himself a place on the notorious Nixon "enemies list." My own experience had toughened me, and I was certain it had done the same for him. If leadership is a product of adversity, and puts "calcium in the spine," as the current President Bush is wont to say, then Kerry's experience in Vietnam had enhanced his own ability to lead America. He has often said that every single day after Vietnam has been a gift, something I have also felt since I left Baghdad in 1991.

Participation in the selection of our nation's leaders, in the celebration of our democracy, is a privilege that I was excited to be a part of. In Iowa, I met voters who were sincerely pondering the country's future, and in New Hampshire I participated in a talk-radio program and loved the give-and-take with callers and the conservative host. That is what the democratic process is all about: not the impugning of the character of those who might not agree with you, but a real discussion of the issues among citizens. I also spoke at a number of fundraisers in New York, Boston, and Washington. I could feel the emotion and the energy in the audiences, all eager to replace the current president.

December 2003 marked the beginning of what I came to call Vindication Month.

On December 24, Walter Pincus, the ever-capable and thorough *Washington Post* reporter, wrote: "The President's Foreign Intelligence Advisory Board has concluded that the White House made a questionable claim in January's State of the Union address about Saddam Hussein's efforts to obtain nuclear materials because of its desperation to show that Hussein had an active program to develop nuclear weapons, according to a well-placed source familiar with the board's findings."

On December 30, Attorney General John Ashcroft recused himself from the investigation into the leak of Valerie's name—an action that clearly indicated what I had been saying since July: this was a grave matter, and it should not be governed by partisan politics.

On January 8, 2004, the Carnegie Endowment for International Peace released a report based on an analysis of all the evidence thus far available, and concluded that while Saddam's WMD programs represented a long-term threat that could not be ignored, they did not pose an immediate threat to the United States, to the region, or to global security. In other words, there had been no need to rush to war; other options had been available to us. The families of the more than 540 dead and 3,000 injured, plus those of the uncounted thousands of Iraqi dead and injured, could take no comfort in the knowledge that their loved ones had been sacrificed unnecessarily.

On the same day, January 8, Colin Powell acknowledged that there was no "smoking gun" connection between Iraq and al Qaeda. The second justification for war—ties to "terrorism with a global reach," to use the president's own words—had now been discredited by one of the most senior officials in his own administration.

On January 11, former Treasury Secretary Paul O'Neill, in an interview with Leslie Stahl on *Sixty Minutes* discussing *The Price of Loyalty,* revealed that the administration had begun serious planning for the overthrow of Saddam as early as the end of January 2001, a mere ten days after coming to power.

On January 12, the *Washington Post* ran a piece reporting on the U.S. Army War College publication of a study by Jeffrey Record, professor at the Department of Strategy and International Security in the U.S. Air Force's Air War College, asserting that the war in Iraq had been "unnecessary." As a result, Record wrote, the U.S. Army was at the breaking point and the war on terrorism was "strategically unfocused."

Finally, on January 23, David Kay, on resigning his post as head of the CIA's Iraq Survey Group, stunned the country by admitting, after nine months of searching, that Saddam Hussein did not have stockpiles of weapons of mass destruction. The original premise for the war was apparently without foundation. While I continue to believe that we were within our rights to insist on satisfying ourselves that Saddam had been disarmed, and that we may still even find some WMD, it is now abundantly clear that we were grossly misled by our political leaders on the seriousness of the threat. It may be true that some of the intelligence was not as good as policy makers might like, but there is no doubt that the administration cherry-picked, exaggerated, and manipulated information often no more credible than gossip to fabricate a justification for war.

For all the vindication I felt in January, I was still chilled to the bone by remembering what President Bush had said in an interview with ABC's Diane Sawyer back on December 16. As Sawyer was trying to make the distinction between actual weapons and capability to produce weapons at some future date, and the threats posed by each, the president responded: "What's the difference?"

It was clear, from this one statement, that the entire war had been a disastrous charade; that the administration, from the president on down, had systematically deceived the American people, Congress, and the world. Most of all, the president had betrayed the soldiers, sailors, airmen, and Marines who so bravely march out when ordered into war to defend our country against imminent threats, or even from grave and gathering dangers. Iraq had posed neither. The difference, Mr. President, I thought, is that war was not the only option, or even the best one. We had gone to war over capacity, not stockpiles, not mushroom clouds, not intent, or, as John Bolton had earlier said more directly, because scientists were on Saddam's payroll. Our troops had died—and were continuing to die—in vain. I came away from this sad revelation resolved that, unlike the other bitterly divisive war debate of my lifetime, over the war in Vietnam, we should admit this terrible fact sooner, rather than later, and thereby revise our national policies accordingly.

I realized that while the leak to Novak, and to the other reporters who chose not to use the information, was an attack on me for writing about what I didn't find in Niger, it was really just the first salvo from an administration desperate to prevent the complete unraveling of the fabric of lies, distortions, and misinformation that it had woven and fed the world to justify its war. My initial speculation that the naming of my wife was designed to discourage others from coming forward seemed accurate; for with every new vindication, there was more evidence that the country had in fact gone to war for no legitimate reason. And for a lot of illegitimate ones.

By February 8, 2004 when the president was interviewed by Tim Russert on *Meet the Press,* he could no longer even pretend that the threat posed by Iraq's weaponry was so urgent as to merit war. The rationale for the invasion of Iraq boiled down to three things: their supposed capacity to make WMD; their alleged intent to transfer them to terrorists; and Saddam's dangerous mental state.

But there *were* no weapons. And in making the case that Saddam could give weapons he did not have to terrorists with whom he was not linked, the president directly contradicted both the National Intelligence Estimate (NIE) of October 2002 and CIA Director Tenet's own testimony that the only time Saddam might hand off his arsenal would be as his regime was about to be overthrown, not before.

Finally, though, the most shocking part of the president's defense of the war was the case that Saddam was a madman. Indeed, Saddam was dangerous, and perhaps mad; but was he an urgent or unique threat to our national security that could be managed only by war? We structure our armed forces to defend our country against foreign threats, not to fight madmen. In reviewing both the U.N. resolution and the congressional use-of-force resolution, there is no reference in either that cites Saddam's mental health or his despicable comportment as justification for war. It was a terrible mistake.

Chapter Twenty-One
A Long Strange Trip

AS OF THIS WRITING, in February 2004, two years have passed since I traveled to Niger. Who could have imagined that journey would lead through such a maze of intrigue, so much deceit on the part of a presidential administration, and such enormous harm to my wife? It has been an existential roller-coaster ride, and the wheels have not yet come to rest. Even so, there are lessons the experience has taught me, and some lessons that I believe the country can learn, from this tragic war of choice that should never have been undertaken, and from the unprecedented disclosure that my wife was an undercover CIA officer.

When in May 2002 I entered the debate on how the United States should confront Iraq, I did so with a mounting sense of unease about the direction in which America was being led by the Bush administration. I began to speak out because I believed that our armed forces would be exposed to unnecessary risk if the administration insisted on marching in to war with the phony coalition then being assembled. I also feared that our credibility and international reputation would suffer greatly and that our position as the global superpower would be undermined, threatening much of the good our foreign policy had achieved since World War II.

Moreover, the suspect rationales being articulated by the administration—weapons of mass destruction, ties to international terrorism with a global reach, and the possibility that Saddam might provide al Qaeda with WMD—just didn't, in my estimation, add up to a legitimate imminent threat or even a grave and gathering danger.

For thirteen months, I never mentioned my trip to Niger in public appearances, in the newspaper commentaries I published, or even in private conversations, until the State Department spokesman claimed that the United States had been fooled by the forged documents. The findings from the Niger mission had not altered the fact that disarmament was a legitimate goal for the international community to pursue, even if force was required to achieve it. It was only when it became clear to me that the claim in the president's State of the Union address referred to Niger, and therefore was untrue, that I had no choice but to insist that my government correct the record.

It was not an act of courage, as some have generously suggested; nor was it a partisan act, as critics have howled. It was a civic duty, pure and simple. If there ever are occasions when our government is justified in lying to its citizens, this was not one of them. Our democracy required that the administration be called to account.

I resisted going public for several months, however, in the futile hope that after it became apparent there was no truth to the Niger uranium claim, and once serious questions were raised in the media, somebody in the administration would come forward and take responsibility for the falsehood. I had no interest in attaching my name and face publicly to any such revelation; I had seen the harm done to bearers of bad tidings in Washington. Even after Condoleezza Rice falsely asserted on *Meet the Press* that "maybe someone knew down in the bowels of the Agency" that the evidence cited in the State of the Union address was suspect, I still hesitated to set the record straight publicly, although I was becoming more determined that the lies be corrected somehow.

A few days after Rice's interview, the House and Senate Intelligence Committees announced that they were going to look into the prewar intelligence, including the uranium claim. I called the staffs of both committees and volunteered to brief them about my trip and findings. I ended up briefing them separately within a few days of each other in mid-June, disclosing what I knew to the appropriate oversight bodies.

A week after those briefings, I learned from a journalist that my name was soon to be made public. I finally decided to write the story myself, and called back David Shipley at the *New York Times* to accept his offer of space on their op-ed page.

I knew that my credibility would be challenged the moment I went public, and I made preparations to defend it. I was not going to let the rabid ankle-biters of the right deny me a voice in the debate or impugn my integrity. I had earned the right to be heard, the same right enjoyed by other responsible citizens. I spoke out confident in the belief that our democracy remains strong precisely because we have a long and proud tradition of citizens challenging our government when it lies to the people.

However, for all the insults I knew I would suffer, I never expected the White House itself to do anything like what it did: come after my wife.

The disclosure of her employment was unprecedented, and the Grand Jury will decide if it was a criminal act. Whether convictions are obtained or not, it was unquestionably beneath the standards of conduct that we have every right to demand from our public servants. But in their attacks on us, the administration was firing at the wrong targets. I had not put the sixteen words in the president's mouth; someone on his staff had, and that is where he should have been taking aim; Valerie had not done anything wrong. And when somebody leaked the fact that she was undercover, thereby putting a national security asset out of commission at a time of war, the president should have demanded swift action to remove the offender from his post. Yet, as in the case of the sixteen words, the president once again demonstrated more loyalty to his staff than they had shown to him. To this day, no one at the White House has apologized for the unwarranted attacks on Valerie and me. And to this day, the person who leaked her name evidently remains in a position where he enjoys the trust of President Bush.

In the end, of course, what has happened to Valerie and me pales in comparison with the harm done to our dead and injured troops and their families, our international standing, and our democracy. Those of us who challenged the neoconservative wave did so out of concern for these potential consequences.

On the international stage, the formulation that "American might makes right" has alarmingly supplanted the rule of law as the operating principle of international relations. In the first flush of battlefield victory, überneocon Richard Perle gloated in an article headlined "Thank God for the Death of the U.N." in the British newspaper *The Guardian* on March 21, 2003: "Saddam Hussein's reign of terror is about to end. He will go quickly, but not alone: in a parting irony, he will take the U.N. down with him. . . . What will die is the fantasy of the U.N. as the foundation of a new world order. As we sift the debris, it will be important to preserve, the better to understand, the intellectual wreckage of the liberal conceit of safety through international law administered by international institutions."

The collective security system that emerged from World War II has served America's ends far more than it has ever impeded our actions. Even while the U.N. is in need of reform—and I agree that it is not appropriately structured to meet the challenges of the post–Cold War era—it is still far superior to the law of the global jungle, under which countries submit to no restraint on their actions. When the U.N. fails to act, it is easy to blame the institution—but in fact the institution reflects the interests of its members. Without it, we would still need to work with other countries who may not share our views. The U.N. provides the forum and the framework within which we can work out differences.

In the case of Iraq, the U.N., belatedly to be sure, was in fact enforcing the will of the international community as stated in Resolution 1441 at the time we decided to short-circuit the process. It turns out, as David Kay and the Carnegie Endowment for International Peace have both stated, the inspection regimes of the 1990s and late 2002 served the world well. Even if we should still find evidence of WMD, they obviously posed no significant threat to us that could not have been managed in a way less destructive than with a military invasion.

I knew, from three decades of experience with conflicts ranging from Angola to Bosnia, that an American invasion was not the best— or the only—option for dealing with Saddam. War, the bluntest of instruments in our foreign policy arsenal, is costly, and it comes with incalculable and unintended consequences.

It is undeniable that the international will to disarm Saddam of his WMD needed to be resuscitated. Inspectors had not been inside Iraq since 1998, and nobody believed that Saddam had changed his ways. He would continue to aspire to build up an arsenal of weapons of mass destruction so long as he was in power. In fact, almost any regime in Iraq would strive to attain such armaments, given that the country lay between two strong and historically aggressive neighbors, Iran and Turkey, and close to what Iraqis had long considered their enemy, Israel, which in fact did have such an arsenal.

No matter who ruled Iraq, we were going to have to monitor the country for a long time, at least until a broader peace emerged in the region—between Iraq and Iran and, farther west, between Israel and its neighbors. The economic sanctions placed on Iraq had proved to be extremely debilitating on the general population but were having virtually no effect on Saddam and the Baathist elite—and international support for them had dissipated. Something had to be done, and the right course of action was indeed to seek international support for the return of a rigorous inspection regime, one backed by a credible threat of force that could and would be implemented if necessary.

While the twelve years of sanctions on his country had not been so airtight that they had prevented Saddam from building palaces, he had not, however much he wished or strived to, been able to rebuild his military. The no-fly zones had effectively denied him sovereignty over much of his country, and his support was eroding from within. A look at photographs of his cabinet meetings showed old men. Saddam's regime was sclerotic. 130,000 American soldiers were not required to topple it; it needed only the resurrection of the inspection regime, supported by the threat of force, and some skillful subversion.

In short, just what was required to ensure the regime's eventual collapse was already happening before the middle of March 2003. We had infiltrated Saddam's intelligence services; we had turned several of his senior military commanders. We were locked and loaded, but we did not need to fire. Not at all. A little patience would have achieved everything we wanted, without creating the whirlwind that we are now reaping in our bloody and chaotic occupation of the country.

Sure, twelve years was a long time for us to put up with the irritation of Saddam. But by way of comparison, the Cold War lasted forty-five years, and Saddam was far less of a threat than several generations of Soviet leaders and the Red Army had been. In fact, the Cold War provided a useful blueprint on how to subvert an oppressive regime and achieve regime change without resorting to brute force.

The Reagan administration, working with the Pope, had been extraordinarily effective in undermining communist rule in Poland, for instance. It was a case study in the use of all the implements in the foreign policy tool kit to bring about desired change. In Poland in the 1980s, we were perceived to be on the side of the people and supportive of their ambitions to overthrow the yoke of communism, yet we neither bombed their capital or their villages nor invaded their countryside in order to achieve our goals. We did not humiliate the Poles with a foreign occupation, or kill thousands of innocent civilians in order to liberate them. Patience, tenacity, and support for those elements that could mobilize opposition from within were appropriate strategies for us in Poland, as they could have been in Iraq.

The president was right to seek U.N. Resolution 1441, for by it he successfully forced Saddam to permit inspectors back into the country. Kenneth Pollack had persuasively argued that coercive containment could not be restored; but to President Bush's credit, it was. Yet, he just would not accept the response of the international community and allow the inspections—which had resumed under Hans Blix—to proceed. The president's hand was exposed: An offensive was of choice could no longer be masked as self-defense.

I harbored no illusion that my views would prevail when I entered the debate over Iraq, but I hoped that my voice, added to the voices of others, might give pause to members of Congress under bombardment by the neoconservatives, for whom nothing short of occupying Baghdad was acceptable. Many moderates from both parties shared our concerns, but the partisan distortions, lies, and misinformation produced a predictable result: a majority of Americans, wanting to trust in the president and his words, actually came to believe that Saddam had nuclear weapons and was somehow responsible for the terrorist attacks of September 11, 2001. The war policy garnered broad support for a time, until the deception, and its massive extent, became apparent to a too-trusting American public.

In our society, the decision to declare war resides correctly with the Congress, the representatives of the people, after a debate based upon a set of commonly accepted facts. The Bush administration subverted the debate on the use-of-force resolution by introducing as facts selective bits of information that had not been vetted by our intelligence analysts, and by pressuring analysts to cast their conclusions in language that would support political decisions already made.

Alan Foley, the recently retired director of the Nonproliferation Center at the CIA, told *Newsweek* reporter Michael Isikoff that there was an item in the report on my trip to Niger that had led him to conclude that there may have been something to the assertion that Iraq had tried to purchase uranium from Niger. I can only assume that he was referring to the conversation a Nigerien source of mine had had with Iraqi Information Minister Mohammed Saeed al-Sahaf, aka "Baghdad Bob," on the margins of an Organization of African Unity (OAU) meeting in 1999. Could it be that we went to war over a conversation in which the word "uranium" was not spoken at all? The only meeting detailed in my Niger report between an Iraqi and a Nigerien official in which even a whiff of uranium arose did not actually include any spoken reference to uranium, only the notion later expressed by my Nigerien contact that maybe, just maybe, at some point in the indeterminate future the Iraqis might, just might, have wanted to raise the subject of uranium. Was that the smoking gun that could supposedly have become a mushroom cloud? And so is it possible that, because of that non-conversation, 549 Americans have already given their lives, countless Iraqis have been killed, and $150 billion of national treasure spent?

The administration's deception of the American people was far more nefarious than mere spin, or a matter of simply putting the best case forward. Instead, the administration engaged in active deception of the United States Congress, the international community, and the American people so that they could go to war for reasons that, had they been honestly and openly debated, would never have been approved.

An example of the administration's shifting rationales for the war is evident in the varying importance officials placed on the allegation that Iraq had purchased uranium, or tried to. In sharp contrast to the president's dire warnings in his September 2002 speech to the U.N., in which he stated, "Should Iraq acquire fissile material, it would be able to build a nuclear weapon within a year," and the subsequent charge that Iraq was actively seeking to purchase uranium from Africa, Condoleezza Rice tried to downplay the importance of the Niger allegation after it came out that it was false. "It is ludicrous to suggest that the president of the United States went to war on the question of whether Saddam Hussein sought uranium from Africa," Dr. Rice said on FOX *News Sunday* on July 13, 2003. "This was part of a very broad case that the president laid out in the State of the Union and other places." But the Niger fabrication was the only allegation of an Iraqi attempt to secure uranium that the administration ever put forward to substantiate the president's charge.

As it turned out, Rice was actually right—if not for the reason she meant—that the Niger allegation was unimportant, because this war was never really about WMD. Paul Wolfowitz, in an interview with *Vanity Fair,* acknowledged as much when he said, "The truth is that for reasons that have a lot to do with the U.S. government bureaucracy we settled on the one issue that everyone could agree on which was weapons of mass destruction as the core reason." (The Pentagon released its own transcript of the interview after they were unhappy with news coverage of the revelations in the published article, but the two versions do not differ on this point).

This enterprise in Iraq was always about a larger neoconservative agenda of projecting force as the means of imposing solutions. It was about shaking up the Middle East in the hope that democracy might emerge—what I had heard Charles Krauthammer call "the coming ashore in Arabia." Whatever one may conclude about the desirability of using our military to bring democracy to the Arab world, the fact is that we went to war without first testing the thesis in serious national debate.

Democratization is a noble goal. I was involved in democratization efforts for most of my diplomatic career. It is a long and hard road that requires institution-building and a significant investment on the part of the local population in a new and different system of governance that is often at odds with tradition. The best description I have heard for the process is that it is like a fine English lawn: you must seed it, you must water it, and if you want it to look really good, you must roll it—for six hundred years. It is not a task that comes naturally to our military, however excellent that institution is.

In perhaps the most eloquent and scathing critique of the consequence of the administration's having lied about why it believed it needed to go to war, Zbigniew Brzezinski observed in an October 2003 speech that during the Cuban missile crisis, Secretary of State Dean Acheson offered to show French President Charles de Gaulle satellite photos of Soviet nuclear missile installations in Cuba to support President Kennedy's request for support in the event we had to go to war. De Gaulle replied that he did not need to see the photographs, as President Kennedy had given his word and his word was good. Who would now ever take an American president at his word, in the way that de Gaulle once did?

So we find ourselves in a disastrous quagmire in a distant land, with our troops suffering fatal wounds and disabling injuries every week, even as we employ ever greater force to subdue an increasingly disgruntled people. And just when we think the numbers of casualties may finally be starting to subside, with our uniformed commanders assuring us that the corner has been turned, that the number of insurgent attacks is at last decreasing, the very lethality of the attacks may in actuality be increasing.

Though peremptorily denied by the administration, our all-volunteer military is suffering long-term damage, as tours of duty are extended with stop-loss orders and as National Guardsmen and Reservists put their civilian lives on hold for longer stretches than they, their families, or their work colleagues ever imagined. Our prestige in the world is sustaining similar damage, notwithstanding the president's claims to the contrary.

The election campaign of 2004 offers the American people an opportunity to engage in a meaningful debate on the merits of this war, and we should so engage. It is long overdue and appropriate, as even the president agreed during his February 8, 2004, interview on *Meet the Press*. It is his judgment, his vision, his policies that are under scrutiny, and that is how it should be in a democracy. Those who attempt to deflect attention from the president's decisions by blaming the quality of the intelligence provided to the administration miss the essential point that it is the president, not the director of Central Intelligence, who made the decision to go to war, and his is the record that must be judged.

The intelligence community provides its estimate of the facts on the ground, but it does not offer policy recommendations or make war decisions. The president and his national security team do. For all the reforms that might be warranted for the intelligence community, we do our spies and analysts incalculable harm when we try to blame them for the bad decisions taken by our political leaders. Unwarranted attacks and finger-pointing debilitate morale and create an adversarial relationship, at precisely the time when we should be working together to effect necessary change in the way we collect and analyze information.

The exposure of a clandestine operative is a reprehensible breach of a trust between our political leadedrship and those who risk their lives to keep America safe. It is a profound betrayal of our country and it has repercussions across the globe. Foreign agents will hesitate before stealing secrets on our behalf for fear that exposure of their American handler may compromise them. American spies will always worry about whether they can trust their own government. Programs will be more difficult to launch and maintain in such a climate. Those who expose an operative must be labeled as what President Bush's father said they are: "the most insidious of traitors."

But even as we debate the merits of what we have wrought, we must not lose sight of how we can best extricate ourselves from this quandary.

The myth that we would be greeted as liberators by the Iraqi population has been definitively dispelled. With the insurrection increasingly requiring heavy-handed military ripostes in which property is destroyed and Iraqi civilians killed or injured, it is unlikely that Middle Eastern history will ever view our invasion as the beneficent mission that President Bush promised it would be: an effort to free Iraqis from the chains of their tyrant. On the contrary, if there is a civil war that results in the violent breakup of the Iraqi state, in the eyes of the Muslim world we will be responsible for having caused it.

We are therefore compelled to see it through, until some semblance of representative government has been installed in Iraq. To cut and run at this chaotic point would guarantee greater instability in the region for the foreseeable future, as various factions vie for power. Yet cutting and running is just exactly what is happening, as the Bush administration has imposed a June 30, 2004, target deadline on itself to transfer sovereignty to the Iraqi people—a timetable geared more to the U.S. election calendar than it is to democratization in Iraq.

Even if that date is moved back, as well it should be, the signal the administration has sent to the Iraqi factions is that we seek an early departure. A precipitous departure before proper institutions have been built; before parameters for acceptable political behavior have been established and accepted; and before a resilient sense of optimism about the future has been fostered within Iraqi society, may well presage a complete breakdown of relations among the many factions that already have armed militias at their disposal. The ill-advised decision of the Coalition Provisional Authority to disband the Iraqi military, one of the country's few unifying national institutions, ensures that there will remain a huge void in the center of Iraqi national life when we leave, unless permanent viable institutions are somehow established and widely accepted by the people of Iraq first. A civil war would fuel independence ambitions among the Kurds, ignite the simmering hostility between the Shia and Sunni, and leave this already-broken country subject to even greater ruin.

And our troops run the substantial risk of being in the middle of it all, trying to defend themselves, and noncombatant Iraqis, who will despair over our continuing inability to provide security and a quality of life better than what they are promised from their indigenous leaders. Lacking a better alternative, they will see no option but to seek protection from within their traditional family and clan structure. We are fighting two wars in Iraq right now, the war against the insurgency and the war to restore public safety and services. If we cannot win the latter, then the ranks of the former will continue to swell daily with bitter citizens.

Wars of liberation are terribly expensive in terms of political capital. One needs only look at the debacle in Somalia, when an American Blackhawk helicopter was shot down in the streets of Mogadishu in 1993. Fewer than twenty deaths resulted from that one urban battle—and the American political will to intervene in African conflicts was stifled for years, as was epitomized by our failure to respond to the genocide in Rwanda that ultimately cost 800,000 Africans their lives in less than four months. No Republican and few Democrats were prepared to argue, during that crisis, that we should intervene militarily. It was only when the number of deaths became too large to ignore that we were shamed into reacting. By then it was too late. We ended up spending $500 million—then roughly 60 percent of our annual development assistance budget for all of Africa—to do little more than bury the dead and purify water for the survivors. We should have done better, but the political will was wanting. It had all been expended in the tragedy of Blackhawk Down.

To avert the possibility of a similarly tragic failure, it behooves us now to make the necessary compromises with those of our friends who have the capability and the will to offer armed forces and police support, so that we can begin to internationalize the presence in Iraq. That internationalization will enable us to credibly argue that ours is a global effort to assist the long-suffering Iraqis. It will also encourage the general population to invest in its own future by facilitating the transfer of responsibility and sovereignty back to Iraq.

A failure in Iraq and any consequent instability in the Middle East must be of grave concern in the region and to the rest of the world. The Europeans and the Asians are even more dependent on oil from the Gulf than is the United States, and more at risk in the event of disruption. A civil war would no doubt prompt an exodus of refugees into neighboring countries, which would in turn provoke tension between the Shia and the Sunni throughout the region. The images of Iraq at war with itself could potentially inflame Muslim populations throughout Europe.

Any internationalization of Iraqi reconstruction will necessarily come at some cost. We should also voluntarily relinquish our monopoly position with respect to contracts awarded for rebuilding the Iraqi infrastructure.

Since this is a self-styled "business administration" administration, an analogy from the corporate world may be appropriate. A goal has been articulated by the president, but it has not been achieved by the plan his managers put into place. Therefore, we need to seek outside equity partners to help us realize the leader's vision. In order to attract those partners, we must be prepared to do what every business does when it goes back into the market: give up seats on the board of directors, give up staff and line positions to the merger partners, and harmonize the vision of the enterprise with that of the outside investors. Moreover, as vulture capitalists well know, the last investor in to save the project takes the largest slice.

None of this means that the United States would sacrifice responsibility or authority to the extent that our interests would be threatened. On the contrary, given the enormous risk of failure, spreading that risk is a good idea. If we succeed, so much the better if that success has a thousand fathers and mothers.

Like a CEO seeking a clean break from a disastrous corporate venture, President Bush should fire Donald Rumsfeld and the entire band of neoconservatives that occupy positions of responsibility under him. This would clear the administration of parasites who are loyal only to their agenda and who have found the Republican party a willing host for more than twenty years.

In the Reagan years, these ideologues pursued a recklessly aggressive arms buildup against an imagined threat from a Soviet Union that most serious analysts understood was a rapidly decaying power, and later they embarrassed us with the arms-for-hostages escapade in Iran and Central America that culminated in the Iran–Contra scandal. They used the same tactics then that they are using to even greater effect now. By creating cells within the government, they maintain direct ties to the political leadership, with the express purpose of circumventing normal reporting channels and undermining the decision-making processes that our government has in place to avoid errors precisely like the ones made in committing our country to war in Iraq. What they have achieved is more than just bringing in fresh eyes to examine the same information base, as some would claim: they have actively subverted the intelligence process by inserting their own ideological biases into the analysis. Greg Thielman, the retired State Department intelligence analyst who had been so critical of Colin Powell after his U.N. speech, was correct when he called it "faith-based intelligence."

The callous use of the tragedy of 9/11 by this recycled band of neoconservatives to promote a war against Iraq was abhorrent. It was also bad policy, as well as a perversion of traditional Republican approaches to international order—the diametric opposite, in fact, of what then-candidate George W. Bush promised in his 2000 campaign: to implement a foreign policy based on international coalition-building, cooperation among traditional friends and allies, humility in dealing with other countries, and a reluctance to impose our values by force. For what are we now but unilateralists who insult our friends, take an "our way or the highway" approach to negotiations, routinely violate the international laws and conventions that we helped draft many years ago, and invade not for the purpose of self-defense but in order to bring American-style democracy to the natives at gunpoint?

The neoconservatives who have taken us down this path are actually very few in number. It is a small pack of zealots whose dedication has spanned decades, and that through years of selective recruitment has become a government cult with cells in most of the national security system. Among those cells are the secretive Office of Special Plans in the Department of Defense (reportedly now disbanded) and a similar operation in the State Department that is managed in the office of Under Secretary for Disarmament John Bolton.

Pat Lang—with whom I had frequently exchanged views on Iraq policy—served his country first as an army officer, rising to the rank of colonel, then as an intelligence officer in the Defense Intelligence Agency in charge of the Middle East before retiring. He once told me about when he was recruited for possible membership in the group.

He described to me a visit, during the administration of the first George Bush, from an elderly couple who dropped in on him unannounced one afternoon at his Pentagon office. They had come, they said, at the suggestion of Paul Wolfowitz, then the Under Secretary of Defense for Policy, who had told them that Colonel Lang was a bright fellow. They introduced themselves as Albert and Roberta Wohlstetter, professors from the University of Chicago, and they made themselves at home for a brief chat.

Albert Wohlstetter, one of the most influential strategists of nuclear weapons policy in the second half of the twentieth century until his death in 1997, was a mentor to Wolfowitz and Richard Perle. In the 1970s he had been an architect of the first effort to bring outside analysts into traditional institutions like the CIA to "reassess" the Soviet threat. This "Team B" effort resulted in the Reagan administration's use of wildly exaggerated claims about Soviet rearmament to justify huge American defense spending increases. By the end of the decade, Wohlstetter had expanded his definition of America's strategic role to include the Middle East. He advocated that the U.S. extend its security umbrella to the Persian Gulf on the grounds that even if no Soviet hand could be seen behind the Islamic revolution in Iran of 1979, the situation there still represented a threat to American interests in the Middle East and Pakistan.

During the Wohlstetters' conversation with Lang, they began to probe the colonel for his views and beliefs. Mrs. Wohlstetter, partner to her husband in academia and in political philosophy as well as in life, pointed out sections in books they had written and asked Lang for his views on the theories espoused in them.

It became apparent to Lang that he was being auditioned— though, as it happened, not to the satisfaction of the Wohlstetters. They soon packed up their books and left.

Lang said that in later conversations with a number of uniformed officers, he learned that many of them had been auditioned as well and, like him, had been found wanting. However, one who did pass the test was former Navy Captain William J. Luti. In the Bush administration he holds the post of Deputy Under Secretary of Defense for Near Eastern and South Asian Affairs. Luti also supervised the Office of Special Plans, described in a seminal 2003 *New Yorker* article by Seymour Hersh as "a separate intelligence unit…in the Pentagon's policy office."

It was through these special offices that so many of the rumors, gossip, and unsubstantiated intelligence about Iraq were passed directly to senior White House officials, notably Vice President Cheney, and were accepted without first being subjected to the rigorous analysis of the $30-billion-a-year intelligence community. American intelligence, which routinely sees and sifts thousands of bits of information daily, has had years of experience developing an analytical capability that can assess precisely whether the information we are receiving is fact or fiction.

Short-circuiting this process—or, in the vivid term Hersh adopted for the title of his disturbing article, "stovepiping" information directly into policy-makers' hands—is dangerous. Addressing his investigation directly to Luti's enterprise, Hersh added: "This office, which circumvented the usual procedures of vetting and transparency, stovepiped many of its findings to the highest-ranking officials" in the administration.

President Bush could fundamentally change the direction of his administration by firing fewer than fifteen senior officials, beginning with those signatories of the Project for the New American Century and those currently holding government posts who signed a 1998 letter that urged President Clinton to wage war on Iraq. They are clustered at the National Security Council (NSC), in the Defense and State Departments, and within Vice President Cheney's own parallel national security office. That particular little-known organization—not accountable to Congress and virtually unknown to the American people—should be completely dismantled. Never in the history of our democracy has there been established such an influential and pervasive center of power with the ability to circumvent long-standing and accepted reporting structures and to skew decision-making practices. It has been described to me chillingly by a former senior government official as a coup d'etat within the State. That's all it would take—firing fewer than fifteen officials, and the scuttling of Cheney's questionable office—to alter this administration's radical course.

But President Bush would have to *want* to make these changes. The fact that he has utterly failed to do so suggests that one popular notion about this president—that he has delegated foreign policy to his "prime minister," Dick Cheney, and that the president is somehow manipulated by him—is doubtful. Even as the criticism mounts and the failure of the war policy becomes ever more evident with every attack on American interests in Iraq, the president refuses to make changes in his lineup. In fact, as one former intelligence officer suggested to me, President Bush may himself be a neoconservative "recruit," and now an active leader of the radical movement rather than a passive follower unable to block it.

The president is not powerless and does not need to demonstrate, as Senator Richard Lugar pleaded on *Meet the Press* in October 2003: "The president has to be president. That means the president over the vice president and over these secretaries [of State and Defense]." On the contrary, he is the president and he is directing his vice president and his cabinet secretaries to do his bidding. He is responsible for what has been wrought in his name.

However our occupation of Iraq plays out over the coming months, a partial list of the significant repercussions coming out of this misadventure can already be drawn up.

The first effect is the increased danger from international terrorism directed at American interests. Terrorist organizations have been able to capitalize on the war in Iraq, with its images of the death and destruction we have dealt out, to enlarge the pool of hard-core recruits—as well as supporters and sympathizers ready to provide cover for the terrorists. In addition to the increased threat of random terrorist attacks on American citizens at home and abroad from already disaffected individuals, we can expect that new and even more determined and diabolically imaginative terrorist groups will emerge from the ashes of the Iraq war and in the aftermath of al Qaeda's eventual defeat. They will adapt their tactics to what they have learned from our reactions to other terrorist feints and attacks.

The second repercussion is that, regrettably, the next generation of American diplomats and warriors will be forced to sing from the music the neoconservatives composed for this war. It may take us more than a generation to recover from the folly that they have foisted upon our country and its ambassadors and soldiers abroad. They have made this a far more dangerous world for Americans, and a far more hostile one.

On September 12, 2001, the world mourned with us and joined us in condemning those who would commit such a horrible crime against humanity. At the United Nations, a decades-old debate on what constituted terrorism was concluded within days of the attack, and nations worldwide stood with us in our grief and anger. Even the French newspaper *Le Monde* expressed its solidarity; it led with a headline crying "We are all Americans." Now we are despised for what we are doing in Iraq, with people around the world fearing the United States more than they do Osama bin Laden. That attitude, coupled with our own insulting behavior toward the rest of the world and the United Nations, will make international cooperation much more difficult to encourage and manage over the long term. We need international intelligence exchanges, police support, and worldwide banking agreements in order to stem the terrorist tide before it swells larger. We will regain that cooperation only if we are perceived as a nation engaging in legitimate activities, not undertaking unjustified actions like the war in Iraq.

For all the jealousy that U.S. power and domination generate overseas, I rarely found any antipathy toward Americans in any place I lived or traveled, even on the streets of Baghdad at the height of Desert Shield. On the contrary, Americans were admired for their openness, their friendliness, and the liberty and freedom that they represented, no matter how controversial the policies of our government might have been. Global resentment engendered by the war and America's current foreign policy has spilled over onto the streets of the world; it has become personal, and our citizens bear the brunt of the anger when they visit foreign countries.

Notwithstanding President Bush's insistence, we are not safer as a result of the war with Iraq, even with Saddam in custody and facing a trial that may help provide Iraq's terrorized population with some catharsis. Nor has our position in the world been enhanced. We no longer inhabit that city on the hill to which people in other lands aspire. In fact, anecdotal evidence already suggests that growing disaffection with the United States is having an impact. Businessmen find their welcome overseas to be less warm, while partnerships designed to isolate and constrain American interests emerge.

However quickly we can roll back the negative effects of our misguided policies, it will not be quick enough. And whatever we are able to do to restore ourselves to a position of international leadership, we may never again be seen as a benign superpower to be respected and admired as a beacon of the future. Rather, we will be viewed as an aggressive, sometimes violent power generally to be wary of and, whenever possible, to be weakened. Other countries of the world will be looking not to follow us but to keep us from again unleashing the dogs of war, possibly on them. And with our international financial indebtedness having risen to historic levels, it may not be long before we begin to see restraints in business abroad take their toll on our standard of living.

This debacle has also had significant repercussions for Israel and all of her friends around the world. Inescapably, Israel remains America's chief ally in the region, and unfortunately it will bear the brunt of the region's negative reaction to what we have done in Iraq. Consequently, resistance to the policies that the Likud government is pursuing toward the Palestinian population will be further inflamed.

Criticism of Israel is all too often expressed in anti-Semitic terms. While not all criticism of Israel is anti-Semitic, many critics resort to ugly and despicable anti-Semitic behavior. In the six decades since the Holocaust, the civilized world has committed to purging this conduct from its midst. There has been progress in this essential effort throughout much of the world, and I am committed to that work. Now, however, I fear that because of the association in the Arab world between America's misguided invasion and occupation of Iraq, and the policies of the Likud government in Israel, we may see an upsurge of hate crimes against Israel and against Jewish populations elsewhere. While this result could not have been anticipated by the policy makers who drove us into the invasion of Iraq, it is potentially an outcome of it just the same. A surge in anti-Semitism such as we are already seeing in Europe and elsewhere, such as the savage synagogue bombings in Istanbul, Turkey, will require a redoubling of our efforts.

The failure of the Camp David process at the end of the Clinton presidency led to a "perfect storm" in the Middle East at the moment George W. Bush took office. Yasser Arafat launched the second intifada with suicide bombers, and the fragile peace between the Palestinians and Israelis that had emerged from the Madrid and Oslo peace processes was shattered. The intifada traumatized Israeli society as well as its friends in America, and it played directly into the hands of radicals on all sides. The moderates were effectively sidelined, and the halting truce that had been generated in the 1990s was lost prior to what, it had been hoped, would be a final agreement. Whatever the controversy over the Madrid–Oslo efforts, the statistics are indisputable: between 1997 and 2000, fewer than 20 Israelis and Palestinians combined died in sectarian violence. In the three years since, more than 600 Israelis and 2,000 Palestinians have perished.

As we learn in *The Price of Loyalty*, from former Treasury Secretary

Paul O'Neill and other administration officials, President Bush downgraded the mediation effort that his father had begun in Madrid after the first Gulf War and that President Clinton had built upon. According to O'Neill, in the new Bush administration's very first National Security Council meeting, the president said, "We're going to correct the imbalances of the previous administration on the Mideast conflict. We're going to tilt it back toward Israel."

Later in the meeting, Colin Powell cautioned that a withdrawal of U.S. involvement "would unleash Sharon." He warned: "The consequences could be dire . . . especially for the Palestinians."

O'Neill remembers that "Bush shrugged," then said, "Maybe that's the best way to get things back in balance." As "Powell seemed startled," Bush concluded the discussion of the Israeli–Palestinian conflict with the observation, "Sometimes a show of strength by one side can really clarify things."

Condoleezza Rice, chairing the NSC meeting, announced that the next topic would be "How Iraq is destabilizing the region, Mr. President." The new administration's agenda for the region was thus prefigured from the start. And so President Bush gave Prime Minister Ariel Sharon, head of Israel's Likud party, free rein to act without even the modicum of restraint that had been observed by no less a hard-liner than fellow Likud Prime Minister Benjamin Netanyahu, whose government cosigned the Wye River Memorandum with Arafat in 1998.

By uncritically favoring Likud, President Bush has done our Israeli friends and allies no favors. Are U.S. interests—or those of Israel—truly served by the forging of an alliance among the Likud party, American neoconservatives, and right-wing American evangelicals, the latter of whom see Israel as a means to their ultimate end: a fervently sought rapture? Our legitimate and unquestioned commitment is not to any one political party in Israel, but to Israel's national security and territorial integrity. I believe that our

war on Iraq coupled with Likud's questionable policies undermines both.

In recent months I have tried to piece together the truth about the
attacks on myself and the disclosure of Valerie's employment by
carefully studying all the coverage and by speaking confidentially
with members of the press who have been following the story. A
number of them have been candid with me in our private conversations but unwilling to speak publicly with the same candor. When I
have asked why the reporting on the story has not been more aggressive, I have received responses that are very disturbing. A reporter
told me that one of the six newspeople who had received the leak
stated flatly that the pressure he had come under from the administration in the past several months to remain silent made him fear that
if he did his job and reported on the leak story, he would "end up in
Guantanamo"—a dark metaphor for the career isolation he would
suffer at the hands of the administration. Another confided that she
had heard from reporters that "with kids in private school and a mort-
gage on the house," they were unwilling to cross the administration.

    In the halcyon days of an aggressive investigative press corps,
journalists saw it as their job "to afflict the comfortable and comfort
the afflicted," as the great Chicago journalist Finley Peter Dunne put
it early in the twentieth century. What does it say for the health of
our democracy—or our media—when fear of the administration's
reaction preempts the search for truth? Mark Fineman, the late *Los
Angeles Times* foreign correspondent who did a profile on me in
Baghdad in 1990, used to call his passion for the truth the search
for the "dirtball" stories—the stories that lay in the soft underbelly
of the public pronouncements, the stories behind the story. Clearly,
many stories lie behind the story of the attacks on my family, but
they have prompted very little "dirtball" reporting. I am disappointed

by the reluctance of the press to make waves and get to the very bottom of the real story.

From everything I have heard, the truth may be found at the nexus between policy and politics in the White House. Whoever made the decision to disclose Valerie's undercover status occupies a position where he—and I believe it is a "he" because Robert Novak's own statements employ the male pronoun exclusively—has access to the most sensitive secrets in our government, and a political agenda to advance or defend. In gumshoe parlance, he's got the means and he's got the motive. Only a few administration officials meet both of these criteria, and they are clustered in the upper reaches of the National Security Council, the Office of the Vice President, and the Office of the President.

After my appearance on CNN in early March 2003, when I first asserted that the U.S. government knew more about the Niger uranium matter than it was letting on, I am told by a source close to the House Judiciary Committee that the Office of the Vice President—either the vice president himself or, more likely, his chief of staff, Lewis ("Scooter") Libby—chaired a meeting at which a decision was made to do a "workup" on me. As I understand it, this meant they were going to take a close look at who I was and what my agenda might be.

The meeting did not include discussion of how the president or his senior staff might address the indisputable, if inconvenient, fact that the allegation I had made was true. In other words, from the very beginning, the strategy of the White House was to confront the issue as a "Wilson" problem rather than as an issue of the lie that was in the State of the Union address. That time frame, from my CNN appearance in early March, after the administration claimed they "fell for" the forged documents, to the first week in July, makes sense, as it allows time for all the necessary sleuthing to have been done on us, including the discovery of Valerie's name and employment.

The immediate effect of the workup, I am told by a member of the press, citing White House sources, was a long harangue against the two of us within the White House walls. Over a period of several months, Libby evidently seized opportunities to rail openly against me as an "asshole playboy" who went on a boondoggle "arranged by his CIA wife"—and was a Democratic Gore supporter to boot.

So what if I'd contributed to the Gore campaign? I had also contributed to the Bush campaign. So what if I'd sat on a Gore foreign policy committee? I had had no political role whatsoever in the campaign. Moreover, my trip to Niger was taken more than two years after the Gore–Bush election, and I had not even been involved in any partisan activities during the campaign. And it was not until the spring of 2003, several months *after* the president's State of the Union address, that I contributed to the Kerry campaign and began to work with his foreign policy committee.

Would a staunch Republican have disregarded the facts and offered findings from Niger that were different than mine? Intelligence collection is not party-specific. Perhaps a Republican would have allowed the lie to pass without comment, but if so, that is a Republican problem. The national security question is always the same: Did we go to war under false pretenses? I am not prepared to argue that Republicans per se endorse the practice of government officials lying and distorting the facts, but it may be that Vice President Cheney and his chief of staff do.

The man attacking my integrity and reputation—and, I believe, quite possibly the person who exposed my wife's identity—was the same Scooter Libby who, before he came into the new administration, was one of the principal attorneys for Marc Rich, ex-fugitive. Rich is the commodities trader who was convicted of having traded petroleum with Iran in violation of sanctions imposed on that country by the United States after the seizure of the American Embassy in Tehran and the taking of more than a hundred American hostages by supporters of Ayatollah Khomeini. Libby is a consummate Republican insider who has bounced back and forth between government posts and his international law practice. He first worked on the Rich case in the mid-1980s, after a stint in the State Department. From 1989 to 1993, Libby worked for Paul Wolfowitz in the Pentagon, before returning to the task of trying to obtain a legal settlement for his fugitive client.

In the late nineties, Libby also participated in the preparation of the Project for the New American Century's seminal document, "Rebuilding American Defenses," which became the neoconservative blueprint for national security policy, much of which has been implemented in the aftermath of 9/11. This ardent neoconservative is a leading participant in the network of hidden cells that funneled so much disinformation to our political decision makers outside normal channels. He is one of a handful of senior officials in the administration with both the means and the motive to conduct the covert inquiry that allowed some in the White House to learn my wife's name and status, and then disclose that information to the press.

The other name that has most often been repeated to me in connection with the inquiry and disclosure into my background and Valerie's is that of Elliott Abrams, who gained infamy in the Iran–Contra scandal during the first Bush administration. Abrams had been convicted in 1991 on two charges of lying to Congress about illegal government support of the Nicaraguan contra rebels. He was pardoned in 1992 by President George H. W. Bush. How unsurprising it would be if Abrams, an admitted perjurer and a charter member of the neoconservative movement, has engaged in unethical or criminal behavior in yet another presidential administration.

According to my sources, between March 2003 and the appearance of my article in July, the workup on me that turned up the information on Valerie was shared with Karl Rove, who then circulated it in administration and neoconservative circles. That would explain the assertion later advanced by Clifford May, the neocon fellow traveler, who wrote that Valerie's employment was supposedly widely known. Oh, really? I am not reassured by his statement. Indeed, if what May wrote was accurate, it is a damning admission, because it could have been widely known only by virtue of leaks among his own crowd.

After the appearance of Novak's article, the subsequent "pushing" of the story by the White House communications office—and by Karl Rove—guaranteed that the allegation would at some point take center stage in the press and would sweep the story behind the sixteen words into the wings. Rove's strategy appears to have been simple—change the subject and focus attention on Valerie and me instead of the White House—but it proved to be seriously flawed. A week after Novak reported the story that the administration pushed to him, David Corn reported that a federal crime might have been committed, and I conveyed that opinion on the *Today* show. I am absolutely certain that Rove and company would have continued trying to convince the public that Valerie and I were motivated by partisanship and somehow responsible for the president's error—ridiculous as that seems—had it not been for the fact that they discovered the outing was quite possibly illegal. Apparently, according to two journalist sources of mine, when Rove learned that he might have violated the law, he turned on Cheney and Libby and made it clear that he held them responsible for the problem they had created for the administration. The protracted silence on this topic from the White House masks considerable tension between the Office of the President and the Office of the Vice President.

The rumors swirling around Rove, Libby, and Abrams were so pervasive in Washington that the White House press secretary, Scott McClellan, was obliged to address them in an October 2003 briefing, saying of Rove: "The president knows he wasn't involved. . . . It's simply not true." McClellan refused to be drawn into a similar direct denial of Libby's or Abrams's possible involvement, however. Later interpretations of the line being taken by the White House spokesman, according to members of the press who have spoken with me, indicate that the administration's defense is extremely narrow: the leakers and pushers of the story did not know the undercover status of Valerie Plame, and therefore, though they may have disclosed her name, they did not commit a crime.

Time will tell if that defense—which strikes me as sophistry and a legal refuge for scoundrels—holds up. Indeed, if the administration has no firm knowledge as to who might have leaked Valerie's name, why would McClellan, and whoever drafted his talking points, address the matter so precisely and try to stay so strictly within the letter of the Intelligence Identities Protection Act? Ignorance of my wife's undercover status may exculpate the leakers and pushers from violations under that act, but as a congressional letter of January 26 to the General Accounting Office makes clear, other laws may have been broken, including statutes relating to the handling of classified material. Even the Patriot Act may have been violated, if Sam Dash's interpretation of that law is correct.

In fact, senior advisers close to the president may well have been clever enough to have used others to do the actual leaking, in order to keep their fingerprints off the crime. John Hannah and David Wurmser, mid-level political appointees in the vice president's office, have both been suggested as sources of the leaks. I don't know either, though at the time of the leak, Wurmser, a prominent neoconservative, was working as a special assistant to John Bolton at the State Department. Mid-level officials, however, do not leak information without authority from a higher level. They would have been instruments, not the makers, of decisions.

Whether the motivation behind the leak was to discredit me or to discourage intelligence officials from coming forward, or both, is immaterial at this stage. What matters is that, as of this writing, the senior administration officials who took it upon themselves to protect a political agenda by exposing a national security asset are still in place. They still occupy positions of trust; they continue to hold full national security clearances. The breach of trust between the administration and its clandestine service will not be healed until they are exposed and appropriately punished.

That no real outrage has been expressed by either the president or Republicans in Congress begs the question of whether our secrets are safe in this administration's hands. By the end of February 2004, efforts to launch congressional inquiries had been voted down in three House committees. Henry Hyde, Republican chairman of the International Relations panel, claimed, "It would be irresponsible for the committee to . . . jeopardize an ongoing criminal investigation." On the contrary, according to congressional sources of mine, Republicans, pressured by the White House, have simply refused to exercise oversight responsibility on this national security matter.

It's a far cry from the days when the House Government Reform committee, chaired by Indiana congressman Dan Burton, held frequent hearings on alleged Clinton administration misdeeds. At a time when all experts on national security agree that we need to strengthen our ability to collect human intelligence, the unwillingness of some to seriously address this act of betrayal is surely damaging that effort.

But as with all cover-ups, such as Watergate and Iran-Contra, the revelation of the whole truth in this matter will likely be a long time coming, and have repercussions none of us can anticipate.

The impact on our family of the disclosures authorized by the administration and reported by Novak has been profound. It is impossible at this stage to know what the future holds for Valerie. The intelligence bureaucracy is not structured to manage surprises like her exposure very well, and while she is an innocent in all of this, her career has nonetheless been irreversibly damaged. Whether the bureaucracy can find some other way to take advantage of her vast talents is still an open question. If it can't, the shame rests with the government and the loss is the country's. Valerie is and always has been a star in her profession.

We worry about our personal security, but there is little we can do. Still, many positive things have happened to Valerie and me as well. Americans of all political persuasions, from William Kristol to Hillary Clinton, have expressed their outrage at what has happened to us and proffered their support.

I was honored to be asked to endorse John Kerry and happy to volunteer my time, unsalaried, to travel the country on his behalf. The campaign trips have taken me to American towns and cities I had never seen before. For somebody who has spent most of his professional career in foreign lands, among foreign peoples, in foreign cultures, it has been an exhilirating experience to learn more about my own land and the people who farm, teach, labor, build, nurse, play, age, and live in it. I have relished the opportunity to discuss with them issues that are important to me but are not often hot topics in election campaigns. My strongly held belief that we are a great and gentle people, fiercely independent but tolerant and courteous even when we disagree with each other, has been reinforced. Thus, this current government of angry and intolerant leaders seems all the more to be an aberration.

For all the complaints we as a people may have about our system and all the vitriol that passes for political discourse these days, we are still the stewards of the most cherished system of government ever known to humankind. The rights of the individual, the protection of minorities, the respect for the law of the land and the constitution, the history that defines the way we view ourselves and our world, imperfections and all—these are what make our experiment in democracy so worth defending and fighting for.

No matter how trying some of the recent times have been for my family and me, and for the country, I come away from the fight I've had with my government full of hope for our future. It takes time for Americans to fully understand when they have been duped by a government they instinctively want to trust. But it is axiomatic that you cannot fool all of the people all of the time and our citizens inevitably react to the deceit. I see that happening wherever I speak around this great land nowadays.

What I have experienced has also inspired me to encourage broader participation in our democracy. Our government reflects the interests of the voters; if you do not vote, you cannot be surprised when the actions the government takes benefit those who voted in your stead. The best way to ensure that our government more fully reflects the views of all of its citizens is through greater participation in the process of selecting our leaders. It is simply untrue that a single vote does not matter. Not only does a vote indicate far more concretely than any other mechanism the concerns of the citizen, the absence of a vote guarantees that those concerns cannot be registered, leading governments to respond to the narrow interests of its vocal supporters rather than the broader concerns of the citizenry in general.

Nations succeed—America included, as our founding fathers understood so well in designing our institutions—when compromises are sought to accommodate as many of the diverse interests in our society as possible. Ours is a great experiment, one that is worth defending, whatever the price, from domestic subversion as much as from foreign enemies. The best defense that each of us has domestically is to be part of the political dialogue in our communities, across our states, and throughout the nation. That is the lesson Valerie and I take away from our experience as we face an uncertain but ever-hopeful future.

When Valerie unpacked her belongings in our new home in Washington in 1998, one of the first items she put out for display in our bedroom was a framed copy of the poem "Ithaka" by C. P. Cavafy, published in 1910. She explained to me that it reflected her own views on life as a journey. While we are not yet on the last leg of that journey, we have certainly encountered our share of Laistrygonians and Cyclops on our way, and the poem speaks to us only more today.

ITHAKA

As you set out for Ithaka
hope your road is a long one,
full of adventure, full of discovery.
Laistrygonians, Cyclops,
angry Poseidon—don't be afraid of them:
you'll never find things like that on your way
as long as you keep your thoughts raised high,
as long as a rare excitement
stirs your spirit and your body.
Laistrygonians, Cyclops,
wild Poseidon—you won't encounter them
unless you bring them along inside your soul,
unless your soul sets them up in front of you.

Hope your road is a long one.
May there be many summer mornings when,
with what pleasure, what joy,
you enter harbors you're seeing for the first time;
may you stop at Phoenician trading stations
to buy fine things,
mother of pearl and coral, amber and ebony,
sensual perfume of every kind—
as many sensual perfumes as you can;
and may you visit many Egyptian cities
to learn and go on learning from their scholars.

Keep Ithaka always in your mind.
Arriving there is what you're destined for.
But don't hurry the journey at all.
Better if it lasts for years,
so you're old by the time you reach the island,
wealthy with all you've gained on the way,
not expecting Ithaka to make you rich.
Ithaka gave you the marvelous journey.
Without her you wouldn't have set out.
She has nothing left to give you now.

And if you find her poor, Ithaka won't have fooled you.
Wise as you will have become, so full of experience,
you'll have understood by then what these Ithakas mean.

Timelines

Diplomatic Career of Ambassador Joseph Wilson

January 1976	Joins United States Foreign Service.
1976–1978	General Services Officer, Niamey, Niger.
1978–1979	Administrative Officer, Lome, Togo.
1979–1981	Administrative Officer, U.S. State Department, Washington, D.C.
1981–1982	Administrative Officer, Pretoria, South Africa.
1982–1985	Deputy Chief of Mission (DCM), Bujumbura, Burundi.
1985–1986	Congressional Fellow, offices of Senator Al Gore and Representative Tom Foley.
1986–1988	DCM, Brazzaville, Republic of the Congo.
1988–1991	DCM, Baghdad, Iraq.
1992–1995	Ambassador to Gabon and São Tomé and Príncipe.
1995–1997	Political Adviser to Commander in Chief U.S. Armed Forces, Europe, Stuttgart, Germany.
1997–1998	Special Assistant to President Clinton and Senior Director for African Affairs, National Security Council, Washington, D.C.

* * *

Events surrounding the "sixteen words" and the disclosure of the undercover status of CIA operative Valerie Plame, wife of Ambassador Joseph Wilson

December 2001–January 2002	First reports of Niger-Iraq uranium connection surface in the Bush administration.
February 2002	Wilson is asked to CIA headquarters to discuss Niger's uranium industry and the possibility of a uranium deal between Niger and Iraq; soon after, he travels to Niger at Agency's request to investigate the claim; in Niger he finds no evidence to substantiate it.
March 2002	Upon returning home from Niger, Wilson briefs CIA and delivers a skeptical report.
September 2002	First public mention of Niger-Iraq uranium connection is made in British white paper.
January 28, 2003	The sixteen words are spoken by President Bush in his State of the Union address: "The British government has learned that Saddam Hussein recently sought significant quantities of uranium from Africa."
March 7, 2003	International Atomic Energy Agency announces that documents provided by U.S. about Niger-Iraq uranium claim are forgeries.
March 8, 2003	State Department spokesman says of forged documents: "We fell for it"; shortly thereafter, Wilson tells CNN that the U.S. government has more information on this matter than the State Department spokesmen acknowledged.
	Sources have informed Wilson that soon after the CNN interview, a decision was made at a meeting in the Office of the Vice President—possibly attended by Dick Cheney, Lewis "Scooter" Libby, Newt Gingrich, and other senior Republicans—to produce a workup on Wilson to discredit him.
June 8, 2003	On *Meet the Press* Condoleezza Rice denies knowledge of how dubious the uranium claim was and dissembles:

"Maybe somebody down in the bowels of the Agency knew about this, but nobody in my circles."

July 6, 2003   Wilson's op-ed, "What I Didn't Find in Africa," is published in the *New York Times*; Wilson appears on *Meet the Press*, describes his trip and why he came away convinced that no attempt by Iraq to purchase uranium from Niger had taken place.

July 8, 2003   Columnist Robert Novak encounters Wilson's friend on Washington, D.C., street and blurts out Valerie Plame's CIA employment.

July 14, 2003   Novak publishes column revealing Plame's status.

July 16, 2003   In *The Nation* David Corn publishes "A White House Smear," explaining that the Intelligence Identities Protection Act may have been violated by leak.

July 20, 2003   NBC's Andrea Mitchell tells Wilson that "senior White House sources" had phoned her to stress "the real story here is not the sixteen words . . . but Wilson and his wife."

July 21, 2003   NBC's Chris Matthews tells Wilson: "I just got off the phone with Karl Rove. He says and I quote, 'Wilson's wife is fair game.' I will confirm that if asked."

September 28, 2003   MSNBC announces that Justice Department has begun a criminal investigation into the leak.

September 29, 2003   *Washington Post* article by Mike Allen and Dana Priest quotes a "senior administration official" who "said that before Novak's column ran, two top White House officials called at least six Washington journalists and disclosed the identity and occupation of Wilson's wife. . . . 'Clearly it was meant purely and simply for revenge,' the senior official said of the leak. . . . A source said reporters quoted a leaker as describing Wilson's wife as 'fair game.' "

October 7, 2003   President Bush states that the Justice Department will "come to the bottom of this."

December 5, 2003   A *Financial Times* article by James Harding quotes a "senior White House official" who says "We have rolled the earthmovers in over this one."

December 30, 2003	Attorney General John Ashcroft recuses himself from the leak investigation.
January 21, 2004	*Time* reports that a federal grand jury has begun hearing testimony.
February 5, 2004	UPI's Richard Sale reports that "Federal law-enforcement officials said that they have developed hard evidence of possible criminal misconduct by two employees of Vice President Dick Cheney's office related to the unlawful exposure of a CIA officer's identity .... The investigation, which is continuing, could lead to indictments, a Justice Department official said."
March 5, 2004	*Newsday*'s Tom Brune reports that the grand jury has issued subpoenas summoning phone logs of Air Force One from July 7-12, from the July 12 press gaggle, and records of the White House Iraq Group from July 6-30.

Acknowledgments

A BOOK, I HAVE LEARNED, is not just the labor of the author's love. There is a whole team of dedicated wordsmiths, editors, marketers, and publicists behind the writer working to make the stories as compelling and readable as possible.

The team at Carroll & Graf and the Avalon Publishing Group is no exception and I offer my heartfelt thanks to everybody who participated in producing this book, particularly Carroll & Graf Editor-in-Chief Philip Turner, Associate Editor Keith Wallman, Publisher Will Balliett, Avalon CEO Charlie Winton, copyeditor Phil Gaskill, indexer Melanie Piper, editors Peter Skutches, Don Weise, and Michele Slung, interior designer Simon Sullivan, Art Director Linda Kosarin, designer Lorie Pagnozzi, Production Director Michael Walters, Senior Managing Editor Claiborne Hancock, and Sandee Roston and Karen Auerbach, Senior Director of Marketing and Director of Publicity, respectively. While errors of fact are a reflection of my own fading memory, if this is a good read, it is largely thanks to their contributions.

Had it not been for Jon Elliot, talk-show radio host on the West Coast, and Barbara Monteiro, a publicist from New York, I never would have written this book. Not only did they encourage me but they also put me in contact with Carroll & Graf, which started the ball rolling.

Kim Fararo, the editor of the Perspective section of the *San Jose Mercury News*, offered me my first opportunity to share my views publicly in an opinion piece. I published three articles in Perspective. Her personal attention and patient editing ensured there was some coherence from the jumbled prose I sent her way. Bruce McLeod, editor of the *Los Angeles Times,* also gave me a chance to speak to readers in my home state, California, and forced me to think about what Saddam really was like, giving rise to the "big cat" metaphor. David Shipley, editor of the *New York Times* opinion section, kept space available for me for weeks while I determined whether I was going to have to attach my own name to the uranium story to make the administration finally come clean with the American people on the fiction of the sixteen words in the president's State of the Union address. Many of the people have told me since that the understated tone of the article added to its impact. Those who know me know that I am not an understated personality, so David was key to helping me find an effective "author's voice." I am most appreciative to all three editors for their help and support. I learned from each.

Chris Wolf has helped my family in too many ways to recount both as our lawyer and as our next door neighbor. His cousin, Audrey Wolf, literary agent, has navigated the publishing waters on my behalf and made it easy for me to concentrate on telling the story.

Lyn and Norman Lear provided us with a warm and welcome refuge in the early days of drafting the book. Their friendship and support during the most intense period of public scrutiny and attention was most welcome. Bill Moyers was kind enough to make the introductions and for that, as well as for giving me a forum on his terrific program, *NOW,* I will be eternally grateful.

Robert Greenwald and Mike Farrell were always there as we tried to add some sanity to a debate dominated by ideologues determined to take the country we love into a destructive and senseless war. The documentary *Uncovered,* produced by Robert, is a stinging indictment of how the Bush administration misled the American people, and I am proud to have participated in it.

Katrina vanden Heuvel and David Corn of *The Nation,* and Tom Andrews, the Executive Director of Win Without War, were other tenacious debaters whose support and friendship throughout has been unflagging. Though we were few in number, we were strong, supported by organizations like MoveOn.org which is doing so much to bring policy debate back to the grassroots. Valerie and I feel privileged to count such patriotic and concerned citizens among our friends.

Thanks also go to Jon Dindas and the team at Greater Talent Network.

Author Ron Suskind was extremely generous in allowing me to quote liberally from his book *The Price of Loyalty: George W. Bush, the White House, and the Education of Paul O'Neill.*

Joshua Micah Marshall's blog, Talkingpointsmemo.com, is a daily source of insight that keeps me and thousands of others informed every day. Special thanks for the letter from his online document collection pictured here on page 359. University of Michigan Professor Juan Cole's Web site is one of the most consistently thoughtful and erudite sources for analysis of the ongoing situation in Iraq.

There are so many friends, acquaintances, and people Valerie and I have never met who have offered their support in the months since we found ourselves under attack by our own government. We are most appreciative. They have reinforced our belief about our country and about the vast majority of its citizens and have been a source of strength as I continue to speak out. Many of those who have been in touch with me were hostages in the first Gulf War, offering their steadfast support. Roland Bergheer, reflecting what many others conveyed to me, said in one interview, "I would give my life for him since he put his on the line for all of us." I an enormously appreciative of this loyalty, but in fact, we all put our lives on the line for our country back then when our government was doing the right thing.

My brother, Willie, a staunch Orange County Republican who was more incensed at what happened to Valerie and me than anybody, has been incredibly supportive throughout the last year. He is so furious that he has promised me that Bush-Cheney will not carry his town, San Clemente, California, in the 2004 election. Only when the Republican party reflects more than the evangelical Right and the neoconservative, illiberal imperialists will he probably revert to his Republican roots.

There is no more intrepid band of public servants than the diplomats who serve their country overseas, often in some of the most challenging countries in the world. Much maligned by those whose foreign experience goes little beyond the plush lobbies of five star hotels in European capitals, the Foreign Service is a noble calling. Who knows how many wars have been prevented or conflicts resolved thanks to imaginative and tenacious diplomacy. This story is as much theirs as it is mine and I hope it is a representative and interesting rendition of life as a diplomat.

My two adult twin children, Sabrina and Joe, have followed me around the world and have always been there for me, through thick and thin. It is a great inspiration to be able to call them friends as well as family. I know that as they make their way in the world, I can be as confident of their patriotism and commitment to our great country as I am in my own.

My other twins, Trevor and Samantha, are too young to understand what we have been through but their unqualified love has been a tonic at the end of many long days. Their good humor is a direct reflection of their mother's patience and unfailing good nature. Their only complaints have come when they occasionally bang on the television telling me to come out of the box, and when they ask when I am going to be finished with the book that has taken me away from park duty. I hope that when they read the book, they will agree that it was worth the time I spent in the basement writing and not rough-housing with them.

Finally, my wife Valerie's most poignant reflection through all of this was when she told me that when she accepted my marriage proposal, she did not count on our years together being such a high profile whirlwind. Like me, she agrees that this is only a chapter in our otherwise rich life as a couple and family, one that has added to it, but hopefully one that will not define us indefinitely. We believe we still have much to contribute, as parents, as citizens, and perhaps as public servants. And we will do it together, for our relationship has been deepened, if that were possible, by the ordeal through which we have been tested. I hope that the story of our love also comes through in these pages.

I have tried to be as accurate as possible in chronicling these events. However, I am fallible, so there may be mistakes of fact. If so, those mistakes are my own.

Newspaper commentaries published by
Ambassador Joseph Wilson before and after
the United States invasion of Iraq in 2003

San Jose Mercury News, October 13, 2002
HOW SADDAM THINKS
By Joseph Wilson

PRESIDENT BUSH HAS made his preference clear: He wants Saddam Hussein's scalp, or at least wants him run out of town—an approach that virtually ensures a bloody American invasion and long occupation of Iraq. And Congress late last week gave the president broad authority to launch that war, with or without United Nations involvement.

The U.N. Security Council, meanwhile, is pursuing a business-as-usual policy, reluctant to put any teeth into the possible resumption of weapons inspections until Saddam cheats yet again.

Both the U.S. and U.N. approaches are dangerously flawed. They ignore crucial lessons we learned in the Persian Gulf War about how Saddam thinks.

If history is any guide, "regime change" as a rationale for military action will ensure that Saddam will use every weapon in his arsenal to defend himself. You need look no further for evidence than his use of chemical weapons to repel Iranian invaders during the Iran–Iraq war. As the just-released CIA report suggests, when cornered, Saddam is very likely to fight dirty.

But history also shows that the less-confrontational approach favored by some on the Security Council—France and Russia—isn't likely to work, either.

Saddam has, after all, repeatedly flouted U.N. resolutions and ignored its demands to let weapons inspectors back into the country for almost four years.

Twelve years ago, I was in charge of the American Embassy in Baghdad. On Aug. 6, 1990, four days after the invasion of Kuwait, I met with Saddam for nearly two hours and listened to him gloat at the overthrow of the Kuwaiti government and threaten to "spill the blood of 10,000 American soldiers in the sands of the Arabian desert" should we counterattack. Over the next several months, my staff and I worked day and night to try to persuade him not just to leave Kuwait, but also to allow Americans in Kuwait and Iraq to go home and to release the hundreds of foreign hostages, including Americans, whom he had taken as "human shields." The lessons we gleaned during that period are applicable to today's looming conflict.

What we learned firsthand is what the CIA psychiatrists have said for years: Saddam is an egomaniacal sociopath whose penchant for high-risk gambles is exceeded only by a propensity for miscalculation. Those psychiatrists, who study the characters of world leaders, believe that he suffers from what is popularly called "malignant narcissism," a sense of self-worth that drives him to act in ways that others would deem irrational, such as invading neighboring countries.

But the trait also makes him highly sensitive to direct confrontation and embarrassment, even as he is contemptuous of compromise.

"In your face" approach

Shortly after the invasion, I met with my senior staff to game out possible outcomes, given the history of Iraq in times of conflict. When the monarchy was overthrown in 1958, foreigners, including Americans, had been dragged from their hotels and hanged in public. At the outbreak of the Iran-Iraq war in 1980, a visiting delegation of Iranians disappeared in Baghdad, never to be seen again. Our conclusion was that some of us attending that meeting would not survive.

We also recognized that the traditional diplomatic methods had not worked; Ambassador April Glaspie had been severely, albeit unjustly, criticized for not being tough enough in her meeting with Saddam just days before the invasion. What she did at that meeting was follow longstanding instructions from Washington to urge, but not demand, that Iraq's dispute with Kuwait over border and oil issues be settled diplomatically. She then left for official business in Washington.

After the invasion, those of us still at the embassy opted for a confrontational "in your face" approach opposite to diplomatic convention, but well-suited to Saddam's understanding of the world. Whenever Saddam tried to garner international sympathy or support, we pushed back hard. Saddam would never yield to traditional diplomatic persuasion, because he equates compromise with weakness. Therefore, we let no action go uncriticized and sought to embarrass him whenever possible, to shame him into concessions.

The first test of this approach came when Saddam tried to portray himself as a host rather than hostage-taker when he appeared on television with a young British boy and his terrified family. We immediately issued statements that true Arab knights, as Saddam liked to be called, did not hide behind women's skirts—mocking his masculinity. Our comments were broadcast to the world and repeated by British Prime Minister Margaret Thatcher in a speech. Just days after Thatcher chided him, Saddam released all women and children. While we could never prove cause and effect, we knew we had succeeded.

Later, when the Iraqi government circulated a diplomatic note threatening to summarily execute anybody harboring foreigners—at a time when the embassy was providing refuge to 125 Americans stuck in Baghdad—I wore a hangman's noose in lieu of a tie to a news briefing. I shared the note with the international media and told them that if the Iraqis wanted to execute me for protecting Americans, I would bring my own rope.

The Iraqis were furious at my black joke and harangued me publicly. Then they withdrew the diplomatic note—another indication that Saddam was thin-skinned in the face of aggressive opposition.

Confrontation worked

At one point, Saddam sought to justify the invasion of his neighbor as a step toward the liberation of Palestine and, in a particularly ludicrous assertion, he claimed to be the champion of the Muslim world against the Christian infidel capitalists. We countered that several hundred thousand Muslim

Pakistanis, Indians and Sri Lankans were languishing in Iraqi refugee camps. Within days, Saddam released all of them.

As we applied these tactics to the task of attempting to reverse the invasion of Kuwait, we understood that the only way to try to avoid a war was to be credible in threatening one. Saddam had announced the annexation of Kuwait on Aug. 8, but by the end of September he was squirming, trying to retain as much of his conquest as possible as we kept beating the drums of war.

We told Saddam that the United States had accepted the fact that the men he was still holding hostage would be killed and convinced him that they were not of any worth to him. On the contrary, we said, they were a liability; if the Iraqis brutalized any of them, American outrage could well trigger a war to avenge the mistreatment.

He released the hostages in early December. Our entire embassy staff and virtually all other foreigners who wanted to leave also were allowed to go before the start of war.

In each case, taking a tough stand worked.

In the end, of course, the United States didn't succeed in peacefully dislodging Iraqi troops from Kuwait. But in the days leading up to Operation Desert Storm the United States again took a confrontational approach that may well have prevented an even deadlier war.

A week before the United States launched the assault on Iraqi forces in Kuwait, Secretary of State James Baker met with Iraqi Foreign Minister Tariq Aziz in Geneva. Throughout December it had become clear that Saddam would fight a military battle that he knew he would lose, calculating that in defeat he could still win the political war. In a region that feels deeply the humiliations it has suffered over centuries at the hands of imperialists, conquerors and more recently Israel, merely standing up to the West is considered a victory.

It fell to Baker to try to deter Saddam from using chemical or biological weapons. In the meeting, Baker made it clear that if Iraq attempted to defend itself in Kuwait by using weapons of mass destruction, the United States would respond by "eliminating the current Iraqi regime"—a not-so-veiled reference to a nuclear strike.

During the war, Saddam launched Scud missiles against Saudi Arabia, set fire to the Kuwaiti oil fields and did everything he could to draw Israel into a broader conflict. But he did not use chemical or biological weapons against our troops. In the end, he prized his own survival above all.

You could argue—and some liberals have—that deterrence alone could work again now, and that neither war nor tough inspections are needed. But effective deterrence requires that world leaders issue ultimatums backed by the credible threat of force, which they have not been willing to do so far.

BUILD ON EXPERIENCE

So the question remains: Can we disarm Saddam this time without risking a chemical attack or a broader regional war that threatens our allies?

The answer, I think, is yes, but only if we reject the approaches favored by many in the Bush administration and by France and Russia, and build instead on the experiences of the gulf war.

An aggressive U.N.-sanctioned campaign to disarm Iraq—bolstered by a militarily supported inspection process—would combine the best of the U.S. and U.N. approaches, a robust disarmament policy with the international legitimacy the United States seeks. Secretary of State Colin Powell is pushing the Security Council to adopt such an approach.

But he will have to overcome French and Russian concerns that other harsh demands in the U.S.–British draft resolution leave Saddam little room to save face and avoid war.

One of the strongest arguments for a militarily supported inspection plan is that it doesn't threaten Saddam with extinction, a threat that could push him to fight back with the very weapons we're seeking to destroy. If disarmament is the goal, Saddam can be made to understand that only his arsenal is at stake, not his survival.

Our message to Saddam can be simple: "You are going to lose your weapons-of-mass-destruction capability either through the inspections or through a sustained cruise-missile assault on the 700 suspicious sites the United Nations has already identified. If you rebuild them, we will attack again. And if you use weapons of mass destruction or attack another country in the region, we will destroy you and your regime." The decision to live or die then becomes his to make.

The ultimate lesson of the gulf war may be that when offered the choice, Saddam will sacrifice almost everything before sacrificing his own life or grip on power.

JOSEPH WILSON *was deputy chief of mission at the U.S. Embassy in Baghdad from 1988 to 1991. He also served as special assistant to President Clinton at the National Security Council and as ambassador to Gabon. He wrote this article for* Perspective.

* * *

Los Angeles Times, February 6, 2003
A 'BIG CAT' WITH NOTHING TO LOSE
Leaving Hussein no hope will trigger his worst weapons, U.S. envoy in historic '90 meeting warns
By Joseph C. Wilson

SADDAM HUSSEIN IS a murderous sociopath whose departure from this Earth would be welcomed everywhere.

I met with Hussein for the last time in a heavily curtained room in the Foreign Ministry late in the morning of Aug. 6, 1990, four days after his invasion of Kuwait. As the senior diplomat in charge of the U.S. Embassy in Baghdad at the time, it was my responsibility to tell him to get out of Kuwait and to let the several thousand Americans, including 150 so-called "human shields," leave the region.

I knew from previous meetings that he always stacked the deck to give himself every advantage, and this session was no different.

I was accompanied by a single embassy note taker, while Hussein had eight senior foreign policy officials with him. But only Tarik Aziz, then the foreign minister, dared speak in his presence. The others were as silent as furniture.

Hussein joined me in the middle of the room with the Iraqi news cameras whirring. Typically, when it came time to shake hands, he deliberately held his low so that to take it I would have to lean over. The cameras would then capture for posterity that his visitor had bowed to the potentate. I kept my back straight.

Later in the meeting, when he turned to others in the room to elicit a reaction, the discomfort was palpable. At one point, he made a move to his ever-present gun. My immediate thought was that I had said the wrong thing. To my relief he took it off, telling me that it hurt his back when he sat. I looked at his people, who were also on edge, watching his every move. He reminded me of a big cat at a watering hole, with the zebra and antelope wondering whether he is there to drink or to eat.

During our session—the last he had with any American official before the war—I listened as he offered his deal through a translator: In exchange for keeping Kuwait, he would give the U.S. oil at a good price and would not invade Saudi Arabia. In a matter-of-fact manner, he dismissed the Kuwaiti government as "history" and scoffed at President Bush's condemnation of him.

He mocked American will and courage, telling me that my country would run rather than face the prospect of spilling the blood of our soldiers in the Arabian Desert.

I was never prouder than when the American response was to confront Hussein and ultimately force him from Kuwait.

Desert Storm was a just war, sanctioned by the international community and supported by a broad multilateral coalition. Today we are on the verge of another conflict with Iraq, but unlike Desert Storm, the goals are not clear—despite Secretary of State Colin Powell's eloquent argument for war in his address Wednesday to the United Nations Security Council.

Is it a war to liberate the people of Iraq, oppressed all these years? Is it a battle in the war on terrorism? Or is it, as President Bush often says, all about disarmament?

Clarity matters, because our goals will determine how Hussein reacts.

By all indications, Hussein is clear in his own mind about our intentions: He believes we are going to war to kill him, whether he disarms or not.

This is a major problem for us. My judgment was—and is—that only power will make him yield, but there also has to be some incentive for him to comply.

During the Gulf War, we were always acutely aware of the need to be confrontational on the issues at hand but to leave Hussein, a proud and vain man, a way to save face.

When he released the women and children hostages, Hussein initially threatened to keep dual Kuwaiti-American citizens. I told his underling that unless all Americans were put on the evacuation flight within half an hour, I would inform the American TV networks that Hussein had again reneged on his promises and was toying with the lives of children.

Hussein relented, and our official statements acknowledged Iraqi cooperation.

There is now no incentive for Hussein to comply with the inspectors or to refrain from using weapons of mass destruction to defend himself if the United States comes after him.

And he will use them; we should be under no illusion about that.

Hussein and Aziz both told me directly that Iraq reserved the right to use every weapon in its arsenal if invaded, just as it had against Iran and later the Kurds.

The fact that thousands of men, women and children had died in these attacks fazed them not one bit. In fact, Aziz could barely be bothered to stop puffing on his Cuban cigar as he made these comments, of so little importance was the use of chemicals to kill people.

It is probably too late to change Hussein's assessment, and that will make any ensuing battle for Iraq that much more dangerous for our troops and for the Iraqis who find themselves in the battlefield.

The assertion that Hussein might share weapons of mass destruction with a terrorist group, however, is counterintuitive to everything I and others know about him. The Iraqi leader is above all a consummate survivalist.

He acts as if he expects the people around him to die for him, but he has long known that every terrorist act, and particularly a sophisticated one, raises the question of his involvement and invites blame. He has nothing to gain and everything to lose. In his mind he is Iraq, Iraq is Hussein, and as long as he survives, Iraq survives.

After then-Secretary of State Jim Baker made it clear to Aziz on the eve of the Gulf War that the United States would destroy Iraq if weapons of mass destruction were used, Hussein did not use them. He is not stupid, and for him living is better than dying in vain.

Now, however, if he feels his death is inevitable, he may well arm extremist groups in an attempt to have a last, posthumous laugh.

Along with our drive toward war, it should also be made clear to Hussein that—in the little time remaining—he still has a choice.

We should do everything possible to avoid the understandable temptation to send American troops to fight a war of "liberation" that can be waged only by the Iraqis themselves. The projection of power need not equate with the projection of force.

JOSEPH C. WILSON, *chief of mission at the U.S. Embassy in Baghdad from 1988 to 1991 and acting ambassador during Operation Desert Shield, is an adjunct scholar at the Middle East Institute in Washington.*

* * *

The Nation, March 3, 2003
REPUBLIC OR EMPIRE?
by Joseph Wilson

AS THE SENIOR American diplomat in Baghdad during Desert Shield, I advocated a muscular U.S. response to Saddam's brutal annexation of Kuwait in flagrant violation of the United Nations charter. Only the credible threat of force could hope to reverse his invasion. Our in-your-face strategy secured the release of the 150 American "human shields"—hostages—but ultimately it took war to drive Iraq from Kuwait. I was disconsolate at the failure of diplomacy, but Desert Storm was necessitated by Saddam's intransigence, it was sanctioned by the U.N. and it was conducted with a broad international military coalition. The goal was explicit and focused; war was the last resort.

The upcoming military operation also has one objective, though different from the several offered by the Bush Administration. This war is not about weapons of mass destruction. The intrusive inspections are disrupting Saddam's programs, as even the Administration has acknowledged. Nor is it about terrorism. Virtually all agree war will spawn more terrorism, not less. It is not even about liberation of an oppressed people. Killing innocent Iraqi civilians in a full frontal assault is hardly the only or best way to liberate a people. The underlying objective of this war is the imposition of a Pax Americana on the region and installation of vassal regimes that will control restive populations.

Without the firing of a single cruise missile, the Administration has already established a massive footprint in the Gulf and Southwest Asia from which to project power. U.S. generals, admirals and diplomats have crisscrossed the region like modern-day proconsuls, cajoling fragile governments to permit American access and operations from their territories.

Bases have been established as stepping stones to Afghanistan and Iraq, but also as tripwires in countries that fear their neighbors. Northern Kuwait has been ceded to American forces and a significant military presence established in Bahrain, Saudi Arabia, Qatar, the United Arab Emirates and Oman. The over-the-horizon posture of a decade ago has given way to boots on the ground and forward command headquarters. Nations in the region, having contracted with the United States for their security umbrella, will now listen when Washington tells them to tailor policies and curb anti-Western dissent. Hegemony in the Arab nations of the Gulf has been achieved.

Meanwhile, Saddam might well squirm, but even without an invasion, he's finished. He is surrounded, foreigners are swarming through his palaces, and as Colin Powell so compellingly showed at the U.N., we are watching and we are listening. International will to disarm Iraq will not wane as it did in the 1990s, for the simple reason that George W. Bush keeps challenging the organization to remain relevant by keeping pressure on Saddam. Nations that worry that, as John le Carré puts it, "America has entered one of its periods of historical madness" will not want to jettison the one institution that, absent a competing military power, might constrain U.S. ambition.

Then what's the point of this new American imperialism? The neoconservatives with a stranglehold on the foreign policy of the Republican Party, a party that traditionally eschewed foreign military adventures, want to go beyond expanding U.S. global influence to force revolutionary change on the region. American pre-eminence in the Gulf is necessary but not sufficient for the hawks. Nothing short of conquest, occupation and imposition of handpicked leaders on a vanquished population will suffice. Iraq is the linchpin for this broader assault on the region. The new imperialists will not rest until governments that ape our worldview are implanted throughout the region, a breathtakingly ambitious undertaking, smacking of hubris in the extreme. Arabs who complain about American-supported antidemocratic regimes today will find us in even more direct control tomorrow. The leader of the future in the Arab world will look a lot more like Pakistan's Pervez Musharraf than Thomas Jefferson.

There is a huge risk of overreach in this tack. The projection of influence and power through the use of force will breed resistance in the Arab world that will sorely test our political will and stamina. Passion for independence is as great in the Arab world as it is elsewhere. The hawks compare this mission to Japan and Germany after World War II. It could easily look like Lebanon, Somalia and Northern Ireland instead.

Our global leadership will be undermined as fear gives way to resentment and strategies to weaken our stranglehold. American businessmen already complain about hostility when overseas, and Arabs speak openly of boycotting American products. Foreign capital is fleeing American stocks and bonds; the United States is no longer a friendly destination for international investors. For a borrow-and-spend Administration, as this one is, the effects on our economic growth will be felt for a long time to come. Essential trust has been seriously damaged and will be difficult to repair.

Even in the unlikely event that war does not come to pass, the would-be imperialists have achieved much of what they sought, some of it good. It is encouraging that the international community is looking hard at terrorism and the proliferation of weapons of mass destruction. But the upcoming battle for Baghdad and the lengthy occupation of Iraq will utterly undermine any steps forward. And with the costs to our military, our treasury and our international standing, we will be forced to learn whether our republican roots and traditions can accommodate the Administration's imperial ambitions. It may be a bitter lesson.

* * *

San Jose Mercury News, April 6, 2003
IRAQ MAY SEE U.S. AS LATEST IN LINE OF CONQUERORS
by Joseph Wilson

WEDNESDAY, U.S. FORCES in An-Najaf were treated to what one officer called a "Macy's Day parade" by several thousand residents happy to see them advancing through the city. But that was the first such celebration in a war the administration said would be fast and easy, partly because Iraqis would welcome U.S. troops as liberators.

There have been plenty of indications that not everyone is as pleased as the revelers in An-Najaf to see U.S. forces. Soldiers have met rather intense resistance by irregulars—and in many places where U.S. troops have prevailed, the populations have been wary of their presence. Even in An-Najaf, the celebration was halted temporarily when a car with men hanging out the windows and pointing AK-47s sped toward the troops.

In short, the picture of how Iraqis feel about this war is anything but simple.

Perhaps in the end, the administration will be proven right. But if U.S. leaders have underestimated the power of nationalism in Iraq, the lack of a liberation "bounce" will vastly complicate not just the war, but also the much more complex and difficult peace.

Having been convinced by exile groups and opposition leaders with their own pro-war agenda that Iraq would fall "like a house of cards," the Bush administration might instead face a population that is far more ungrateful for our efforts than some accuse the French of being for the Allied liberation of France in World War II.

If the level of resentment is high, U.S. troops who occupy the country, maybe for years to come, could face guerrilla warfare or terrorist attacks. It might also undermine one of the administration's reasons for going to war: to establish a democracy in Iraq that would create a domino effect in a region populated with authoritarian rulers. It will not be easy to build that model democracy if a large part of the Iraqi population is hostile, or just sullen.

Even if the Iraqis are thrilled at the overthrow of Saddam Hussein, that jubilation could wane quickly as the United States passes from the role of liberator to occupier. The Iraqis are a proud people steeped in their history and their contributions to civilization. They remember their conquering heroes Saladin and Nebuchadnezzar as if their reigns were yesterday, rather than centuries before our own George Washington.

And the Iraqis have been difficult vassals in the past. Ottoman dictionaries, from the time when the Turks ruled what is now Iraq, reportedly defined arrogance as "walk like a Baghdadi." And the British—who took over from the Turks after World War I—soon moved to install a Hashemite king to act as their agent during their colonial rule. Direct rule had been too difficult and costly.

So the vital question is this: Will a people free of outside control for less than a century, after several centuries of domination, live with an occupation, even if it is temporary?

WHAT IRAQIS FEAR

It's not clear yet whether most Iraqis will welcome Americans in what they see as their initial role, as liberators. Some American commentators and government officials have explained away the relative silence from the Iraqi population as temporary. They suggested that Iraqis are so frightened of Saddam—and a possible repeat of his crackdown of rebellions in 1991—that the celebrations will begin only when his head is paraded on a pike.

Of course Iraqis are afraid. Saddam has always ruled by fear, and terror is the key weapon in his arsenal to keep people in check, and to discourage dissent. In my years as a diplomat in Baghdad, just before the Persian Gulf War, Iraqis simply would not talk about the government or Saddam, other than to utter ritualistic praises about his enlightened rule and popularity.

There were at least seven intelligence agencies, several of which spied on the others. Every neighborhood had its government agents to watch and report on neighbors. Nobody was exempt from government prying.

One professor friend of mine recounted how he had entertained a senior government official at dinner. The next day, my friend and his wife were summoned to the local security headquarters for interrogation about what was discussed and what the official had said. Paranoia is entrenched at all levels of society. Torture, arbitrary executions and disappearances reinforced the reign of terror.

Still, fear of Saddam and his thugs may not be the only reason Iraqis are less than jubilant about their pending liberation. A long history of having conquered and being conquered has left the Iraqis jaded, cynical and suspicious of foreigners' stated goals.

They joined the fight against the Ottomans in the first world war, alongside the British, only to have their national ambitions betrayed and their historic borders carved up to maximize British political and economic interests, including the hiving off of Kuwait as a separate emirate. At the time, the British claimed they knew what was best for the Iraqis: a jodhpurs-and-pith-helmet colonial rule.

The Iran–Iraq war, so often portrayed as an example of Saddam's wanton aggression, was viewed by most Iraqis as a decadelong sacrifice to keep out possible new conquerors, in that case the Persians. Virtually all Iraqi families lost loved ones in that brutal conflict fought with equal courage by the Shiites and the Sunnis. The Shiites, for all their justifiable grievances against Sunni rule, proved themselves in that war to be Iraqis first in the face of an external enemy, and opponents of Saddam second.

Suspicions raised

Given that history, Iraqis may well be skeptical that liberation is the objective of the U.S. invasion. Once Saddam is gone and we remain, they may well see us as only the latest in a long line of conquerors with designs on their land.

When I worked in Iraq in the late 1980s and early '90s, one of the common themes in conversations from the bazaar to the ministries was that self-interest is the motivating factor in the policies of all governments. The United States supported Saddam during the Iran–Iraq war because it was in its self-interest to do so, not because it was being altruistic. The United States gave the Iranians weapons in the same war because it was in its self-interest to do so.

"Why should we believe you are motivated by other than self-interest now?" my Iraqi friends would ask after that war.

There is even more recent history that has stirred bitterness. For the past 12 years, Iraqis have suffered from debilitating economic sanctions, first put into place by the United States and subsequently by the United Nations. The goal was initially to pressure Saddam to withdraw from Kuwait, and later to force disarmament of weapons of mass destruction.

Those who supported the sanctions saw them as a way to avoid war, but the Iraqis didn't necessarily agree they were being spared suffering—especially as the policy dragged on without a foreseeable end.

It is not an accident that gold jewelry in Baghdad's Khadamiya market is cheaper than anywhere else in the world. In Iraqi society, heirlooms are passed from generation to generation; gold is not just bangles and accessories, but serves as families' savings accounts. The sanctions have forced many families to liquidate those accounts to put food on the table.

SADDAM'S WAGER

Iraqis have been told for years that the Americans are responsible for the destruction of the personal wealth of the nation. Consequently, the hatred of Saddam, which is widespread after 30 years of tyranny, does not necessarily translate into affection for or even trust of those who have reduced them to such dire straits.

Saddam's endgame wager this time is the same as during the 1991 gulf war, even as his strategy and tactics have changed. When I met with him on Aug. 6, 1990, four days after his invasion of Kuwait, he told me he did not believe that the United States had the political will or the tenacity to either accept the deaths of 10,000 soldiers in the Arabian desert—or to remain there as long as it would take to defeat his forces.

In that war, he made the mistake of leaving his troops exposed in the desert where U.S. forces could pick them off at will—as they did, without exposing themselves to the prospect of high casualties. This time, he has taken a page out of the Stalin handbook, drawing American forces deep into the country, stretching their supply lines and trying to force them into urban killing fields. His idea is surely to kill or injure enough Americans so that we will go away.

If he cannot hurt the United States militarily, the alternative is to hold out long enough so that the war of attrition in Baghdad wears away the political support for the war, and turns the Muslim world so against Americans that international opposition will be impossible to ignore.

To succeed, Saddam needs his people's support, as well as popular support in the Arab world.

Unlikely to survive

It is unlikely Saddam will survive as leader of Iraq in any case. But it's also not yet clear—and may not be clear for a long time—whether the United States will score the full victory it says it wants. A military win is one thing. But to bring democracy to Iraq—and to avoid a disastrous long-term struggle with its Arab neighbors—the United States will need to win the battle for people's hearts and minds.

So far, we have lost that battle in the greater Muslim world. The leaders of many neighboring countries were willing to go along with the war, but many of their fellow citizens do not agree with the war. Some Arabs are even willing to join Saddam in battle. Newspapers last week reported that hundreds of men from across the Arab world were trying to get to Baghdad to fight coalition troops.

We are likely to lose more support during the battle for Baghdad if it is as bloody as some predict. The juxtaposition of Baghdad burning under American air assault with photos of two Iraqi peasants who say they shot down Apache helicopters leaves the impression that this is a war not to liberate but to conquer, a realization of Arabs' worst nightmares.

There are ways to ameliorate those fears, and perhaps even begin to regain some trust. One way would be to make the rebuilding of Iraq's institutions a truly international project involving a significant role for the United Nations, our estranged allies, and even Iraq's neighbors, including Syria and Iran. Only by having everybody involved in a positive way can we hope to avoid attempts to undermine our efforts.

The other way to generate good will would be to quickly reinvigorate the peace process between Israelis and the Palestinians, acknowledging that this is an issue of vital concern among many Arabs.

We should be under no illusions; the road to democracy will be long and tough. Iraqis of all stripes will quickly learn to speak to their American occupiers in the mellifluous tones of democracy.

But the real game will be, as it has long been, about power—who has it, how to get it and how to use it for the benefit of family, clan, tribe and religion. Brokering deals among these competing interests will take all of our ingenuity and acumen.

* * *

The New York Times, July 6, 2003
WHAT I DIDN'T FIND IN AFRICA
by Joseph C. Wilson 4th

DID THE BUSH administration manipulate intelligence about Saddam Hussein's weapons programs to justify an invasion of Iraq?

Based on my experience with the administration in the months leading up to the war, I have little choice but to conclude that some of the intelligence related to Iraq's nuclear weapons program was twisted to exaggerate the Iraqi threat.

For 23 years, from 1976 to 1998, I was a career foreign service officer and ambassador. In 1990, as chargé d'affaires in Baghdad, I was the last American diplomat to meet with Saddam Hussein. (I was also a forceful advocate for his removal from Kuwait.) After Iraq, I was President George H. W.

Bush's ambassador to Gabon and São Tomé and Príncipe; under President Bill Clinton, I helped direct Africa policy for the National Security Council.

It was my experience in Africa that led me to play a small role in the effort to verify information about Africa's suspected link to Iraq's nonconventional weapons programs. Those news stories about that unnamed former envoy who went to Niger? That's me.

In February 2002, I was informed by officials at the Central Intelligence Agency that Vice President Dick Cheney's office had questions about a particular intelligence report. While I never saw the report, I was told that it referred to a memorandum of agreement that documented the sale of uranium yellowcake—a form of lightly processed ore—by Niger to Iraq in the late 1990's. The agency officials asked if I would travel to Niger to check out the story so they could provide a response to the vice president's office.

After consulting with the State Department's African Affairs Bureau (and through it with Barbro Owens-Kirkpatrick, the United States ambassador to Niger), I agreed to make the trip. The mission I undertook was discreet but by no means secret. While the CIA paid my expenses (my time was offered pro bono), I made it abundantly clear to everyone I met that I was acting on behalf of the United States government.

In late February 2002, I arrived in Niger's capital, Niamey, where I had been a diplomat in the mid-70's and visited as a National Security Council official in the late 90's. The city was much as I remembered it. Seasonal winds had clogged the air with dust and sand. Through the haze, I could see camel caravans crossing the Niger River (over the John F. Kennedy bridge), the setting sun behind them. Most people had wrapped scarves around their faces to protect against the grit, leaving only their eyes visible.

The next morning, I met with Ambassador Owens-Kirkpatrick at the embassy. For reasons that are understandable, the embassy staff has always kept a close eye on Niger's uranium business. I was not surprised, then, when the ambassador told me that she knew about the allegations of uranium sales to Iraq—and that she felt she had already debunked them in her reports to Washington. Nevertheless, she and I agreed that my time would be best spent interviewing people who had been in government when the deal supposedly took place, which was before her arrival.

I spent the next eight days drinking sweet mint tea and meeting with dozens of people: current government officials, former government officials, people associated with the country's uranium business. It did not take long to conclude that it was highly doubtful that any such transaction had ever taken place.

Given the structure of the consortiums that operated the mines, it would be exceedingly difficult for Niger to transfer uranium to Iraq. Niger's uranium business consists of two mines, Somair and Cominak, which are run by French, Spanish, Japanese, German and Nigerian interests. If the government wanted to remove uranium from a mine, it would have to notify the consortium, which in turn is strictly monitored by the International Atomic Energy Agency. Moreover, because the two mines are closely regulated, quasi-governmental entities, selling uranium would require the approval of the minister of mines, the prime minister and probably the president. In short, there's simply too much oversight over too small an industry for a sale to have transpired.

(As for the actual memorandum, I never saw it. But news accounts have pointed out that the documents had glaring errors—they were signed, for example, by officials who were no longer in government—and were probably forged. And then there's the fact that Niger formally denied the charges.)

Before I left Niger, I briefed the ambassador on my findings, which were consistent with her own. I also shared my conclusions with members of her staff. In early March, I arrived in Washington and promptly provided a detailed briefing to the CIA. I later shared my conclusions with the State Department African Affairs Bureau. There was nothing secret or earth-shattering in my report, just as there was nothing secret about my trip.

Though I did not file a written report, there should be at least four documents in United States government archives confirming my mission. The documents should include the ambassador's report of my debriefing in Niamey, a separate report written by the embassy staff, a CIA report summing up my trip, and a specific answer from the agency to the office of the vice president (this may have been delivered orally). While I have not seen any of these reports, I have spent enough time in government to know that this is standard operating procedure.

I thought the Niger matter was settled and went back to my life. (I did take part in the Iraq debate, arguing that a strict containment regime backed by the threat of force was preferable to an invasion.) In September 2002, however, Niger re-emerged. The British government published a "white paper" asserting that Saddam Hussein and his unconventional arms posed an immediate danger. As evidence, the report cited Iraq's attempts to purchase uranium from an African country.

Then, in January, President Bush, citing the British dossier, repeated the charges about Iraqi efforts to buy uranium from Africa.

The next day, I reminded a friend at the State Department of my trip and suggested that if the president had been referring to Niger, then his conclusion was not borne out by the facts as I understood them. He replied that perhaps the president was speaking about one of the other three African countries that produce uranium: Gabon, South Africa or Namibia. At the time, I accepted the explanation. I didn't know that in December, a month before the president's address, the State Department had published a fact sheet that mentioned the Niger case.

Those are the facts surrounding my efforts. The vice president's office asked a serious question. I was asked to help formulate the answer. I did so, and I have every confidence that the answer I provided was circulated to the appropriate officials within our government.

The question now is how that answer was or was not used by our political leadership. If my information was deemed inaccurate, I understand (though I would be very interested to know why). If, however, the information was ignored because it did not fit certain preconceptions about Iraq, then a legitimate argument can be made that we went to war under false pretenses. (It's worth remembering that in his March "Meet the Press" appearance, Mr. Cheney said that Saddam Hussein was "trying once again to produce nuclear weapons.") At a minimum, Congress, which authorized the use of military force at the president's behest, should want to know if the assertions about Iraq were warranted.

I was convinced before the war that the threat of weapons of mass destruction in the hands of Saddam Hussein required a vigorous and sustained international response to disarm him. Iraq possessed and had used chemical weapons; it had an active biological weapons program and quite possibly a nuclear research program—all of which were in violation of United Nations resolutions. Having encountered Mr. Hussein and his thugs in the run-up to the Persian Gulf war of 1991, I was only too aware of the dangers he posed.

But were these dangers the same ones the administration told us about? We have to find out. America's foreign policy depends on the sanctity of its information. For this reason, questioning the selective use of intelligence to justify the war in Iraq is neither idle sniping nor "revisionist history," as Mr. Bush has suggested. The act of war is the last option of a democracy, taken when there is a grave threat to our national security. More than 200 American soldiers have lost their lives in Iraq already. We have a duty to ensure that their sacrifice came for the right reasons.

* * *

San Jose Mercury News, September 14, 2003
EX-U.S. DIPLOMAT SAYS WHITE HOUSE IS IN FULL
RETREAT FROM IRAQ REALITY
Seeking honesty in U.S. policy
by Joseph Wilson

DURING THE GULF war in 1991, when I was in charge of the American Embassy in Baghdad, I placed a copy of Lewis Carroll's "Alice in Wonderland" on my office coffee table. I thought it conveyed far better than words ever could the weird world that was Iraq at that time, a world in which nothing was what it seemed: The several hundred Western hostages Saddam Hussein took during Desert Shield were not really hostages but "guests." Kuwait was not invaded, but "liberated."

It is clearly time to dust the book off and again display it prominently, only this time because our own government has dragged the country down a rabbit hole, all the while trying to convince the American people that life in newly liberated Iraq is not as distorted as it seems.

It is returning to normal, we are assured, even as we are asked to ante up an additional $75 billion and pressure builds to send more troops and extend the tours of duty of those who are there. Deputy Defense Secretary Paul Wolfowitz tells Congress that all we need is to project a little confidence. The Mad Hatter could not have said it better.

President Bush's speech last Sunday was just the latest example of the administration's concerted efforts to misrepresent reality—and rewrite history—to mask its mistakes. The president said Iraq is now the center of our battle against terrorism. But we did not go to Iraq to fight Al-Qaida, which remains perhaps our deadliest foe, and we will not defeat it there.

By trying to justify the current fight in Iraq as a fight against terrorism, the administration has done two frightening things. It has tried to divert attention from Osama bin Laden, the man responsible for the wave of terrorist attacks against American interests from New York and Washington to Yemen, and who reappeared in rugged terrain in a video broadcast last week. And the policy advanced by the speech is a major step toward creating a dangerous, self-fulfilling prophecy and reflects a fundamental misunderstanding of the facts on the ground.

This is an insurgency we're fighting in Iraq. Our 130,000 soldiers in Iraq now confront an angry but not yet defeated Sunni Muslim population who, although a minority in Iraq, had been in power for a century. We are now also beginning to face terrorists there, but it is our own doing. Our attack on Iraq— and our bungling of the peace—led to the guerrilla insurgency that is drawing jihadists from around the Muslim world. The "shock and awe" campaign so vividly shown on our television screens has galvanized historic Arab envy, jealousy and resentment of the United States into white-hot hatred of America.

Where once there were thousands, now there are potentially millions of terrorists and sympathizers who will be drawn into this campaign.

We've seen other examples of the kind of insurgency we're now facing. One was in Afghanistan against the Soviets in the 1980s, and we all should know the end of that story by now. Bin Laden was one of the outside jihadists drawn into that battle; he emerged as the head of a group of hardened soldiers he called Al-Qaida.

It is perhaps not surprising that the administration is trying to redefine why we went to Iraq, because we have accomplished so little of what we set out to do—and severely underestimated the commitment it would take to deal with the aftermath of war.

The president told us in his seminal speech in Cincinnati in October 2002 that Iraq "possesses and produces chemical and biological weapons . . . is seeking nuclear weapons . . . has given shelter and support to terrorism, and practices terror against its own people."

He dismissed the concerns raised by critics of his approach as follows: "Some worry that a change of leadership in Iraq could create instability and make the situation worse. The situation could hardly get worse, for world security and for the people of Iraq. The lives of Iraqi citizens would improve dramatically if Saddam Hussein were no longer in power."

Now we know that even if we find chemical or biological weapons, the threat that they posed to our national security was, to be charitable, exaggerated.

It all but disappeared from the president's speech last week and Defense Secretary Donald Rumsfeld, one of the leading proponents of the threat, now tells us that he didn't even ask the chief weapons-of-mass-destruction sleuth in Iraq, David Kay, for a status report during his recent trip to Baghdad, relegating such weapons to the same dark corner as bin Laden, whose name rarely passes the lips of our leaders these days.

Indeed, in the most telling revision of the justification for going to war, the State Department's undersecretary for arms control, John Bolton, recently said that whether Saddam's government actually possessed weapons of mass destruction "isn't really the issue. The issue, I think, has been the capability that Iraq sought to have . . . WMD programs."

In other words, we're now supposed to believe that we went to war not because Saddam's arsenal of weapons of mass destruction threatened us, but because he had scientists on his payroll.

And the cakewalk post-war scenario that had been painted by some in the administration is anything but. More Americans have died since the president announced the end of major combat operations than during the war itself. The cost runs $1 billion per week in military support alone, and some experts say our deployment is already affecting future military preparedness.

Iraqis live in chaotic conditions as crime flourishes in the unpatrolled streets and family squabbles are settled vigilante style; basic services such as electricity remain unavailable to large segments of the urban population.

The truth is, the administration has never leveled with the American people on the war with Iraq.

It is true that many people outside the administration, including me and many leading Democrats, thought Saddam had residual stocks of weapons of mass destruction; disarmament was a legitimate international objective supported unanimously by the United Nations Security Council. But we did not need to rush to war before exploring other, less risky options.

Invasion, conquest and occupation was always the highest-risk, lowest-reward choice. The intrusive U.N. inspections were disrupting Saddam's programs and weakening him in the eyes of his key supporters, including in the Iraqi military. That would explain why the United States, according to reports, was able to thoroughly infiltrate the army before the onset of hostilities and obtain commitments from Iraqi generals to send their troops home rather than have them fight.

The administration short-circuited the discussion of whether war was necessary because some of its most powerful members felt it was the best option—ostensibly because they had deluded themselves into believing that they could easily impose flowering democracies on the region.

A more cynical reading of the agenda of certain Bush advisers could conclude that the Balkanization of Iraq was always an acceptable outcome, because Israel would then find itself surrounded by small Arab countries worried about each other instead of forming a solid block against Israel. After all, Iraq was an artificial country that had always had a troublesome history.

One way the administration stopped the debate was to oversell its intelligence. I know, because I was in the middle of the efforts to determine whether Iraq had attempted to purchase uranium "yellowcake"—a form of lightly processed ore—from Africa.

At the request of the administration I traveled to the West African nation of Niger in February 2002 to check out the allegation. I reported that such a sale was highly unlikely, but my conclusions—as well as the same conclusions from our ambassador on the scene and from a four-star Marine Corps general—were ignored by the White House.

Instead, the president relied upon an unsubstantiated reference in a British white paper to underpin his argument in the State of the Union address that Saddam was reconstituting his nuclear weapons programs. How many times did we hear the president, vice president and others speak of the looming threat of an Iraqi mushroom cloud?

Until several months ago, when it came out that the country was Niger, I assumed that the president had been referring to another African country. After I learned, belatedly to be sure, I came forward to insist that the administration correct the misstatements of fact. But the damage had already been done.

The overblown rhetoric about nuclear weapons inspired fear and drowned out the many warnings that invasion would create its own formidable dangers.

Middle East experts warned over and over again that Iraq's many religious and ethnic factions could start battling each other in a bloody struggle for power. Former British foreign secretary Douglas Hurd fretted that we would unleash a terrorist-recruiting bonanza, and former U.S. national security adviser Brent Scowcroft warned of a security meltdown in the region.

The U.S. army's top general at the time, Eric Shinseki, meanwhile, questioned the cakewalk scenario. He told Congress that we would need several hundred thousand soldiers in Iraq to put an end to the violence against our troops and against each other. His testimony was quickly repudiated by both Rumsfeld and Wolfowitz.

As we now know, he was close to the mark. Our 130,000 soldiers are failing to stem the violence. Even as Rumsfeld says jauntily that all is going well, Secretary of State Colin Powell is running to the United Nations to try to get more foreign boots on the ground. One of the administration's staunchest supporters, British Foreign Secretary Jack Straw, says ominously that we risk strategic failure if we don't send reinforcements.

And the infighting that Middle East experts feared could still erupt. The majority Shiite Muslim population, brutalized during Saddam's rule, is content with a tactical truce with our forces so long as they are free to consolidate their control and the United States continues to kill Sunni Muslims so that they don't have to. That truce is threatened not only by Shiite political ambition but also by ongoing skirmishes with the Sunnis.

The recent car bomb at the An-Najaf mosque that killed one of Shiite Islam's most influential clerics and head of the largest Shiite party in Iraq almost resulted in the outbreak of civil war between the two groups. Widespread belief that Sunni elements were behind the assassination and that the United States failed in its responsibilities for security has brought Shiite armed militias back onto the streets, actively seeking to avenge the death of their leader. Such a war within a war would make our occupation infinitely more dangerous.

Some now argue that the president's speech Sunday represents a change of course. Even if the administration won't admit it made any mistakes, the mere call for international involvement should be enough to persuade the world to accept the burden of assisting us, as we continue to control both the military and the economic reconstruction.

That may well be true, but we cannot count on the international community to do our bidding blindly. While the administration scurries back to the United Nations for help, our historic friends and allies still smart from the gratuitous insults hurled at them nine months ago. This is the same United Nations which Richard Perle, a not-so-invisible hand behind the war, recently called an "abject failure."

As Zbigniew Brzezinski, who was President Carter's national security adviser, has pointed out, at a time when our military might is at its zenith, our political and moral authority is at its lowest ebb. Essential trust has been broken, and it will take time to repair. At a minimum, we need to jettison the hubris that has driven this policy, the pretensions of moral rectitude that mask a jodhpurs-and-pith-helmet imperialism that cannot succeed.

In the meantime, we must demonstrate that we understand that more than military might is required to tame the anger in the region. This includes both the internationalization of the reconstruction effort and the redoubling of efforts to ease tensions on the Israeli–Palestinian front.

That is the thorn that must be pulled from the side of the region. The road to peace in the Middle East still goes through Jerusalem.

But before we can hope to win back international trust or start down a truly new path in Iraq, the administration has to start playing it straight, with the American people and with the world. Recent administration statements, including the president's speech, suggest that it still prefers to live in a fantasy world.

Bibliography

BOOKS

al-Khalil, Samir. *Republic of Fear: The Inside Story of Saddam's Iraq.* New York: Century Hutchinson, 1989.

Baker, James A., with Thomas M. DeFrank. *The Politics of Diplomacy: Revolution, War, and Peace, 1989–1992.* New York: Putnam, 1995.

Bush, George H. W., and Brent Scowcroft. *A World Transformed.* New York: Knopf, 1998.

Cleland, Max. *Strong at the Broken Places.* (Updated edition). New York: Longstreet Press, 2000.

Crocker, Chester A. *High Noon in Southern Africa: Making Peace in a Rough Neighborhood.* New York: W. W. Norton, 1992.

Culbertson, Roberta, and W. Nathaniel Howell. *Siege: Crisis Leadership: The Survival of U.S. Embassy Kuwait.* Charlottesville: Virginia Foundation for the Humanities, 2001.

Freedman, Lawrence, and Efraim Karsh. *The Gulf Conflict, 1990–1991: Diplomacy and War in the New World Order.* Princeton: Princeton University Press, 1993.

Hare, Paul J. *Angola's Last Best Chance for Peace: An Insider's Account of the Peace Process.* Washington: United States Institute of Peace Press, 1998.

Hochschild, Adam. *King Leopold's Ghost: A Story of Greed, Terror, and Heroism in Colonial Africa.* Boston: Houghton Mifflin, 1998.

Jackson, Steve. *Lucky Lady: The World War II Heroics of the USS* Santa Fe *and* Franklin. New York: Carroll & Graf, 2003.

Jentleson, Bruce. *With Friends Like These: Reagan, Bush, and Saddam, 1982–1990.* New York: W. W. Norton, 1994.

Pakenham, Thomas. *The Scramble for Africa, 1876–1912.* New York: Random House, 1991.

Pollack, Kenneth M. *The Threatening Storm: The Case for Invading Iraq.* New York: Random House, 2002.

Powell, Colin L., with Joseph E. Persico. *My American Journey.* New York: Ballantine, 2003.

Prendergast, John. *Crisis Response. Humanitarian Band-Aids in Sudan and Somalia.* London and Chicago: Pluto Press, 1997.

_____. *Front-Line Diplomacy: Humanitarian Aid and Conflict in Africa.* Boulder: L. Rienner, 1996.

Rather, Dan with Mickey Herskowitz. *The Camera Never Blinks Twice: The Further Adventures of a Television Journalist.* New York: William Morrow, 1994.

Record, Jeffrey. *Bounding the Global War on Terrorism.* Army War College, 2004.

Sciolino, Elaine. *The Outlaw State: Saddam Hussein's Quest for Power and the Gulf Crisis.* New York: Wiley, 1991.

Suskind, Ron. *The Price of Loyalty: George W. Bush, the White House, and the Education of Paul O'Neill.* New York: Simon & Schuster, 2004.

U.S. News & World Report. *Triumph Without Victory: The Unreported History of the Persian Gulf War.* New York: Times Books, 1992.

Wiener, Robert. *Live From Baghdad: Gathering News at Ground Zero.* New York: Doubleday, 1992.

Woodward, Bob. *Bush at War.* New York: Simon & Schuster, 2002.

Miscellaneous Sources

Foreign Affairs Oral History Project. Interview with Ambassador Joseph C. Wilson, conducted by Charles Stuart Kennedy, January 8, 2001. Arlington, Virginia: Association for Diplomatic Studies and Training, 2002.

The Fertel Foundation and The Nation Institute. *The Ron Ridenhour Awards: Fostering the Spirit of Courage and Truth* (program booklet). The Ron Ridenhour Prize for Truth-Telling: Joseph Wilson; The Ron Ridenhour Book Prize: Deborah Scroggins; and The Ron Ridenhour Courage Award for Lifetime Achievement: Daniel Ellsberg. October 15, 2003, National Press Club, Washington, D.C.

Newspaper, Magazine, and Internet Articles

Jan. 26, 1998. Letter to President Clinton on removing Saddam Hussein from power in Iraq, signed by Elliott Abrams, Richard L. Armitage. William J. Bennett, Jeffrey Bergner, John Bolton, Paula Dobriansky, Francis Fukuyama, Robert Kagan, Zalmay Khalilzad, William Kristol, Richard Perle, Peter W. Rodman, Donald Rumsefeld, William Schneider, Jr., Vin Weber, Paul Wolfowitz. R. James Woolsey, Robert B. Zoellick. *Newamericancentury.org.* Available at http://www.newamerican century.org/iraqclintonletter.htm.

March 31, 2003. Seymour Hersh. "Who Lied to Whom?" *New Yorker.* Available at http://www.newyorker.com/fact/content/?030331fa—fact1.

May 6, 2003. Nicholas Kristof. "Missing in Action: Truth." *New York Times,* A-31.

June 12, 2003. Walter Pincus. "CIA Did Not Share Doubt on Iraq Data Bush Used Report of Uranium Bid." *Washington Post,* A-1.

June 22, 2003. Walter Pincus. "Report Cast Doubt on Iraq Al Qaeda Connection." *Washington Post,* A-1.

July 9, 2003. Robert Scheer. "A Diplomat's Undiplomatic Truth: They Lied." *The Nation.* Available at http://www.thenation.com/doc. mhtml%3Fi=20030721&s=scheer20030708.

July 11, 2003. Clifford D. May. "Scandal!" *National Review Online.* Available at http://www.nationalreview.com/may/may071103.asp.

July 14, 2003. Robert Novak. "Mission to Niger." *Chicago Sun-Times* (syndicated column).

July 15, 2003. David Corn. "A White House Smear." *The Nation.* Available at http://www.thenation.com/capitalgames/index.mhtml?bid=3&pid=823.

July 17, 2003. Matthew Cooper, Massimo Calabresi, and John F. Dickerson. "A War on Wilson?" *Time.* Available at http://www.time.com/time/ nation/article/0,8599,465270,00.html.

July 18, 2003. Clifford D. May. "No Yellowcake Walk." *National Review Online.* Available at http://www.nationalreview.com/may/may071803.asp.

July 22, 2003. Timothy M. Phelps and Knut Royce. "Columnist Blows CIA Agent's Cover." *Newsday.* Available at http://www.newsday.com/ news/nationworld/nation/ny-uscia0722,0,2346857.story?coll=ny-top-headlines.

July 26, 2003. Mark Matthews. "Wilson, A Man on the Spot." *Baltimore Sun*. Available at http://www.johnkerry.com/honesty/ baltimore_sun. html.

July 30, 2003. Josh Marshall. "Investigation? No, Bush Should Pick Up the Phone." *The Hill*. Available at http://www.hillnews.com/marshall/ 073003.aspx.

Aug. 15, 2003. John W. Dean. "Bush Administration Adopts a Worse-Than-Nixonian Tactic." *Findlaw.com*. Available at http://writ.news.findlaw. com/dean/20030815.html.

Sept. 28, 2003. Mike Allen and Dana Priest. "Bush Administration Is Focus of Inquiry." *Washington Post*, A-1.

Sept. 29, 2003. Howard Kurtz. "Media Review Conduct After Leak." *Washington Post*, A-4.

Sept. 29, 2003. Clifford D. May. "Spy Games." *National Review Online*. Available at http://www.nationalreview.com/may/may200309291022.asp.

Sept. 30, 2003. Greg Miller. "Leak Accusation Stirs White House." *Los Angeles Times*, A-1.

Sept. 30, 2003. "Criminal Probe of CIA Leak." *CBSNews.com*. Available at http://www.cbsnews.com/stories/2003/12/30/national/main590737.shtml.

Oct. 1, 2003. Tom Hamburger, Greg Hitt, and Gary Fields. "Diplomat at Eye of Storm." *Wall Street Journal*.

Oct. 1, 2003. Robert Novak. "Columnist Wasn't Pawn for Leak." *Chicago Sun-Times* (syndicated column).

Oct. 1, 2003. "Washington Post ABC News Poll: Probe Into CIA Leak." *Washington Post*.

Oct. 1, 2003. Ken Fireman. "Dispute Over Source Unfolds Amid Probe." *Newsday*. Available at http://www.newsday.com/news/nationworld/ nation/ny-usbox1001,0,3587459.story?coll=ny-top-headlines.

Oct. 1, 2003. Robert Novak. "The CIA Leak." *Townhall.com*. Available at http://www.townhall.com/columnists/robertnovak/rn20031001.shtml.

Oct. 2, 2003. James Gordon Meek and Kenneth R. Bazinet. "She's the Perfect Spy." *NY Daily News*. Available at http://www.nydailynews.com /front/v-pfriendly/story/122875p110377c.html

Oct. 2, 2003. Steve Turnham. "GOP Senator: Ashcroft Should Consider Recusal on Leak Probe." *CNN.com/Inside Politics*. Available at http://www.cnn.com/2003/ALLPOLITICS/10/02/leak.main/.

Oct. 2, 2003. "Betrayal of Trust." Editorial. *Denver Post*, B-6.

Oct. 2, 2003. Peter Beinart. "Theater of the Absurd." *New Republic.* Available at https://ssl.tnr.com/p/docsub.mhtml?i=express&s=crowley111303.

Oct. 2, 2003. "Americans Want Special Counsel on CIA Leak." *Associated Press.* Available at http://www.theksbwchannel.com/news/2527075/ detail.html.

Oct. 2, 2003. Eric Boehlert. "Robert Novak's Desperate Damage Control." *Salon.com.* Available at http://www.salon.com/news/feature/2003/ 10/02/novak/index_np.html.

Oct. 3, 2003. Eric Boehlert. "Suspicion Centers on Lewis Libby." *Salon.com.* Available at http://www.salon.com/news/feature/2003/ 10/03/libby/index_np.html.

Oct. 4, 2003. Robert Novak. "The Wilsons for Gore." *CNSNews.com.* Available at http://www.cnsnews.com/ViewCommentary.asp?Page=%5 CCommentary%5Carchive%5C200310%5CCOM20031004a.html.

Oct. 5, 2003. Lynette Clemetson. "Adviser to Bush's Father Redefines Himself as Wary Whistle-Blower." *New York Times,* sect. 1, pg. 22.

Oct. 6, 2003. "A Sense of Betrayal." *ABC News.* Available at http://www.commondreams.org/headlines03/1007-12.htm.

Oct. 6, 2003. "Envoy Says Leak Endangers CIA Wife." *CBS News.* Available at http://www.cbsnews.com/stories/2003/10/07/national/main576877. shtml.

Oct. 6, 2003. William Rivers Pitt. "Fair Game." *Truthout.org.* Available at http://www.truthout.org/docs_03/printer_100603A.shtml.

Oct. 7, 2003. David Jackson. "Bush Aides Will Review Leak Notes." *Dallas Morning News.* Available at http://www.dallasnews.com/ sharedcontent/dallas/washington/topstory/stories/100703dnnatcialeak.11b0f.html

Oct. 7, 2003. Scott Lindlaw. "Bush Expresses Doubt That Leaker of CIA Official's Name Will Be Caught." *Associated Press.* Available at http:// www.signonsandiego.com/news/nation/20031007-1712-cialeak.html.

Oct. 7, 2003. Dana Milbank. "Novak Leak Column Has Familiar Sound." *Washington Post,* A-23.

Oct. 8, 2003. Richard Leiby and Dana Priest. "The Spy Next Door." *Washington Post,* A-1.

Oct. 8, 2003. Jennifer C. Kerr. "Wilson Working on Book on Life as a Diplomat—and the Leak." *Associated Press.* Available at http://www. sfgate.com/cgi-bin/article.cgi?f=/news/archive/2003/10/08/ national1701EDT0771.DTL.

Oct. 9, 2003. "Wilson Leak Looking More Like Big Nothing." *Rushlimbaugh.com*. Available at www.rushlimbaugh.com/home/eibessential1/wilsonleak.guest.helpWin.html.

Oct. 9, 2003. "Does Wilson Know the Ending?" *Rushlimbaugh.com*.

Oct. 9, 2003. Paul Heise. "Time for Answers from Bush Bunch." *Lebanon (Pennsylvania) Daily News*.

Oct. 9, 2003. Anne Schroeder. "Joe Wilson's Other Agent." *Washington Post*.

Oct. 12, 2003. Warren P. Strobel. "Leak of CIA Officers Leaves Trail of Damage." *Knight Ridder Newspapers*. Available at http://www.commondreams.org/headlines03/1011-01.htm.

Oct. 12, 2003. Robert Collier. "Uneasy Bedfellows in Investigation of CIA Leak." *San Francisco Chronicle*. Available at http://globalsecurity.com/global_security/uneasy_bedfellows.htm.

Oct. 12, 2003. Robert Koehler. "Secrets and Leaks: A Formula for Scandal." *Tallahassee Democrat*. Available at http://www.tallahassee.com/mld/democrat/news/opinion/6974616.htm.

Oct. 12, 2003. Joshua Micah Marshall. *Talkingpointsmemo.com*. Available at http://www.talkingpointsmemo.com/archives/week_2003_10_12.html.

Oct. 13, 2003. Michael Duffy. "Leaking With a Vengeance." *Time*. Available at http://www.time.com/time/archive/preview/from_covers/0,10987,1101031013-493240,00.html.

Oct. 14, 2003. David Corn. "I Am No Novak." *The Nation*. Available at http://www.thenation.com/capitalgames/index.mhtml?bid=3&pid=1007.

Oct. 15, 2003. *Ron Ridenhour Awards booklet*.

Oct. 16, 2003. Joseph L. Galloway and James Kuhnhenn. "Bush Orders Officials to Stop the Leaks." *Philadelphia Inquirer*. Available at http://www.philly.com/mld/inquirer/news/nation/7023679.htm.

Oct. 16, 2003. Robert Novak. "CNN's Novak Tells Students: Protect Your Sources." *Orlando Sun-Sentinel*, 3-B.

Oct. 16, 2003. Timothy M. Phelps. "Agent No Longer Out of Sight." *Newsday*. Available at http://www.geocities.com/yando.geo/blogtown.htm.

Oct. 16, 2003. Reilly Capps. "Paying Homage to Truth and Its Consequences. *Washington Post*, C-1.

Oct. 16, 2003. Michael Tomasky. "Papered Over." *The American Prospect*. Available at http://www.prospect.org/webfeatures/2003/10/tomasky-m-10-16.html.

Oct. 17, 2003. Rich Holmes. "Turmoil in the Cabinet." *North Shore Sunday*.

Oct. 18, 2003. "Don't Ask, Don't Know." Editorial. *Boston Globe.* Available at http://www.boston.com/news/globe/editorial_opinion/editorials/ articles/2003/10/18/dont_ask_dont_know/.

Oct. 22, 2003. Thomas E. Ricks. "Iraq War Planner Downplays Role." *Washington Post,* A-27.

Oct. 22, 2003. Julian Borger. "The Spy Who Was Thrown Into the Cold." *The Guardian.* Available at http://www.guardian.co.uk/usa/story/ 0,12271,1068124,00.html.

Oct. 23, 2003. "Rove, McClellan Interviewed in CIA Probe." *ABCNews.com.* Available at http://asia.news.yahoo.com/031023/ap/ d7uc3nmg0.html.

Oct. 23, 2003. Curt Anderson. "White House Remains Focus of Leak Investigation." *Washington Post.*

Oct. 23, 2003. "Bush Should Come Clean on Spy Outing." Editorial. *Tahlequah (Oklahoma) Daily Press.*

Oct. 24, 2003. "Ex-Agents: CIA Leak a Serious Betrayal." *CNN.com/Inside Politics.* Available at http://cnn.com/2003/ALLPOLITICS/10/24/ cnna.leak/index.html.

Oct. 24, 2003. William Rivers Pitt. "Memo to Central Intelligence Agency." *Truthout.org.* Available at http://www.truthout.org/docs_03/printer_ 102503A.shtml.

Oct. 27, 2003. Seymour M. Hersh. "The Stovepipe." *New Yorker.* Available at http://www.newyorker.com/fact/content/?031027fa_fact.

Oct. 28, 2003. David Corn. "The Wilson-CIA Leak, WMDs, and the Dems." *The Nation.* Available at http://www.thenation.com/capital games/ index.mhtml?pid=1035.

Oct. 31,2003. Joshua Micah Marshall. *Talkingpointsmemo.com.* Available at http://www.talkingpointsmemo.com/archives/002145.html.

Nov. 3, 2003. Eric Alterman. "Abrams and Novak and Rove? Oh My!" *The Nation.* Available at http://www.thenation.com/doc.mhtml?i=2003 1103&s=alterman.

Nov. 5, 2003. "Former Watergate Counsel Doubts FBI Will Solve Alleged CIA Leak Case." *Washington News.*

Nov. 21, 2003. Harry Jaffe. "Bush People Will Talk, But What Are Their Names?" *Washingtonian Online.* Available at http://www.washingtonian. com/inwashington/buzz/bushpeople.html.

Dec. 7, 2003. Dan Chapman. "Ray McGovern, Former CIA Analyst: 'We're Trying to Spread a Little Truth.'" *Atlanta Journal-Constitution.* Available at http://www.ajc.com/print/content/epaper/editions/sunday/issue_f32d89a7b145407000cc.html.

Dec. 9, 2003. Michelle Goldberg. "Now Playing in 2,600 Home Theaters: Bush Lies about Iraq." *Salon.com.* Available at http://www.salon.com/news/feature/2003/12/09/uncovered/ index_np.html.

Dec. 12, 2003. James Harding. "The Agent's Tale: From Hoo-ha to Ho-hum." *Financial Times.*

Dec. 29, 2003. Lee Hockstader. "Army Stops Many Soldiers from Quitting." *Washington Post,* A-1.

Dec. 30, 2003. David Stout. "Ashcroft to Remove Himself from Inquiry into CIA Leak." *New York Times.* Available at http://www.nytimes.com/2003/12/30/politics/30CND-LEAK.html?ex=1077858000&en=675517f77F462953&ei=5070.

Dec. 31, 2003. Eric Lichtblau. "Special Counsel Is Named to Head Inquiry on CIA Leak." *New York Times,* A-1.

Jan. 2004. Vicky Ward. "Double Exposure." *Vanity Fair.* Available at http://www.jimgilliam.com/2004/01/vanity_fairs_profile_on_joseph_wilson_and_valerie_plame.php.

Jan. 2004. "Plame Them," "Josh Marshal," and "Some More Plame." *Complex Now Blog.* Available at http://www.complexnow.com/mt/archives/2004_01.html.

Jan. 1, 2004. David Johnston. "Large File of Evidence Is Available in CIA Leak Case." *New York Times,* A-18.

Jan. 2, 2004. Kelli Arena. "FBI Seeks Confidentiality Waivers from Bush Staffers." *CNN.com.* Available at http://www.cnn.com/2004/US/01/02/cia.leak.probe/.

Jan. 2, 2004. Mike Allen. "Justice Could Decide Leak Was Not a Crime." *Washington Post,* A-4.

Jan. 3, 2004. David Johnston. "Investigators Into CIA Leak Ask Officials to Waive Private Talks With Reporters." *New York Times,* A-10.

Jan. 5, 2004. Mike Allen. "No Word From Bush on Forms in Leak Probe." *Washington Post,* A-4.

Jan. 6, 2004. John F. Dickerson. "A Shifting Probe?" *CNN.com.* Available at http://www.cnn.com/2004/ALLPOLITICS/01/06/timep.probe.tm.

Jan. 6, 2004. "Leak Probe: Call for Loose Lips." *CBSNews.com.* Available at http://www.cbsnews.com/stories/2004/02/10/national/main599179. html.

Jan. 6, 2004. Joshua Micah Marshall. *Talkingpointsmemo.com.* Available at http://www.talkingpointsmemo.com/archives/week_2004_01_04.html.

Jan. 7, 2004. Joshua Micah Marshall. "Plame Leak Shameful No Matter How the White House Spins It." *The Hill.* Available at http://www.hillnews.com/marshall/010704.aspx.

Jan. 7, 2004. Barton Gellman. "Iraq's Arsenal Was Only on Paper." *Washington Post,* A-1.

Jan. 9, 2004. John W. Dean. "Why Did Ashcroft Remove Himself from the Valerie Plame Wilson Inquiry?" *Salon.com.* Available at http://www.salon.com/opinion/feature/2004/01/09/dean_ashcroft/index_np.html.

Jan. 12, 2004. Joshua Micah Marshall. *Talkingpointsmemo.com.* Available at http://www.talkingpointsmemo.com/archives/week_2004_01_11.html.

Jan. 15, 2004. David Corn. "Not-So-Special Counsel." *The Nation.* Available at http://www.thenation.com/doc.mhtml%3Fi=20040202&s=corn.

Jan. 22, 2004. Douglas Jehl. "Ex-Intelligence Group Presses for Congressional Inquiry on Disclosure of CIA Officer." *New York Times,* A-21.

Jan. 22, 2004. John Dickerson and Viveca Novak. "Grand Jury Hears Plame Case." *Time.* Available at http://www.time.com/time/nation/article/0,8599,581456,00.html.

Jan. 22, 2004. Eric Boehlert. "Bad News." *Salon.com.* Available at http://www.salon.com/news/feature/2004/01/22/confidentiality/index_np.html.

Jan. 22, 2004. "Democrat Urges White House to Do More to Help Investigators Probing CIA Leak." *World Now.*

Jan. 28, 2004. Greg Mitchell. "Editorials Question Bush's Role in 'Cooking Up' a War." *Editor & Publisher.*

Feb. 4, 2004. Joshua Micah Marshall. *Talkingpointsmemo.com.* Blog entry on the CIA's reply to a request from Representative John Conyers on information over the Justice Department's investigation of the leak. Available at http://www.talkingpointsmemo.com/archives/week_2004_02_01.html.

Feb. 5, 2004. "America Misled into War." Editorial. *Charleston (West Virginia) Gazette.*

Feb. 5, 2004. Richard Sale. "Cheney's Staff Focus of Probe." *United Press International.* Available at http://www.commondreams.org/headlines 04/0205-12.htm.

Feb. 11, 2004. Tom Brune. "Panel Questions White House Aides." *Newsday.* Available at http://www.newsday.com/news/printedition/nation/ny-usleak113665063FEB11,0,4128876.story?coll=ny-nationalnews-print.

Feb. 12, 2004. Murray S. Waas. "Did Robert Novak Willfully Disregard Warnings That His Column Would Endanger Valerie Plame? Our Sources Say 'Yes.'" *American Prospect.* Available at http://www.prospect.org/ webfeatures/2004/02/waas-m-02-12.html.

Feb. 17, 2004. Jim Lobe. "Dear Mr. Prosecutor." *AlterNet.org.* Available at http://www.alternet.org/story.html?StoryID=17874.

Feb. 22, 2004. Roger Patches. "Truth at Stake in President's Decision to Investigate." *York Daily Record.* Available at http://ydr.com/story/op-ed/19174/.

Feb. 23, 2004. David Goldstein. "Inquiries Putting Pressure on Bush." *Kansas City Star,* A-1.

March 5, 2004. Tom Brune. "Air Force One Phone Records Subpoenaed." *Newsday.* Available at http://www.newsday.com/news/nation/ny-usleak 0305,0,2896503.story?coll=ny-top-span-headlines.

March 5, 2004. "A Timeline of the Case." *Newsday.* Available at http:// www.newsday.com/ny-ustime053695945mar05,0,3791461.story?coll= ny-top-headlines.

NEWSPAPER COMMENTARIES BY AMBASSADOR JOSEPH WILSON

Oct. 13, 2002. "How Saddam Thinks." *San Jose Mercury News.* Available at http://www.mercurynews.com/mld/mercurynews/news/editorial/ 4277734.htm.

Feb. 6, 2003. "A 'Big Cat' With Nothing to Lose." *Los Angeles Times.* Available at http://www.johnkerry.com/honesty/la_times.html.

March 3, 2003. "Republic or Empire?" *The Nation.* Available at http://www.thenation.com/doc.mhtml%3Fi=20030303&s=wilson.

April 6, 2003. "Iraq May See U.S. as Latest in Line of Conquerors." *San Jose Mercury News.*

July 6, 2003. "What I Didn't Find in Africa." *New York Times,* sect. 4, pg. 9.

Sept. 14, 2003. "Seeking Honesty in U.S. Policy." *San Jose Mercury News.*

Index